PRAISE FOR *BUSINESS ANALYTICS WITH PYTHON*

For business school students learning about business analytics, and business professionals seeking practical guidance concerning the skills and techniques that business analytics require, this comprehensive volume is quite simply a must-read. It goes beyond mere theory to illuminate the practical uses of business analytics applicable to real-world situations. This volume is thoughtful, intelligent, well-written and curated, yet readily accessible, providing clear explanations and pertinent insights, while ensuring that the mathematical content remains at a level that readers can understand. I have found it to be invaluable and illuminating, making business analytics intelligible to the interested reader who may not yet be familiar with all that business analytics has to offer.
Mairi Maclean, Professor of International Business, School of Management, University of Bath

Business Analytics with Python stands out as a rare resource that successfully bridges the gap between theoretical concepts and real-world applications – something few tools manage to accomplish today. Its step-by-step approach and meticulously crafted examples ensure that readers don't just learn about business analytics in the abstract, but actually gain the skills to apply these methods and techniques in practice. The hands-on guidance throughout makes advanced data analysis accessible, even to those without a strong quantitative background. In an era where actionable analytics skills are increasingly essential, this book serves as both a solid educational foundation and a practical reference, empowering students and professionals alike to confidently solve complex business problems with Python.
Nedko Krastev, Founder and CEO, 365 Data Science

This book is a clear and practical blueprint for incorporating machine learning insights into business operational decisions. Drawing on my experience in operations management and business analytics, I appreciate how the authors seamlessly blend fundamental Python skills, advanced modelling techniques and actionable business strategies. Their guidance empowers readers to streamline processes, improve effi
and translate predictive insights into tangible, real-world results. This is
for anyone serious about leveraging machine learning to drive
data-driven decisions.
Yufei Huang, Associate Professor in Operations Manageme
Trinity Business School, Trinity College Dublin

This is a must-read for professionals and students looking to harness the power of Python in solving real-world business challenges. The book masterfully bridges the gap between programming fundamentals and practical applications in business analytics, providing readers with step-by-step guidance and hands-on examples. With its clear explanations, accessible approach and industry-relevant use cases, this book empowers readers to confidently use Python to derive insights, make data-driven decisions and drive strategic outcomes. Whether you're a beginner or looking to enhance your existing skills, this is an invaluable resource for staying competitive in today's data-driven world.
Wei Zhou, Professor of Information and Operations Management, ESCP Business School

In the FinTech industry, data fuels innovation and informed decision-making. This book equips students and professionals with the essential tools to analyse financial and business data, optimize operations and uncover actionable insights through predictive analytics. It is an invaluable resource for those striving to excel in this fast-paced and highly competitive field.
Yu Zheng, Associate Professor of Fintech, School of Finance, Southwestern University of Finance and Economics, and CEO of Inboc Technologies

Business Analytics with Python

Essential Skills for Business Students

Bowei Chen and Gerhard Kling

KoganPage

First published in Great Britain and the United States in 2025 by Kogan Page Limited

Kogan Page
Kogan Page Ltd, 2nd Floor, 45 Gee Street, London EC1V 3RS, United Kingdom
Kogan Page Inc, 8 W 38th Street, Suite 90, New York, NY 10018, USA
www.koganpage.com

EU Representative (GPSR)
Authorised Rep Compliance Ltd, Ground Floor, 71 Lower Baggot Street, Dublin D02 P593, Ireland
www.arccompliance.com

Kogan Page books are printed on paper from sustainable forests

ISBNs
Hardback 978 1 3986 1728 5
Paperback 978 1 3986 1717 9
Ebook 978 1 3986 1727 8

British Library Cataloguing-in-Publication Data

A CIP record for this book is available from the British Library.

Library of Congress Control Number
2024058291

Typeset by Integra Software Services, Pondicherry
Print production managed by Jellyfish
Printed and bound by CPI Group (UK) Ltd, Croydon CR0 4YY

CONTENTS

PART THREE Applications and Tools

ABOUT THE AUTHORS

Bowei Chen

Bowei Chen is an Associate Professor of Marketing Analytics and Data Science at the Adam Smith Business School, University of Glasgow, where he is also the Programme Director of the MSc in Business Analytics. He obtained his PhD in Computer Science from University College London and has a wide range of research interests, focusing on the use of probabilistic modelling and machine learning in business, particularly in marketing and finance. Previously, he was an Assistant Professor at the School of Computer Science at the University of Lincoln. He has also undertaken work and research visits at institutions including Copenhagen Business School, Trinity College Dublin, University College London, Aarhus University, Bucharest University of Economic Studies, University of La Sabana, Université de Technologie de Belfort-Montbéliard, University of Bath, National University of Singapore, and Microsoft Research Cambridge.

Gerhard Kling

Gerhard Kling is a Professor in Finance at the University of Aberdeen. He has worked in higher education for over 20 years (SOAS, University of Southampton, UWE, Utrecht University). As a Practice Specialist in Corporate Finance at McKinsey & Company, he mainly focused on firm valuation and mergers and acquisitions. Since January 2022, he has been the Managing Director of YUNIKARN LTD, an educational content creation and consulting firm. YUNIKARN publishes courses in Data Science using Python and Stata on YouTube and Udemy. He has provided consulting services for McKinsey, HMRC, Industrial Bank (China), Brunello Cucinelli, China State Shipbuilding Corporation, Third Bureau of Supervision of SASAC, and Economic Research Institute for ASEAN and East Asia (ERIA), among others. He has a background in Economics (PhD, BSc/MSc) and Mathematics (BSc/MSc). His current interests focus on machine learning (ML), artificial intelligence (AI), and their applications in FinTech and Green Finance.

PREFACE

Data-driven methods have gained widespread adoption in analysing various types of business data to extract insights and facilitate informed business decision-making. This book provides a comprehensive guide to the practical techniques and skills required for business analytics. It is specifically designed for two key audiences: (i) business school students engaged in analytics-related courses or programmes and (ii) business professionals seeking actionable guidance in this domain. For business school students, this book can be a useful resource. It is beneficial for those at the senior undergraduate and postgraduate levels studying analytics in disciplines such as economics, finance, and management. The book delves into topics and concepts relevant to these areas, equipping students with the knowledge and skills imperative for academic excellence. Furthermore, the book transcends theoretical knowledge by emphasizing practical applications. It guides students in applying analytics methods and techniques to real-world situations, utilizing publicly available or synthetic datasets, thereby preparing them for future professional challenges. Business professionals may also find this book valuable. Whether they aim to enhance their current expertise or to gain a deeper understanding of analytics, the book offers practical insights that can be seamlessly integrated into their professional practices. It serves as an essential reference guide for professionals across a variety of industries who are keen to employ analytics in driving data-informed decision-making and achieving enhanced business outcomes. The content is thoughtfully curated to address the unique requirements of these two groups, providing relevant insights, hands-on methods, and techniques integral to business analytics. While encompassing both theoretical and practical aspects, the book primarily concentrates on practical applications and business cases, ensuring that mathematical content is maintained at a basic level.

ACKNOWLEDGEMENTS

The content of this book has emerged from many years of teaching and research. Over the years, our students have learned about machine learning tools, their implementation, and applications in business. However, teaching is the most effective way of learning. Being challenged by students (and ChatGPT) in class is an excellent way to deepen our own understanding. Hence, we wish to thank our students – keep pushing us.

WALKTHROUGH OF FEATURES AND ONLINE RESOURCES

Learning Outcomes

A bulleted list at the beginning of each chapter summarizes what you can expect to learn, to help you to track your progress.

> By the reading of this chapter, you will be able to:
>
> - Gain a clear understanding of what business analytics is and its different types.
> - Differentiate between the scopes and focal points of data science, machine learning, and statistics.
> - Understand how these disciplines converge and complement each other in the field of business analytics.
> - Identify and understand the various types of machine learning.
> - Recognize the five diverse communities within the field of machine learning, each with its unique approach and methodologies.
> - Comprehend the CRISP-DM framework and its significance in the analytics process.

Worked Examples

Step-by-step examples and code take you through the key tasks and enable you to apply your knowledge and develop your coding skills.

> These data types can change depending on your code dynamically. So, it is important to check and monitor data types.

```
#Type function
#Python is dynamically typed
print(type(a))
print(type(b))
```

Exercise Questions

These can be used in tutorials or small study groups to stimulate debate and critical thinking.

> Exercise
>
> 1 Identify and describe the different types of analytics.
>
> 2 What is machine learning? Describe its main types.
>
> 3 Detail the key phases involved in the CRISP-DM.
>
> 4 What is an IDE in programming?

Key Terms Boxes

These boxes give explanations of key terms and concepts in the book to highlight them for your learning.

> **BOOLEANS: TELL THE TRUTH**
>
> *Booleans* are either True or False. Python assesses objects as 'falsy' or 'truthy', which is used in many operations (e.g. if statements).

References

Detailed references provide quick and easy access to the research and underpinning sources in the book.

Online Resources

This book includes online resources for lecturers comprising datasets. These resources can be accessed at **www.koganpage.com/BusinessAnalyticsWithPython.**

PART ONE
Introduction and Preliminaries

1 | Introduction

This chapter presents an introductory overview of business analytics. It lays the foundation by introducing essential concepts and terminology, distinctly differentiating between related fields, and thoughtfully placing this book within the broader spectrum of business analytics. By the reading of this chapter, you will be able to:

- Gain a clear understanding of what business analytics is and its different types.
- Differentiate between the scopes and focal points of data science, machine learning, and statistics.
- Understand how these disciplines converge and complement each other in the field of business analytics.
- Identify and understand the various types of machine learning.
- Recognize the five diverse communities within the field of machine learning, each with its unique approach and methodologies.
- Comprehend the CRISP-DM framework and its significance in the analytics process.

1.1 What is Business Analytics?

Business analytics refers to the use of data-driven methods to analyse business data and gain insights that inform decision-making and strategy. It involves the application of statistical analysis, data mining, machine learning, and other advanced analytics techniques to understand and solve business problems. The primary goal of business analytics is to transform data into actionable findings for business planning and operations.

Business intelligence is closely related to business analytics, but they have distinct focuses and serve different purposes in the business environment. Business intelligence primarily deals with the collection, integration, analysis, and presentation of business information. It typically involves data aggregation from various sources, data warehousing, reporting, and querying software that allows users to interact with their data, create reports, and visualize data in an accessible way, along with descriptive analytics. Business intelligence is often seen as a more foundational and descriptive approach, focusing on what has happened and what the current state is, based on available data. In contrast, business analytics extends beyond the descriptive nature of business intelligence to include more advanced techniques. The focus of business analytics is more on understanding why things are happening, predicting what will happen in the future, and determining what actions should be taken. However, as both fields are somewhat interdisciplinary and their scopes evolve over time with the development of the underlying technologies, the terms have sometimes been used interchangeably in recent times.

1.2 Types of Analytics

Analytics, in its broadest sense, is the systematic computational analysis of data. It is used for the discovery, interpretation, and communication of meaningful patterns in data. More importantly, it aids in decision-making across various sectors including business, science, and technology. There are primarily four types of analytics: descriptive, diagnostic, predictive, and prescriptive. Each type offers a different perspective on the data, enabling businesses and organizations to make informed decisions. Understanding these categories is crucial for effectively applying analytics in any field.

Descriptive analytics is the simplest and most commonly used form of analytics. It involves summarizing past data to understand what has happened in a given period. This type of analytics answers the question 'What has happened?' Common techniques used in descriptive analytics include data aggregation and data mining. The primary goal is to find patterns and relationships in historical data. For example, a retail company uses descriptive analytics to understand its sales patterns over the last year. By analysing data from sales records, the company can identify trends, such as which products were the best sellers, and what times of year.

Diagnostic analytics goes a step further than descriptive analytics by not only summarizing past data but also providing reasons for past events. This type of analytics answers the question 'Why did it happen?' It involves more in-depth data analysis techniques like drill-down, data discovery, correlations, and causality analysis. Diagnostic analytics is crucial for understanding the root causes of events and behaviours. If using the same retail company as an example, they notice a significant drop in sales in a particular quarter. Using diagnostic analytics, they analyse various data points like marketing activities, customer feedback, and market trends during that period. They discover that the decline was due to a competitor's aggressive marketing campaign at the same time.

Predictive analytics uses statistical models and machine learning techniques to understand the likelihood of future outcomes based on historical data. This type of analytics answers the question 'What is likely to happen?' Predictive analytics is used to make informed guesses about future events, and it involves techniques such as regression analysis, forecasting, multivariate statistics, pattern matching, predictive modelling, and forecasting. For example, a commercial bank uses predictive analytics to determine the risk of loan default. By analysing past data of loan repayments and defaults, along with customer credit scores and economic conditions, they can predict which loan applicants are at higher risk of defaulting in the future.

Prescriptive analytics is the most advanced form of analytics. It not only predicts future events but also suggests actions to achieve desired outcomes. This type of analytics answers the question 'What should we do?' and employs complex algorithms, computational modelling, business rules, and machine learning to recommend actions. Prescriptive analytics is used for decision optimization and to provide advice on possible outcomes. As another example, a healthcare provider could use prescriptive analytics for patient care. By analysing medical records, treatment outcomes, and patient characteristics, the system can recommend personalized treatment plans for patients, such as the most effective medication for a patient with specific health conditions and history. Two further examples of prescriptive analytics are Netflix and Amazon. They use prescriptive analytics to suggest movies and TV shows to their users. By analysing a user's viewing history, preferences, and even the viewing habits of similar users, their recommender systems can prescribe a list of titles that the user is likely to enjoy. This not only enhances the user experience but also increases the time spent on the platform.

Figure 1.1 summarizes these four types of analytics, highlighting their focuses and characteristics. The value of these analytics types increases as one moves from descriptive to prescriptive, but so does the complexity of the algorithms involved. Descriptive analytics is valuable for understanding the basic context of business performance, while diagnostic analytics provides insights into factors influencing that performance. Predictive analytics is highly valuable for planning and forecasting, allowing businesses to anticipate changes and trends. Prescriptive analytics, being the most advanced, offers the highest value by enabling informed decision-making and strategic planning based on predictive insights and business intelligence. However, the complexity of algorithms in predictive and prescriptive analytics also means they require more data, computational resources, and expertise to implement effectively. This complexity can pose challenges in terms of data quality, model accuracy, and the interpretability of results, which are crucial for making informed business decisions.

Figure 1.1 Types of analytics

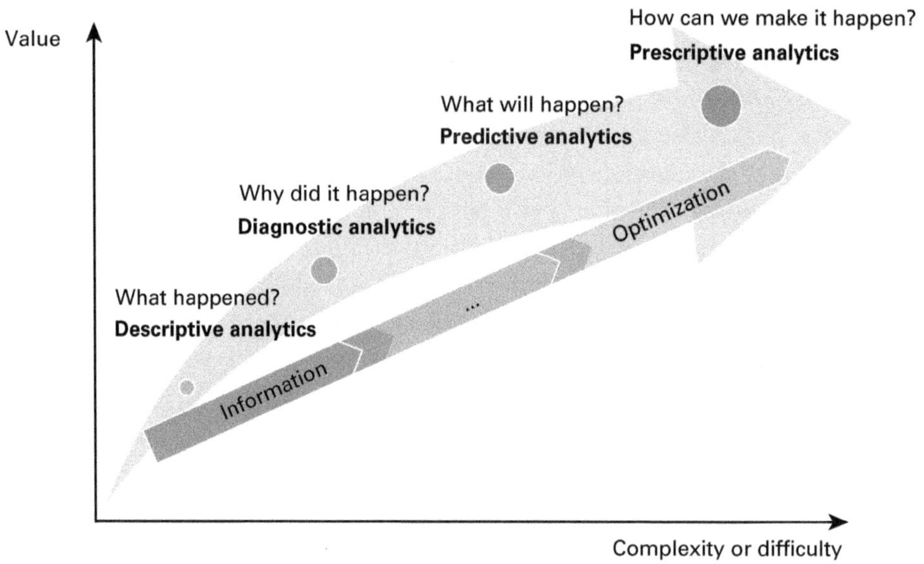

1.3 Statistics and Machine Learning

Methods and techniques used in business analytics primarily derive from the fields of statistics and machine learning. These two fields have significant overlaps, often converging in their methods, objectives, and applications. At their core, both disciplines are concerned with understanding and making predictions based on data. *Statistics* is a field with a long history in mathematics, and focuses on making inferences from data, testing hypotheses, and providing measures of confidence and uncertainty. It traditionally emphasizes understanding the underlying processes and generating insights about data through models that are interpretable and theoretically sound. Statistical methods are foundational in analysing and interpreting data, and they provide the theoretical underpinnings for many machine learning algorithms. *Machine learning*, a subset of artificial intelligence, focuses on the development of computer programmes that can access data and learn autonomously. It is more concerned with prediction and action based on data analysis.

Table 1.1 Comparison of terminology in statistics and machine learning

Concept	Statistics	Machine learning
Model training	Estimation	Training
Model testing	Validation	Testing
Input data	Predictor or independent variable	Feature
Output data	Response or dependent variable	Label or target variable
Model evaluation	Goodness of fit	Performance measure
Error measurement	Residuals	Loss function
Data splitting	Sampling	Training/test split
Overfitting handling	Shrinkage methods	Regularization
Model complexity	Degrees of freedom	Model capacity

Statistics and machine learning share a deep and intricate connection. Both fields aim to extract valuable insights and predictions from data, using a range of tools and techniques. As mentioned, this shared objective results in significant overlap in their theoretical foundations and practical applications. Statistics provides the bedrock upon which many machine learning algorithms are built. Statistical concepts like probability and parameter estimation form the core of various machine learning models. For instance, linear regression, a fundamental machine learning technique, relies heavily on statistical principles for understanding relationships between variables and making predictions. Furthermore, machine learning extends and complements statistical methods. While classical statistics often focuses on interpretability and understanding the underlying relationships within data, machine learning prioritizes accuracy and prediction, even if the model's inner workings are less transparent. This allows machine learning to tackle complex problems that may be intractable using traditional statistical techniques. In essence, machine learning and statistics are not isolated disciplines, but rather two sides of the same coin. They work in tandem to unlock the secrets hidden within data, contributing significantly to scientific discovery, technological advancements, and our understanding of the world around us. Some concepts have different terminology names in machine learning and statistics. To assist the reader, certain concepts that are termed differently in statistics and machine learning are summarized in Table 1.1 for convenience and clarity. These terms are sometimes used interchangeably in various textbooks.

1.4 Types of Machine Learning

The recent shift in focus within business analytics towards machine learning algorithms is a significant development. This shift is also the central focus of the methods introduced in this book. In the following, we will lay down some fundamental concepts of machine learning, including the three main types of machine learning: supervised learning, unsupervised learning, and reinforcement learning. Each of these types of machine learning has its unique characteristics and is suited for different kinds of problems. Understanding these types is crucial for applying the right machine learning techniques to the right problem, ensuring effective and efficient solutions.

Supervised learning involves providing the algorithm with labelled data, meaning each data point has a known outcome or target variable. The algorithm learns the relationship between the input data and the target variable by analysing numerous examples. Imagine a child learning to identify fruits. You show them various fruits, labelling each one as an apple, banana, or orange. By analysing these labelled examples, the child gradually grasps the defining characteristics of each fruit. Similarly, in supervised learning, the algorithm learns from labelled data, where each data point has a known value of the target variable. This enables the algorithm to identify patterns and relationships within the data and utilize them to predict future outcomes for unseen data. Common techniques in supervised learning include linear regression, logistic regression, decision trees, random forest, neural networks, and so on. Supervised learning is used in applications like fraud detection in banking, customer churn prediction, and image recognition. For instance, in healthcare, it can be used to predict whether a patient has a certain disease based on their symptoms and medical history.

Figure 1.2 Types of machine learning

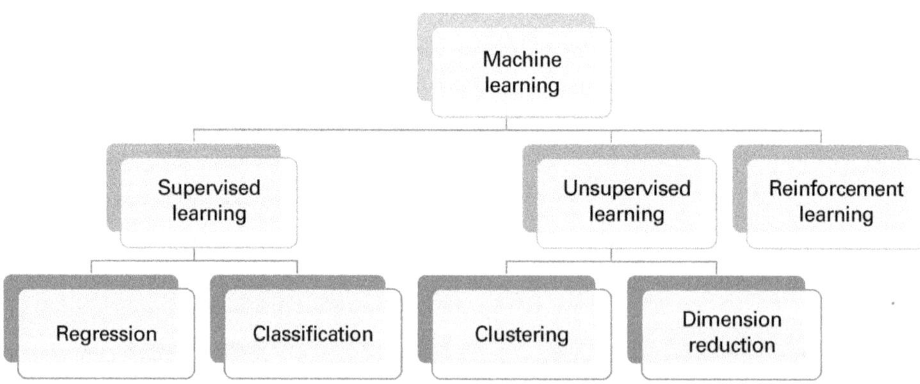

In supervised learning, two types of problems are commonly addressed: regression and classification. Both use labelled datasets for training, but they differ in the nature of the output or prediction they are designed to make. Regression is used when the target variable is a real or continuous value, such as salary, weight, sales, or stock price. The goal of regression is to predict a continuous quantity. The algorithm tries to find the best possible mapping function from the input variables to the numerical output (i.e. target variable). This involves determining a line, curve, or some kind of mathematical formula that best fits the given data points. Common regression techniques include linear regression, polynomial regression, neural networks, decision trees, and random forest, among others. On the other hand, classification problems involve predicting a discrete label or category, such as spam or not spam in an email filtering system. The target variable in classification is categorical. The algorithm learns from the training data and then uses this learning to classify new observations. This involves determining the boundaries or decision rules that best separate the different classes in the dataset. Techniques used in classification include logistic regression, support vector machines, decision trees, and neural networks. Classification is used in a variety of applications, such as email spam detection, image recognition, and medical diagnosis, like classifying tumours as benign or malignant. It is worth mentioning that some algorithms, like neural networks, decision trees, and random forest, can be used in both regression and classification problems. Details will be introduced in the corresponding chapters in Part Two.

Unsupervised learning is a type of machine learning where algorithms learn patterns from data without any explicit labels or instructions. Unlike supervised learning where the data has desired outputs, unsupervised learning works with unlabelled data. This means the algorithms do not have any pre-defined expectations or goals, allowing them to explore the data freely. Therefore, the goal of unsupervised learning is to identify patterns and relationships within the data. This can involve grouping similar data points together, finding hidden clusters, or identifying anomalies. Unsupervised learning has two types of algorithms: clustering and dimensionality reduction. The former aims at grouping similar data points together (for customer segmentation, fraud detection, or anomaly detection) while the latter reduces the number of features in the data to make it easier to analyse and visualize. Unsupervised learning is often used for exploratory data analysis, customer segmentation, and market basket analysis. For example, in retail, unsupervised learning can help identify customer segments with similar buying behaviours, which can be targeted with specific marketing strategies.

Reinforcement learning is a type of machine learning where a machine learns to make decisions by performing certain actions and observing the rewards or penalties that result from those actions. It is about learning from interaction with an environment to achieve a goal or maximize some notion of cumulative reward. It involves three key components: the agent (the learner or decision-maker), the environment (everything the agent interacts with), and actions (what the agent can do). The agent makes decisions, the environment responds to those actions and presents new situations to the agent, and the agent receives rewards. These rewards are the basis for altering the agent's decision-making process. Reinforcement learning has been successfully used in various domains, including robotics for industrial automation, in recommendation systems where an algorithm learns to recommend products or content that maximizes user engagement, and in gaming to develop AI that can beat humans in complex games. A notable example of this is AlphaGo (Silver et al., 2016), a ground-breaking artificial intelligence programme developed by Google DeepMind. AlphaGo represents a paradigm shift in artificial intelligence, showcasing the power of reinforcement learning as its cornerstone technology. Through meticulous training and strategic decision-making, AlphaGo achieved unprecedented success in mastering the complexities of the ancient game of Go. Its ground-breaking victory against the legendary world champion Lee Sedol in 2016 marked a significant milestone in the advancement of AI capabilities. This achievement captured the attention of both the scientific community and the general public, highlighting the immense potential of reinforcement learning to tackle complex real-world problems.

This book will introduce several widely used algorithms from the realms of both supervised and unsupervised learning. These have been selected for their substantial relevance in addressing a wide array of challenges in business analytics. Notably, certain algorithms, such as linear regression and logistic regression, represent an intersection between machine learning and statistics. However, their development, evaluation, and interpretation differ across these two fields. Importantly, this book does not cover reinforcement learning, which involves more advanced mathematical and programming concepts, as it extends beyond the remit of this text.

1.5 Tribes of Machine Learning

The concept of 'tribes' in machine learning became widely accepted following the publication of the book from Domingos (2015) *The Master Algorithm: How the quest for the ultimate learning machine will remake our world*. This concept refers to the various schools of thought and approaches within the field of machine learning. Each tribe has its own unique perspective and methodologies, often influenced by historical developments and foundational theories. Domingos (2015) identifies five distinct tribes in machine learning, as summarized in Table 1.2.

Specifically, the Symbolists, tracing their lineage back to logic and philosophy, view learning as the inverse of deduction and focus on the manipulation of symbols to create knowledge. Notable algorithms in this tribe include decision trees,

Table 1.2 Summary of tribes in machine learning

Tribe	Focus	Techniques
Symbolists	Logic and symbolic representation	Decision trees, logic programming
Connectionists	Brain structure and function	Neural networks
Evolutionaries	Evolutionary biology	Genetic algorithms
Bayesians	Probabilistic reasoning	Bayesian networks, Markov models
Analogizers	Learning by analogy and similarity	Support vector machines

rule-based systems, and inductive logic programming. They pioneered early artificial intelligence and expert systems. The Connectionists, inspired by neuroscience and the workings of the human brain, model learning as a process of forming connections in artificial neural networks. Their key techniques, artificial neural networks and particularly recent deep learning, have made significant contributions in fields like image and speech recognition, playing a central role in the current artificial intelligence boom. The third tribe, the Evolutionaries, draw from evolutionary biology and the principles of natural selection and genetics. They use computer simulations to mimic evolution, optimizing solutions to problems. Genetic algorithms, their main technique, are particularly useful in optimization problems and areas where explicit programming is challenging. The Bayesians, stemming from Thomas Bayes' work on probability theory, focus on learning as a form of probabilistic inference using Bayes' Theorem. Their key techniques, including Bayesian networks and Markov models, are influential in areas that require uncertainty modelling and decision-making under uncertainty. The final tribe, the Analogizers, unlike other tribes with distinct characteristics, draw from various fields, including statistics, mathematics, computer science, and engineering. They learn by drawing analogies between different instances and inferring new information. Notable techniques in this tribe, such as support vector machines and k-nearest neighbors, are effective in classification and regression tasks, especially when the data volume is not large.

Each tribe offers a unique perspective on machine learning, contributing to the field's richness and diversity. Historically, these tribes have sometimes been viewed as competing or mutually exclusive. However, in modern machine learning, there is a growing trend towards hybrid approaches that combine the strengths of multiple tribes, leading to more robust and versatile algorithms.

Figure 1.3 CRISP-DM

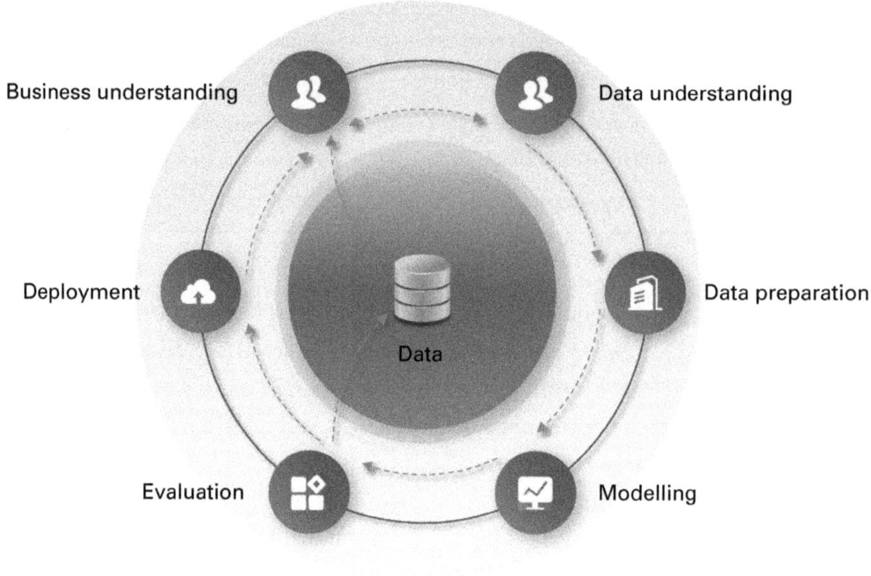

1.6 CRISP-DM

Cross-industry standard process for data mining (CRISP-DM) is a widely recognized framework that provides a structured approach for planning, executing, and evaluating data mining projects. It is incredibly valuable for business analytics, as it ensures a systematic and efficient way to extract meaningful insights from data and translate them into actionable business decisions. As demonstrated in Figure 1.3, there are six major phases of CRISP-DM, forming a cyclical process that encourages iterative learning and adaptation.

This initial phase is *business understanding*, which focuses on comprehending the project objectives and requirements from a business perspective. It involves defining the problem, determining the project's aims, and establishing a preliminary plan to achieve these objectives. For instance, a telecom company aiming to predict customer churn to identify customers at risk of leaving and implement retention strategies might apply the CRISP-DM methodology. Their business goal is to reduce customer churn and increase customer lifetime value, e.g. decreasing the churn rate by 10% within 12 months.

Concurrent with business understanding, the second phase, *data understanding*, involves collecting initial data and proceeding with activities to get familiar with the data, identify data quality issues, and discover preliminary insights into the data. It is about understanding the data's potential and limitations. For the telecom company, this might include analysing customer demographics, usage patterns, and service quality metrics to identify potential churn factors. This phase is iterative and may loop back to business understanding as new data insights prompt a reevaluation of business objectives or reveal additional business questions. In the meantime, checking for missing values, outliers, and inconsistencies in the data can also be proceeded in this phase.

The third phase, *data preparation*, is perhaps the most time-consuming as it encompasses all activities required to construct the final dataset from the initial raw data for developing analytics models. This includes tasks such as handling missing values, transforming categorical variables, and scaling numerical variables. This phase also includes feature engineering (e.g. creating new features based on customer behaviour and service usage patterns) and dividing the data into training, validation, and testing sets.

Once the dataset is prepared, the fourth phase, *modelling*, involves developing analytics models. Various statistical and machine learning algorithms can be trained to address the predefined problem. For instance, developing logistic regression, decision trees, random forests, neural networks, and so on for predicting customer churn. As many advanced algorithms contain parameters that need to be pre-specified and can significantly influence their performance (known as *hyperparameters*), tuning these hyperparameters to optimize model performance on the validation set is a crucial step in this phase.

After developing analytics models, the subsequent phase is *evaluation*. This phase has two aims. First, it involves evaluating the developed models against a set of evaluation metrics such as mean squared errors, accuracy, precision, recall, and the area under the ROC curve. Second, it entails interpreting the model results in the context of the business objectives defined in the first phase, ensuring that the initial business questions can be answered. The model with the best accuracy and interpretability on the test set would then be selected from all the examined models.

The final phase, *deployment*, involves deploying the model into a real-world environment. This can range from a simple report of the findings to implementing a repeatable data mining process across the organization. For the latter, the telecom company could integrate the chosen churn prediction model into its customer relationship management (CRM) system and develop a scoring mechanism to identify high-risk customers based on the model's predictions. This will allow the company to regularly monitor the model's performance and update it as necessary to adapt to changes in customer behaviour or company offerings such as personalized offers or improved customer service for at-risk customers.

Throughout this process, particularly in the early phases, there is a fluid back-and-forth movement between business understanding and data understanding. As new data insights are gained, they may influence and refine the business objectives and questions, leading to a more targeted and effective data solution. The topics discussed in this textbook cover all six phases of CRISP-DM, with a special focus on data understanding, data preparation, modelling, and evaluation. The other two phases, business understanding and deployment, depend heavily on context, so they are lightly covered through business cases and applications.

1.7 Data Scientist Tools

When it comes to the practice of business analytics, a pivotal consideration is the selection of an appropriate data analytics tool. This involves choosing the right data programming or analysis language and its corresponding software that can operate efficiently. The rationale for considering tools favoured by data scientists lies in their proven effectiveness and versatility in handling a broad range of data analysis tasks. It is also noteworthy to mention *data science*, an expansive and interdisciplinary field that utilizes scientific methods, processes, algorithms, and systems to extract knowledge and insights from both structured and unstructured data. This domain encompasses a wide array of techniques drawn from diverse fields such as mathematics, statistics, machine learning, information science, and computer science. The choice of tools in data science is critical, as it directly impacts the efficiency and effectiveness of the business analytics process.

Data scientists typically opt for tools that offer robust functionality, scalability, and strong community support. Figure 1.4 presents a summary of Kaggle data science and machine learning surveys from 2018 to 2022 regarding programming languages. It reveals that the most popular tools in the data science community are Python, SQL, and R. Python is renowned for its simplicity and versatility, supported by a vast array of libraries such as Pandas, NumPy, scikit-learn, Matplotlib, and statsmodels, making it ideal for data manipulation, analysis, and machine learning. Therefore, it is without doubt that Python is our selected data programming language for business analytics practice.

An *integrated development environment (IDE)* is a software application that provides comprehensive facilities to computer programmers for software development. An IDE typically integrates a variety of tools into one cohesive package, facilitating an integrated experience for development. For Python, several IDEs are popular due to their features and ease of use, including Jupyter Notebook, PyCharm, Visual Studio Code, Spyder, and so on. Each of these IDEs has its strengths and is suited to different types of Python projects. The choice of an IDE often depends on the specific requirements of the project, personal preference, and the level of programming expertise. In this book, we have adopted Jupyter Notebook for sharing the source codes for business analytics. It is an open-source web application that enables one to create and share documents containing live code, equations, visualizations, and narrative text. It is ideally suited for business analytics scenarios and also for us to share and demonstrate practices with the intended audience.

Figure 1.4 Most popular programming languages from Kaggle's data science and machine learning surveys, 2018–2022

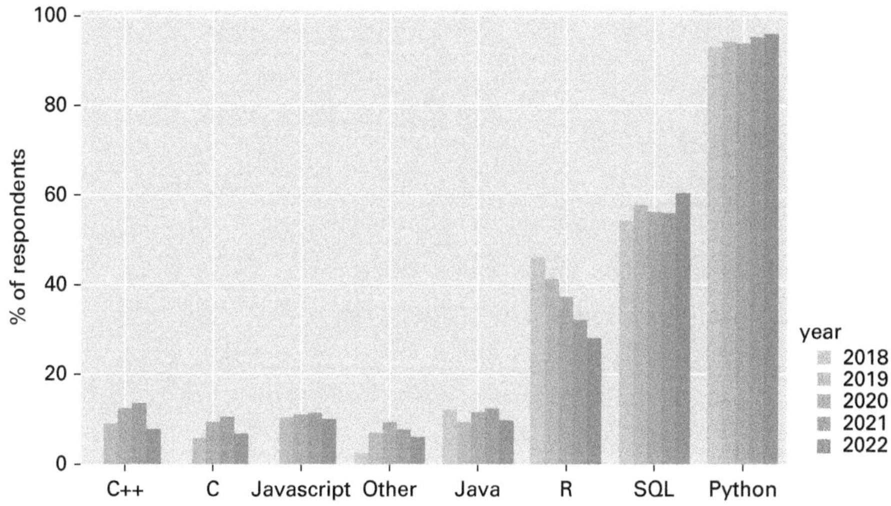

SOURCE www.kaggle.com/c/kaggle-survey-2022

1.8 Outline of this Book

This book, organized into three parts and 16 chapters, offers a comprehensive guide to business analytics, blending theoretical concepts with practical applications. Part One lays the foundation by first introducing business analytics, discussing its types and significance in decision-making. It is followed by a review of the essential mathematics necessary for understanding business analytics. Next, the chapter covers Python programming, which is indispensable for data manipulation and analysis, and data wrangling techniques, crucial for preparing data for meaningful analysis. The part concludes with an introduction to data visualization using Python, underscoring its importance in presenting data insights effectively. Part Two delves into various analytical methods and techniques. It begins with linear and logistic regression, essential for understanding relationships between variables and modelling outcomes. The book then explores advanced topics like neural networks, k-nearest neighbours, Naïve Bayes, and tree-based methods, each crucial for specific types of data analysis tasks in business. Support vector machines and principal component analysis are also covered, offering insights into classification, regression, and dimensionality reduction. The part concludes with a focus on cluster analysis, a key technique for data segmentation. Part Three applies these concepts in real-world scenarios. It presents case studies in fintech and green finance, demonstrating the application of data-driven methods in solving business problems. The final chapter discusses the development of machine learning web tools, guiding readers in building interactive dashboards and ML-powered web applications for effective data-driven decision-making. This book is a valuable resource for understanding and applying business analytics techniques, blending theoretical knowledge with practical skills.

1.9 Exercise

1. Identify and describe the different types of analytics.
2. What is machine learning? Describe its main types.
3. Detail the key phases involved in the CRISP-DM.
4. What is an IDE in programming?

2 Mathematical Foundations of Business Analytics

This chapter provides a quick review of the core mathematics that are essential for developing a good understanding of data analytics in a business context, including calculus, linear algebra, probability, and statistics.

After studying this chapter, you should be able to:

- Understand the basic concepts of calculus, including real numbers, functions, and derivatives.
- Execute elementary vector and matrix operations, which are essential for straightforward data analysis tasks.
- Learn to represent tabular data in matrix form, understanding that more sophisticated techniques will require further exploration beyond this introductory review.
- Understand what probability is and its basic properties.
- Identify random variables and acquire a preliminary understanding of their probability distributions, which is adequate for basic applications and sets the stage for more advanced studies.
- Calculate the basic expectation and variance of random variables, laying the groundwork for more in-depth statistical analysis.

In line with the aims of this book, we have deliberately limited the mathematical content to ensure that students with a business background can quickly develop data analytics skills. As a result, we have not extensively covered some topics related to mathematical foundations, though these can be explored in greater depth if required. For readers keen to delve deeper into these areas, we recommend various textbooks in the following sections.

2.1 Calculus

Calculus is fundamental for analysis as it provides the mathematical framework necessary for dealing quantitatively with rates of change and accumulation. This section concentrates solely on the basic calculus concepts, rules, and theorems relevant to business analytics.

2.1.1 *Cartesian Coordinates and Equations of Lines*

Calculus fundamentally relies on the properties of the real number system. Real numbers are numbers that can be expressed as decimals, such as

$$-\frac{1}{4} = -0.25, \quad \frac{2}{3} = 0.66666..., \quad \sqrt{2} = 1.41421356...,$$

where ... indicates that the sequence of decimal digits continues indefinitely. Geometrically, real numbers are represented as points on a number line known as the *real line*, which is usually denoted by $\mathbb{R}$ in many books.

Consider two real lines that intersect perpendicularly at their zero points, where one line is horizontal and the other vertical. The horizontal line is referred to as the *x-axis*, and the vertical line as the *y-axis*. The intersection point of these lines is known as the *origin*. The coordinate system established by these axes is commonly called *Cartesian coordinates*.

Figure 2.1 Example of Cartesian coordinates and the slope of the line $y = 3x - 2$

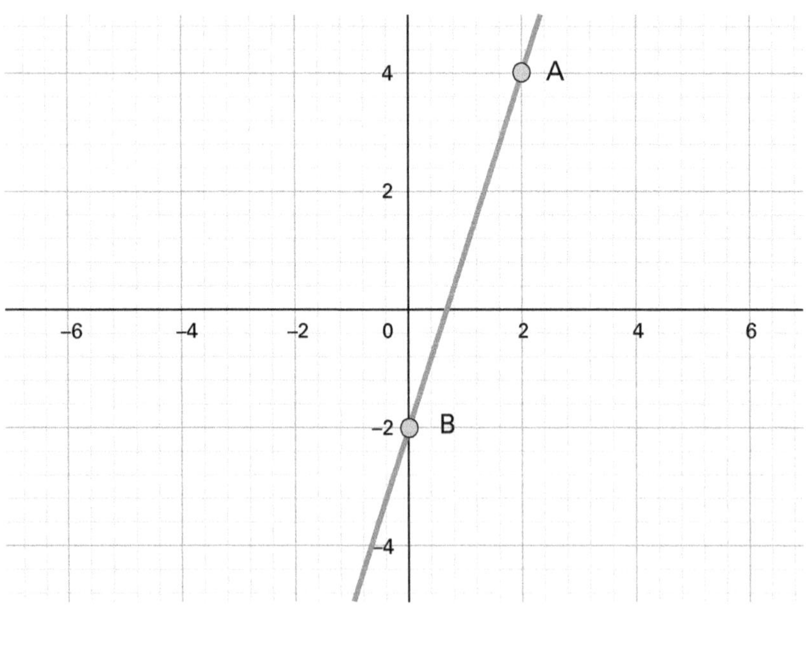

Figure 2.1 illustrates how the axes are used to represent points. For instance, point A on the plane is denoted as the pair (2, 4), and point B is represented by (0, –2). Between point A and point B, the increments (net changes) in the x– and y– coordinates are as follows

$$\Delta x = 0 - 2 = -2, \quad \Delta y = -2 - 4 = -6.$$

Here the symbols Δx and Δy represent the difference in the x– and y– coordinates, respectively.

We can draw a line that passes through any two points in the plane, then the *slope* of the line – the rate at which the line ascends or descends along the y-axis as one moves along the x-axis – can be calculated from the changes in coordinates. In the example of Figure 2.1, the slope is

$$\frac{\Delta y}{\Delta x} = \frac{-6}{-2} = 3.$$

As all the points in the line have the same slope, we can use an equation to represent this line based on the slope. The equation can be expressed as

$$y - y_1 = m(x - x_1),$$

where m is the slope, and (x_1, y_1) represents a point that the line passes through. In the example of Figure 2.1, the line has the slope 3 and passes through the point (0, –2), so

$$y - (-2) = 3(x - 0),$$

then we obtain $y = 3x - 2$, which is the equation for the line. It should be noted that horizontal and vertical lines can be simply expressed as $y = y_1$ and $x = x_1$.

2.1.2 Functions and Their Graphs

In mathematics, a function is a relation between a set of inputs and a set of permissible outputs, with each input related to exactly one output. We can use the symbol f to denote the function, whose input x coming from the domain D, and the output of the function $f(x)$ make up the function range R. We often write $f(x) : D \rightarrow R$. In business analytics, functions model relationships between variables. For example, a sales function might relate advertising expenditure (input) to sales revenue (output).

The point (x, y) in the plane, representing the input-output pairs of the function $y = f(x)$, forms the graph of the function. Figure 2.2 shows the graph of the function $y = x^3$ over the interval $-2 \leq x \leq 2$. Here the domain x can extend over the entire set of real numbers.

Figure 2.2 Example of the function $y = x^3$

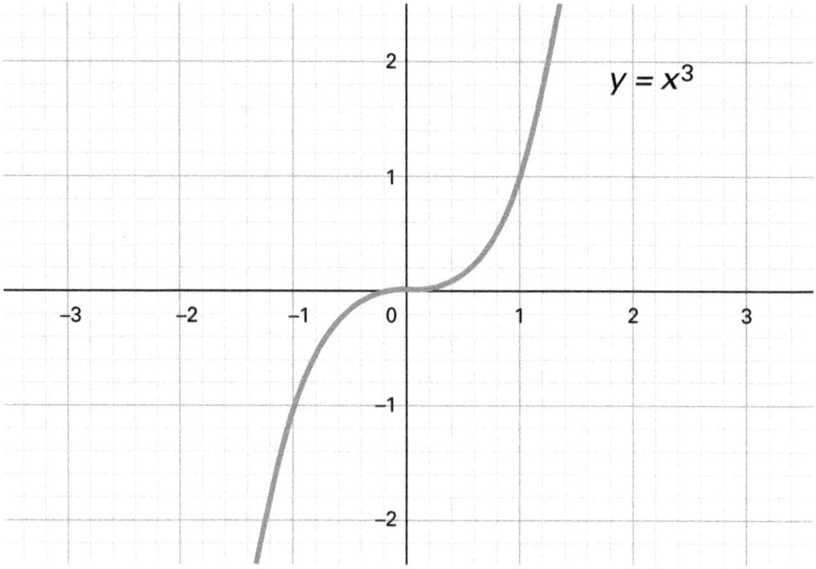

Suppose the outputs of a function g can be used as inputs for another function f. By connecting g and f, we create a new function whose inputs are those of g and whose outputs are given by $f(g(x))$. This function, denoted $f(g(x))$, is called the *composite* of g and f, formed by first applying g and then f. The conventional notation for this composite function is $(f \circ g)(x)$ or $f(g(x))$. For example, if we have $g(x) = x^2$, and $f(x) = x + 10$, then $f(g(x)) = x^2 + 10$.

2.1.3 Derivatives

The *average rate of change* of a function over a specified interval is a measure of how much the function's value changes between two points. For function $y = f(x)$ over the interval $[x_1, x_2]$, its average rate of change can be calculated as

$$\frac{\Delta y}{\Delta x} = \frac{f(x_2) - f(x_1)}{x_2 - x_1} = \frac{f(x_1 + h) - f(x_1)}{h}, h \neq 0.$$

It is essentially the *slope* of the line that connects these two points on the graph of the function. The slope of a curve $y = f(x)$ at any point $(x_0, f(x_0))$ can be described mathematically as follows

$$m = \lim_{h \to 0} \frac{f(x_0 + h) - f(x_0)}{h},$$

where m represents the slope of the tangent line at the point $(x_0, f(x_0))$. This tangent line is the straight line that intersects the curve exactly at this point and has the slope m. As shown in Figure 2.3, for function $y = x^2$, if $x_0 = 1$, then $f(x_0) = f(1) = 1$, and its slope at the point $(x_0, f(x_0))$ is

$$m = \lim_{h \to 0} \frac{f(x_0 + h) - f(x_0)}{h}$$

$$= \lim_{h \to 0} \frac{x_0^2 + 2x_0 h + h^2 - x_0^2}{h}$$

$$= 2x_0 + h = 2x_0 = 2.$$

Then it is not difficult to find a line with the slope $m = 2$ that passes through the point $(x_0, f(x_0))$, which is $y = 2x - 1$.

In the above example, x_0 can be any value of x. That is, at any point $(x, f(x))$ on the function $f(x) = x^2$, the slope is $m = 2x$, which is the derivative of this function. For any arbitrary function $f(x)$, if the limit exists

Figure 2.3 Example of derivative of the function $y = x^2$ at the point (1, 1)

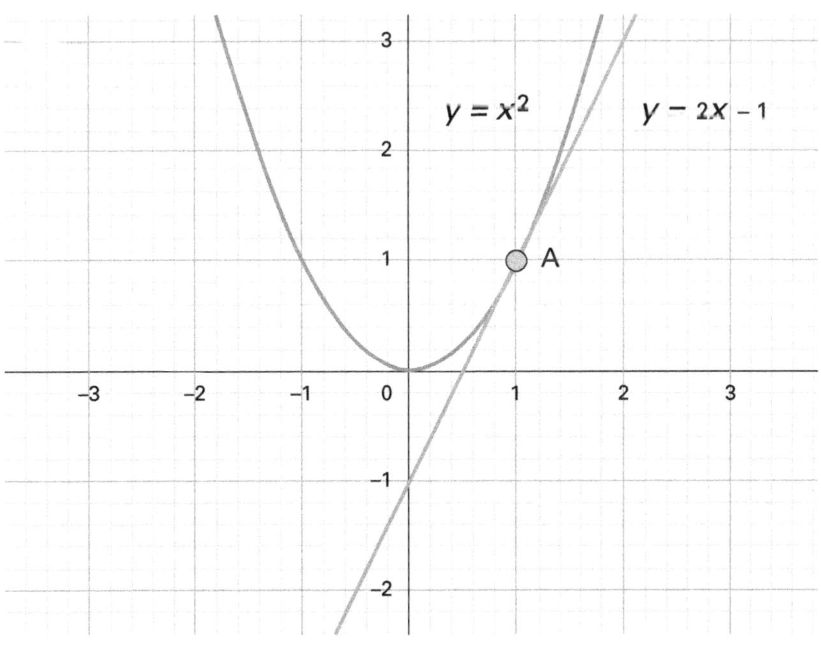

$$\lim_{h\to 0}\frac{f(x+h)-f(x)}{h},$$

it is *differentiable* at the point x, and then its *derivative* $f'(x)$ is defined as

$$f'(x)=\lim_{h\to 0}\frac{f(x+h)-f(x)}{h}.$$

To highlight that differentiation is an operation applied to a function, we often employ alternative notations for the derivative $f'(x)$. These include $\frac{df(x)}{dx}$, $\frac{d}{dx}f(x)$, $D_x f(x)$, and $\frac{\partial f(x)}{\partial x}$. The derivative represents the rate at which a function's output changes as its input changes.

RULES OF DERIVATIVES

1 Constant rule:

$c' = 0$, if c is a constant.

2 Linear rule:

$$\left(f(x) \pm g(x)\right)' = f'(x) \pm g'(x).$$
$$\left(cf(x)\right)' = cf'(x).$$

3 Product rule:

$$\left(f(x)g(x)\right)' = f'(x)g(x) + f(x)g'(x).$$

4 Quotient rule:

$$\left(\frac{f(x)}{g(x)}\right)' = \frac{f'(x)g(x) - g'(x)f(x)}{\left(g(x)\right)^2}$$

5 Chain rule:

$$\left(f(g(x))\right)' = f'(g(x))g'(x).$$

There are several fundamental rules for calculating derivatives, succinctly summarized in the highlight box. Detailed proofs of these rules can be found in Hass et al. (2022). To effectively apply these rules, first identify the specific form of the function to be differentiated. Then, select the appropriate rule or combination of rules that best fits the function's structure. Finally, execute the differentiation process step by step. Each rule addresses different functional operations, allowing for systematic computation of derivatives across a broad spectrum of functions.

In business settings, grasping the concept of derivatives enables individuals to forecast alterations in costs, revenues, or profits when faced with changes in factors such as production volume or pricing. Additionally, derivatives act as the cornerstone of optimization techniques in many machine learning algorithms, providing valuable insights into how functions behave. By providing information about the rate of change of these functions, derivatives facilitate the application of efficient optimization algorithms like gradient descent. Within the realm of machine learning, where models continuously refine their parameters to minimize errors, derivatives play a crucial role in guiding this iterative process. They indicate the direction of the steepest descent, helping to steer the model towards the optimal solution. This process lies at the heart of training neural networks and other complex models, enabling them to learn from data and generate accurate predictions. For example, understanding the chain rule of derivatives is essential in comprehending back-propagation during neural network training, highlighting the importance of derivatives in machine learning.

2.1.4 Integration

Integration enables the efficient computation of various quantities by dividing them into smaller segments and subsequently summing the contributions from each segment. It has widespread applications across fields such as statistics, economics, science, and engineering.

If a function $f(x)$ is non-negative and integrable over a closed interval $[a, b]$, then the area under the curve is the *integral* of f from a to b, that is

$$\int_a^b f(x)dx,$$

where the notation $\int$ is the integral sign, a is the lower limit of the integration, and b is the upper limit of the integration. Therefore, if $f(x)$ is continuous on $[a, b]$, then $F(x) = \int_a^x f(t)dt$ is continuous on $[a, b]$, and differentiable, and its derivative is $f(x)$, that is

$$F'(x) = \frac{d}{dx}\int_a^x f(t)dt = f(x).$$

From another perspective, we can have

$$\int_a^b f(x)dx = F(b) - F(a).$$

For example, $\int_a^b x^2 dx = \frac{b^3}{3} - \frac{a^3}{3}$. Essentially, integration is simply the opposite of differentiation. Therefore, many of the basic rules that apply to derivatives also apply to integrals. For instance, the product rule for derivatives is fundamental to the formula for integration by parts. However, as these are not the main focus of this review, we will not go into further detail here.

2.1.5 Other Topics in Calculus

Calculus encompasses a wide range of fundamental concepts and advanced theorems essential for understanding the behaviour of functions and their derivatives. Other topics include asymptotes, L'Hôpital's rule, Taylor series, and limits of numerical sequences. Moreover, calculus extends its reach into more advanced territories, such as multivariable calculus, where functions of several variables are studied. This branch of calculus explores topics like partial derivatives, gradients, and multiple integrals, enabling the analysis of phenomena in spaces of higher dimensions, which would be particularly useful for understanding machine learning algorithms. As mentioned earlier, those interested in exploring calculus further can find comprehensive explanations in Hass et al. (2022), Thomas and Finney (1992), and Rudin (1976).

2.2 Linear Algebra

Linear algebra is highly valuable in business analytics, offering essential tools for efficiently representing and manipulating data in the forms of vectors and matrices. This enables rapid computations that are vital for handling extensive datasets. Fundamental machine learning algorithms leverage linear algebra for critical tasks like prediction, pattern recognition, and feature extraction. It also underpins optimization techniques crucial for training these algorithms. Furthermore, advanced deep learning techniques, widely used in image and speech recognition, depend on manipulating tensors, a concept stemming from linear algebra.

2.2.1 Vectors

In linear algebra, a *vector* is an ordered collection of numbers. These numbers can be arranged vertically in column form or horizontally in row form, enclosed within parentheses or square brackets. For example

$$\begin{pmatrix} 420 \\ 292.5 \\ 3 \\ 1 \end{pmatrix} \quad or \quad (420, 292.5, 3, 1) \quad or \quad \begin{bmatrix} 420 \\ 292.5 \\ 3 \\ 1 \end{bmatrix} \quad or \quad [420, 292.5, 3, 1].$$

Typically, unless otherwise specified, a vector is assumed to be a column vector. Each numerical value within the vector is referred to as an *element* (or *entry*). The *size of the vector* corresponds to the number of elements it encompasses. It is worth noting that the meanings of the numbers in a vector are usually defined by its creator or user. For example, in the above instances, a vector could represent price, apartment size, number of bedrooms, and number of bathrooms in holiday resort accommodation booking data.

Lowercase bold symbols are employed to denote vectors; for instance, we can use $\boldsymbol{x}$ to denote a vector with size n

$$\boldsymbol{x} = \begin{bmatrix} x_1 \\ \vdots \\ x_n \end{bmatrix},$$

where $x_1, \ldots, x_n$ represents the elements (without specifying their specific values) corresponding to positions 1 through n, respectively.

Various arithmetic rules govern the manipulation and interaction of vectors, facilitating efficient operations and aiding in the comprehension and resolution of complex problems across different fields. Summarized within the highlight box are the fundamental arithmetic rules of vectors. Essentially, vectors of equal size can be added or subtracted by combining their corresponding elements, resulting in a new vector of the same size, referred to as their sum or difference. The scalar multiplication rule governs the scaling of a vector by multiplying each of its components by a scalar value, thereby adjusting its magnitude while retaining its direction. Additionally, the pointwise product rule, also recognized as the *Hadamard product*, denoted by $\odot$, entails the element-wise multiplication of two vectors of equal size. This yields a new vector wherein each element represents the product of the corresponding elements from the input vectors. Moreover, the *inner product*, also called the *dot product*, delineates a scalar quantity derived from the summation of the products of corresponding elements from two vectors. The symbol $\top$ denotes the transpose of a vector, that is $\boldsymbol{u}^\top = [u_1, \ldots, u_n]$.

There are some special vectors. For example, a vector that has all elements equal to 0 is called the *vector of zeros*, denoted by $\mathbf{0}$ (or $\mathbf{0}_n$ to emphasize its size). A vector with all values of 1 is called the *vector of ones*, often denoted by $\mathbf{1}$ (or $\mathbf{1}_n$ to emphasize its size). Additionally, if a vector has a length of 1, it is called the *unit vector*.

Here, the *length of a vector* is also called its *norm*. It represents the distance from the origin to the point represented by the vector. Mathematically, for a vector x, its norm can be represented using the double vertical bars symbol $\| x \|$, given by

$$\| x \| = \sqrt{x_1^2 + x_2^2 + \ldots + x_n^2}.$$

2.2.2 Matrices

A *matrix* is a mathematical concept used to organize and manipulate data in a structured format, which consists of numbers arranged in rows and columns within a rectangular array. Therefore, a vector can be depicted as a one-dimensional matrix. In the context of the holiday resort accommodation booking example in section 2.2.1, the subsequent matrix can accommodate multiple bookings. Each row within the matrix serves as a vector representing a booking, while the columns denote variables such as price, apartment size, number of bedrooms, and number of bathrooms.

$$\begin{bmatrix} 420 & 292.5 & 3 & 1 \\ 660 & 208.0 & 3 & 1 \\ 660 & 194.0 & 3 & 2 \\ \vdots & \vdots & \vdots & \vdots \\ & & & \end{bmatrix}.$$

Matrices are often denoted by uppercase bold letters, such as $\mathbf{X}$, $\mathbf{Y}$, $\mathbf{Z}$. The size of a matrix $\mathbf{X}$ is specified as $n \times m$, where n is the number of rows and m is the number of columns. Therefore, a matrix $\mathbf{X}$ can also be denoted by $[x_{ij}]_{n \times m}$, where x_{ij} represents the element in the i-th row and j-th column of the matrix. The following summarizes different expressions of a matrix

$$\mathbf{X} = [x_{ij}]_{n \times m} = \begin{bmatrix} x_{11} & x_{12} & \cdots & x_{1m} \\ x_{21} & x_{22} & \cdots & x_{2m} \\ \vdots & \vdots & \ddots & \vdots \\ x_{n1} & x_{n2} & \cdots & x_{nm} \end{bmatrix}.$$

If $m = n$, then the matrix,

$$\mathbf{X} = \begin{bmatrix} x_{11} & x_{12} & \cdots & x_{1n} \\ x_{21} & x_{22} & \cdots & x_{2n} \\ \vdots & \vdots & \ddots & \vdots \\ x_{n1} & x_{n2} & \cdots & x_{nn} \end{bmatrix},$$

is called the *square matrix*. The elements $x_{11}, x_{22}, \ldots, x_{nn}$ is called the *diagonal elements*. If $x_{ij} = x_{ji}$, where $i, j = 1, \ldots, n$, then the matrix is called the *symmetric matrix*. If the off-diagonal elements are all 0, then the matrix is called the *diagonal matrix*. If

RULES FOR VECTORS

1. Addition rule:

$$\text{If } \boldsymbol{u}=\begin{bmatrix}u_1\\ \vdots\\ u_n\end{bmatrix}, \boldsymbol{v}=\begin{bmatrix}v_1\\ \vdots\\ v_n\end{bmatrix}, \text{ then } \boldsymbol{u}+\boldsymbol{v}=\begin{bmatrix}u_1+v_1\\ \vdots\\ u_n+v_n\end{bmatrix}.$$

2. Subtraction rule:

$$\text{If } \boldsymbol{u}=\begin{bmatrix}u_1\\ \vdots\\ u_n\end{bmatrix}, \boldsymbol{v}=\begin{bmatrix}v_1\\ \vdots\\ v_n\end{bmatrix}, \text{ then } \boldsymbol{u}-\boldsymbol{v}=\begin{bmatrix}u_1-v_1\\ \vdots\\ u_n-v_n\end{bmatrix}.$$

3. Scalar multiplication rule:

$$\text{If } \boldsymbol{u}=\begin{bmatrix}u_1\\ \vdots\\ u_n\end{bmatrix}, c \text{ is a constant, then } c\boldsymbol{u}=\begin{bmatrix}cu_1\\ \vdots\\ cu_n\end{bmatrix}.$$

4. Pointwise multiplication rule:

$$\text{If } \boldsymbol{u}=\begin{bmatrix}u_1\\ \vdots\\ u_n\end{bmatrix}, \boldsymbol{v}=\begin{bmatrix}v_1\\ \vdots\\ v_n\end{bmatrix}, \text{ then } \boldsymbol{u}\odot\boldsymbol{v}=\begin{bmatrix}u_1v_1\\ \vdots\\ u_nv_n\end{bmatrix}.$$

5. Inner product rule:

$$\text{If } \boldsymbol{u}=\begin{bmatrix}u_1\\ \vdots\\ u_n\end{bmatrix}, \boldsymbol{v}=\begin{bmatrix}v_1\\ \vdots\\ v_n\end{bmatrix}, \text{ then } \boldsymbol{u}^\top\boldsymbol{v}=u_1v_1+u_2v_2+\ldots+u_nv_n.$$

a diagonal matrix has diagonal elements equal to 1, then the matrix is called the *identity matrix*, denoted by $\boldsymbol{I}$ (or $\boldsymbol{I}_n$ to emphasize its size).

Matrices share similarities with vectors in their manipulation, as outlined in the highlighted box. These basic operations pave the way for advanced matrix manipulations, facilitating tasks spanning from solving systems of equations to data transformations in diverse applications. Addition and subtraction of matrices involve combining or differentiating corresponding elements, respectively, resulting in new matrices of the same size. Scalar multiplication scales a matrix by a constant factor, affecting all its elements uniformly. The transpose rule in matrix operations involves switching the rows and columns of a given matrix. Pointwise multiplication involves multiplying corresponding elements of two matrices to obtain a new matrix with products at each position. Matrix multiplication, however, is more intricate, requiring careful alignment and computation. It involves multiplying rows of the first matrix by columns of the second and summing the results to produce each element of the resulting matrix. Therefore, $\boldsymbol{UV} \neq \boldsymbol{VU}$.

RULES FOR MATRICES

1 Addition rule:

$$\boldsymbol{U} + \boldsymbol{V} = [u_{ij}]_{n\times m} + [v_{ij}]_{n\times m} = [u_{ij} + v_{ij}]_{n\times m}.$$

2 Subtraction rule:

$$\boldsymbol{U} - \boldsymbol{V} = [u_{ij}]_{n\times m} - [v_{ij}]_{n\times m} = [u_{ij} - v_{ij}]_{n\times m}.$$

3 Scalar multiplication rule:

$c\boldsymbol{U} = [cv_{ij}]_{n\times m}$, where c is a constant.

4 Transpose rule:

$$\boldsymbol{U}^\top = \begin{bmatrix} u_{11} & \cdots & u_{n1} \\ \vdots & \ddots & \vdots \\ u_{1m} & \cdots & u_{nm} \end{bmatrix}.$$

5 Pointwise multiplication rule:

$$\boldsymbol{U} \odot \boldsymbol{V} = \left[u_{ij}v_{ij}\right]_{n\times m}.$$

6 Matrix multiplication rule:

$$\boldsymbol{UV} = \left[u_{ij}\right]_{n\times p} \times \left[v_{ij}\right]_{p\times m} = \begin{bmatrix} \sum_{k=1}^{p} u_{1k}v_{k1} & \cdots & \sum_{k=1}^{p} u_{1k}v_{km} \\ \vdots & \ddots & \vdots \\ \sum_{k=1}^{p} u_{nk}v_{k1} & \cdots & \sum_{k=1}^{p} u_{nk}v_{km} \end{bmatrix}.$$

2.2.3 System of Linear Equations, Inverse Matrix, and Determinant

Consider there is a system of n linear equations

$$a_{11}x_1 + a_{12}x_2 + \cdots + a_{1n}x_n = b_1,$$

$$a_{21}x_1 + a_{22}x_2 + \cdots + a_{2n}x_n = b_2,$$

$$a_{n1}x_1 + a_{n2}x_2 + \cdots + a_{nn}x_n = b_n,$$

where $x_1,\ldots, x_n$ are unknown. Based on matrix multiplication, the above system of linear equations can be rewritten as below

$$\underbrace{\begin{bmatrix} a_{11} & a_{12} & \cdots & a_{1n} \\ a_{21} & a_{22} & \cdots & a_{2n} \\ \vdots & \vdots & \ddots & \vdots \\ a_{n1} & a_{n2} & \cdots & a_{nn} \end{bmatrix}}_{A} \underbrace{\begin{bmatrix} x_1 \\ x_2 \\ \vdots \\ x_n \end{bmatrix}}_{x} = \underbrace{\begin{bmatrix} b_1 \\ b_2 \\ \vdots \\ b_n \end{bmatrix}}_{b},$$

that is

$$\boldsymbol{Ax} = \boldsymbol{b}.$$

By moving $\boldsymbol{A}$ to the right-hand side, we can solve the equation, yielding the formula for **x**. The solution involves an important concept, *inverse matrix*, which is a matrix that, when multiplied with the original matrix $\boldsymbol{A}$, yields the identity matrix $\boldsymbol{I}$. For simplicity, the inverse matrix of $\boldsymbol{A}$ can be simply denoted by $\boldsymbol{A}^{-1}$ such that

$$\boldsymbol{A}^{-1}\boldsymbol{A} = \boldsymbol{A}\boldsymbol{A}^{-1} = \boldsymbol{I}.$$

It is important to note that this identity holds true irrespective of the multiplication order, underscoring the commutative property of matrix multiplication when involving an inverse.

Not all matrices have inverses. A matrix is said to be *invertible* if and only if it can be transformed into an upper triangular matrix via the Gaussian elimination method, with all elements on the main diagonal being non-zero. Alternatively, the necessary and sufficient condition for a matrix to have an inverse is that it must be *non-singular*, which means that its determinant is non-zero. The determinant of a matrix A, denoted by $\mathbf{det}(\boldsymbol{A})$ or $|\boldsymbol{A}|$, is defined as follows

$$\det(\boldsymbol{A}) = \sum_{j=1}^{n} a_{ij}(-1)^{i+j}\det(\boldsymbol{A}_{ij}),$$

where $\boldsymbol{A}_{ij}$ represents the sub-matrix that deletes row i and column j from $\boldsymbol{A}$.

The computational methods for finding the inverse matrix include using the adjugate matrix and the determinant, or applying numerical methods like Gaussian elimination. The properties of inverse matrices are symmetric, meaning that the inverse of the inverse of a matrix is the matrix itself, and the inverse of a product of matrices is the product of their inverses in reverse order. Understanding and applying these rules effectively allows for the exploration of system solutions, matrix equations, and other higher-level operations in mathematical contexts.

Several foundational properties of inverse matrices are summarized in the box [above/on the previous page]. First, the primary characteristic is that the product of a matrix and its inverse results in the identity matrix so $(\boldsymbol{U}^{-1})^{-1} = \boldsymbol{U}$. Also, the inverse of the transpose of a matrix is the transpose of the inverse. When a scalar multiplication is involved, the inverse of $c\boldsymbol{U}$ is given by $\frac{1}{c}\boldsymbol{U}^{-1}$, where c is a non-zero

RULES FOR INVERSE MATRICES

1 $(\boldsymbol{U}^{-1})^{-1} = \boldsymbol{U}$.
2 $(\boldsymbol{U}^{\top})^{-1} = (\boldsymbol{U}^{-1})^{\top}$.
3 $(c\boldsymbol{U})^{-1} = \frac{1}{c}\boldsymbol{U}^{-1}$ if c is a constant.
4 $(\boldsymbol{UV})^{-1} = \boldsymbol{V}^{-1}\boldsymbol{U}^{-1}$.

scalar. For products of matrices, the inverse of the product is the product of the inverses in reverse order. These properties enable the reversal and algebraic manipulation of matrix operations, facilitating the resolution of complex problems across various tasks.

2.2.4 Other Topics in Linear Algebra

In addition to the reviewed fundamental concepts, there are many other useful topics in linear algebra. For example, the rank of a matrix, providing insights into the dimensionality of the vector space spanned by the matrix's columns or rows, is crucial for solving systems of linear equations, determining solution existence and uniqueness, and characterizing the behaviour of linear transformations. Eigenvectors and eigenvalues, on the other hand, are pivotal in various applications, such as principal component analysis and spectral decomposition of matrices. Matrix decomposition involves expressing a matrix as a product of simpler matrices with specific properties, facilitating efficient numerical computations, solving linear systems, and extracting meaningful information from data matrices in applications like image processing, signal processing, and machine learning. For a thorough understanding of these topics and their real-world applications, it is advisable to refer to Strang (2023) and Boyd and Vandenberghe (2018).

2.3 Probability and Statistics

Probability and statistics are vital in business analytics for making informed, data-driven decisions. Probability underpins statistical theory, which determines the likelihood of various event scenarios and aids in forecasting and risk assessment. Statistics then allow businesses to analyse trends, assess variability, and understand data distributions, essential for interpreting past performance and predicting future outcomes.

2.3.1 Probability Measure

Probability quantifies uncertainty and is expressed as a number – such as a fraction, decimal, or percentage – ranging between 0 and 1, where 0 denotes impossibility and 1 denotes certainty. Consider the act of rolling a fair die to evaluate the likelihood of rolling a 4 or a 6. In probability terms, this action is called the *experiment*. The complete set of all possible outcomes from this experiment is known as the *sample space*, represented by $\Omega = \{1, 2, 3, 4, 5, 6\}$. Each individual outcome within the sample space is termed an *elementary event*, while any subset of the sample space is defined as an *event*.

Mathematically, a *probability measure*, denoted by $\mathbb{P}$, is a function from the sample space Ω to the range $[0, 1]$, which satisfies the following three axioms:

1 $0 = \mathbb{P}(\emptyset) \leq \mathbb{P}(E) \leq 1$, where $\emptyset$ is the empty set and E is the event.

2 For all disjoint events $E_1, E_2, E_3, \ldots, E_n$, $\mathbb{P}(E_1 \cup E_2 \cup \ldots \cup E_n) = \sum_{i=1}^{n} \mathbb{P}(E_i)$.

3 $\mathbb{P}(\Omega) = 1$.

Let's look at the following example to understand how to compute probability. Suppose we randomly select two balls from a box containing 8 white, 4 black, and 2 orange balls. We win £2 for each black ball selected and lose £1 for each white ball selected. Let X represent our winnings. What are the possible values of X, and what probabilities correspond to each of these values?

Let W, B, and O represent the number of white, black, and orange balls drawn, respectively. Then,

$$\mathbb{P}(X - -2) = \mathbb{P}(W = 2, B = 0, O = 0) = \frac{\binom{8}{2}}{\binom{14}{2}},$$

$$\mathbb{P}(X = -1) = \mathbb{P}(W = 1, B = 0, O = 1) = \frac{\binom{8}{1}\binom{2}{1}}{\binom{14}{2}},$$

$$\mathbb{P}(X = 0) = \mathbb{P}(W = 0, B = 0, O = 2) = \frac{\binom{2}{2}}{\binom{14}{2}},$$

$$\mathbb{P}(X=1)=\mathbb{P}(W=1,B=1)=\frac{\binom{8}{1}\binom{4}{1}}{\binom{14}{2}},$$

$$\mathbb{P}(X=2)=\mathbb{P}(B=1,O=1)=\frac{\binom{4}{1}\binom{2}{1}}{\binom{14}{2}},$$

$$\mathbb{P}(X=4)=\mathbb{P}(B=2,O=0)=\frac{\binom{4}{2}}{\binom{14}{2}}.$$

The notation $\binom{n}{k}$ in the above solution is known as a *binomial coefficient*, and represents the number of ways to choose k elements from a set of n elements without considering the order of the elements. It is a key concept in combinatorics, used to solve problems involving combinations. The computation of $\binom{n}{k}$ is expressed as

$$\binom{n}{k}=\frac{n!}{k!(n-k)!},$$

where $n!$ denotes the *factorial* of a non-negative integer n, defined as the product of all positive integers up to n, i.e. $n! = n \times (n-1) \times \ldots \times 1$.

2.3.2 Conditional Probability

We often need to calculate probabilities when only partial information regarding the outcome of an experiment is at hand. In these circumstances, the probabilities we ascertain are conditional. *Conditional probability* quantifies the likelihood of an event occurring, given the prior occurrence of another event.

Let E and F denote two events, such that $\mathbb{P}(F) > 0$. Then, the probability of event E occurring given that F has occurred can be computed as

$$\mathbb{P}(E \mid F)=\frac{\mathbb{P}(E \cap F)}{\mathbb{P}(F)},$$

where $\mathbb{P}(E \cap F)$ is the probability of both E and F occurring together. If two events E and F are *independent*, the occurrence of one event does not affect the occurrence of the other event, that is $\mathbb{P}(E \cap F) = \mathbb{P}(E)\,\mathbb{P}(F)$, and

$$\mathbb{P}(E \mid F) = \frac{\mathbb{P}(E)\mathbb{P}(F)}{\mathbb{P}(F)} = \mathbb{P}(E).$$

Consider a further example. Suppose a box contains 50 defective light bulbs, 100 partially defective light bulbs (lasting only 5 hours), and 250 fully functional light bulbs. If a bulb from this box is used and it does not immediately fail, what is the probability that the bulb is in good condition?

The conditional probability is computed as follows

$$\mathbb{P}(\text{Good} \mid \text{Not Defective}) = \frac{\mathbb{P}(\text{Good} \cap \text{Not Defective})}{\mathbb{P}(\text{Not Defective})} = \frac{250/400}{350/400} = 5/7.$$

The Law of Total Probability is a key rule in probability theory that lets us calculate the likelihood of an event by using the probabilities of other events that cover all possible outcomes. This rule is very useful when an event can happen in different

LAW OF TOTAL PROBABILITY

Let E be an event, and let $F_1, F_2, \ldots, F_n$ be partitions of Ω, that is

1 $F_1, F_2, \ldots, F_n$ are mutually disjoint, i.e. $F_i \cap F_j = \emptyset$ for any $1 \le i, j \le n$,
2 $\cup^n_{i=1} F_i = \Omega$.

Then, $E = \cup^n_{i=1} (E \cap F_i)$ and

$$\mathbb{P}(E) = \sum_{i=1}^{n} \mathbb{P}(E \cap F_i) = \sum_{i=1}^{n} \mathbb{P}(E \mid F_i)\mathbb{P}(F_i).$$

BAYES' THEOREM

Let E be an event, and $F_1, F_2, \cdots, F_n$ be partitions of Ω, then

$$\mathbb{P}(F_j \mid E) = \frac{\mathbb{P}(F_j \cap E)}{\mathbb{P}(E)} = \frac{\mathbb{P}(E \mid F_j)\mathbb{P}(F_j)}{\sum_{i=1}^{n} \mathbb{P}(E \mid F_i)\mathbb{P}(F_i)}.$$

ways or under different conditions. It also helps derive Bayes' theorem, which is vital for evaluating risks, making forecasts, and carrying out tests in many scientific and practical areas.

Consider this example: within a black box, there are two coins, one fair and one with two heads. A gambler randomly selects a coin from the box. If he flips the coin a third time and it lands on tails, what is the probability that he has chosen the fair coin?

Let F denote the event where the fair coin is flipped, U represent the event where the two-headed coin is flipped, H indicate the event that shows heads, and T denote the event that shows tails. Then

$$\mathbb{P}(F \mid HHT) = \frac{\mathbb{P}(HHT \mid F)\mathbb{P}(F)}{\mathbb{P}(HHT \mid F)\mathbb{P}(F) + \mathbb{P}(HHT \mid U)\mathbb{P}(U)} = \frac{1/8 \times 1/2}{1/8 \times 1/2 + 0 \times 1/2} = 1.$$

2.3.3 Random Variable

Random variables are fundamental to probability theory and statistics, which tackle uncertainty using quantifiable and analytical methods, thus supporting structured decision-making and predictions in situations of randomness. A *random variable* X is a function with domain Ω and codomain $\mathbb{R}$ (we can simply write it $X: \Omega \to \mathbb{R}$).

Consider the experiment of rolling two dice, where the sample space is defined as

$$\Omega = \{(i, j) : i, j = 1, \ldots, 6\}$$

Within this context, several random variables can be defined. For example, let $X = i + j$; then X can take values ranging from 2 to 12. Similarly, define $Y = |i - j|$; consequently, Y can assume values from 0 to 5.

A random variable X can be determined by its *cumulative distribution function* $F_X: \mathbb{R} \to [0, 1]$, which is defined as $F_X(x) = \mathbb{P}(X \le x) = \mathbb{P}(\{\omega \in \Omega : X(\omega) \le x\})$. In conventional notation, capital letters are used to denote random variables, while the corresponding lowercase letters represent a realization, or a specific value, of the random variable. Additionally, the CDF is often referred to simply as the *distribution function.*

The CDF of a random variable possesses several essential properties, outlined in the box, not only delineating the behaviour of the CDF but also offering practical

PROPERTIES OF THE CDF

1. F_X is non-decreasing, that is if $a < b$ then $F_X(a) \leq F_X(b)$.
2. $\lim_{x \to -\infty} F_X(x) = 0$ and $\lim_{x \to \infty} F_X(x) = 1$.
3. $F_X(\cdot)$ is right continuous, that is $\lim_{h \to 0} F_X(x + h) = F_X(x)$.

methodologies for computing probabilities and analysing the behaviour of random variables, whether they are discrete or continuous.

A random variable X is *discrete* if its range is countable, i.e. it has a finite or infinitely countable number of possible values. For a discrete random variable, we define the *probability mass function (PMF)* as

$$f_X(x_i) = \mathbb{P}(X = x_i), \quad \text{for } i = 1, 2, \ldots,$$

where $0 \leq f_X(x_i) \leq 1$ for all i, and $\Sigma_i f_X(x_i) = 1$, and its CDF can be expressed as

$$F_X(x) = \sum_{i: x_i \leq x} \mathbb{P}(X = x_i).$$

A random variable is *continuous* if it can take on any value in an interval of numbers. A continuous random variable has the *probability density function (PDF)*, f_X, defined as

$$\mathbb{P}(a < X < b) = \int_a^b f_X(x)dx,$$

where we must have that the integral under the f_X curve equals to 1, that is

$$\mathbb{P}(-\infty < X < \infty) = \int_{-\infty}^{\infty} f_X(x)dx = 1.$$

2.3.4 Expectation and Variance

Expectation and variance are fundamental statistical concepts that underpin our understanding of random variables. They shed light on central tendency and variability, crucial information which equips us to make informed decisions and predictions.

Let X be a random variable with range $\mathbb{R}$. The *expectation* of X calculates the mean or average value of a random variable over many trials or in a probabilistic context. It is often denoted by $\mathbb{E}[X]$ and is defined as

$$\mathbb{E}[X] = \begin{cases} \sum_i x_i \mathbb{P}(X = x_i), & \text{if } X \text{ is discrete,} \\ \int x f_X(x)dx, & \text{if } X \text{ is continuous.} \end{cases}$$

Consider an experiment in which two coins are to be flipped. The first coin will land on heads with probability 0.6, the second with probability 0.7. Assume that the results of the flips are independent, and let X equal the total number of heads that result. What is $\mathbb{E}[X]$?

Note that X can take the values 0, 1, or 2. We can begin by deriving the PMF of X

$$p_X(x) = \begin{cases} \mathbb{P}(T,T) = 0.4 \times 0.3 = 0.12 & \text{if } x = 0, \\ \mathbb{P}(H,T) + \mathbb{P}(T,H) = 0.6 \times 0.3 + 0.7 \times 0.4 = 0.46 & \text{if } x = 1, \\ \mathbb{P}(H_1, H_2) = 0.6 \times 0.7 = 0.42 & \text{if } x = 2, \end{cases}$$

Thus, $\mathbb{E}[X] = \sum_{x=0}^{2} x p_X(x) = 1.3$.

The *variance* of X is denoted by $\text{Var}[X]$, and is defined as

$$\text{Var}[X] = \mathbb{E}[(X - \mathbb{E}[X])^2] = \begin{cases} \sum_i (x_i - \mathbb{E}[X])^2 \mathbb{P}(X = x_i), & \text{if } X \text{ is discrete,} \\ \int (x - \mathbb{E}[X])^2 f_X(x)dx, & \text{if } X \text{ is continuous.} \end{cases}$$

Variance measures how spread out the data is in relation to its average value. It is sometimes used alongside the *standard deviation*, which is the square root of variance and is expressed in the same units as the original data.

While the expectation and variance are different measures characterizing various aspects of a random variable's behaviour, the computation of variance hinges on the concept of expectation. Expanding upon this, a broader scenario involves computing the expectation of a function of a random variable. Let $h(X)$ be a function of a random variable X. Then

$$\mathbb{E}[h(X)] = \begin{cases} \sum_i h(x_i)\mathbb{P}(X = x_i), & \text{if } X \text{ is discrete,} \\ \int h(x) f_X(x)dx, & \text{if } X \text{ is continuous.} \end{cases}$$

Thus, variance is the case that $h(X) = (X - \mathbb{E}(X))^2$.

PROPERTIES OF EXPECTATION

1. $\mathbb{E}[c] = c$ if c is a constant.
2. $\mathbb{E}[cg(X)] = c\mathbb{E}[g(X)]$ for a constant c, where $g(\cdot)$ is a function of X.
3. $\mathbb{E}[c_1 g_1(X) + c_2 g_2(X)] = c_1 \mathbb{E}[g_1(X)] + c_2 \mathbb{E}[g_2(X)]$ for constants c_1 and c_2, where $g_1(\cdot)$ and $g_2(\cdot)$ are functions of X.
4. $\mathbb{E}[g_1(X)] \leq \mathbb{E}[g_2(X)]$ if $g_1(x) \leq g_2(x)$ for all x.

Expectation is a linear operator, whose properties encapsulate fundamental principles guiding its computation and interpretation in probability theory. As outlined in the box, firstly, the expectation of a constant is simply itself, reflecting the preservation of constants under the expectation operator. Secondly, the linearity property extends this notion to functions of a random variable X, affirming that a constant multiplied by such a function can be factored out of the expectation. Moreover, this linearity extends to the sum of multiple terms involving functions of X, emphasizing the additive nature of expectations. Lastly, the property of monotonicity ensures that if one function of X is pointwise less than or equal to another, then their expectations follow the same ordering. These properties collectively form the foundation for computing and understanding expectations within the realm of probabilistic analysis.

Table 2.1 Summary of the special univariate distributions

Discrete distributions	Continuous distributions
Uniform	Uniform
Bernoulli	Normal/Gaussian
Binomial	Exponential
Geometric	
Poisson	

2.3.5 *Special Univariate Distributions*

Many random variables adhere to specific probability distributions, each characterized by its mathematical form and parameters. Familiarity with these special univariate distributions can greatly simplify analysis and computation, thus facilitating the development of statistical methods, hypothesis testing, and parameter estimation techniques. Typically, we consider three key aspects regarding these distributions: (i) the specific definition of each distribution; (ii) the notable properties or outcomes associated with them; and (iii) the scenarios or types of problems in which each distribution is applicable. While Table 2.1 summarizes some popular special univariate distributions, this section does not exhaustively cover them all. For a more comprehensive discussion, readers are encouraged to refer to references such as Ross (2009) and Casella and Berger (2002).

The *discrete uniform distribution* is a probability distribution that describes an experiment where there are a finite number of equally likely outcomes. In other words, each outcome has the same probability of occurring. For example, consider rolling a fair die. Each outcome has a probability of ⅙ of occurring. This is a classic example of a discrete uniform distribution. We usually denote a random variable X follows a discrete uniform distribution by $X \sim \text{Uniform}(N)$, and its PMF is

$$\mathbb{P}(X = x) = \begin{cases} \dfrac{1}{N} & x = 1, 2, \ldots, N, \\ 0, & \text{otherwise.} \end{cases}$$

Then its expectation and variance are $\mathbb{E}[X] = \dfrac{N+1}{2}$ and $\text{Var}(X) = \dfrac{N^2 - 1}{12}$, respectively.

Many real-world situations can be modelled as sequences of decisions with binary outcomes, also known as *Bernoulli trials*. For instance, coin tosses, the effectiveness of medical treatments, online advertisement clicks, and so on. A random variable X following the *Bernoulli distribution* can be represented as $X \sim \text{Ber}(p)$, with its PMF given by

$$\mathbb{P}(X = x) = \begin{cases} p^x (1-p)^{1-x} & \text{for } x = 0, 1, \text{where } 0 \le p \le 1, \\ 0 & \text{otherwise.} \end{cases}$$

Subsequently, the expectation and variance are $\mathbb{E}[X] = p$ and $\text{Var}(X) = p(1 - p)$, respectively. Both the binomial distribution and geometric distribution are linked to sequences of independent Bernoulli trials. The former describes the count of successes k in a fixed number n of independent trials, each with a success probability of p. The latter models the number of trials needed until the first success occurs.

Another noteworthy distribution worth mentioning is the normal distribution (or Gaussian distribution). It stands out as one of the most fundamental and extensively utilized probability distributions across various domains, including economics, finance, management, natural sciences, and engineering. Its prevalence in numerous natural phenomena, as demonstrated by the central limit theorem, coupled with its mathematical tractability, underscores its significance. When a random variable X follows a *normal/Gaussian distribution*, we denote it as $X \sim N(\mu, \sigma^2)$, where μ and σ represent the mean and standard deviation, with its PDF expressed as

$$f_X(x) = \frac{1}{\sqrt{2\pi\sigma^2}} e^{-\frac{(x-\mu)^2}{2\sigma^2}} \quad \text{for} \quad x \in \mathbb{R}.$$

This definition of the PDF renders the normal distribution a symmetric bell-shaped curve when plotted on a graph.

2.3.6 Other Topics in Probability and Statistics

There are many other valuable topics within probability and statistics that are not covered in this section. For instance, in probability theory, understanding the limiting behaviour of random variables, such as the central limit theorem (CLT), Markov's inequality, Chebyshev's inequality, and the weak law of large numbers, can be immensely beneficial. Additionally, in statistics, various sampling techniques, such as simple random sampling and stratified sampling, merit discussion. Sampling distribution, a cornerstone concept, offers crucial insights into the variability of sample statistics and forms the basis for making statistical inferences about the population. Proficiency in understanding sampling distributions is pivotal for conducting statistical analysis and deriving accurate interpretations from sample data. Statistical inference entails drawing conclusions or making predictions about a population based on data collected from a sample. Point estimation involves estimating unknown population parameters, such as the population mean or proportion, from sample data. Conversely, interval estimation provides a range of values within which the population parameter is believed to lie, accompanied by a level of confidence. These estimation methods enable researchers to quantify uncertainty and make informed decisions based on sample data. Hypothesis testing, a formal procedure, evaluates the strength of evidence against a null hypothesis, typically representing a default assumption. It encompasses specifying null and alternative hypotheses, collecting sample data, and employing statistical tests to ascertain the likelihood of observing the sample data if the null hypothesis were true. Hypothesis testing facilitates the assessment of theories' validity, comparison between groups, and drawing conclusions about population parameters. Analysis of variance, a statistical tool, is employed to compare means across two or more groups to determine if there are statistically significant differences among them. For readers seeking an in-depth exploration of probability theory and statistics, references such as Ross (2009) and Casella and Berger (2002) offer comprehensive insights.

2.4 Summary

We have reviewed essential mathematical concepts relevant to data analytics in business contexts, covering key areas such as calculus, linear algebra, probability, and statistics. Fundamental topics in calculus include real numbers, Cartesian coordinates, functions, derivatives, and integration, all of which are important for understanding rates of change, optimization, and machine learning algorithms. In linear algebra, we focus on vector and matrix operations, which are crucial for organizing data, solving systems of equations, and implementing machine learning tasks. Finally, in probability and statistics, we explore probability measures, random variables, and core concepts such as expectation and variance, which underpin data-driven decision-making and predictions in uncertain situations. Key distributions, including binomial and normal, are discussed, along with their real-world applications. As highlighted in the chapter, these are foundational topics, and while we aim to keep the mathematics accessible for a broad audience, further exploration of these areas is possible through the references provided.

2.5 Exercise

1 What is the limit of the following?

(a) $\lim_{x\to-\infty}\frac{4}{x^2}$.

(b) $\lim_{x\to c}(x^2+10)$.

(c) $\lim_{x\to c}\frac{x^3+4x^2-3}{x^2+5}$.

(d) $\lim_{x\to 2}\frac{x^3-8}{x^2-4}$.

2 If a bike manufacturer produces x bikes per week, the cost function is given by $c(x) = x^3 - 6x^2 + 10x$ pounds. Suppose the manufacturer is currently producing 10 bikes a week, how much additional cost will be incurred to produce one more bike a week?

3 What is the derivative of the following?

(a) $y = x^4 + 12x.$

(b) $y = x^3 + 3x^2 - 5x + 1.$

(c) $y = \dfrac{x^2 - 1}{x^2 + 1}.$

(d) $y = \dfrac{x^4}{4} + \dfrac{x^3}{3} + \dfrac{x^2}{2} + x + 2.$

(e) $y = \left(1 - \dfrac{x}{7}\right)^7.$

(f) $y = (2x - 5)^4 (x + 1)^8.$

4 Calculate the following vector and matrix operations:

(a) $\boldsymbol{U} = \begin{bmatrix} 1 & 2 & 1 & 5 \\ 3 & 2 & 4 & 1 \\ 3 & 1 & 4 & 1 \end{bmatrix}, \boldsymbol{V} = \begin{bmatrix} 7 & 1 \\ 1 & 5 \\ 1 & 2 \\ 2 & 3 \end{bmatrix}$, what is $\boldsymbol{UV}$?

(b) $\boldsymbol{U} = \begin{bmatrix} 4 & 3 & 1 \\ 1 & -2 & 3 \\ 5 & 7 & 0 \end{bmatrix}, \boldsymbol{V} = \begin{bmatrix} 7 \\ 2 \\ 1 \end{bmatrix}$, what is $\boldsymbol{UV}$?

(c) $\boldsymbol{U} = \begin{bmatrix} 1 & 1 & 1 \\ 1 & 1 & -1 \\ 1 & -1 & 1 \end{bmatrix}, \boldsymbol{V} = \begin{bmatrix} 1 & 2 & 3 \\ -1 & -2 & 4 \\ 0 & 5 & 1 \end{bmatrix}$, what is $\boldsymbol{U}^\top \boldsymbol{V}$?

5 If $\boldsymbol{U} = \begin{bmatrix} 1 & 2 \\ 1 & 3 \end{bmatrix}$, and $\boldsymbol{V} = \begin{bmatrix} 1 & 0 \\ 1 & 2 \end{bmatrix}$ please could you check if these equations are correct?

(a) $\boldsymbol{UV} = \boldsymbol{VU}.$
(b) $(\boldsymbol{U} + \boldsymbol{V})^2 = \boldsymbol{U}^2 + 2\boldsymbol{UV} + \boldsymbol{V}^2.$
(c) $(\boldsymbol{U} + \boldsymbol{V})(\boldsymbol{U} - \boldsymbol{V}) = \boldsymbol{U}^2 - \boldsymbol{V}^2.$

6 If $\boldsymbol{U} = \begin{bmatrix} 1 & 0 \\ c & 1 \end{bmatrix}$, calculate $\boldsymbol{U}^k$, where c and k are constant.

7 Roll a die and then flip that number of fair coins. What is the probability of getting exactly 3 heads?

8 Bob has three children, each of which is equally likely to be a boy or a girl independently of the others. Define the events:

A = All the children are of the same sex
B = There is at most one boy
C = The family includes a boy and a girl

(a) Show that A is independent of B, and that B is independent of C.
(b) Is A independent of C?
(c) Do these results hold if Bob has four children?

9 Let X denote a random variable that takes on any of the values –1,0, and 1 with respective probabilities $\mathbb{P}(X = -1) = 0.2$, $\mathbb{P}(X = 0) = 0.5$ and $\mathbb{P}(X = 1) = 0.3$. Compute $\mathbb{E}[X^2]$.

10 The random variable X has the PDF

$$f(x) = \begin{cases} ax + bx^2, & 0 < x < 1, \\ 0, & \text{otherwise.} \end{cases}$$

Assume that $\mathbb{E}[X] = 0.6$.
(a) Find a and b.
(b) Find $\mathbb{P}(X < 1/2)$.
(c) Find Var$[X]$.

3 Getting Started with Python

This chapter briefly introduces Python, focusing on the basics to get you started. As outlined in the introduction, Python has emerged as the dominant programming language in the context of machine learning and its applications in business and finance. This chapter teaches you Python but also programming in general, or, to be more precise, algorithmic thinking.

Right from the start, working on problems or projects is the best way of learning. You will quickly understand the purpose of your coding. Understanding the process and thinking about ways to solve problems is a lot more important than trying to memorize syntax. The latter can be found online easily. In addition, many AI-enhanced tools offer convenient ways to access information. However, you need to understand what you are looking for to use these tools effectively. Put differently, you need to learn how to ask the right question and ChatGPT or its superior cousins will be able to help with the syntax.

In professional life, it is likely that you will learn many programming languages. In contrast to human language, programming languages are much easier to learn after learning how to code in one language. What does this chapter cover?

- Installing and running Python.
- Using integrated development environments or text editors.
- Updating Python and installing packages.
- Creating, activating, and replicating virtual environments.
- Understanding data structures and types.
- Developing loops to automate repetitive tasks.
- Writing conditions.
- Creating functions and objects.

3.1 Installation and Setup

How to get started with Python? We need to install Python and set up ways to work with Python effectively. There are two common ways to install Python. One can argue that users interested in data science and machine learning tend to prefer installing Python through Anaconda. You can download Anaconda for free (www.anaconda.com). Anaconda offers an installation of Python and includes several *integrated development environments (IDEs)*, including *Spyder* and *Jupyter Notebook* (Project Jupyter).

For many applications in data science, machine learning, or business analytics, *R* is another prominent programming language. Anaconda provides access to *R* and *R Studio* without any additional installation. Apart from *Spyder* and *Jupyter Notebook*, *PyCharm* is a popular alternative IDE for Python, which can be downloaded from JetBrains (www.jetbrains.com). For projects that require several programming languages, Visual Studio Code (https://visualstudio.microsoft.com/) is a favourite choice. Every IDE has benefits and disadvantages (e.g. integration with *GitHub*). This book focuses on applications in *business analytics*. Hence, *GitHub* and its role in software development are beyond the scope of this book. Of course, there is much more to learn in the broader area of machine learning or software development. We will suggest additional sources for readers who want to explore specific areas further.

Alternatively, Python can be installed directly on your system, offering more flexibility. Before installing Python, it is recommended to check whether your machine already has a version of Python installed. Open the command line and use the following code.

```
python -V
```

If the terminal displays the version number, Python is ready to be used. Otherwise, navigate to (www.python.org/downloads) and download the latest version of Python. Once the installation is completed, enter the Python shell by typing *python* in the command line.

3.2 'Hello World!'

Now, you operate in Python. It is customary to display 'Hello World!' when starting a new programming language. The print function accomplishes this task. Note that Python functions have open and closed brackets. These brackets might be empty or contain a so-called argument, which refers to the function's input.

```
print("Hello World!")
```

Depending on the function, something or nothing might be returned. In this case, the terminal displays our text as expected. Text is stored as a *string*, which is a data type that contains a sequence of characters. Double or single quotation marks are required to indicate that 'Hello World!' is a string. This is the first type we encounter. More will follow in subsequent sections. You can exit the Python shell by typing the following command, which also seems to be a function.

```
exit()
```

Using the Python shell is one way to work with Python. This is fine for certain tasks but not always convenient. We can type and save our Python code in a file using the extension *.py*. You can use any text editor (e.g. Notepad or Word) to write and edit your code as long as you add the file extension *.py* when saving the file.

For instance, we write our print function in any text editor and save it as *main.py*. You can use the File Explorer (Windows OS) to navigate to the folder where you saved this file. Next, open the command line by typing *cmd* in the window that displays the path to your folder. Alternatively, you can use the change directory command to move to the correct directory. Then, execute the file using the following line of code in the terminal.

```
python main.py
```

This is a common way to run Python scripts. You can use more advanced text editors, which facilitate writing your code. A good choice is *Sublime Text*, which can be downloaded for free (www.sublimetext.com). Scripts can be executed using the command line.

In summary, you can get started with Anaconda, which provides everything in one package, or use a standalone installation of Python. There are many IDEs and text editors to explore, and the code used in this book works on all of them.

3.3 Pip Installer or Conda

Anaconda manages updates, packages, and dependencies. Packages can be installed using *Conda*. The *pip installer* can be used if you work with your standalone Python installation. However, it is advisable to work with virtual environments to control the versions of installed packages. The following section addresses this issue in detail.

However, some Python packages might not be available on Anaconda. In many applications, running your standalone Python installation and using virtual environments to handle packages for different projects remains essential.

To install the *pip installer*, start the command line using *cmd* in the 'type here to search' bar. Then, use the following command, which refers to a so-called *curl*, which transfers data from servers. The second line unpacks the installation for Python.

```
curl https://bootst/rap.pypa.io/get-pip.py-oget-pip.py
python get-pip.py
```

3.4 Virtual Environments

The following experience is an analyst's nightmare. You invested months in developing your code. It all works perfectly. Then, suddenly, error messages indicate unexpected problems. What has happened? The issue is that your code relies on many packages maintained by others.

Virtual environments address this issue effectively. They can save you time and frustration as packages and dependencies change with unforeseen consequences for your code. Let's create and activate our virtual environment following the simple steps outlined below.

We create a new folder where we keep our virtual environment. Navigating to the folder and typing *cmd* into the window that shows the path opens the command line in the selected folder. Before using virtual environments in Python, we run the following code in the command line, which installs *virtualenv* using the *pip installer*.

```
pip install virtualenv
```

After this is completed, we can create the virtual environment, which we call 'MyEnv', as follows.

```
python -m venv MyEnv
```

The installation might take a few minutes. Once completed, a new folder 'MyEnv' emerges, which contains your virtual environment. To activate your virtual environment, use the following code in the command line.

```
MyEnv\Scripts\activate
```

You should see the name of your virtual environment in parentheses displayed in the command line. This indicates that your virtual environment is active. Now, you can install additional packages using the pip installer while your virtual environment remains active.

Closing the command line deactivates your virtual environment. You can also close your virtual environment using *deactivate*. It is common practice to isolate projects using virtual environments.

Over time, you might install a large number of packages. These packages require installation to run your code on other machines. The *requirements.txt* file offers a convenient way to achieve the replication of your virtual environment on other machines. This file contains a list of packages installed in your virtual environment.

How can we create the *requirements.txt* file? With your active virtual environment, we use the following code in the command line.

```
pip freeze > requirements.txt
```

You can inspect the created file, which contains a list of the packages installed in our virtual environment. Most importantly, the installed versions of each package are mentioned. This ensures version control and that your code runs even if packages change over time.

To replicate your environment, we create and activate a new virtual environment using the steps outlined above. This new environment might be located on a different machine. It is common to share the *requirements.txt* file on *GitHub*. Nowadays, *GitHub* hosts most projects due to its powerful tools, facilitating collaboration, storage, and code execution. The main objective is to ensure that others can replicate your code. Good documentation and a *requirements.txt* file are essential for your collaborators or end-users. There is a common saying among programmers:

> Only God and I know how my code works. After two weeks, only God knows.

So please document your code. This book provides plenty of examples. Let's create a *requirements.txt* file by executing the following line of code with the new virtual environment activated.

```
pip install to-requirements.txt
```

This replicates your setup on other machines. Your code should run on the activated new virtual environment.

3.5 Your First Python Session

After installing Python, IDEs, or text editors, we are ready for our first session. Ideally, you follow the steps on your machine while reading the book. This is the most effective way of learning. Horizontal lines separate text and code in this book. Our code appears in a different font, which is colour-coded based on specific keywords. The book will explain all keywords in detail. The online sources provide all *scripts* (i.e. files that contain code). Hence, you can run each code example while going through each chapter.

Open your favourite IDE or text editor and start assigning *variables*. A *variable* is a 'container' that stores information. In the following example, *a* is a variable. This variable is *assigned* assignment indicated by the equal to symbol. The equal to is followed by the number 10. Typing the number 10 provides information. Information includes the value of a variable. Python interprets 10 as an *integer*, a data type. Moreover, 10 is the variable's value.

```
#Assignment
a = 10
b = 'ball'
#Print function
print(a)
print(b)
```

Single or double quotation marks indicate *strings* (i.e. text). Typing numbers are understood as *integers* or *floats*, depending on the value. So, if you assign 7.2, Python knows this is not an *integer*. Instead, Python interprets the input as a *float*. A *float* refers to numbers with one or more decimal places. This is also called a floating-point number.

Without the print functions, nothing is displayed on the terminal. If you use *Spyder* as your *IDE*, the assigned variables *a* and *b* can be inspected without using the print function. The variable explorer window also provides the type of each variable. Note that comments can be added using a hashtag (#) or a doc string (three double quotation marks to open and close the comment, which can be several lines).

Python is *dynamically typed*, which might require a bit of 'getting used to' depending on your prior programming experience. This means that the assignment, such as *a*=10, is understood in the following manner. The variable *a* is an integer based on the value 10, which has been assigned. Hence, the type of *a* is an integer, <class 'int'>, whereas *b* is a string, <class 'str'>. Note that everything is an object in Python. Section 3.14 on *object-oriented programming (OOP)* explores this further. The type function reveals the type of variables (objects), which reveals data types. These data types can change depending on your code dynamically. So, it is important to check and monitor data types.

```
#Type function
#Python is dynamically typed
print(type(a))
print(type(b))
```

As Python is dynamically typed, the type of an object can change after reassignment. The following code runs in Python without causing any *TypeError* as types are modified in line with the input provided. Dynamically typed languages offer flexibility, but there is no protection for types. Hence, checking types, e.g. after an object is passed to a function, is a common feature in Python programming.

```
#Reassign variable - this changes its type
a = 7/8
print(type(a))
print(a)
```

```
b = 2
print(type(b))
```

To illustrate the difference between mathematical and Pythonian thinking, the following example is useful.

```
#Reassign b, taking the old value of b and adding 3
b = b + 3
print(b)
```

Mathematically, this statement is incorrect, but Python follows the following logic. First, it assesses the terms after the equality sign, which refers to an assignment and not the assessment of equality. Python sees *b*, which has a value of 2. Based on this assignment, *b* is an integer. Python then adds 3 to the integer 2 and evaluates the result as 5. The result of 5 is assigned to the variable *b*. Hence, *b* is reassigned, which is permitted. Thus, after this operation, *b* has the value of 5.

It is tempting to use symbolic calculations. For instance, we write *b* equals *x* plus *x* to the power of 2, written as two asterisks in Python. However, this code does not run, and a *NameError* is raised. The error is because *x* is not defined prior to the assignment. Python tries to assess the right-hand side of the assignment first and does not know *x*.

```
#Symbolic calculations are not permitted
#You need to specify a function
b = x + x**2
```

Such statements can be handled using functions and data structures. In addition, there are Python packages that permit symbolic calculations. This section introduced variables, assignments, and data types. The subsequent sessions introduce more advanced data types and explain how they offer better ways to store information.

3.6 Booleans

Let's talk about relationships – well, of the interesting kind – between objects. First, we assign values to two variables, *a* and *b*. Next, we ask Python to check several conditions, including whether the value of *a* is larger, smaller, equal to, or not equal to the value of *b*.

```
a = 7
b = -2
#Assert relationships
print(a > b)
```

```
5 print(a <= b)
6 print(a == b)
7 print(a != b, end = "!!!\ n")
```

The print function in line 7 uses a second argument. What does that mean? Some functions accept more than one argument. Not all arguments might be required. In this case, the argument is called *end*. Arguments can be positional arguments, defined by the order in which they appear inside the brackets, or they can be named. The *print()* function allows options to modify how inputs are displayed. This line tells Python to display whether *a* is not equal to *b* and to end the display with three exclamation marks followed by a line break.

When you run the code, you notice that the statements displayed are of a different type, called *Booleans*. Statements are either *True* or *False*. *Booleans* can be assigned directly, for instance, *c=True*. *True* or *False* seems to be text. However, using quotation marks tells Python to treat *True* or *False* as *strings*. In contrast, *True* or *False* indicates the truth. Python recognizes these keywords as a unique data type called *Booleans*.

Booleans can be assigned directly or result from an assessment, as shown in the following example. Note that the brackets around (*a*>*b*) are not required, but they might make the code more readable. Adding separators such as additional brackets or space tends to make it easier to read code. You will see many examples throughout this book.

```
#Assign Booleans
d = False
c = (a > b)
```

Next, we explore logical comparisons such as *and*, *or*, and *not*. Combining various conditions becomes essential once we introduce *if* statements in section 3.11.

```
#And, or, not
e = not d
f = not d and c
g = d or c
```

BOOLEANS: TELL THE TRUTH

Booleans are either True or False. Python assesses objects as 'falsy' or 'truthy', which is used in many operations (e.g. if statements).

For instance, the integer 0 is 'falsy' but any other value is 'truthy'. Any string is 'truthy', except the empty string, written with open and closed quotation marks without any space between them. You will see this behaviour in action in many applications, which are explained in detail.

```
#Bool function: is it falsy or truthy?
print(bool(0))
print(bool(118))
print(bool("word"))
print(bool(""))
```

Let's explore some more weird but useful objects in subsequent sections.

3.7 Lists

Lists are flexible and powerful tools for many tasks. They contain other objects, which can have different types. For instance, we could combine *a*=3, *b*="*apple*", and *c*=*False* in a list. These collections of objects are useful for storing and accessing data (using *indexing* and *slicing*). We can go through a list item-by-item using *loops*, which will be discussed in subsequent sections.

It is sometimes useful to start with an empty list, which serves as a container for items to be added later. We specify several objects of different types. Then, we apply the *append()* method to add each item to the list.

This is the first example of *object-oriented programming*. The object, the empty list, can be modified by applying a *function* (called a *method* as this function only operates on lists). The *append()* method takes the object inside its brackets (the *argument*) and adds it to the list as the last item.

FUNCTIONS AND METHODS: CHANGE IS COMING

A function takes the object(s) provided inside its brackets (arguments) and might return a new object. A method operates similarly, but only works on certain types of objects.

```
#Empty list
empty = [] #alternative list()
#Add item to list
a = 7
b = 8
```

```
c = -2
d = "fun"
#Append method and dot operator
empty.append(a)
empty.append(b)
empty.append(c)
empty.append(d)
```

THE DOT OPERATOR: WHAT IS THE POINT?

In almost every code example, you will see the dot operator, which is simply a dot after variable names. The dot operator signals that we want to modify the variable (object).

Note that the *dot operator* is added after the name of the object, *empty*, followed by the method, *append()*. The *len()* function takes a list as an argument. It is a function, not a method, i.e. you cannot combine *len()* using the dot operator after the name of a list. The list enters the brackets as an argument. The *len()* function returns the number of items stored in the list.

LOST IN TRANSLATION

The terminology is confusing in the beginning, but it is essential to get used to it, which you will after some practice.

```
len(empty)
```

3.7.1 Indexing and Slicing

Items stored on a list can be returned using indexing, assuming the position of the item is known. We refer to the list followed by rectangular brackets which include the index (position). Note that Python counts from 0, which might cause confusion initially if you are used to programming languages that count from 1 (e.g. Stata/Mata). We can use the index –1 to obtain the last item stored.

```
#Indexing
print(empty[0])
#To get the last entry
```

```
print(empty[-1])
#Alternative
print(empty[len(empty)-1])
```

The *pop()* method can be applied to lists using the dot operator, as shown below. The argument –1 points to the last item stored in the list. The *pop()* method returns this item and modifies the original list, i.e. removes the last item.

```
empty.pop(-1)
```

If you want to obtain several stored items from a list, slicing is a useful approach. Similar to indexing, the start position of your slice is added in rectangular brackets. The start position is included (inclusive) in the returned slice. This is followed by a colon and the end position. Note that the end position is excluded (exclusive) from the returned slice. Slicing returns a list. The default is to move by one integer from the start position until the end position is reached, which is excluded. However, you can specify your own step change using a colon after the end position followed by an integer.

```
#Slicing
print(empty[0 : 1])
print(empty[0 : 2])
print(empty[: 2])
print(empty[1 :])
#Steps (third entry; default is 1)
print(empty[0 :: 2])
```

3.7.2 Copies

Python can make copies of objects. Note that there are different kinds of copies. The following is an example of a shallow copy, which does not contain nested objects. In more advanced sessions, we will explore this further.

```
#Shallow copy
copy = empty[:]
```

The order of items stored in a list can be modified as lists are mutable. The *reverse()* method can be applied to a list using the dot operator. This method reverses the order of items.

```
#Reverse order
copy.reverse()
```

3.7.3 *In or Not In*

Finally, we can check whether an item can be found in a list using the *in* and *not in* operators.

```
#The in and not in operator
print(d in empty)
print(d not in empty)
```

There are many ways to sort, reshuffle, and modify lists, which we introduce later when needed. Understanding the basic properties of lists is sufficient to get started.

3.8 Tuples and Sets

Tuples are a good choice if you want to preserve the order of items. For instance, storing a postal address requires that the different parts of an address remain in the same place (e.g. street name followed by house number). Again, we can start with an empty tuple using open and closed brackets.

```
first_tuple = ()
```

Items can be added using the plus operator. Note that brackets and commas are needed to indicate a tuple.

```
#Add one item to a tuple using +
item_one = "First name"
item_two = "Last name"
item_three = "Position"
#Note the comma!
updated_tuple = first_tuple + (item_one, ) \
+ (item_two, ) + (item_three, )
```

Sometimes, it might be useful to convert a tuple into a list using the *list()* function.

```
updated_list = list(updated_tuple)
```

Indexing and slicing work in the same way as in the case of lists.

```
print(updated_tuple[0])
print(updated_tuple[:2])
```

However, tuples are not mutable, i.e. the order of items is preserved. This might be a useful feature if the order carries meaning. For instance, you might like to store the name and email address of users, where names always come first followed by the associated email address. Hence, the order of items matters.

Another useful feature is to unpack tuples into items and lists. Note the asterisk in front of *other* indicating that all other items go into this category, which is returned as a list. After unpacking, you can use the print function to explore *first_name* and *other*.

```
#Unpacking a tuple into items and lists
first_name, *other = updated_tuple
```

Sets are a different data structure. They are useful for storing unique items, i.e. duplicates are not allowed, which differs from tuples and lists. Furthermore, the order of items is irrelevant. Sets can contain mutually exclusive choices (e.g. colours of tiles). Note that indexing or slicing does not work as the order is not fixed.

Again, we can start with an empty set using *set()*. We can add items to the set by applying the *add()* method to the set. You notice the use of the dot operator. The argument provided is added to the set. Adding the same argument twice does not lead to a duplicate entry.

```
first_set = set()
#Adding colours to a set of colours
first_set.add("red")
first_set.add("blue")
first_set.add("green")
first_set.add("red")
print(first_set)
```

Finally, we can use the *in* and *not in* operators to check whether an item is already an element of the set. A Boolean is returned.

```
print("red" in first_set)
print("blue" not in first_set)
```

3.9 Dictionaries

The final data structure that has many valuable applications refers to *dictionaries*. A dictionary is a comma-separated list of *key:value* pairs inside curly brackets. Dictionaries are indexed by keys and not positions. Values can be extracted using the associated key, as shown in the following example.

```
my_dict = {"Name": "Tom"}
print(my_dict["Name"])
```

Dictionaries can be updated using the *update()* method, which takes a *key:value* pair inside curly brackets as an argument.

```
my_dict.update({'Age': 43})
print(my_dict)
```

The *list()* function applied to a dictionary returns a list containing the keys of the dictionary. This is useful in some applications.

```
list_keys = list(my_dict)
print(list_keys)
```

The *sorted()* function applied to a dictionary provides a sorted list of keys.

```
list_keys = sorted(my_dict)
print(list_keys)
```

To construct a dictionary, applying the *dict()* function is sometimes helpful. This function takes a list of tuples, as shown below. The first item of each tuple refers to the key, whereas the second item is the value.

```
new_dict = dict([('Name', 'Amy'),
('Position', 'Data nerd')])
print(new_dict)
```

Dictionaries can also be constructed using keyword arguments.

```
new_dict = dict(Name = 'Amy', Position = 'Data nerd')
print(new_dict)
```

These basic data structures solve many problems we will encounter later in the book. Before we can work on our first project, we need a basic understanding of loops and branching.

3.10 Loops

The main benefit of programming is delegating boring and repetitive tasks to a machine. *Loops* provide instructions to execute the same commands repeatedly until all cases are covered or a break occurs (e.g. a certain condition is met). Loops are essential in the context of algorithms used in machine learning.

LOOPS: DO IT AGAIN AND AGAIN

Virtually all problems in business analytics do not have a closed-form solution. Hence, we rely on numerical solutions, i.e. trying to minimize or maximize a target function and repeating the process after incremental adjustments again and again until we find an 'acceptable' solution. Loops can handle these iterations.

This section covers the most common types of loops, starting with *for loops* using the *range()* function. This example prints the index *j* starting with the first integer 0 as Python counts from zero. Note that the argument in the *range()* function, i.e. the integer 10 is exclusive. Thus, after 10 iterations, the loop stops, and the last integer printed is 9.

```
for j in range(10):
  print(j)
```

INCLUSIVE OR EXCLUSIVE

Python includes or excludes items. For instance, *range(12)* excludes 12 but includes all integers starting from 0.

Loops can run over iterable objects such as lists or tuples. The index *food* in this example iterates through the list named *foods* starting with the first item. Variables can be embedded into a string for display. This can be achieved using a formatted string, i.e. an *f* is placed in front of the quotation mark, and the variable is embedded in curly brackets. These curly brackets act as a *placeholder*. Placeholders allow us to update our formatted strings based on the latest value of a variable.

```
foods = ['apples', 'pizza', 'bread']
for food in foods:
  print(f"I like to eat {food}")
```

FIBONACCI NUMBERS: LOOPS IN ACTION

Fibonacci numbers refer to a series of integers. Each integer is created by the sum of the two preceding integers. Accordingly, the Fibonacci sequence is 0, 1, 1, 2, 3, 5, 8, ...

To understand the power of loops, let's explore a worked example. We develop a Python code that can generate Fibonacci numbers. In many contexts, including forecasting stock markets, Fibonacci numbers are often regarded as 'magical'. This application is not successful; otherwise, the authors would have accumulated substantial wealth by exploiting the predictive power.

Python can create a Fibonacci series of any length using a *while loop*. A *while loop* keeps iterating until the condition stated after the keyword *while* becomes false. In the example below, the condition states that the previous number is less than 10,000. The variable *fib* refers to a list which starts with the two initial integers.

The next integer is created by adding these two initial values. The new integer is then appended to the existing list using the *append()* method. Indexing with position –1 selects the last entry of the list. This last integer is compared with the value 10,000. Once the condition becomes false, the while loop stops.

```
fib = [0, 1]
while fib[-1] < 10000:
  fib.append(fib[-2] + fib[-1])
print(fib)
```

Next, we explore *if* statements, which make our code more responsive.

3.11 Branching

Branching checks whether conditions are met and then executes a block of code. Python uses *indentation* (tab) to structure code into blocks. An *if* statement starts with the keyword *if* followed by a condition and a colon. Then, an indentation follows, which starts the block of code associated with the *if* statement. This block of code only runs if the condition is true. Otherwise, the block is ignored.

In the example below, the text 'As expected' is only printed if the condition is true. The *print()* function on line 7 that states 'That cannot be true' is always executed.

```
1 #Define variables
2 a = 7
3 b = -2
4 #if statement
5 if a > b:
6     print("As expected")
7 print("That cannot be true")
```

An *if* statement can be followed by an *else* statement. Note that a colon must follow the keyword *else*. Python assesses whether the *if* statement is true. A true statement triggers the block of code following the *if* statement. A false statement moves to the next line of code, which refers to the *else* statement. The block inside the *else* statement is executed. A true *if* condition means that Python 'jumps' over the *else* statement and its associated block of code.

```
#The if-else statement
if a > b:
    print("As expected")
else:
    print("That cannot be true")
```

More refined behaviour can be created using an *if elif else* statement. Note that the *elif* statement is only assessed if the first *if* statement is false. Python checks the *elif* condition next. Again, a false statement means that Python moves to the *else* statement.

```
#the if - elif - else statement
if a > b:
    print("As expected")
elif a == b:
    print("Equal")
else:
    print("That cannot be true")
```

Branching can become complicated as various statements can be nested or combined with loops. Now that we have covered all the basics, it is time to apply our knowledge to solve our first problems.

BRANCHING NEEDS TESTING

Using *if*, *else*, and *elif* statements makes our code responsive to certain conditions (e.g. user input). However, always test your code and check whether the behaviour is intended.

3.12 First Project: The Takeaway Challenge

Working on projects is the best way to learn Python and programming in general. Solving problems offers learning opportunities. Let's focus on the following task.

YOUR TASK

Build an application running in the terminal that takes customers' names and food orders. The application calculates the total price. Interaction with customers occurs in the terminal.

We recommend that you attempt this task before exploring our implementation. You might come up with better ideas. Our solution is one of many possible ways to address this task.

It is helpful to start building a few ‘containers’ to store information about food items sold and their prices. There are many different ways to address this problem. For instance, lists can be used to store this information. They could be stored in two separate lists or a list containing tuples.

```
#Create a list of food items
food_list = [
        ‘pizza’,
        ‘pasta’,
        ‘burger’
        ]

#Create a list of prices
price_list = [
    10,
    7.5,
    5]
```

The code above creates a list of food items *food_list* and a list of prices *price_list*. Using *lower_snake_case* to name variables in Python is common. Yet, this is only a convention. This design has its flaws as the order of items can be changed. This would mess up the link between food items and their prices, which is based on the position in the list.

Next, we display a welcome message using the *print()* function, and ask for customers' names using the *input()* function. Note that inputs are always regarded as strings by Python. To store inputs, we need a variable. In line 3, we assign *name* to the return value of the *input()* function. So the information is stored for later use.

```
1 #The input function
2 print(‘Welcome to Cheap Cuts’)
3 name = input(‘Enter your name: ’)
```

We start with an empty list to collect the items ordered, which we call *order_list*. Then, we go through all food items using a loop, which iterates over our list of food items, *food_list*.

We ask customers using their names, which a formatted string accomplishes, whether they want the first food item. If they type *‘y’*, the order list is appended with the integer 1. The *elif* statement checks whether customers input *‘n’*. In this case, the order list is appended with a zero. If customers input neither *‘y’* or *‘n’*, the *else* statement is triggered. A warning message is displayed.

```
#Make an order
order_list = []

for food in food_list:
    order = input(f‘{name} do you want {food}?: [y/n] ’)
    if order == ‘y’:
        order_list.append(1)
    elif order == ‘n’:
        order_list.append(0)
    else:
        print(f‘sorry {name} I do not understand’)
```

Our initial attempt has a few shortcomings. First, it handles an exception if customers input an invalid response. However, the loop just continues and does not start again. Customers cannot correct their invalid input. Second, we do not permit that customers want many pizzas, so only one item is added.

The first issue can be fixed using a *while loop*. The loop keeps going until the condition becomes false. Hence, we can specify a Boolean *order_incomplete = True* and then start the *while loop* referring to the Boolean, which is initially true. Then we go through our *if-elif-else* sequence and switch the Boolean *order_incomplete* to false if we recognize a valid customer response. This ensures that we repeat questions until valid responses are collected.

```
#Make an order
order_list = []

for food in food_list:
    order_incomplete = True
    while order_incomplete:
        order = input(f‘{name} do you want {food}?: [y/n] ’)
    if order == ‘y’:
        order_list.append(1)
        order_incomplete = False
    elif order == ‘n’:
        order_list.append(0)
        order_incomplete = False
    else:
        print(f‘sorry {name} I do not understand’)
```

The second issue is easy to fix by adding another *input()* function, which asks for the number of items customers wish to order. Note that all inputs are regarded as strings.

Hence, we need the *int()* function to convert the input into an integer, which is added to the order list.

```
#Make an order
order_list = []

for food in food_list:
      order_incomplete = True
      while order_incomplete:
            order =
            input(f'{name} do you want {food}?: [y/n] ')
            if order == 'y':
                 num =
                 input(f'How many {food}s do you want? ')
                 order_list.append(int(num))
                 order_incomplete = False
            elif order == 'n':
                 order_list.append(0)
                 order_incomplete = False
            else:
                 print(f'sorry {name} I do not understand')
```

This is certainly an improvement, but there are still issues. What if customers respond to the question 'How many pizzas do you want?' with an invalid input that cannot be converted into an integer? Additional exception handling is needed to address these issues. Alternatively, we could restrict users' inputs using a graphical user interface (GUI) (e.g. a horizontal slider that only permits integers). We will explore GUIs provided by desktop and web applications later in this book.

Finally, we calculate the total costs using *list comprehension*. We can create new lists from existing lists. For instance, we can select even numbers from a list of integers and store the result in a new list.

```
list_num = [2 , 4 , 5]
list_even_num =
[num for num in list_num if num % 2==0]
```

List comprehension offers a compact way to write loops. The same could be achieved by writing several lines of code.

LIST COMPREHENSION

List comprehension is a powerful tool to make your code more concise.

```
list_num = [2, 4, 5]
list_even_num = []
for num in list_num:
    if num % 2==0:
        list_even_num.append(num)
```

You must get used *to* the syntax of *list comprehension*. They are used frequently in more advanced code.

For our problem, we use a different kind of loop. A *zip()* goes through two lists item-by-item simultaneously. Hence, it looks at the number of items ordered and the associated price. Both are multiplied. Finally, the *sum()* function is applied to the new list created by the *list comprehension*.

```
print(f'\nThanks {name} for ordering {order_list[0]} \
food_list[0]}s')
print(f'{order_list[1]} {food_list[1]}s and \
order_list[2]} {food_list[2]}s')

total_price = sum([order * price for order, \
price in zip(order_list, price_list)])

print(f'Please pay GBP {total_price}')
```

To complete the task, we interact with customers using formatted strings and display the total price of the order. This completes *our* first Python project.

LEARNING BY DOING

Projects *are* a great way to learn. Challenge yourself with your own project, or explore free Python projects on our GitHub pages.

3.13 Functions

Thus far, we have reassigned variables and applied built-in Python functions. However, Python also offers user-made *functions*. Let's consider the following example. We assign two integers x and a and want to calculate x^a. This operation can *be* executed as follows, and the result is displayed using a formatted string.

```
x = 5
a = 3
result = x**a
print(f'{x} to the power of {a} is {result}.')
```

What if you want to apply the same operation to a different value of x and a? You can reassign variables and re-run the code by copy-pasting it. However, this is not an efficient approach.

Python enables you to define your own functions. A function is introduced using the keyword *def* followed by the user-defined name of the function. Open and closed brackets are required even if the function requires no arguments. In our case, we want to input two integers, which we specify inside the brackets. After the function is named and arguments are specified, an indentation must follow, which starts a block. Any code inside the block is only executed once the function is called.

We create a local variable named *out*. This local variable only exists inside the function (block). It has a local *scope*. Hence, if you call the function, you cannot print *out*, except the function returns this variable.

SCOPE: WHERE DO YOU EXIST?

Scope is an important concept in programming. A variable introduced in a block of code (e.g. a function) only exists inside this block of code. It has a local scope. Local variables can be returned by functions to be used outside their functions. Alternatively, we can declare that a variable has a *global* scope by using the keyword *global* before the variable name.

```
def power(x, a):
    out = x**a
    print(f'{x} to the power of {a} is {out}.')
```

When you execute the above code, nothing seems to happen. To see any output, we must invoke or call the function.

```
power(5, 3)
power(x = 5, a = 3)
```

To call the function, we use its name followed by open and closed brackets. There are two ways to pass arguments. First, we can use positional arguments. The order follows how the function was defined, i.e. x is first followed by a. Second, keywords that need to match our definition can be used. Working with keywords permits changing the order of arguments.

Our function does not return anything. So if we assign a variable to the function, the variable is of type *none*. The function, however, displays the outcome using the *print()* function. The function can provide a return value using the keyword *return*. This can be used in assignments.

```
def power(x, a):
    out = x**a
    print(f'{x} to the power of {a} is {out}.')
    return out
```

Accordingly, we can specify a variable that takes the return value of our function.

```
out = power(5, 3)
```

Functions help to simplify the structure of your code. It is common to keep functions in separate files and import them into your main script if needed. We will explore this in more advanced problems. Let's do another coding challenge to practise our skills.

YOUR NEXT TASK

Your task is to write a function that asks for user input. Users should input integers. The function returns the sum and product of all integers entered. The process stops when the user enters 0.

It might be convenient to split this function into two. The first function checks whether users' input is valid and returns an integer. The second function uses the validation function and completes the remaining tasks.

```
def input_num():
    invalid_input = True

    while invalid_input:
        num = input("Please enter an integer. \
        Enter 0 to stop: ")
        try:
            num = int(num)
            invalid_input = False
        except:
            print('Invalid input')
    return num
```

The function *input_num()* handles our input validation. Again, we use a *while* loop until users input a valid response. We make use of the *try-except* exception handling approach. The keyword *try* followed by a colon starts a block. Indentation is required. So Python tries to run this block. If it fails, it moves to the block after the keyword *except*. In our case, we try to apply the *int()* function, which converts users' input into an integer. This fails if users do not respond with a number. The Boolean *invalid_input* is switched to false once the users' input is converted into an integer successfully. Finally, the function returns the integer.

The second function *sum_product()* calls the *input_num()* function, which returns a valid integer provided by the user. Remembering that 0 is evaluated as false, we use *num*, the valid input from users, to stop the *while* loop. So users can stop the process by responding with a zero as requested. Finally, integers are added and multiplied. The result is displayed using formatted strings. The function does not return anything.

```
def sum_product():
    #Sum and product of numbers entered
    sum_num = 0
    prod_num = 1

    #Call first number
    num = input_num()

    while num:
        sum_num += num
        prod_num *= num
        num = input_num()

    print(f"The sum of integers is {sum_num}")
    print(f"The product of integers is {prod_num}")
```

To test our functions, we call the function. Users' inputs are requested, validated, and passed to the *sum_product()*. This completes our coding challenge.

```
sum_product()
```

Thus far, we used built-in classes such as lists or tuples. Next, we will explore user-defined classes with a brief introduction to *object-oriented programming (OOP)*.

3.14 Object-Oriented Programming

Let's imagine that you want to build a staff management system. What do you need in a staff management system? What tasks should it be able to perform?

First, you will need staff. What do you need to know about members of staff? It would be useful to identify them, which might be accomplished by names or staff numbers. Furthermore, it might be helpful to know how many hours they work.

It is always a good idea to start with the first object and continue adding features, depending on your requirements. We start a new class using the keyword *class*. It is common to add open and closed brackets. In addition, convention dictates that classes are written in *UpperCamelCase*. The following code creates the *Staff* class. The keyword *pass* after indentation is useful to create an empty shell, i.e. a class without any attributes, methods, or other features.

ABOUT SNAKES AND CAMELS

Programming in Python follows certain conventions. Names of functions tend to be in *lower_snake_case*, whereas classes use *UpperCamelCase*. Hence, if you read the name *MyNewClass()* or *my_new_function()*, you should know whether it is a class or function.

```
class Staff():
    pass
```

Running this code does not seem to do anything. To start using the new class, a so-called *instance* needs to be initialized, which refers to assigning a variable to the class.

```
new_staff = Staff()
```

This creates a member of staff. All information (well, at the moment, nothing) is stored in *new_staff*, and the *type()* reveals that this object is an instance of the new class *Staff()*.

Using the *print()* function on *new_staff* displays a code. Basically, it points to a place in memory. No other information is displayed. Again, there is no information yet to display, and Python does not know how to display information.

We need to store information about the name and hours worked. This can be achieved using *attributes*. To add attributes, we use a so-called *magic method*, the *__init__(self)* method. This method is just written like a function using the *def* keyword followed by the name and open and closed brackets. Arguments look different as *self* must be included as the first positional argument. The argument *self* refers to the instance (the self). Note that attributes can be accessed using the dot operator without open and closed brackets. So when we assign initial values to attributes, we can refer to *self*, the instance of the class, use the dot operator and state the attribute's name. Then, we assign a value, which can be passed using arguments.

```
class Staff():
    def __init__(self, name, hours):
        self.name = name
        self.hours = hours
```

If we want to initialize an instance, the revised class demands two positional arguments. The argument self is not counted as it does not need to be passed.

```
new_staff = Staff('Amy', 40)
```

The new staff member has the attributes *name* and *hours*. In the process of initialization, values are assigned to both attributes and the information is stored on the instance. Thus, using *print(new_staff.name)* will display 'Amy'. However, *print(new_staff)* only shows the location in memory as we have not told Python what to display.

We add another magic method, the *__ repr __(self)* method. Magic methods are also called *dunder methods*. Note that dunder refers to a double underscore. The reason for using double underscores is that it is unlikely that users will name their own methods in the same way. Otherwise, magic methods could be overwritten.

```
class Staff():
    def __init__(self, name, hours):
        self.name = name
        self.hours = hours
    def __repr__(self):
        return f'{self.name} works for {self.hours} hours'
```

Adding this magic method tells Python to print a formatted string, which includes the attributes when using the *print()* function on an instance of the class.

Next, our staff management system might be used in different companies. Each firm employs several staff. Firms should be able to add new staff. This functionality could be handled by a new class, which we call *Firm()*. We could start a new firm with zero employees, and the staff details could be stored on each firm instance. Finally, we need a method that acts on an instance, such as adding a new staff member.

```
class Firm():
    def __init__(self):
        self.staff_list = []

    def add_staff(self, staff):
        self.staff_list.append(staff)
```

The *__ init __(self)* method initializes an instance of the *Firm()* class with the attribute *staff_list*. Initially, the list is empty. So, we do not include an argument in the __init__(self). Staff are added by applying the *add_staff(self, staff)* method on an instance of the *Firm()* class. This method changes the attribute by appending the list of staff. Staff is an instance of the *Staff()* class.

Accordingly, the members of staff stored in *staff_list* are instances of the *Staff()* class. Writing a loop that iterates through the attribute *staff_list* can access the attributes of each item on the list, including the name and hours worked.

We conclude this section with an extensive test of our new classes.

```
#Instance
staff1 = Staff('Amy', 40)
staff2 = Staff('Tom', 35)
print(f'{staff1.name} works for {staff1.hours} hours.')

#Start firm
my_firm = Firm()
print(my_firm.staff_list)

#Add staff to list
my_firm.add_staff(staff1)
my_firm.add_staff(staff2)

#Show our list
print(my_firm.staff_list)
```

Object-oriented programming (OOP) can be helpful in structuring your code. You will have many choices when implementing your code. Many more features are a little advanced. These will be introduced later in the book.

3.15 Summary

Well done for completing this chapter. Getting used to Python is a longer process. So, do not expect to master Python programming in a few weeks. It will take a lot of practice. If you are totally new to programming, you might find the playlist on *Python for Data Science* helpful as it offers a very gentle and detailed introduction.

THE BEST WAY TO LEARN PYTHON

- Do not memorize code.
- Try to use code to solve problems.
- Work on projects as soon as possible.

If you want to work on more projects, we suggest the *Blackjack: First Python Project* playlist. If you need a more advanced challenge, you can try the *Families of Florence: Python Project* playlist. The latter explores user interfaces, which this book covers in later chapters. Each playlist has its own GitHub repository, providing free access to the code.

We suggest that you attempt the exercises at the end of this chapter. This will allow you to experiment with coding in Python. A section on possible solutions details each task. Of course, there are many alternative ways to address each task. Time to explore.

3.16 Exercise

You will need to learn about importing Python packages using the *import* keyword at the top of your Python script. Your task is to build a simple dice game step by step. Our online sources provide the solution in the Python file *dice.py*. Now, make Python roll the dice for you!

3.16.1 Random Numbers

Generate a random number from 0 to 1 using the *random* Python package. Assign this random number to a variable.

3.16.2 Create a Player Class

Create a player class with two attributes: the player's name and the number of armies, which refers to an integer.

3.16.3 Initialize Two Players

Create two instances of the player class. 'Amy' has 5 armies, whereas 'Tom' has only 4 armies.

3.16.4 Start a Conflict

For each army, the player can roll the 'dice,' i.e. obtain a random number from 0 to 1. The random numbers are added up, giving the player a score. The player with the highest score wins. Your code should print a statement about the game's winner to the terminal.

4 Data Wrangling

Data wrangling is the process of obtaining data, shaping it into the desired shape, and addressing data-related issues such as outliers and missing values. After more than 20 years of working with data, we stress the importance of data handling. If your dataset has issues (e.g. measurement errors, incomplete data, etc.), fixing the consequences at the data analysis stage will be very hard or impossible.

Machine learning relies on high-quality data. Training and test data require careful data preparation, which is even more important if you want to work with unstructured data (e.g. text obtained from PDF files). You need to think very carefully about your research design (data sources, sampling, inherent biases, etc.), data structures (time series, panel data, etc.), and data-related issues (missing values, extreme values, etc.).

This chapter introduces *NumPy* and *Pandas*. Both libraries offer a wide range of tools, which are essential in the context of handling and managing data. Next, we explore various ways to import data. Getting data from online sources has emerged as a powerful alternative to traditional databases. *APIs* (application programming interfaces) play a major role in providing convenient access to data from online sources such as Reddit or Yahoo Finance to name a few.

Identifying *outliers*, i.e. extreme observations, is important in practice. We discuss common methods and their advantages and disadvantages. *Missing values* affect most datasets. Should we ignore missing values, delete cases, or try to predict missing values from existing data?

Finally, this chapter briefly outlines the applications of *synthetic data* (e.g. testing) and simulations. Both can be useful in solving problems in business analytics. In summary, you will learn the following after completing this chapter:

- Understanding arrays and numerical methods in NumPy.
- Using Pandas to import, reorganize, and manage data.
- Obtaining data from social media platforms using APIs.
- Getting financial data for free from Yahoo Finance.
- Exploring PDF documents to retrieve data.

- Detecting and handling outliers.
- Dealing with missing values.
- Generating synthetic data for testing.
- Running experiments using simulations.

Before diving into data analysis and modelling, note the following:

- Always check your data.
- Understand the data structure and format.
- Are values missing?
- Can you observe unusual or extreme values?

4.1 NumPy

The previous chapter introduced Python and covered basic data types, including lists and tuples. However, additional 'tools' offered by Python libraries are crucial to work with data efficiently. NumPy is a library containing many functions and operations on arrays.

THE POWER OF NUMPY

You will notice that operations in NumPy are much faster than in 'pure' Python. NumPy is based on the programming languages C and C++, which provide a significant speed advantage.

At first glance, arrays look similar compared to lists. They also contain items (e.g. integers). However, operations on arrays in NumPy are much faster, and data is stored more efficiently in arrays than in lists. Consequently, machine learning algorithms tend to require NumPy arrays as inputs. Moving between data types, e.g. converting lists into NumPy arrays, is often a useful strategy to speed up your code.

Before we can use NumPy, the library needs to be imported. Note that NumPy does not need to be installed if you use the Anaconda distribution. In other cases, you might need to install NumPy using the pip installer (*pip install numpy*).

The previous chapter introduced the *pip installer*. A virtual environment is unnecessary because NumPy does not depend on other packages.

```
import numpy as np
```

The *import* statement adds *as np*, which is not required. However, *as np* means that NumPy functions can be accessed using *np.* instead of *numpy.*, which is more convenient. You can use any acronym, but *np* is the convention. Once imported, we can use NumPy's square root function *np.sqrt()*.

For instance, we assign integers to variables a and b. Then, we apply a NumPy function to one of the variables.

```
a = 7
b = 2
print(np.sqrt(a))
```

If you have done a course in linear algebra, you should be familiar with vectors (row or column vectors) and matrices. Arrays can be regarded as vectors or matrices. We use arrays to handle data, e.g. the data matrix X is an array with N rows (observations) and k columns (independent variables and the all-one vector if a constant term is added to the model).

There are many functions that can be used to create NumPy arrays. For instance, the function *np.zeros(d)* determines a column vector, i.e. d rows and one column, which contains zeros. This all-zero array might be useful as a container for subsequent value changes. Basically, the container defines the dimension (e.g. iterations or observations) of the problem, followed by an algorithm that derives entries replacing the zeros.

The function *np.ones(d)* established the all-one array with dimension d. An all-one-column vector is useful for calculations (e.g. it is common to add an all-one column to a data matrix if a constant term is needed). Using indexing, entries in arrays can be reassigned.

The *np.array()* function assigns arrays in one line. In practice, arrays are created from imported data. Data can be imported directly as arrays using NumPy. In many applications, however, data imports are managed in Pandas, another Python library covered in the following section. Pandas objects such as *DataFrames* can easily be converted into NumPy arrays.

```
vector = np.zeros(5)
ones = np.ones(5)
vector[0] = a
vector[-1] = b
vector_a = np.array([1, 2, 34, 7])
```

When developing algorithms, starting with loops over arrays or lists tends to be more intuitive. This is acceptable for development but loops are slow to execute. It is common to refactor an initial algorithm to replace loops with operations on arrays. This process is called *vectorization*. As shown below, NumPy can apply functions to arrays, which is more efficient than applying a function to each item in a loop.

```
sqrt_vector = np.sqrt(vector)
```

An array representing a matrix with all-zero entries can be created, where the first integer refers to rows and the second integer to columns. Entries can be reassigned using indexing. Note that depending on the dimension of the array, several indices might be required to identify an entry uniquely. In our example, we need to specify the row and column numbers, noting that Python counts from zero.

```
matrix = np.zeros((3, 4))
matrix [0, 1] = a
```

NumPy arrays such as *matrix* have shape and size attributes. You can access these attributes using the dot operator followed by the attribute without open and closed brackets. Note that shape returns a list with two entries in our example. The first entry refers to the number of rows, and the second is the number of columns. We can use indexing to access the number of rows. Hence, we can construct a suitable all-one-row vector, which can be pre-multiplied to our array.

```
print(matrix.shape)
print(matrix.size)
ones = np.ones((1, matrix.shape[0]))
```

Matrix multiplication can be executed as follows. In the context of matrix operations, constructing the identity matrix is useful (the neutral element in matrix multiplication).

```
matrix_new = np.matmul(ones, matrix)
matrix_identity = np.eye(5)
```

Several methods can be applied to arrays using the dot operator. For instance, we can obtain descriptive statistics from a data matrix (array), including the mean and standard deviation.

```
print(matrix.sum())
print(matrix.mean())
print(matrix.std())
```

The following NumPy functions generate a range for loops or an x-axis for graphs. The third integer can adjust steps. The function *np.linspace()* determines the optimal step size based on the start, endpoint, and number of steps. Note that the endpoint is included.

```
idx = np.arange(1, 10, 0.1)
ldx = np.linspace(1, 10, 100)
```

Horizontal and vertical stacks merge data stored as arrays (data matrix). A horizontal stack refers to adding additional variables (columns) to a dataset where the number of observations matches (rows). A vertical stack adds observations based on the same number of columns (variables). For instance, observing several time series might increase the investigation period.

```
matrix_a = np.array([[1, 2, 3], [3, 6, 8]])
matrix_b = np.array([[0, -2, 3], [4, -5, 1]])
print(matrix_a, matrix_b, sep = “ and \ n”)

print(“Horizontal”)
print(np.hstack([matrix_a, matrix_b]))

print(“Vertical”)
print(np.vstack([matrix_a, matrix_b]))
```

NumPy offers many methods that operate on arrays that modify dimensions or entries. The following example can be used to flatten arrays into a single dimension.

```
print(matrix_a.ravel())
print(matrix_a.flatten())
```

Note that the methods *ravel()* and *flatten()* look the same, but we are careful as *flatten()* returns a copy. You might change your original matrix if values are resigned. Try the following example in Python.

```
rav = matrix_a.ravel()
flat = matrix_a.flatten()

#Changing rav and flat
flat[2] = 99
rav[2] = 99
```

It is virtually impossible to cover all aspects of NumPy. We will introduce new functions and methods when needed later in the book. By now, the basics are covered, and we should be ready to use NumPy's arrays and convert various data types into arrays.

4.2 Pandas

Pandas has emerged as the favourite Python library for importing data, reshaping data structures, and analysing data. If you do not work with Anaconda, you can install Pandas using the *pip installer*.

```
pip install pandas
v
```

After installation, the package Pandas needs to be imported. It is common to use the acronym *pd*.

```
import pandas as pd
```

In most applications, the first step is to import data from other files. Pandas can handle different data formats, including Excel, Stata (dta files), MAT files, etc.; however, the most common data format is comma-separated values (CSV) files. Many data sources or statistical software packages can export data as csv files.

If you keep your data files in a different directory compared to your Python script, a change of the working directory is needed to locate the data. The *os* library manages the interaction with your operating system, including changing directories. This library is imported, and the path to your data files is specified as a string, requiring quotation marks. Then, the function *chdir()* is called. It is advisable to store data in the same folder where your Python script is located. Hence, you do not need to change the directory.

If you specify the full path to your data files (absolute import), this path only works on your machine. Using your code on a different machine with a different file structure will result in errors. Generally, it is better to use relative import, which relates to your current location. For instance, you might store your data files in the folder *data*. For instance, you can access this folder using *"./data/hh_data.csv"*. Note the use of backslash or forward slash depends on your operating system.

```
import os
path = ""
os.chdir(path)
```

The Pandas function *pd.read_csv()* imports data from csv files. The object *data* refers to a Pandas *DataFrame*. *DataFrames* come with many useful attributes and methods to modify your data.

```
data = pd.read_csv ("hh_data.csv")
```

After a data import, displaying the first or last five observations of your dataset is good practice. This provides an overview, capturing the data structure (e.g. time series) and variables. Some IDEs (e.g. Spyder) can display data in the variable explorer.

```
data.head()
data.tail()
```

Visualizing your data is usually the first step in data analysis as many features (e.g. non-linear patterns, outliers) can be detected at this stage. Scatter plots show two-dimensional relationships. Figure 4.1 depicts household income and fixed assets in our example. The *plot.scatter()* method does not require any additional library. However, if you want to save and export the figure *matplotlib.pyplot* is required. Note that the *show()* function has to follow the *savefig()* function. This displays the figure if the script is executed using the command line. Some IDEs store figures in separate output windows.

```
import matplotlib.pyplot as plt
data.plot.scatter(x = 'FIX_A', y = 'INC')
plt.savefig(r"DW_scatter.png")
plt.show()
```

Figure 4.1 Scatter plot: income and fixed assets

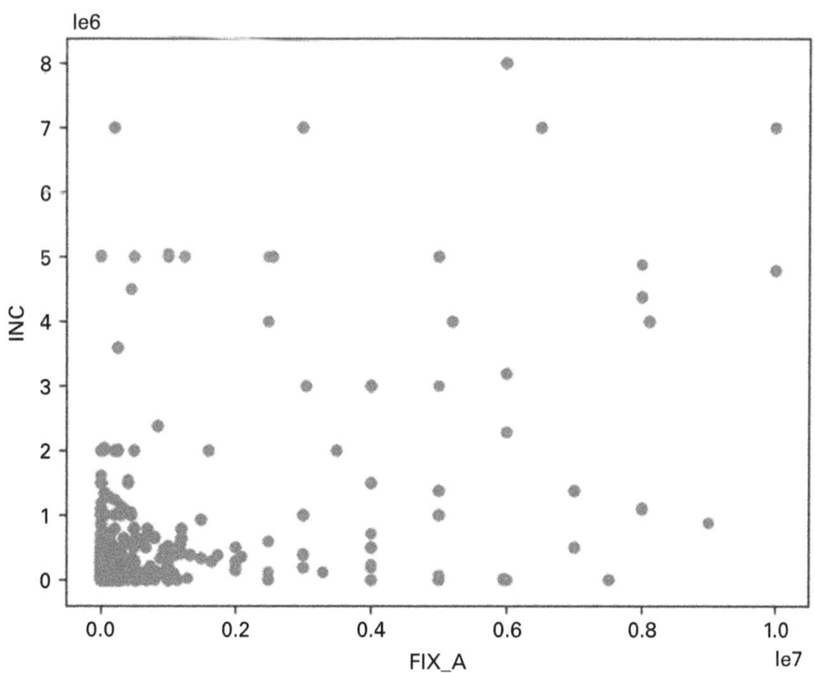

We can select variables from our dataset, the Pandas *DataFrame*, using keys (i.e. the name of the column or variable) or attributes (i.e. columns or variables become attributes of the *DataFrame*). The resulting Pandas object is a Pandas *series*.

```
income = data['INC']
income = data.INC
```

Indexing works when we apply the *iloc[]* method. The entries refer to the data structure, i.e. rows followed by columns. In this example, we focus on the first column and select all or the first 100 observations.

```
income = data.iloc[:, 0]
income = data.iloc[:100, 0]
```

Conditions can be applied when selecting variables. Conditions can be combined; however, note that the bitwise operator & is used rather than the logical operator *and*. The reason is that Pandas *Series* contains many entries. The same applies to NumPy arrays.

```
income = data.INC[data.INC > 100000]
data = data[(data.INC > 100000) & (data.FIX_A > 100000)]
```

Finally, we can convert a Pandas *Series* into a NumPy array using the *values* attribute. This is required before applying many machine learning algorithms.

```
income = data.INC.values
```

Understanding these basic ideas is sufficient to get started with Pandas. Later sections will explore many more features.

4.3 Data Downloads Using APIs

There are many ways to obtain data, including access to databases, web scraping, and APIs. The latter can be convenient and often for free. A word of caution is warranted. There are a vast number of APIs. Sadly, not all are reliable or safe to use. You need to do your research and check the documentation carefully. Finally, APIs keep changing. You might need to adjust your code or control versions of packages using virtual environments.

This section demonstrates the use of the Yahoo Finance API, which provides free access to financial data. First, we suggest to create and activate a virtual environment as outlined in the previous chapter. Using the command line and *python -m venv yahoo*, we create the environment called *yahoo*. This environment is activated using *yahoo Scripts Activate* and is ready for installation. Second, we install the Python package *yfinance* using the *pip* installer.

```
pip install yfinance
pip install matplotlib
```

After installation, we import the Python package *yfinance* and *matplotlib.pyplot*. The latter library offers many functions and methods for data visualization. Chapter 5 on data visualization covers more advanced tools and alternative Python libraries.

```
import yfinance as yf
import matplotlib.pyplot as plt
```

To obtain financial data, we can use the *download* function, which takes the ticker symbol, period, and interval, among others, as arguments. Note that you can also specify start and end dates using the format *YYYY-MM-DD*. By default, daily data is downloaded but you can obtain intra-daily data restricted to the last 30 days.

```
data = yf.download("BTC-USD", period = "1d", interval = "1m")
print(type(data))
```

The object *data* contains the downloaded financial data. In our example, we selected the value of Bitcoin in USD for a one-day period and a one-minute interval. The *type()* function reveals that the object *data* is a Pandas *DataFrame*. The *head()* method is useful to explore the data structure. Apparently, our download provides intra-daily data for prices (open, high, low, close, and adjusted close) as well as trading volume.

```
print(data.head())
```

We plot closing prices using the attribute *Close* to refer to the Pandas *Series*, which is the argument for the *plot()* function. Finally, we save the figure and display Figure 4.2.

```
plt.plot(data.Close)
plt.savefig(r"DW_bitcoin.png")
plt.show()
```

The next section explores a different API and combines country-level data in Pandas.

Figure 4.2 Intra-day Bitcoin price in USD

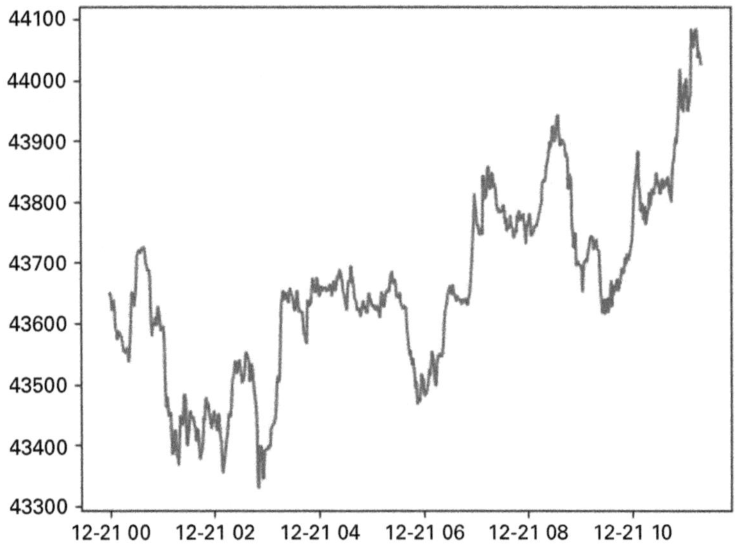

4.4 Merging

Berkeley Earth (https://berkeleyearth.org/data/) provides access to global climate data. Data is available on country levels and based on geographical location (gridded data). Let us explore time series data for India and the UK. Following the links on the website, we navigate to a url that provides the country-level data as in a *txt* format.

Our first task is to download the data from the url using the *requests* library. Again, it is useful to create and activate a virtual environment called *web*, followed by installing the *requests* library.

```
python -m venv web
web\Scripts\activate
pip install requests
pip install numpy
pip install pandas
pip install matplotlib
```

All installed Python libraries are imported, followed by a list of countries and an empty list that will store our Pandas *DataFrames*.

```
import requests
import numpy as np
import pandas as pd
import matplotlib.pyplot as plt
#Country list
countries = [
    'india',
    'united - kingdom'
    ]
#Empty list of Pandas DataFrames
dfs = []
```

We construct urls from three strings. The first and the last part are identical for different countries. Hence, looping through the list of countries, we concatenate a unique string pointing to the respective url for each country. Then, we use the *requests* library and obtain the data as a text file. Country-specific file names are constructed, and the data is written to txt files. These text files are loaded as Pandas *DataFrames*. Finally, we name each *DataFrame* using the country name stored in the list of countries. Note that this code can be easily modified by adding additional country names. Each *DataFrame* is added to the list of *DataFrames* called *dfs* using the *append()* method.

```
for country in countries:
  url_part1 = 'https://berkeley - earth -
        \temperature.s3.us - west - 1.amazonaws.com/
     Regional/TAVG/'
  url_part2 = '-TAVG - Trend.txt'
  url = url_part1 + country + url_part2
  response = requests.get( url, allow_redirects = True)
  #Obtains strings
  strings = response.text
  file_name = country + '_output.txt'
  open(file_name, 'w').write(strings)
  #Load data to obtain DataFrame
  data = np. loadtxt( file_name, comments = '%')
  df_name = 'df' + '_country'
  df_name = pd.DataFrame(data[:,:6], \
        columns = ['year', 'month', 'm_ano', \
        'm_temp', 'a_ano', 'a_temp'])
  dfs.append(df_name)
  print(df_name.head())
```

The data download contains many variables. We need the year and months to identify the observation uniquely. Apart from the identifiers, the monthly temperature anomaly, which refers to a deviation from historical averages, is obtained. Line 2 shows a list comprehension to reassign the list of *DataFrames* to datasets that contain the identifiers and the monthly temperature anomaly. Renaming the column to make it unique for different countries is useful. This is achieved using a loop over the *zip()* of *DataFrames* and countries. The datasets with renamed variables are then added to a new list called *dfs_renamed*.

There are many different ways to merge datasets in Pandas. We use the *merge()* method in this example. Starting with the first dataset in the list of *DataFrames*, we merge the second dataset. The index can be readjusted. Finally, we check the data structure using the *head()* and *tail()* methods.

```
1 #Merge data
2 dfs = [df[['year', 'month', 'm_ano']] for df in dfs]
3 #Rename variable
4 dfs_renamed = []
5 for df, country in zip(dfs, countries):
6   df = df.rename(columns={'m_ano': country})
7   dfs_renamed.append(df)
8
9 #Merge DataFrames
10 df_merged = dfs_renamed[0].merge(dfs_renamed[1])
11 df_merged.reindex(['year', 'month'])
12 print(df_merged.head())
13 print(df_merged.tail())
```

Merging the data was successful. The following code creates a subplot comparing temperature anomalies across countries. Of course, the chapter on data visualization covers many ways to modify the appearance of the subplots.

```
#Plot temperatures
fig, axes = plt.subplots(nrows = 1, ncols = 2, sharey = True)
df_merged ['india'].plot(ax = axes [0], color = 'red')
df_merged ['united - kingdom'].plot(ax = axes[1], color =
'blue')
#Modifications
axes[0].set_xlabel('Time')
axes[1].set_xlabel('Time')
axes[0].set_ylabel('Anomaly')
```

```
axes[0].set_title('India')
axes[1].set_title('UK')
plt.savefig('DW_climate.png')
plt.show()
```

Figure 4.3 Monthly temperature anomalies

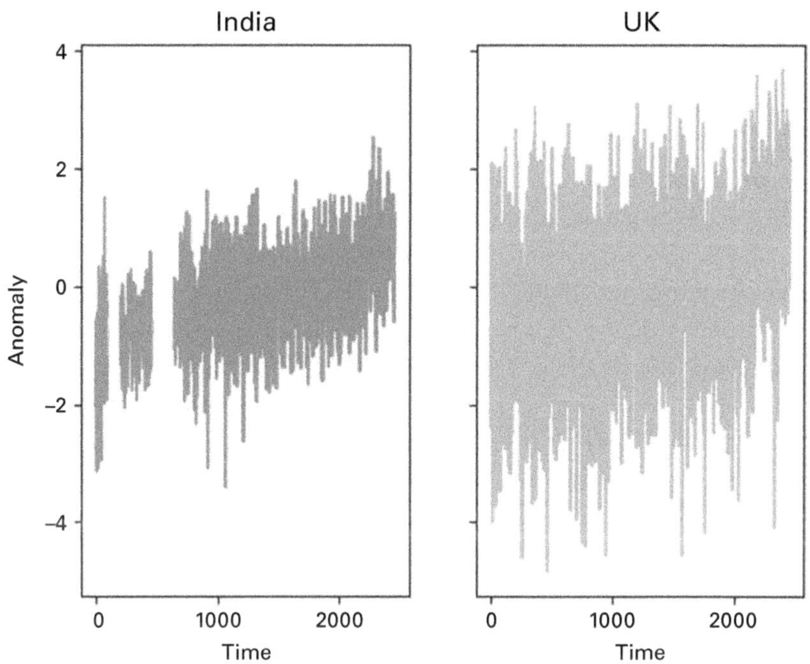

Figure 4.3 depicts deviations of monthly temperatures from their historical averages for India and the UK.

Berkeley Earth offers a wide range of data on climate measures, which can be used for free. Climate risk has become an active research area and has emerged as an important driver of risk such as default risk.

4.5 Outliers and Missing Values

Outliers are observations with 'extreme values', which can affect the robustness of statistical models. Some methods are more robust (e.g. quantile regressions) if outliers are present. Scatter plots such as Figure 4.1 can identify outliers, which are 'far away' from other observations.

It is good practice to start your data analysis with descriptive analyses of your variables. The following code can be applied to Pandas *Series* and the whole *DataFrame*. Note that we continue our analysis of household data. Minimum and maximum values provide the range of a variable. Percentiles such as the 25-percentile and 75-percentile determine the interval that captures 50% of all observations.

```
print("\nDescriptive statistics: Pandas Series\n")
stats = data['INC'].describe()
print(stats)

print("\nDescriptive statistics: Pandas DataFrame\n")
stats = data.describe(include = 'all')
print(stats)
```

Outliers are usually defined as values that are ±3 standard deviation below or above the average value. What should we do with outliers after they are identified? Many practitioners drop them from the dataset. However, this can be problematic as we do not know the underlying reason for extreme values. Reasons include genuine mistakes (e.g. measurement errors) but also events that affect certain variables (e.g. economic shock or policy change). The latter can be modelled using dummy variables as outlined in the chapter on linear regressions.

Before outliers are removed, we suggest to explore the distribution of variables. Variables can be transformed (e.g. log transformation) if negative or positive skewness is present. For instance, household income tends to exhibit positive skewness, i.e. a few large income values can be observed, with the majority of incomes below the mean. This positive skewness can be addressed by applying a natural logarithm. NumPy can transform a Pandas *Series* as well as the Pandas method *transform()* in combination with Python's *lambda* functions. Note that *lambda* functions are unnamed functions in Python. They tend to be simple enough to fit into one line of code.

```
# Log transformation using two different approaches
data['ln_INC'] = np.log(data['INC'])
data['ln_INC'] = data['INC'].transform(lambda x: np.log(x))
```

Figure 4.4 compares the original variable, household income, with the log-transformed variable. The histograms clearly show that the log transformation shifts large positive values to the centre of the distribution. Hence, the skewness is reduced. This might be sufficient to address issues arising from outliers.

Figure 4.4 Before and after log-transformation

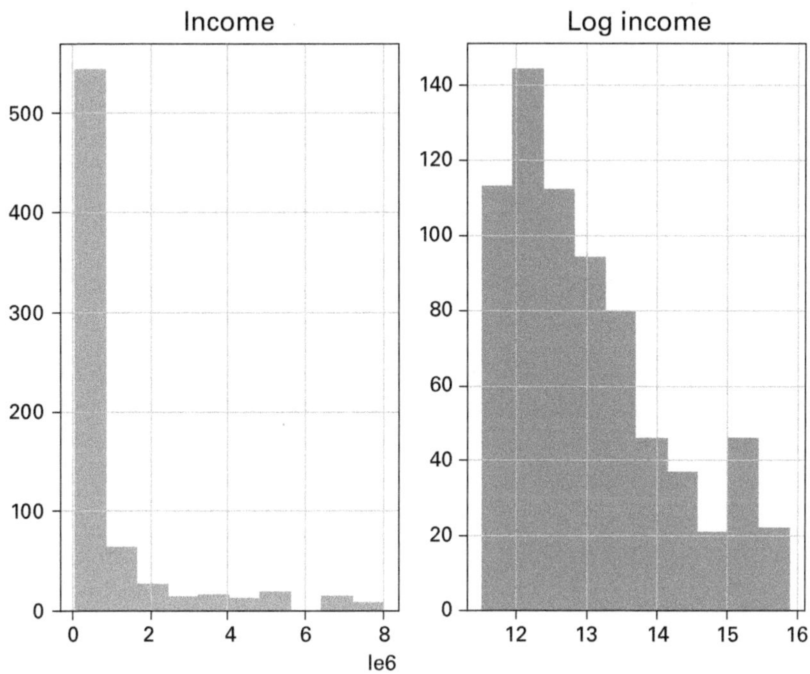

The following code replicates Figure 4.4. Apart from histograms, box plots or Kernel density might be used to illustrate the distribution of variables.

```
#Histograms
fig, axes = plt.subplots(nrows = 1, ncols = 2)
data['INC'].hist(ax = axes[0], color = 'red')
data['ln_INC'].hist(ax = axes[1], color = 'blue')
#Add titles and save the graph
axes[0].set_title('Income')
axes[1].set_title('Log income')
plt.savefig('DW_transform.png')
plt.show()
```

If transformations or dummies fail to mitigate the impact of outliers, *winsorization* can be attempted. Winsorization replaces extreme values with the value at the 5-percentile and 95-percentile. Other cut-off points are common. Alternatively, robust methods can reduce or eliminate the effect of outliers on parameter estimates.

Missing values is another common problem in data wrangling. Basically, there are two options: (i) ignore missing values or (ii) try to predict missing values using existing data. In most applications in business analytics, missing data is ignored. To be precise, we adopt list-wise deletion, i.e. the observation (row) is removed from the model if one of the variables has missing values. This approach makes sense if data is easily available (e.g. data downloads).

In some disciplines, data is expensive to collect (e.g. medical trials). Accordingly, data imputation techniques have emerged for various data structures. In this book, we tend to adopt the list-wise deletion approach in line with most of the literature in business analytics.

4.6 Simulations

Apart from analysing actual data, simulated data offers useful insights in many applications. Theoretical models might not predict deterministic outcomes but probabilistic insights can be derived. This is the case in many areas of business analytics. Many asset pricing or risk management models refer to stochastic modelling, where outcomes depend on stochastic processes.

This section illustrates the use of simulations to generate interest rates. The Vasicek (1977) model provides the underlying theory, which describes a continuous-time stochastic process. Time is continuous (in theory); hence, the letter d denotes the change in some variable. For instance, a basic continuous-time stochastic process for describing the dynamics of the short rate (r) is given by equation (4.1):

$$dr = bdt + \sigma dz \tag{4.1}$$

Note that r is the short rate, and dr denotes the change in the short rate. The change in time refers to dt or, equivalently, the length of the time interval (for a very small interval of time). Finally, dz denotes a random process, and b is the expected direction of the rate change. The impact of the random process is scaled by σ.

The random nature of the change in the short rate stems from the random process dz. The assumptions are that the random process follows a normal distribution with a mean of zero and a standard deviation of one (i.e. is a standardized normal distribution). Furthermore, the change in the short rate for any two different short intervals of time is independent. The expected value of the change in the short rate is equal to b, the drift term.

The Vasicek (1977) model modifies equation (4.1), assuming that interest rates are mean-reverting. The parameter β may be regarded as the equilibrium level of the short-term interest rate around which it evolves. When r falls far below (above) its long-term value β, the expected instantaneous variation of r is positive (negative). In this case, the short-term rate will tend to move up (down). It will move towards its long-term value quickly when it is far from it and when the parameter α, the speed of return to the long-term mean, is high. Finally, dW refers to a so-called Wiener process (Brownian Motion).

$$dr = \alpha(\gamma - r)dt + \rho dW \tag{4.2}$$

How can we simulate interest rates based on equation (4.2)? The main trick is to derive a discrete version of equation (4.2) as time is not continuous in programming. So we note that $dr \approx \Delta r_t = r_t - r_{t-1}$. We start by importing Python libraries.

```
import numpy as np
import matplotlib.pyplot as plt
```

Then, we specified a new class that would do the simulation for us. As discussed in the section on object-oriented programming, we use the *dunder __ init __()* method to define a set of attributes, our model parameters. These attributes include the number of iterations for our simulation *N*, the time step *dt* (time is discrete), the parameters α, β, γ (see equation (4.2)), and an initial value for the interest rate r_0. The latter is needed as we require to know r_{t-1}. Starting our simulation at time $t = 1$ suggests an initial value r_0, which is assigned to 4% as a default. Note that all arguments have default values (provided using an equal sign followed by the value). When we initialize an instance of the class, these default values apply, except we decide to use our own values.

```
class Rate ():
    def __init__(self, N=1000, dt=0.05, \
    rho=0.001, alpha=10, gamma=0.04 , r0=0.04):
        """
        Parameters
        ----------
        N : Number of steps
        dt : Time steps
        rho : Scale
        alpha : Speed of adjustment
        gamma : Long - term equilibrium
        r0: Current interest rate
        """
        self.N = N
        self.dt = dt
        self.rho = rho
        self.alpha = alpha
        self.gamma = gamma
        self.r0 = r
```

There are different ways to implement equation (4.2). Usually, it is a good idea to separate processes as they could be re-used for other simulations. Accordingly, we add a method *wiener(self)* to our class that returns a Wiener process. You notice the use of attributes in this method to incorporate parameter values.

```
def wiener(self):
    """
    Wiener process
    Returns
    -------
    Array of realisations of Wiener process
    """
    #Result vector
    out = np.zeros(self.N)

    #Initial value
    out[0] = np.sqrt(self.dt) * self.rho * np.random.normal
    (0, 1)

    for j in range(1, self.N):
        out[j] = out[j - 1] + np.sqrt(self.dt) * self.
    rho * np.random.normal (0, 1)

    return out
```

Next, we use the *wiener(self)* method in our second method *vasicek(self)*, which completes the simulation.

```
def vasicek(self):
    """
    Returns
    -------
    Array of simulated interest rates
    """
    #Result vector
    out = np.zeros(self.N)

    #Initial value
    out[0] = self.r0

    #Wiener process
    w = Rate()
    w = w.wiener()
```

```
        for j in range(1, self.N):
            out[j] = out[j - 1] + self.alpha*(self.gamma -
        out[j - 1])*self.dt + w[j]

        return out
```

Finally, we initialize an instance and call the *vasicek(self)* method. The result is plotted in Figure 4.5.

```
#Initialise rate instance
rate = Rate()

#Apply Vasicek method
rate = rate.vasicek()

#Plot
plt.plot(rate)
plt.savefig('DW_rate.png')
plt.show()
```

Figure 4.5 illustrates a stochastic process with mean-reversion. Simulated interest rates are driven by a stochastic element but tend to go back to their long-term average.

Figure 4.5 Simulated interest rates

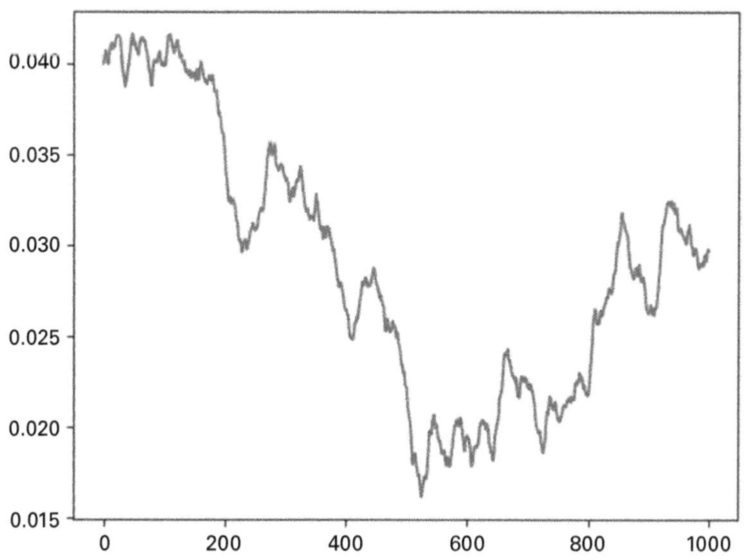

4.7 Synthetic Data

Obtaining real data can be expensive and, in some settings, challenging (e.g. unobserved phenomena, rare events). Simulated data is an option if you have a theoretical model to derive the data. Basically, you need a data-generating process.

In the absence of a data-generating process, synthetic data might be an option. Synthetic data has many applications in testing and machine learning. We suggest creating and activating a new virtual environment, called *fake*, followed by installing the *scikit-learn* (in short sklearn) and several other libraries.

```
python -m venv fake
web\Scripts\activate
pip install scikit - learn
pip install numpy
pip install pandas
pip install matplotlib
```

After the installation is complete, we make the following import statements. Note that we only import the *make_classification* class.

```
import numpy as np
import pandas as pd
from sklearn.datasets import make_classification
```

Then we initialize an instance of the *make_classification* class, which requires two variables: the data matrix X and the array or classifications y, the dependent variable. Note that the *make_classification* class provides default settings for arguments. In our example, we make a few changes. For instance, we only want two dimensions (features or independent variables) and no redundant features. Redundant features are variables that do not contain any information. They are constructed from informative features using linear models with random coefficients. Finally, we create 200 artificial observations. Note that the resulting data matrix X and classifications y are NumPy *arrays*.

```
#Data matrix X and response y
X, y = make_classification(
    n_samples = 200,
    n_features = 2,
    n_redundant = 0,
    n_clusters_per_class =1,
 )
#Data matrix
print(X)
```

```
print(type(X))
#Response (classification)
print(y)
print(type(y))
```

We convert the NumPy *arrays* into a Pandas *DataFrame* and a Pandas *Series* using the respective function and passing the arrays. The resulting list is an argument in the *concat()* function, which merges the Pandas objects horizontally, indicated by the *axis=1* option. It is useful to change the column names and check the synthetic data.

```
#Merge converted DataFrame and Series
df = pd.concat([pd.DataFrame(X), pd.Series(y)], axis=1)
#Rename columns
df.columns = ['x1', 'x2', 'y']
print(df.head())
print(df.tail())
```

There are many alternative Python packages, e.g. *faker*, that generate synthetic data. However, given its importance in machine learning, *scikit-learn* is a prominent choice.

4.8 Summary

This chapter introduced data wrangling and introduced the most prominent Python libraries, including NumPy, Pandas, and scikit-learn. Each library has been extensively covered in the literature (McKinney, 2012; Molin, 2019). We focused on a brief introduction, stressing the importance of problem-based learning at an early stage in your learning journey.

Data wrangling includes downloading or collecting data, exploring data structures, reshaping data, checking for outliers, and addressing missing values. These are essential tasks. Sadly, we have seen many cases in applied and academic research where crucial steps in the process were skipped. Even the best machine learning tool will struggle if you feed it with low-quality data.

SYMPTOMS AND UNDERLYING CAUSES

Observing violations of model assumptions (e.g. non-linear relationships in linear models) is very common. Frequently, the symptoms are treated without understanding the underlying reasons. Data wrangling can identify some causes, such as outliers.

4.9 Exercise

Imagine you are trying to develop a strategy to win at Roulette. The idea is the following. You only bet using 50 : 50 bets. Of course, one has to note that they are not quite 50 : 50 as the green 0 ensures that the bank has an advantage. You start with a fixed bet of x, which you can modify at the start of the game.

If you win, you continue with your initial bet. If you lose, you double your bet in the next round. After winning, you adjust your bet back to the initial bet. The idea is that you can recover from any loss using this betting strategy. Historically, some casinos banned this strategy. As far as we know, this strategy is no longer considered against the rules.

Your task is to build a Python code that can run a simulation of this strategy. Implement the strategy based on betting on even or odd numbers. Your initial cash position, the number of simulated games, and the initial value of the bet should be model parameters. Your simulation should show the gambler's cash position. Will the gambler escape the gambler's ruin? You will find it out.

5 Data Visualization

This chapter introduces data visualization in Python using *Matplotlib*, *Seaborn*, and *Plotly*. The code discussed in the remainder of the book primarily relies on *Matplotlib* or *Seaborn* to plot data. However, Plotly has emerged as a serious contender, offering a huge library of high-quality graphs. The library is open source and available on https://plotly.com/python. *Plotly* integrates well with *Dash*, which creates dashboards for interactive charts. These dashboards can be embedded into web applications that run on *Flask*. Chapter 16 on user interfaces and web applications will provide an introduction to Flask. Accordingly, acquiring a basic understanding of Plotly is useful in business analytics and its applications. Of course, *Power BI* or *Tableau* tend to be predominately used in business analytics. Discussing those alternatives is beyond the scope of this chapter. Python can also be used in both applications. Python still rules.

The area of data visualization is evolving rapidly, and there are more than 10 Python libraries that offer tools to make your data more accessible. Most of these libraries focus on niche applications, e.g. *geoplotlib* offers tools to analyse geographical data. Moreover, many packages provide alternative ways to display figures on web applications (e.g. *Gleam*).

This chapter starts by highlighting the purpose of data visualization. Apart from being a powerful communication tool, visualizing your data provides clues and insights in the context of data analysis. Chapter 4 on data wrangling stresses the importance of cleaning your data to avoid or mitigate the impact of extreme observations (outliers). Data visualization (e.g. scatter plots or box plots) can be used to detect outliers. Moreover, many models assume that the relationships between variables are linear, which might be violated in practice. Plotting your data can reveal non-linear patterns, which might be overlooked otherwise. Chapter 6 on linear regressions discusses the importance of 'looking at your data' to ensure our model assumptions are reasonable. Apart from diagnostics, figures and interactive charts aid in decision-making. As with any tool, figures can be revealing or misleading. Hence, understanding the limitations and being transparent about inherent biases is essential to data analysis.

Data types determine – to a large extent – the most effective chart. This chapter covers the most common data types that you will encounter in business analytics, such as time series, panel data, and cross-section. In two or three dimensions, graphs can capture the essence of your data or model predictions. In higher dimensions, more advanced techniques, such as dimensionality reduction, might be applied prior to data visualization. The chapter on principal component analysis discusses machine learning tools to condense dimensions without losing crucial information.

Finally, we explain the Python code used to create 'classic charts', including line charts, bar charts, scatter plots, and heat maps. This chapter concludes with exporting and integrating figures, followed by a brief summary and exercises. Consequently, after completing this chapter, you will learn the following:

- Data visualization to facilitate decision-making.
- Plotting data in diagnostics.
- Data types and recommended charts.
- Python code to create line charts, bar charts, scatter plots, and heat maps.
- Saving and exporting figures for other applications.

5.1 What is the Purpose of Data Visualization?

Data visualization plays a major role in diagnostics. The previous chapter on data wrangling focused on outlier detection using scatter plots. Moreover, histograms or density plots capture a variable's distribution. Depending on the skewness and kurtosis, transformations might be necessary to achieve a more symmetric distribution or mitigate the impact of extreme observations (e.g. winsorization). Scatter plots can also reveal non-linear relationships, as discussed in the chapter on linear regression models. There are many additional applications of data visualization. We outline a few examples and highlight limitations. Section 5.3 explores the Python code to create the most important charts used in business analytics.

Correlations between variables of a model can suggest inherent challenges in the context of multivariate regressions. It is common to report correlations using a table; however, a heat map can capture the essence of a correlation matrix, visualizing variables with high degrees of similarities. Combining them might make it hard to detect the separate impact of a variable, as discussed in the next chapter on linear regressions. Figure 5.1 depicts a heat map based on correlations.

Figure 5.1 Heat maps visualize a correlation matrix

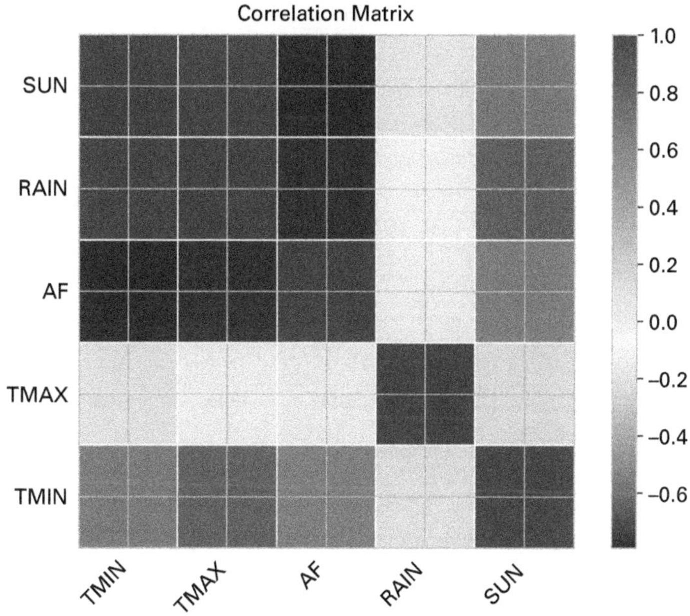

We will encounter many challenges when trying to forecast the impact of variables in this book. Sadly, once estimated, model parameters do not remain constant over time. Some parameters can exhibit time-varying behaviour. There are many examples in practice. For example, estimating companies' cost of capital is tricky because beta coefficients are often unstable. Figure 5.2 plots a line chart to illustrate parameter estimates and their upper and lower boundaries based on percentiles.

Surface charts plot three-dimensional relationships as illustrated in Figure 5.3. Three-dimensional figures look impressive and have their purpose in communicating results. However, in most applications, a two-dimensional representation of three-dimensional problems simplifies the visualization.

A contour plot is a good example of a two-dimensional chart capturing a three-dimensional problem. Figure 5.4 shows multivariate probability density functions with two random variables denoted R and T. The third dimension refers to the probability density. Subplots compare a theoretical probability density derived from a mathematical model with a simulated probability density. Contours are easier to compare than surface plots.

Data visualization can be a powerful tool for detecting violations of model assumptions, checking the reliability of predictions, illustrating relationships between variables, and assisting decision-making in business analytics. Various Python libraries help you make your figures stand out; however, Python cannot fix every problem. The following guidelines proved useful in academic publishing, consulting projects, and policy reports.

Figure 5.2 Illustration of parameter stability

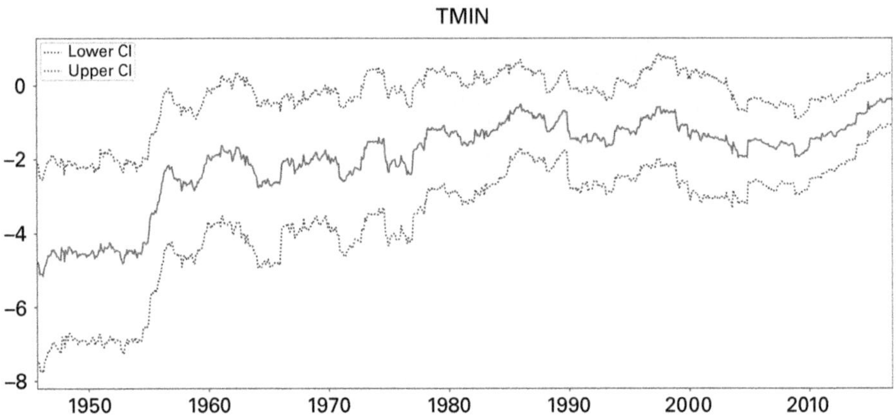

Figure 5.3 Surface plots

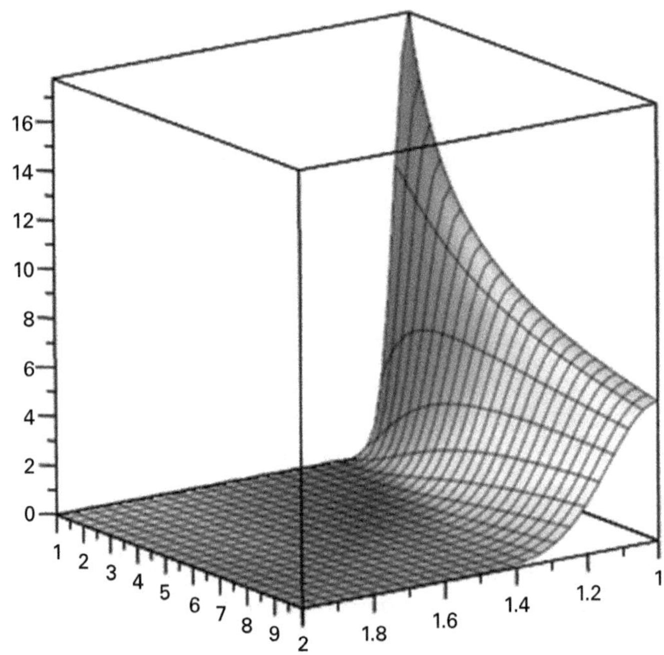

Figure 5.4 Contour plots to compare probability density functions

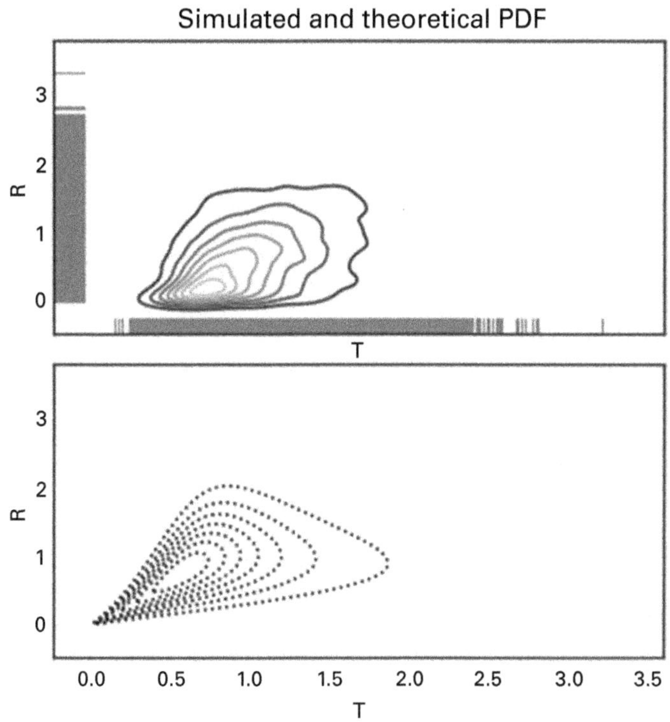

5.2 Data Structures and Types

Our ability to visualize data depends on data structures and types. Not all types are suitable for visualization without further modification (e.g. qualitative data). Moreover, some data structures might benefit from aggregation or multi-level modelling (e.g. nested data). This section explores common data structures, including time series, panel, and cross-sectional data. We also explore different data types.

Let's get some data to explore data structures and types. This chapter will focus on climate change and its impact on businesses. This is a growing research area with many important business applications, including risk management (e.g. ratings) and disclosure (e.g. ESG investing). For instance, Kling et al. (2021) demonstrates the effect of climate risk on the cost of capital. The file *co2_emissions.csv* contains data compiled by the Global Carbon Budget on countries' CO2 emissions. The dataset can be downloaded from our online sources. Starting with importing *Pandas*, we load the CSV file into a new *DataFrame* object.

GUIDELINES TO MAKE YOUR FIGURES STAND OUT

The main aim is to make a figure understandable without reading the text. It can stand on its own and convey its message. To achieve this aim, we suggest applying the following guidelines:

- Each axis needs a label.
- Use headings and subheadings in subplots.
- Capture three-dimensional problems in two dimensions.
- In subplots, use the same scale to ensure comparability.
- Add notes to figures explaining acronyms (e.g. labels).

```
1 import pandas as pd
2
3 #Import data as DataFrame
4 df = pd.read_csv("co2_emissions.csv")
5
6 print(df.head())
```

The data structure refers to panel data, where countries' CO2 emissions are recorded over time. Due to missing values, the panel dataset is unbalanced, i.e. the number of years with observed data varies between countries. Moreover, the dataset also contains groups of countries (e.g. by geography), i.e. some data entries are aggregated over certain countries.

Pandas offers the *plot()* method, which can be applied to objects such as a Pandas *Series* or *DataFrame*. The *plot()* method relies on Matplotlib. Accordingly, we import *matplotlib.pyplot* to gain access to functions and methods that work on figures, such as saving or displaying figures.

After the additional import statement, we set an index, but which index should be used? To obtain an overview, we start with an aggregated time series; hence, only the time dimension, i.e. years, is required to identify observations uniquely. Line 4 reassigns the *DataFrame*, which updates the index.

The dataset contains the aggregated global CO2 emissions. Lines 9 to 11 look rather convoluted, but it is a nice example of object-oriented programming in Python. Starting with the variable of emissions (i.e. a Pandas *Series*), a condition is embedded that applies to the column with entity names. Entities refer to countries or aggregates of countries. Finally, the *plot()* method is applied to the filtered column, and further options determine the figure's appearance. These options include a title, a label for the y-axis, and log-transformed y-values. By default, the *plot()* method selects a line chart. The resulting figure is saved and displayed.

```
import matplotlib.pyplot as plt
import itertools

#Set index
df = df.set_index(df[‘Year’])

print(df.head())

#Aggregated data over time
df[‘Emission’][df[‘Entity’] == ‘World’].
plot(title = ‘Global Emissions’,
ylabel = ‘CO2 Emission’, logy = True)

#Save figure
plt.savefig(‘DV_world.png’)
plt.show()
```

Figure 5.5 shows the increase in CO2 emissions globally. A log transformation makes it easier to see changes in the trend. Emissions tend to grow exponentially in line with economic growth. The slope of the graph reveals the growth rate in different periods. Until 1900, growth rates seem to be higher than in later periods. Interestingly, there seems to be a period with stable emissions, which coincides with the 1890s, WWI, the interwar period, and WWII. This is followed by a similar growth pattern, which slowly diminishes over time.

Given the large number of entities, visualizing different trajectories among countries can be challenging. Hence, we focus on the top five countries regarding CO2 emissions in 2022 and compare their progression since 1900. We select only the rows that refer to countries to accomplish this task. The column *Code* has missing values for all aggregated indices – except for the global level, which is denoted *OID_WRL*. Consequently, we use the *dropna()* to deal with the majority of indices and also add the condition that entries in the *Code* column are not equal to *OID_WRL*. Finally, we only focus on 2022, the most recent year available. The conditions are separated by brackets and combined using &. A new object, *df_top*, contains this filtered dataset.

```
#Top 5 countries by emission 2022
#Drop missing values
#Ignore aggregated indices
df_top = df[(df[‘Code’] != ‘OWID_WRL’) &
(df[‘Year’] == 2022)].dropna ()
```

Next, we sort the resulting *DataFrame* by CO2 emissions by applying the *sort_values()* method. The top five countries are selected by row numbers using slicing for which the *iloc()* method is required. A print statement checks this step of our analysis. After identifying the five countries with the highest emissions, we create a list named *countries* from the *Entity* column of the dataset. This is accomplished using the *tolist()* method. The usual suspects are China, the USA, India, Russia, and Japan.

Figure 5.5 Illustration of the global trend

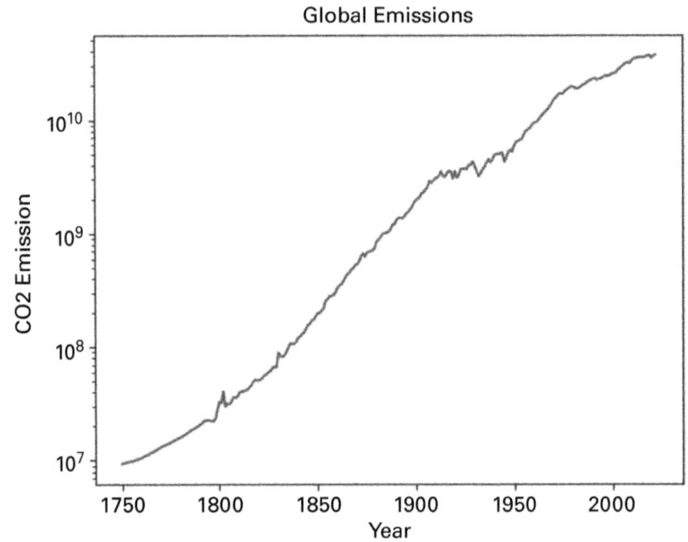


```
#Sort by CO2 emissions in 2022
#Select top 5
df_top = df_top.sort_values(by = ['Emission'],
ascending = False).iloc[:5,:]
print(df)

#Add selected countries to a list
countries = df_top['Entity'].tolist()
print(countries)
```

With this knowledge, we return to our original dataset and select the top five countries. Applying the same conditions, we ignore aggregated indices and start in 1900. The *isin()* method checks whether the country is on our countries list.

```
#Plot top 5 countries over time
#Ignore aggregated indices
df = df[(df['Code'] != 'OWID_WRL') & (df['Year']>=1900)].
dropna()
df = df[df['Entity'].isin(countries)]
print(df)
```

For panel data, the *groupby()* method is convenient in defining the panel variable, i.e. the country level. Alternatively, one can work with hierarchical or multi-level indexing. Finally, line charts plot each country's emissions in the top five since 1950 using a *for loop*. The *key*, i.e. the country code, serves as a label for the legend.

```
#Linestyles in list
style = itertools.cycle(["-","--","-.",":","."])

grouped = df.groupby('Code')
for key, group in grouped:
         plt.plot(group.Year, group.Emission,
"k"+next(style), label = key)
plt.legend()
plt.savefig('DV_top_5.png')
plt.show()
```

Figure 5.6 shows the sudden surge in China's emissions from offshore manufacturing outsourcing in the 1990s and the recent domestic market expansion. In line with India's economic success, emissions have increased lately. Of course, the USA and other developed countries that dropped out of the top five emitters have significantly contributed to total CO2 emissions since the beginning of industrialization.

Data visualization can aid decision-making; however, figures can also mislead. The main challenge is to justify the measures you used. Should we account for differences in population or the size of the economy? When should we start our analysis?

Figure 5.6 Top five countries based on CO2 emissions in 2022

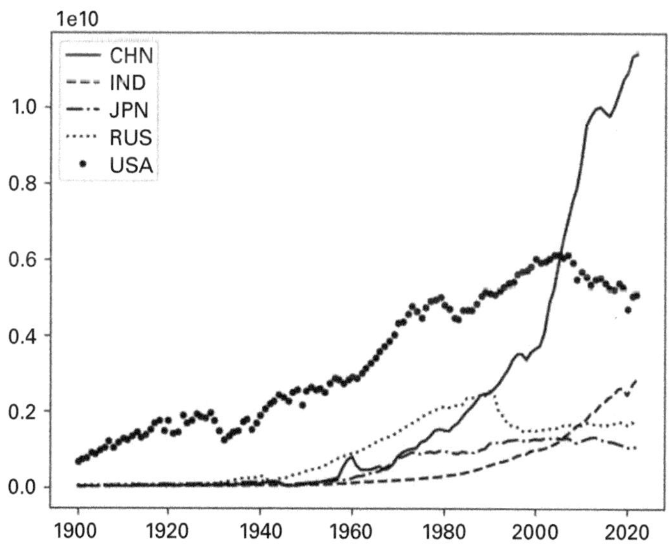

DO FIGURES MISLEAD?

Figures can send a message and move policymakers. However, figures can also contribute to bad decision-making. Finding good measures is essential to address these issues.

- Can the variable of interest be observed directly (e.g. latent variables)?
- Does the measure depend on size (population, economy, etc.)?
- Can the measure be applied consistently over time and across units of observation?
- Do effects vanish over time or do they accumulate?

Recent CO2 emissions can be accurately measured and allocated to countries. Even trade can be accounted for; outsourcing production and importing goods still count as emissions. Consistency over time and across countries is more of a challenge as standards have evolved considerably. Regarding CO2 emissions and their impact on climate change, one has to acknowledge the cumulative effect over extended periods. Apart from size adjustments (e.g. relative measures of emissions), adding emissions over time illustrates the cumulative impact of countries.

The following code applies the *cumsum()* method, which has a profound impact on our interpretation of the empirical facts.

```
#Cumulated emissions
grouped = df.groupby('Code')
print(grouped)
for key, group in grouped:
        plt.plot(group.Year,
group.Emission.cumsum(), "k"+next(style),
label = key)
plt.legend()
plt.savefig('DV_top_5_cum.png')
plt.show()
```

After combining all emissions over time, the cumulative impact of the USA is evident. Of course, the starting point of the analysis is even more crucial. Finally, any measurement errors will be amplified by adding up estimated emissions. Figure 5.7 depicts the cumulative emissions since 1900. The Python script *emissions.py* replicates this section.

The examples discussed in this section focus on a single variable (i.e. emissions) over time. In practice, you might encounter datasets with many variables (dimensions); hence, more advanced methods are needed to visualize the data and capture

Figure 5.7 Cumulative emissions of the top five countries since 1900

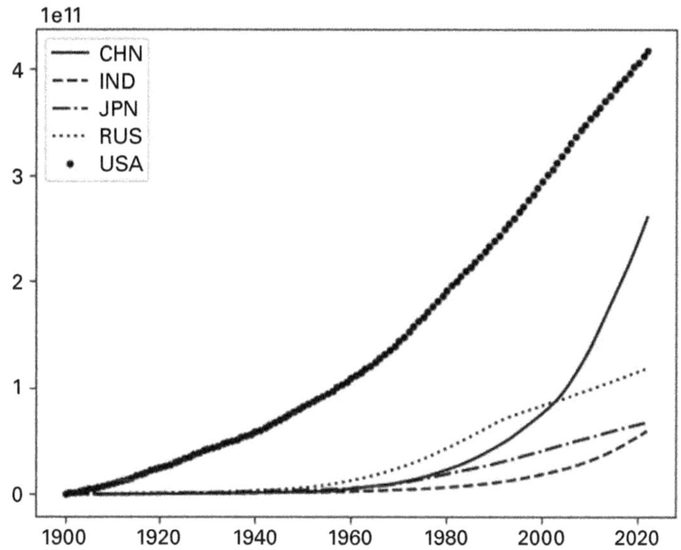

the essential information. The chapter on principal component analysis introduces machine learning tools that reduce dimensions. These methods can help visualize data in lower dimensions without losing too much information.

Furthermore, we addressed the heterogeneity of countries in our panel dataset by using a subgroup of countries or combining countries into indices. Cluster analysts, covered in Chapter 14, offer alternative methods to identify similarities between observations (e.g. countries).

5.3 Creating Figures in Python

5.3.1 *Line Charts*

The previous section used line charts to illustrate the trend in global CO2 emissions and showcase the five countries with the highest emissions. Line charts are ideal for capturing developments over time in time series and panel data, which requires aggregation or selection of a sub-sample. Thus far, we created line charts in Pandas using the *plot()* method, which is based on Matplotlib.

The following example introduces Seaborn, which offers useful features. However, the differences between basic line charts are minimal. As an installation is required, we create a virtual environment called *plot*, which we activate. Using the pip installer,

Seaborn is installed with all its dependencies. It is not required to create a virtual environment as the installation could be done in *conda* or using *pip* on your system. However, we suggest practising virtual environments as they pay off in more advanced projects.

```
python -m venv plot
plot\Scripts\activate
pip install seaborn
```

In the context of climate risk, food prices matter, as prices are closely related to oil prices. Sudden jumps in food prices have triggered social unrest, contributing to political risk. The latter is priced in sovereign bond markets and affects investment flows. Let's get some more data on food prices. The Food and Agriculture Organization of the United Nations provides the FAO Food Price Index. This index combines various food items and tracks their prices since 1961. The dataset *food_price_index.csv* contains two time series of the index. The nominal index does not adjust for inflation, whereas the real index accounts for consumer price changes.

We start with import statements and obtain a *DataFrame* using the *read_csv()* method. You notice that we still rely on Matplotlib, which we also import. Inspecting the data already offers interesting insights. As expected, nominal food prices have surged, but in real terms, food prices have moved marginally, albeit exhibiting pronounced cycles.

```
import pandas as pd
import seaborn as sns
import matplotlib.pyplot as plt

#Import data as DataFrame
df = pd.read_csv("food_price_index.csv")

print(df.head())
```

A line chart plotting both time series can capture our initial observation, which we generate as follows in Seaborn.

```
#Set index
df = df.set_index(df['Year'])

#Multiple lines
sns.lineplot(data = df[['Nominal', 'Real']],
palette = ['red', 'blue'],
markers = True, dashes = True)

plt.savefig('DV_food.png')
plt.show()
```

Figure 5.8 Nominal and real food prices since 1961

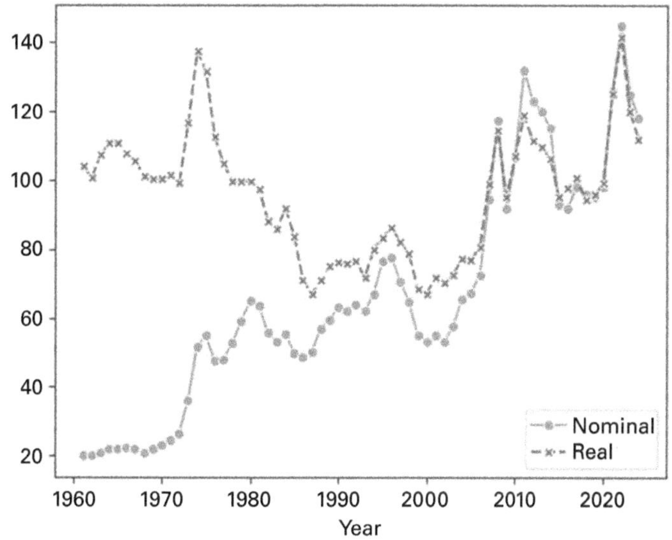

As in the previous example, we use the *Year* column as our index. The *lineplot()* function creates our chart, which we modify with markers, line patterns, and colours. Figure 5.8 shows the recent increase in nominal and real food prices. Over the long term, however, food price inflation was in line with other price changes. Yet, sudden changes in price, i.e. spikes in variance, can have real consequences (e.g. food insecurity, poverty, instability).

The Python script *food.py* replicates this section. Depending on your message and intention, showing nominal food prices demonstrates a crisis, whereas real prices paint a different picture. Moreover, one needs to consider other ways of measurement, e.g. expressing food prices relative to wages. Finally, food price indices and inflation are averages, ignoring inequalities and heterogeneity across groups. Data visualization is a tool, but you need to think carefully about the measure used and how it is displayed. Does a figure inform or indoctrinate? Transparency, i.e. discussing your measures and assumptions, is essential.

5.3.2 Bar Charts, Box Plots, and Subplots

Many variables cannot be observed directly; they are latent. For instance, the rule of law or the ability to enforce environmental standards are hard to measure. Statistical methods, such as measurement models or expert surveys, try to quantify latent variables. For instance, Pesqué-Cela et al. (2021) develop a Confirmatory Factor Analysis to measure a country's level of financial inclusion, i.e. the access to formal financial services.

Environmental policies must be evaluated in the context of climate and country risk analysis. The World Bank conducts the Country Policy and Institutional Assessment (CPIA). World Development Indicators contain several CPIA ratings apart from many macroeconomic variables. Ratings are in the range of 1, indicating low quality, to 6, the highest quality of policies and institutions. Hence, the variable is categorical with a minimum step of 0.5. Values of a categorical variable need to be interpreted with care. Orderings are meaningful, e.g. a value of 2.5 is lower than a value of 5. However, we cannot say that a value of 5 is 'double as good' than a value of 2.5. After creating charts, we will return to this problem and critically discuss measurement issues. The CSV file *policy_ranking.csv* contains ratings on policies and institutions for environmental sustainability. Our online sources provide access to this dataset.

After the usual import statements, the CSV file is read into Pandas and assigned to the variable *df*, a *Pandas DataFrame*. Ratings are only available from 2005, and many countries exhibit missing values. Therefore, we apply the *dropna()* method to the dataset, which we reassign. The *rename()* method shortens the name of columns. Inspecting the data reveals that years are floats (e.g. 2005.0); thus, a redundant decimal is added while importing the data. The *astype()* with the argument *int* for integer converts the floats into integers. Finally, the *head()* and *tail()* methods display the first and last five rows of the dataset to check data structure and consistency.

```
import pandas as pd
import seaborn as sns
import matplotlib.pyplot as plt

#Import data as DataFrame
df = pd.read_csv("policy_ranking.csv")

#Remove missing values
df = df.dropna()

#Change column name
df = df.rename(columns = {"Country Name": "Country",
"Time": "Year", "Value": "CPIA"})

#Change float to integer for Year
df['Year'] = df['Year'].astype(int)

#Check the data structure
print(df.head())
print(df.tail())
```

Bar charts can capture trends or compare across units of observations (e.g. countries). With a large time dimension, line charts are the better option to explore behaviour over time. However, policy ratings and, in fact, many categorical variables (e.g. credit ratings) are 'sticky' in the sense that variation is limited over short time horizons. To capture the medium- to long-term trend, we select four points in time, which are stored in a list. The *isin()* method filters all rows associated with elements of the list, selecting a sub-sample for further analysis.

```
#Define a list of years
years_selected = [2005, 2010, 2015, 2022]

#Select years
df = df[df[‘Year’].isin(years_selected)]
```

In Seaborn, the overall theme and colour scheme can be modified. The documentation outlines many options, and we suggest you experiment with different project settings. Bar charts can detect the overall pattern of change in a sample of countries; however, the values displayed refer to averages. Accordingly, the chart does not provide any information about the heterogeneity among countries or any changes in terms of convergence or divergence from an overall trend. Box plots provide more insights as outliers and percentiles are captured, providing a snapshot of the distribution of the rating at different points in time.

Matplotlib's *subplots()* function offers a powerful tool that combines several plots into a single figure. We can use the same x- and y-axes to facilitate comparing graphs. In this example, the subplots are arranged in one row and two columns (horizontally). The *ax* argument in each subplot assigns the respective chart to the axis (i.e. the location on the matrix with one row and two columns).

```
#Subplots
#Combine barplot and boxplot
sns.set_theme(style = “whitegrid”)
sns.color_palette(“Spectral”, as_cmap = True)

#Define figure with two subplots and axes
fig, axes = plt.subplots(1, 2, sharex = True,
figsize = (9, 6))
fig.suptitle(‘Ratings over time’)
axes[0].set_title(‘Barplot’)
axes[1].set_title(‘Boxplot’)

#Barplot
sns.barplot(
    data = df,
    x = “Year”, y = “CPIA”, hue = “Year”,
    legend = False, ax = axes [0])

#Boxplot
sns.boxplot(
    data = df,
    x = “Year”, y = “CPIA”, hue = “Year”,
    legend = False, ax = axes[1])
plt.savefig(‘DV_rating.png’)
plt.show()
```

Figure 5.9 Bar plots compared to box plots

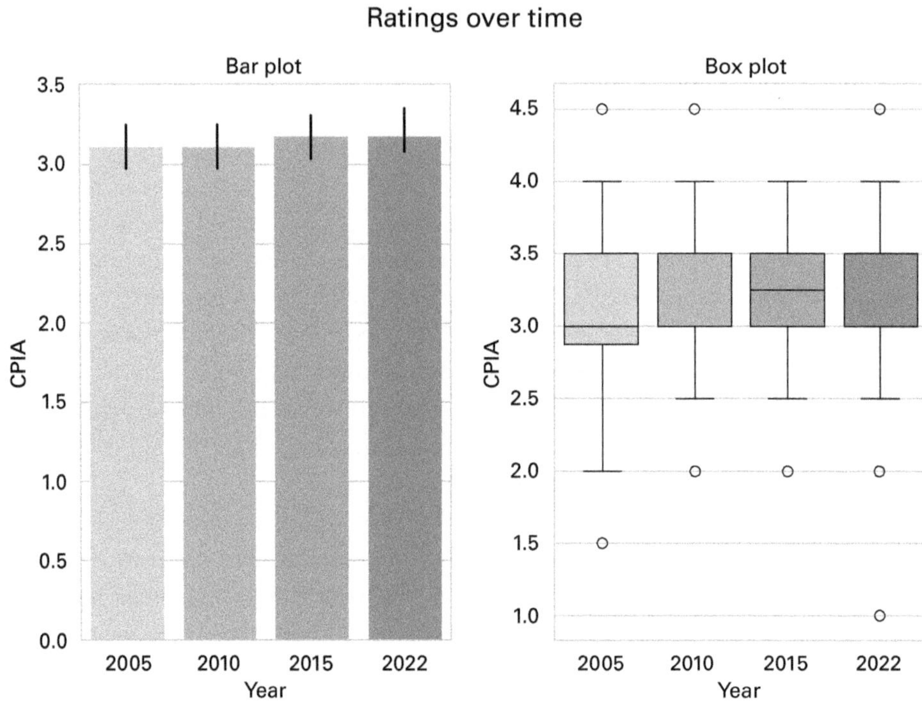

Figure 5.9 depicts the bar chart and the box plot of ratings for the four points in time. The bar chart seems to suggest that ratings improved on average. Inspecting the box plots provides further clues. The alleged improvement in overall ratings has been driven by fewer outliers, i.e. countries with very low ratings. Does that mean that the countries with the lowest ratings improved the most? Before we draw this conclusion, we must investigate whether countries with the lowest ratings in earlier years remain in the sample. It is not uncommon that missing values do not miss at random. So, a sample selection bias needs to be ruled out.

Finally, a word of caution. As we rely on a categorical variable, consistency over time and across countries needs to be ensured. Put differently, has the methodology of the rating progressed over time? Who provides the assessment? In summary, data visualization might not provide the answers you are looking for but suggests even more questions that should be explored.

5.3.3 Scatter Plots

Scatter plots simply show the data (e.g. points in two- or three-dimensional space) directly without aggregation (e.g. percentiles). As discussed in the previous chapter on data wrangling, looking at the whole dataset with scatter plots might detect outliers. Moreover, scatter plots are a feature in many machine learning tools, such as the model fit or predictions can be compared to actual training or test data.

For a change, we introduce another Python library for data visualization called Plotly. Of course, scatter plots can be created in Matplotlib and Seaborn as well. Plotly, however, offers interactive charts and can be used with Dash to create data-driven web applications.

We start by installing Plotly in our active virtual environment using the pip installer. This is followed by the same steps as in the previous section as we continue exploring the policy ratings. The Python script *scatter.py* replicates the example in this section.

```
pip install plotly
```

After importing *plotly.express*, the *scatter()* function takes the *DataFrame* and the two axes as arguments. The scatter plot shows the values at different points in time. With a categorical variable, this type of chart is less useful as many countries have the same rating in the same year. However, a scatter plot only shows one observation without providing the number of identical cases. Again, this example stresses the importance of understanding your data structure and types before visualizing your data.

```
import plotly.express as px
fig = px.scatter(df, x = "Year", y = "CPIA")
fig.show()
```

When you execute this code, you notice that your default browser opens and displays the scatter plot. Plotly is built for web applications and offers interactive charts. You will find a menu of various tools in the top right corner of the browser. These tools allow you to zoom and explore different areas of the chart. This can be a useful feature in large datasets. You can also download a static picture of your chart in standard formats, including PNG or PDF. Plotly offers a very different experience compared to Matplotlib or Seaborn. Section 5.4 discusses exporting and embedding charts in more detail.

5.3.4 Heat Maps

Heat maps visualize similarities between two variables. They are most frequently used in combination with correlation coefficients, which measure the linear interrelationship between them. To illustrate the use of heat maps, we explore oil and gas reserves in the UK. They seem to be dwindling rapidly. Yet, one needs to be careful with this interpretation, as the UK does not permit fracking. The USA experienced a similar decline in reserves, which has been reversed due to fracking and the discoveries of significant shale gas reserves.

The Office for National Statistics (ONS) provides estimates of the UK's oil and gas reserves. It is common to classify reserves into proven, probable, and possible, depending on the likelihood of recovering oil or gas at reasonable costs.

After the usual import statements, we import the CSV file and inspect the data structure. Next, we drop the year column as we do not require an index and calculate the correlation matrix using the *corr()* method.

```
import pandas as pd
import seaborn as sns
import matplotlib.pyplot as plt

#Import data as DataFrame
df = pd.read_csv(“uk_reserves.csv”)

#Check the data structure
print(df.head())
print(df.tail())

#Drop Year
df = df.drop(columns = [‘year’])

#Correlation matrix
corr_matrix = df.corr()
```

Seaborn’s *heatmap()* function takes the *DataFrame* as argument, generating a heat map based on the correlation coefficients. All observed correlation coefficients exceed 0.75, indicating a high degree of co-movement of the time series.

```
#Heat map
sns.heatmap(corr_matrix)
plt.savefig (‘DV_heat.png’)
plt.show()
```

Figure 5.10 depicts the heat map representing the correlation matrix. A heat map can replace a table with correlation coefficients for academic or policy-focused outputs. Coefficients can be displayed in the cells of the heat map if required, setting the argument *annot* to true.

5.4 Exporting and Embedding Figures

Matplotlib's *savefig()* function is our default approach. It saves figures in standard formats, including PNG, PDF, EPS, and SVG; however, other common formats, such as JPG, are unavailable. Nevertheless, charts in PNG format can be converted into a JPG format in Python by using *Pillow*, a fork of PIL, the Python Imaging Library.

Once saved, charts can be imported into other applications, including LaTeX, Word, or PowerPoint. If you require frequent updates of figures, LaTeX is the best choice in our view. Figures and tables can be kept and updated in separate files. Once you complete your analysis, the updated outputs are recompiled without additional editing.

Figure 5.10 Visualizing correlations between different types of oil and gas reserves

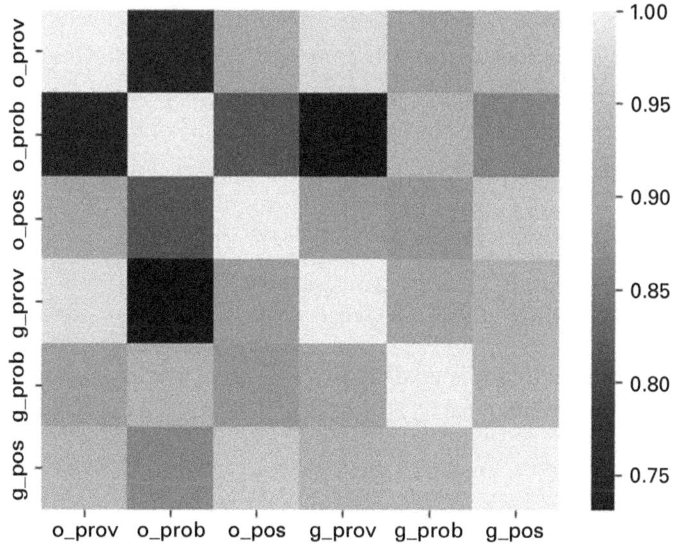

Despite the option to rerun your code and update your figures, exported and embedded outputs using the *savefig()* function remain static. End-users cannot easily manipulate the charts or request an updated version. The chapter on user interfaces and web applications explores the interaction with end-users. You will build desktop applications in *Tkinter* and web applications in Flask.

If more interactivity is desired, Plotly together with Dash might be a good starting point. Interactive charts can enhance the user experience and are an important aspect of creating natural user interfaces. This book offers both rigorous modelling and packaging your models in a way that simplifies their use.

5.5 Summary

Data visualization can identify violations of model assumptions without conducting statistical tests. For instance, scatter plots might identify non-linear relationships between variables, or heat maps of a correlation matrix highlight multicollinearity between explanatory variables. Relying on statistical tests to identify issues overstates their precision, as test statistics rely on assumptions. Always visualize your data; you might be surprised by what you find.

Apart from diagnostic tests, data visualization aids in conveying information. Line charts, bar plots, and scatter plots capture model predictions or distinct patterns in your data. Tables might contain the same information as figures, but a figure is easier to interpret if you follow these suggestions.

In many reports and academic papers, figures are difficult to interpret, or there are simply too many elements, so the core message is lost. Finally, it is all about applying the correct measures, which is often overlooked. So, think about how variables are measured and whether they can be observed directly or latent. Frequently, figures mislead as only a selected number of observations are shown to convey a certain narrative. Ideally, you focus on the long-term behaviour of variables to provide the whole picture and not just cherry-pick periods to make a point.

ONE FIGURE – ONE MESSAGE

It is tempting to add too many features to a chart (e.g. increasing the number of subplots). More is not better in data visualization. Ask yourself the following questions:

- Can the figure be understood without reading the text?
- Can you describe the message conveyed by the figure in one sentence?
- Is the figure necessary (i.e. is the message important)?

5.6 Exercise

You will explore the Maddison Project Database 2023. The complete dataset, covering the economic growth of 169 countries, can be downloaded from the project website for free. If you are interested in long-term economic development, the Maddison Project Database is a good starting point for your analysis. The CSV file *gdp.csv* contains a sub-sample of the GDP per capita data for five countries, including Argentina (ARG), Austria (AUS), Australia (AUT), Brazil (BRA), and the United Kingdom (GBR). Our online source provides access to the CSV file, and a Python script *gdp.py* showcases a possible solution. Try to address the following tasks.

5.6.1 *Importing the Data and Data Wrangling*

Import the CSV file, set an appropriate index, convert floats to integers, and check your dataset. Export the figure as a PNG picture.

5.6.2 Line Charts

Using Seaborn, depict GDP per capita of all countries over time.

5.6.3 Do Countries Converge or Diverge?

Calculate sigma convergence, which is defined as the standard deviation of the log of GDP per capita of the sample in a given year. Plot the change in sigma convergence over time and interpret the result.

PART TWO
Methods and Techniques

6 Linear Regression

This chapter introduces *linear regression*, which offers an initial assessment of linear relationships in your data. Linear regression has a long history dating back to the early 19th century, based on publications by Gauss and Legendre. Stigler (1981) provides a detailed account of the history of least squares, which is a fascinating read. Nowadays, linear regression is regarded as a supervised learning method and has been used in classification problems.

This chapter provides a brief overview of linear regression, starting with the main idea, interpreting regression outputs, implementing it in Python, and its limitations. Many books in econometrics are dedicated to the fine-grained detail of regression analysis. It is tempting to dedicate much time to deriving the *ordinary least squares (OLS)* estimator and go through each assumption. However, Hayashi (2011) provides a detailed account of the underlying algebra of linear regression. Moreover, Hayashi (2011) derives all assumptions. In practice, most, if not all, assumptions tend to be violated. Accordingly, our focus is on implementing and interpreting results. Most importantly, we will explore the inherent limitations of linear regression models.

Finally, unlike econometricians, we are not interested in causal inference. A fine correlation is good enough as long as it enhances our predictability. In the context of business analytics and machine learning, our main concerns are model fit and predictability. Hence, many issues related to the violation of assumptions, which affect the reliability of hypotheses tests, are often neglected.

What will you learn after completing this chapter?

- Understanding of the ideas and principles behind regression analysis.
- Interpretation of regression output.
- Implementation in Python.
- Limitations of linear regression.

In spite of their inherent limitations, linear regressions remain a useful tool in our arsenal. Follow these recommendations to use this tool wisely.

HOW TO USE LINEAR REGRESSIONS?

Linear regressions provide a first glimpse into relationships between variables after data wrangling and correlation analysis. In many applications, a rough idea about linear relationships (e.g. linear approximations) is all you need to identify important drivers of your target variable.

6.1 The Main Idea

A regression model attempts to explain a *dependent variable* using one or more *independent variables*. There are many misconceptions regarding the alleged purpose or power of regression models. The most problematic misconception is the following.

CAUSALITY

A linear regression model suggests that a set of independent variables explains a dependent variable. However, this relationship does not have to be causal. It is not a test of causality.

We consider a linear model that tries to explain a dependent variable y using one or more independent variables denoted x_j with $j = 1, \ldots, k$. Linearity simplifies our model but it might oversimplify the true relationship between variables. The section on limitations will explore this issue in more detail.

Depending on the data structure, we might observe the variables for a cross-section of N observations denoted $i = 1, \ldots, N$, a time series with $t = 1, \ldots, T$, or panel data. The following equation shows a linear regression model with one independent variable for a cross-sectional dataset.

$$y_i = \alpha + \beta x_i + \varepsilon_i, \quad i = 1, \ldots, N \tag{6.1}$$

This model describes a straight line with two coefficients α and β. If $x_i = 0$, $y_i = \alpha$; hence, we call α the intercept (or constant term). Then, β measures the change in y if x is changing. $\beta > 0$ indicates a positive relationship, whereas $\beta < 0$ shows a negative relationship.

Linear models can be regarded as approximations of the true relationship between variables. These approximations work reasonably well for small changes of y

and x. If things change entirely, for instance, in a crisis or due to a sudden shift in policy, linear models will struggle to capture the nature of the relationship. So, one needs to be aware of the limitations.

However, linearity is not as restrictive as one might initially assume. Many problems can be converted into a linear model using transformations. For instance, the Cobb-Douglas production function, $y = AL^{\alpha}K^{\beta}$, can be transformed using the log into a linear model $\ln y = \ln A + \alpha \ln L + \beta \ln K$.

IT IS A MODEL, NOT THE TRUTH

Note that the linear model is only a model – it is not the true relationship.

As we deal with a model, there is an element of uncertainty. We add an error term to the equation denoted ε_i to capture this fact. We assume that, on average, the model is correct. This implies that the expected value of the error term is zero, $E(\varepsilon_i) = 0$. Note that we cannot observe error terms directly as we do not know the true value of the coefficients α and β or the true functional form. For instance, the true relationship might not be linear.

However, we can measure *residuals* ('leftovers'). The idea is to estimate α and β and use these estimates to predict the value of the dependent variable y_i. Then we compare the actual value of y_i with its predicted value denoted $\hat{y}_i$. The difference between these values refers to the residuals (i.e. the unexplained component), shown in equation (6.2).

$$\hat{\varepsilon}_i = y_i - \hat{y}_i = y_i - \hat{\alpha} - \hat{\beta}x_i, \quad i = 1,\ldots,N \tag{6.2}$$

6.1.1 The Visualization of a Regression Model

Observations can be visualized as points in a multidimensional space. The number of variables defines the dimensions. We restrict our discussion to two dimensions to make it easier to visualize the main principles. Hence, we have one dependent variable y and one independent variable x. Each observation has values x_i and y_i and can be mapped in a two-dimensional space. We aim to fit a straight line that best describes these points. Figure 6.1 plots a few observations and a straight line ($y_i = 0.7x_i$). Based on 'guesswork', we selected a constant term $\alpha = 0$ and $\beta = 0.7$, but is this a 'good' or 'optimal' choice? How can we derive these estimated coefficients?

Figure 6.1 Illustration of linear regression

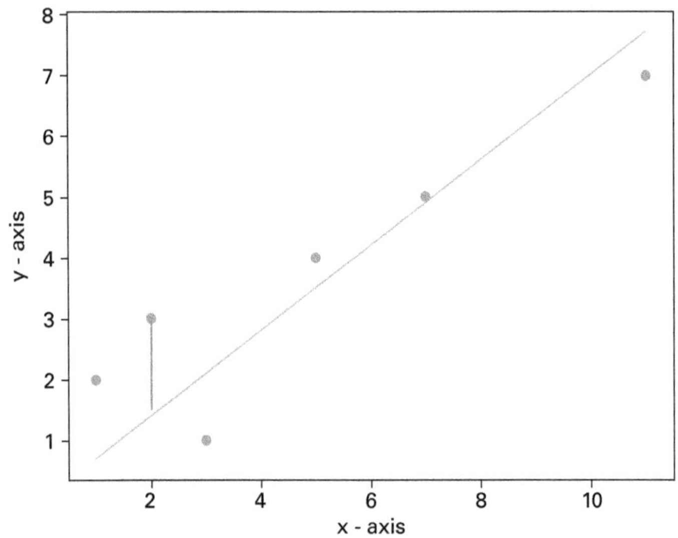

The following code generates Figure 6.1. We added a few comments to explain our approach.

```
import matplotlib.pyplot as plt
import numpy as np

#Independent variable x axis
x = np.array([1, 5, 3, 7, 2, 11])
#Dependent variable y axis
y = np.array([2, 4, 1, 5, 3, 7])
#Scatter plot
plt.scatter(x, y)
#Naming axes
plt.xlabel('x - axis')
plt.ylabel('y - axis')

#Straight line
y_hat = 0.7*x
plt.plot(x, y_hat, color='green')

#Example deviation
x1 = np.array ([2, 2])
y1 = np.array ([2.9, 1.5])
plt.plot (x1, y1, color='red')

```

```
#Save figure
plt.savefig("reg_illustration.png")
plt.show()
```

A straight line cannot fit all the data perfectly, and mistakes occur. These mistakes refer to the difference between y_i and its predicted value $\hat{y}_i = 0.7x_i$. The predicted value is on the straight line, called the regression line. The vertical line in Figure 6.1 shows the mistake made when predicting the value of y given $x = 2$.

6.1.2 Deriving the Regression Line

How exactly do we find the regression line? Linear regression applies an ordinary least squares (OLS) estimator. The OLS estimator minimizes a so-called loss function, which is based on the observed mistakes, i.e. deviations from the straight line. A loss function determines the loss we incur if we make mistakes. The 'mistakes' are captured in our residuals. Equation (6.3) shows the minimization problem.

The choice of loss function matters. OLS determines the coefficients so that the sum of squared residuals is minimized. By taking the squared value, we treat positive and negative deviations from the regression line in a similar way. In addition, larger mistakes have a higher impact on the loss function. This also suggests that outliers can affect our estimated regression line quite substantially.

$$\min_{\hat{\alpha},\hat{\beta}} \sum_{i=1}^{N} \hat{\varepsilon}_i^2 = \min_{\hat{\alpha},\hat{\beta}} \sum_{i=1}^{N} (y_i - \hat{y}_i)^2$$

$$= \min_{\hat{\alpha},\hat{\beta}} \sum_{i=1}^{N} \left(y_i - \hat{\alpha} - \hat{\beta}x_i\right), \quad i = 1, \ldots, N \tag{6.3}$$

Estimated coefficients are so-called *point estimates* and indicate the partial impact of the independent variable on the dependent variable. For instance, $\hat{\beta}_k = \frac{\partial y}{\partial x_k}$ if the model uses several independent variables k. These are estimates, they are not precise. They have a distribution – the true value should be in the centre of the distribution. The standard error refers to the estimated standard deviation of the coefficient denoted $\hat{\sigma}_{\hat{\beta}}$. It is a measure of the precision of the point estimate.

In our case with one independent variable, the estimated slope coefficient denoted $\hat{\beta}$ in our model captures the alleged partial impact of x on y. This coefficient is estimated. How do we know that the true slope coefficient β is actually positive or negative, implying that x has an impact on y? We need to conduct a hypothesis test.

We select a null hypothesis, which we try to reject. The null hypothesis is that $\beta = 0$, i.e. the partial impact of x on y is zero. Note that we will make mistakes as β

is only estimated following the minimization problem described in (6.3). Our focus is on controlling the mistake made when rejecting the null hypothesis. We restrict this mistake to the so-called level of significance. It is common to use 0.1%, 1%, or 5% for the level of significance. The level of confidence refers to one minus the level of significance. This translates into a level of confidence of 99.9%, 99%, or 95%.

Hypothesis tests can be conducted in two manners: (i) using a test statistic, which has a distribution under the null hypothesis, and (ii) using confidence intervals. The null hypothesis that $\beta = 0$, suggests a test statistic $t = \frac{\hat{\beta}}{\hat{\sigma}_{\hat{\beta}}}$ which has a *Student distribution* under the null. Confidence intervals are an alternative tool to conduct hypothesis tests.

The confidence interval refers to $[\hat{\beta} \pm 1.96 \times \hat{\sigma}_{\hat{\beta}}]$. It determines the range (upper and lower limit) of the true partial impact; hence, with a probability of 95%, the true partial impact is an element of the confidence interval. If zero is inside the 95% confidence interval, then we cannot reject the null hypothesis.

Hypothesis tests can be assessed by looking at t- and p-values of coefficients. The t-values are test statistics and are defined as the coefficient divided by standard error. If $|t| = \left|\frac{\hat{\beta}}{\hat{\sigma}_{\hat{\beta}}}\right| > 2$, the coefficient is significantly different from zero. The p-values indicate the probability that the true partial impact is outside the confidence interval. If p-value < 0.05, the coefficient is significantly different from zero with a 95% level of confidence or a 5% level of significance.

R-squared and adjusted R-squared (adjusted for degrees of freedom) are measures of the quality of the model (model fit); e.g. an R-squared of 70% means that the model can explain 70% of the observed variability of the dependent variable. Note that we do not use the R-squared in isolation to select 'good' models. Additional tests, such as F-tests and other specification tests, are required. The F-test refers to a joint null hypothesis that all coefficients are equal to zero ('model is useless'). If you can reject the null hypothesis (p–value < 0.05), it means that the model has explanatory power. Enough theory, let's move to the application in Python.

6.2 Modelling Sales Volumes of UK Properties

To illustrate the application of linear regression models, we try to predict sales volumes of existing and new properties in the UK using past house price changes. A more in-depth analysis would benefit many additional issues, such as non-stationary time series, causal order, and seasonality.

In this section, we simplify the problem and focus on applying linear regression in Python, interpreting regression outputs, and briefly discussing this approach's inherent limitations.

The data on house prices and sales volumes is collected by the Land Registry and provided by the ONS (https://landregistry.data.gov.uk/). The dataset is public, and a cleaned version is available on the book's website as a CSV file. As outlined in our chapter on data wrangling, CSV files can be imported using Pandas. The explicit print statement is needed (line 5) if you run the code in some text editors (e.g. Sublime text) or IDEs.

```
1 import pandas as pd
2
3 file = "uk_property_data.csv"
4 df = pd.read_csv(file)
5 print(df.head())
```

The variable (Pandas series) *time* contains strings that show the year (four characters) followed by a hyphen and the month (two characters). We can use the *split()* method, which operates on strings, to split the content using hyphens as separators. The *split()* method returns lists, and we can assign the first item of each list to a new variable, *year*, which we add to the Pandas *DataFrame*. The second item of each list contains the month, which creates a new column in our *DataFrame*. Finally, we use the *head()* to check our data structure.

```
df['time_split'] = df.time.str.split("-")
print(df.time_split)

df['year'] = df.time_split.apply(lambda x: int(x[0]))
df['month'] = df.time_split.apply(lambda x: int(x[1]))

df = df.drop('time_split', axis=1)

print(df.head())
```

Prior to modelling, it is useful to plot the time series of house prices and sales volumes. There are two types of sales: existing houses and new-build homes. Our example focuses on sales of existing homes.

Figure 6.2 shows the long period of house price growth followed by sharp corrections. Sales volumes exhibit a strong seasonal pattern and seem to dip after price drops. The following code replicates Figure 6.2. To show years and months on the x-axis, we set our index to the variable *time*.

```
df = df.set_index('time')
fig1, axes = plt.subplots(nrows=2, ncols=1)
df.price.plot(ax=axes[0])
df.volume.plot(ax=axes[1], color='red')
```

```
plt.tight_layout()
fig1.savefig("reg_series.png")
plt.show()
```

Figure 6.2 Property prices and sales volume

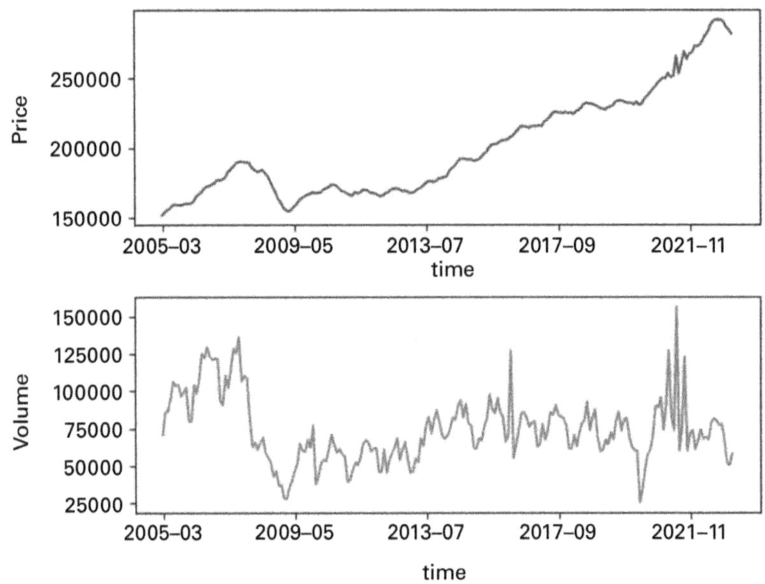

We need to address two issues before implementing a linear regression in Python. First, seasonality matters as we work with monthly time series, as shown in Figure 6.2. Second, house prices are likely affected by sales volume and vice versa. Hence, the causality of this relationship is not clear.

Seasonality can be modelled explicitly using a set of dummy variables derived from our variable *month*, which suggests a fixed seasonal pattern. Many alternative approaches include ARIMA models (autoregressive integrated moving average). However, the easiest approach is to construct first-differenced time series, which compares values in a particular month with the value of the same month in the previous year. The first-difference takes the form $x_t - x_{t-12}$ in the case of monthly data. The following code applies this method to house prices and sales volume. Finally, Figure 6.3 plots the change in sales volume without and with seasonal adjustment.

```
df['adj_price'] = (df.price-df.price.shift(12)).shift(1)
df['adj_volume'] = df.volume-df.volume.shift(12)
df['d_volume'] = df.volume.diff()
```

```
fig2, axes = plt.subplots(nrows=2, ncols=1)
df.d_volume.plot(ax=axes[0], color='green')
df.adj_volume.plot(ax=axes[1], color='red')
plt.tight_layout()
fig2.savefig("reg_adjustment.png")
plt.show()
```

Figure 6.3 Seasonal adjustment of changes in sales volume

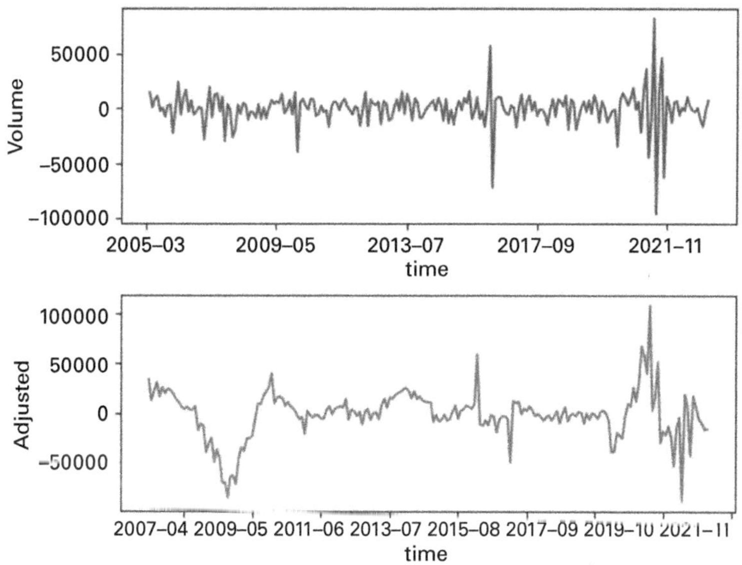

Figure 6.3 shows the unadjusted change in sales volume in the first panel, which is more dominated by the seasonal pattern. More pronounced changes emerge in the adjusted time series depicted below. House price changes might explain these.

To address the issue of causality, we use a lagged independent variable. Hence, the seasonally adjusted change in house prices in the previous period refers to our independent variable. Lagging by one period means that the variable is pre-determined (or observed). This ensures that the model is *weakly exogenous*, which is sufficient to conduct regression analyses. Using lagged variables is a common approach in applied time series analysis.

Equation (6.4) shows our linear regression model, where the change in sales volume denoted Δv_t is explained using lagged house price changes Δp_{t-1}. Finally, the error term ε_t is added, and the time dimension refers to $t = 1, \ldots, T$.

LAGGED VARIABLES

In practice, ensuring that independent variables are truly independent is challenging. Using lagged variables observed in the previous period (i.e. $t - 1$) guarantees that the current values of other variables cannot influence the variable.

$$\Delta v_t = \alpha + \beta \Delta p_{t-1} + \varepsilon_t, \quad t = 1, \ldots, T \tag{6.4}$$

Next, we implement the linear regression model (6.4) in Python, obtain regression tables, and interpret the outputs.

6.3 Implementation in Python

6.3.1 *Regressions in Statsmodels*

The Python package Statsmodels (https://pypi.org/project/statsmodels/) provides descriptive statistics and multivariate models, including linear regression. After installation using pip or Conda, we can import the package. OLS regressions refer to *smf.ols()*. The model is specified, fitted, and we can report the summary statistics.

```
pip install statsmodels
import statsmodels.formula.api as smf
```

To estimate our regression model (6.4), we use *smf.ols()* and specify the regression equation, defining the dependent variable *adj_volume* and the lagged independent variable *adj_price*. Then the *fit()* method is called on the OLS model object *mod1*. Finally, we display the regression table.

```
mod1 = smf.ols('adj_volume ~ adj_price', data=df)
res1 = mod1.fit()
print(res1.summary())
```

Based on our inspection of the time series, it seems to be likely that the Global Financial Crisis had a pronounced impact on property sales. To capture this alleged crisis effect, we add dummy variables for the years 2008 and 2009. The following code creates dummies from the categorical variable *year* adding the prefix Y. The year dummies are added to the *DataFrame* using the *join()* method. Finally, the resulting dataset is inspected.

```
year_dummies = pd.get_dummies(data = df.year, prefix = 'Y')
df = df.join(year_dummies)
print(df.head())
```

Two year dummies are added to an alternative model specification. Both specifications are combined into a single table, which we export as a LaTeX file (other formats are possible). The following code accomplishes these tasks.

```
1 from statsmodels.iolib.summary2 import summary_col
2 mod2 = smf.ols(‘adj_volume ~ adj_price + Y_2008 + Y_2009’\
3 , data=df)
4 res2 = mod2.fit()
5 print(res2.summary())
6
7 info_dict={‘N’:lambda x: “{0:d}”.format(int(x.nobs)), \
8 ‘R2’:lambda x: “{:.2f}”.format(x.rsquared)}
9 dfoutput = summary_col([res1, res2], stars=True, float_
  format=“%0.3f”, \
10 model_names=[‘Reference’, ‘Year’], info_dict=info_dict, \
11 regressor_order=[‘const’,‘adj_price’,‘Y_2008’,‘Y_2009’])
12 print(dfoutput)
13 dfoutput.as_latex()
14 with open(‘reg_table1.tex’,‘w’) as tf:
15     tf.write(dfoutput.as_latex())
```

The two dummies are added to the model specification with plus signs. To run line 8, we need to import *summary_col* in line 1. The table layout, order of variables, statistics, and formats can be modified easily. This is an efficient approach to automate the generation of regression tables. These tables can be inputs of a LaTeX document. Hence, every time you re-run your regression models, all tables reflect the latest changes.

6.3.2 Regressions in scikit-learn

There are many alternative ways to conduct linear regressions in Python. For instance, *scikit-learn* offers linear regressions among its linear models. Required inputs refer to the data matrix **X** and the dependent variable **y**. Both need to be NumPy arrays. The data matrix can be constructed from a Pandas *DataFrame* using the attribute *values* to convert Pandas objects into NumPy arrays. Installation is required using the pip installer or Conda.

```
pip install scikit - learn
```

Note that *LinearRegression()* in *scikit-learn* does not permit missing values. Hence, we need to drop missing values using listwise deletion, applying the *dropna()* method on our dataset. The data matrix X has the dimension $N \times k$, where N refers to the number of rows (observations) and k is the number of independent variables. If a constant term is desired, an all-one-column vector can be added to the data matrix. This operation is sometimes included in Python packages. Accordingly, the independent variables are selected from the *DataFrame* in line 6 (see below), and using the attribute *values* converts the *DataFrame* into a NumPy array. In a similar manner, we select the dependent variable. The *fit(X,y)* method takes the data matrix and the array containing the dependent variable. This method returns the results of the linear regression. These results can be displayed or used in other forms of output, such as tables. For instance, we can print the estimated coefficients, which are stored in the attribute *coef_*.

```
1 from sklearn.linear_model import LinearRegression
2 #Remove missing values
3 df = df.dropna()
4 #Define data matrix from DataFrame
5 #Convert to NumPy array
6 X = df[[‘adj_price’, ‘Y_2008’,‘Y_2009’]].values
7 #Select dependent variable
8 y = df[‘adj_volume’].values
9 reg = LinearRegression().fit(X, y)
10 #Show coefficients
11 print(reg.coef_)
```

6.3.3 Regression Using NumPy

NumPy's *polyfit()* function offers an alternative approach, which can be used to derive linear regression lines by specifying a linear fit (polynomial of order 1). Adjustments for missing values are not needed, and *polyfit()* works with Pandas series and *DataFrames*. The following code re-estimates our model using NumPy. The *polyfit()* function returns OLS estimates of the intercept *alpha* and slope coefficient *beta*.

```
beta, alpha = np.polyfit(df[‘adj_price’], \
df[‘adj_volume’], 1)
```

Apart from *LinearRegression()* in *scikit-learn* or NumPy's *polyfit()*, many packages perform linear regressions. In addition, developing your own linear regression class is often useful if you require further features (e.g. time-varying coefficients). The *LinearRegression()* function is not our favourite approach as it is less convenient to specify models. For instance, the data matrix needs to be changed using slicing, and additional modification might be required. Finally, you might prefer different layouts to showcase the outputs of your models.

Table 6.1 Regression table

	Reference	Year
adj_price	0.604***	0.378**
	(0.145)	(0.168)
Y_2008		-51029.742***
		(6434.173)
Y_2009		6105.346
		(7632.353)
Intercept	-6081.489***	-1738.994
	(1951.281)	(2247.723)
R-squared	0.079	0.326
R-squared Adj.	0.074	0.316
N	204	204

Standard errors in parentheses. * $p<.1$, ** $p<.05$, *** $p<.01$

6.4 Interpretation

Table 6.1 summarizes our two linear regressions. The reference model displayed in the second column shows that past adjusted changes in house prices *adj_price* have a positive impact on adjusted changes in sales volume. So, a price drop in the previous period can be used to predict a decline in volume. The coefficient has a magnitude of impact of $\hat{\beta}=0.604$. The standard error is $\hat{\sigma}_{\hat{\beta}} = 0.145$. Dividing the point estimate by its standard error yields the t-statistic, $t = \frac{0.604}{0.145} \approx 4.17$. As the absolute value exceeds two, it indicates that the null hypothesis that $\beta=0$ can be rejected.

It is common to indicate significance levels using one, two, or three asterisks. Depending on the discipline, 10%, 5%, and 1% or 5%, 1%, and 0.1% are frequently reported levels. In most recent academic papers across disciplines, reporting p-values instead of standard errors has become the norm. The main benefit of p-values is that they are easier to interpret without deriving t-statistics.

GIVE ME P-VALUES, NOT T-VALUES

In recent published empirical studies, displaying p-values is the norm. A p-value is directly related to significance or confidence levels and, hence, is easier to interpret than a t-value.

The reference model also includes a constant term or intercept, $\hat{\alpha}$, which is the predicted value of sales volumes if house prices remained constant in the previous period. The number of observations $N=204$ needs to be considered based on the context (e.g. many independent variables require more observations to estimate all coefficients). For small samples, $N<30$, OLS regressions become unreliable.

The adjusted R-squared is 0.074, which suggests that only 7.4% of the observed variability of the dependent variable can be explained by the model. Hence, more than 90% remain unexplained. Additional statistics, such as the F-test, can be reported. The reference model has an F-test statistic of 17.30 with an associated p-value of 0.000, indicating that the joint hypothesis that all coefficients of the model are equal to zero can be rejected. In summary, the model has some explanatory power, but past house price changes cannot explain the vast majority of observed changes in sales volume.

Clearly, limiting the model to a single independent variable is not sufficient. This might also lead to an omitted variable bias, which requires further testing, e.g. the Ramsey RESET test. The second model specification incorporates two dummy variables, *Y_2008* and *Y_2009*. Both dummies have coefficients pointing in different directions. The initial shock triggered a sharp drop in sales volume, followed by a modest recovery. Adding the two dummies increases model fit considerably with an adjusted R-squared of 0.316.

Dummy variables can capture exogenous shocks, such as financial crises or policy changes. This approach can be extended to assess the timing of effects, including the anticipation of policy changes and time lags. For instance, extensions include intervention models, which are common in political science. In many applications, using dummies is sufficient to improve model fit. However, improved model fit does not always translate into better forecasting abilities, as discussed in the limitations section.

6.5 Limitations

This section explores the most important limitations of linear regression analysis. Honestly, in most applied work, linear regressions are all that is needed to capture the relationships between variables. Linear regressions tend to be easier to interpret and communicate. However, it is essential to understand the inherent limitations.

6.5.1 Causality

It is important to understand that the linear model shown in equation (6.4) implies a direction of influence (causality). The independent variable, the change in house prices in the previous period, affects the dependent variable, the change in sales volume. As we argued, we lagged the independent variable by one period. Hence, a variable observed at time $t - 1$ can affect the dependent variable's current value at time t. However, the dependent variable cannot influence the past realization of the independent variable. Therefore, lagging independent variables ensure causal order, i.e. the past affects the present, but the present cannot affect the past. Of course, this assumes that time travel is not possible. If any of you reading this book invented time travel in the future, please appear before me right now, and I will correct my statement. Yes, the past tense is correct in this case. Jokes aside, causal order is a useful concept based on Granger causality. In applications, causality is usually not a major concern. The focus is on predictability.

6.5.2 *Multicollinearity*

The slope coefficient β captures the partial impact. The partial impact assumes that we can change one variable and hold all other variables constant. This, of course, is a given in our two-dimensional model. Yet, this is not guaranteed if you have many independent variables. This assumption is also called 'ceteris paribus' (other things being equal). This assumption is violated in real-life settings, i.e. without strict experimental designs. Put differently, if one independent variable changes in value, others are likely to change as well. Independent variables tend to be correlated. If correlation coefficients in absolute value exceed 0.85, this problem, called multicollinearity, can become severe. This means that it might be more difficult to estimate coefficients and partial impacts. It is common to explore the correlation matrix to ensure that correlation coefficients remain within ±0.85.

In addition, variance inflation factors (VIF) can be derived. Common cut-off points tend to be 5 or 10. VIFs can detect relationships between more than two variables. They are more reliable compared to inspecting the correlation matrix. In business analytics, identifying partial impacts is often not the main concern. In summary, multicollinearity might not be important to consider if your objective is to achieve high overall model fit and predictability.

6.5.3 *Linearity*

Non-linear relationships can be captured using transformations. However, linearization is often not a suitable approach. After a regression model is fitted, Ramsey RESET tests are recommended. These tests add the squared fitted values (or squared independent variables) to the regression model. Then a joint hypothesis test is conducted, assessing whether all coefficients associated with squared values are equal to zero. If the resulting F-test can reject the null hypothesis, one can conclude that a non-linear relationship might be present. This test also detects an omitted variable bias. If the regression model ignores an important independent variable, an omitted variable bias can occur. It is not always easy to distinguish between an omitted variable bias and an alleged non-linear relationship. The best approach is to inspect fitted values and residuals.

The following code re-estimates our regression model using NumPy. It plots observations using a scatter plot and depicts the fitted regression line.

```
beta, alpha = np.polyfit(df['adj_price'], df['adj_volume'], 1)
#Scatter plot
plt.plot(df['adj_price'], df['adj_volume'], 'o', \
color = 'gray', markersize = 2)
#Add regression line
plt.plot(df['adj_price'], alpha + beta*df['adj_price'], \
color = 'orange')
plt.savefig("reg_predict.png")
plt.show()
```

Figure 6.4 shows that the regression line is a reasonable approximation for most observations. However, outliers seem to be present. Some of these 'extreme' values can be explained using dummies (e.g. caused by exogenous shocks such as the Global Financial Crisis). Moreover, the pattern of deviations from the regression line does not suggest any systematic behaviour. If you observe consistent over- or

Figure 6.4 Fitted and actual values

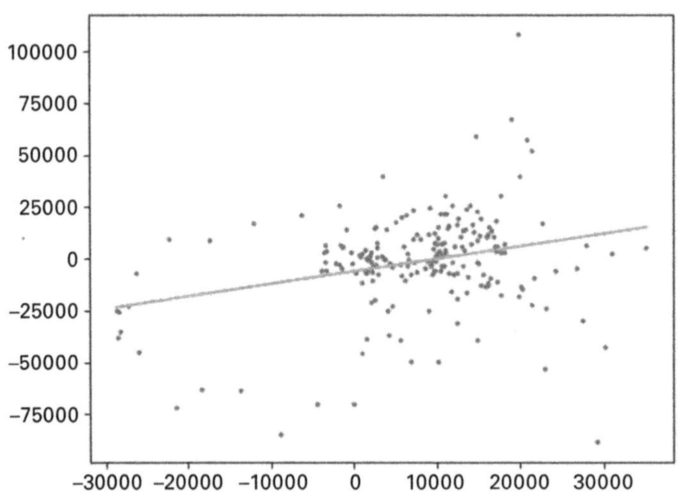

understatement of actual values, non-linear relationships might be the underlying reason. In summary, our model is a reasonable start. Additional independent variables should be considered to ensure that an omitted variable bias can be ruled out.

6.5.4 Heteroskedasticity

Violations of OLS assumptions are very common. These assumptions include heteroskedasticity and serial correlation. Linear regression assumes that the error term ε_t in our model (6.4) has the same standard error. So, mistakes are random and are not dependent on the value of independent variables. Furthermore, observing an error term at time $t-1$ does not help us to predict current or future values. Put differently, error terms do not exhibit serial correlation. In practice, both assumptions are likely to be violated. Violations affect the reliability of hypothesis tests. However, identifying partial impacts of independent variables is often not the main objective.

In addition, robust estimation procedures exist that address unknown forms of heteroskedasticity and serial correlation (Newey-West estimator). For instance, the Python package Statsmodels offers the *sandwich_covariance.cov_hac* method, which can be applied to regression results. It is easy to adjust for heteroskedasticity and serial correlation. In fact, robust estimation tends to be the default setting even before conducting further post-estimation tests.

TEST, TEST, TEST, ...

A word of caution is needed. Do not rely on tests in isolation. Every test needs a set of assumptions. It is best practice to explore fitted values and residuals as outlined above. These inspections can reveal the underlying reasons for violated assumptions.

6.5.5 Categorical or Binary Outcome

In our case, the dependent variable, the change in sales volume, is continuous. The dependent variable can take, in principle, any real value. There are no boundary conditions. Linear regressions provide fitted values on the real axis. In some problems, we want to predict a categorical or binary outcome. For instance, we might be interested in decision-making, where the observed outcome refers to a yes or no decision. Linear regression is less suitable for binary dependent variables because fitted values are not constrained to binary outcomes. The next chapter on logistic regressions offers a better modelling approach.

6.6 Summary

Linear regressions have been used long before the recent emergence of machine learning tools. A linear regression fitted with OLS might be regarded as a supervised learning algorithm as the dependent variable, i.e. the classification, is known. Hence, we can provide feedback regarding the errors made by fitting a linear regression line. So, how does the machine learn in this case? Well, by making mistakes. Mistakes are assessed based on the sum of squared deviations comparing fitted and actual values.

Of course, OLS requires a long list of assumptions to be fulfilled to ensure the reliable estimation of coefficients and test statistics. In practice, assumption violations are the norm, not the exception. Nevertheless, OLS is a useful starting point for exploring the relationships between variables in your dataset. OLS is fast because it is actually a closed-form solution to an optimization problem. More advanced machine learning tools require many iterations to estimate relationships. Convergence is not guaranteed in these cases. In summary, start with regression models before moving to more advanced methods. Categorical dependent variables (e.g. Likert scales) are often treated like continuous variables in regression models. However, logistic regressions are the better starting point if your dependent variable is binary (e.g. a yes-no answer to a question).

6.7 Exercise

You will explore a panel dataset, which includes several country-level variables observed over time. We used the dataset to conduct a research project for The Economic Research Institute for ASEAN and East Asia (ERIA). Additional material on GitHub includes STATA, Python code, and links to YouTube videos. The Python script *health.py* contains a possible solution. As discussed in this chapter, there are many ways to conduct a regression analysis in Python. Accordingly, you can achieve the same results following different paths.

The dataset contains the country code (*iso*), real GDP per capita (*r_gdp*), total employment (*emp*), hours worked per employee (*hours*), total hours worked (*t_hours*), the size of the population (*pop*), health expenditure (*h_exp*), and a digital healthcare index (*DHI*). The index captures the degree of digital healthcare provision in the respective country.

6.7.1 Setup

Your first task is to create and activate a virtual environment, followed by the installation of Python packages. We recommend installing Statsmodels, but many packages can conduct linear regression analyses. The choice is yours.

6.7.2 Data Import

Import the CSV file *health.csv* and check the data structure.

6.7.3 Data Wrangling

Remove missing values using list-wise deletion.

6.7.4 Regressions

Conduct linear regression models to explain countries' level of health expenditure (*h_exp*). You can try different model specifications. What explains health expenditure? Can you interpret your results?

7 Logistic Regression

This chapter delves into logistic regression, which is a powerful analytics method used for binary classification tasks like predicting customer churn and detecting credit card fraud, allowing us to predict the probability that an observation belongs to one of two categories based on one or more input variables.

After studying this chapter, you should be able to:

- Grasp the fundamentals of logistic regression and how it contrasts with linear regression.
- Understand the logistic function and its S-shaped curve.
- Interpret the coefficients of a logistic regression model in terms of odds ratios.
- Assess the fit of a logistic regression model using tools like the confusion matrix, classification report, ROC curve, and Area Under the Curve (AUC).
- Apply logistic regression to real-world problems, such as credit scoring, disease prediction, and customer churn prediction.
- Use Python to perform logistic regression for business analytics.

7.1 Business Analytics Example: Predicting Online Ad Clicks

We introduce logistic regression within the context of a business analytics case study focused on predicting online advertisement (in short ad) clicks. As shown in Figure 7.1, we delve into a credit card company's strategy aimed at targeting Amazon customers, utilizing a dataset named *ad_click.csv* obtained from Amazon. This dataset encompasses crucial details such as recent spending and age, alongside indicators of whether users clicked on the ads. These variables are summarized as below.

Figure 7.1 Example of online advertisement on Amazon webpage

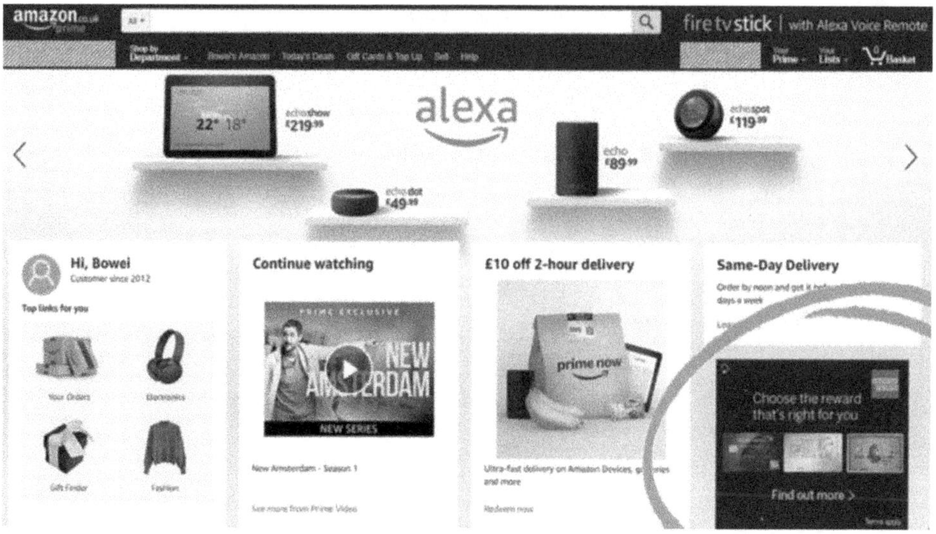

Variable	Description
Spending	The amount of money that a user has spent on the recent purchase
Age	The age of the user
Click	A binary variable indicating whether the user clicked (1) or did not click (0) on the credit card banner advertisement

The primary objective of the credit card company is to construct a model capable of predicting the likelihood of a user clicking on their credit card advertisement, thereby augmenting its marketing efficacy. The predictive capabilities of this model will be pivotal in facilitating the company's efficient allocation of advertising resources, allowing for targeted outreach to users exhibiting the highest propensity to engage with the advertisement.

7.2 Preliminary Analysis

To get started we need to know what data we have so the first step is to import the dataset. By using Python, specifically the Pandas package, we load the dataset into a Jupyter notebook. This allows us to examine the variables and understand the dataset's framework including its dimensions. This step is essential to create a robust baseline for any subsequent data analysis or predictive model development.

Figure 7.2 Jupyter output of data loading and variable checking

	Spending	Age	Click
0	9.5	14	0
1	20.2	21	1
2	9.7	10	0
3	18.3	14	1
4	12.3	15	1

(200, 3)

```
import pandas as pd

df = pd.read_csv("data/ad_click.csv")
df.head()
df.shape
```

We then check the distribution of each variable (including input variables *Spending* and *Age*, and the target variable *Click*). A pairs plot allows us to see both distribution of single variables and relationships between two variables. Creating a pairs plot is simple. We load in the Seaborn package and call the *pairplot* function, passing it our data frame *df*.

```
import matplotlib.pyplot as plt
import seaborn as sns
import numpy as np

sns.set_style("darkgrid")
g = sns.pairplot(df, height=2.5, corner=True)
def corr(x, y, **kwargs):
    coef = np.corrcoef(x, y)[0][1] # Calculate the value
    label = r" $\rho$ = " + str(round(coef, 2)) # Make the label
    ax = plt.gca() # Add the label to the plot
    ax.annotate(label, xy=(0.25, 0.75), size=11, xycoords=ax.transAxes)
g.map_lower(corr)
plt.show()
```

Several findings can be seen from Figure 7.3. First, the positive (i.e. click) and negative (i.e. no click) samples in the response variable Click are relatively balanced in the

Figure 7.3 Output of the pairs plot

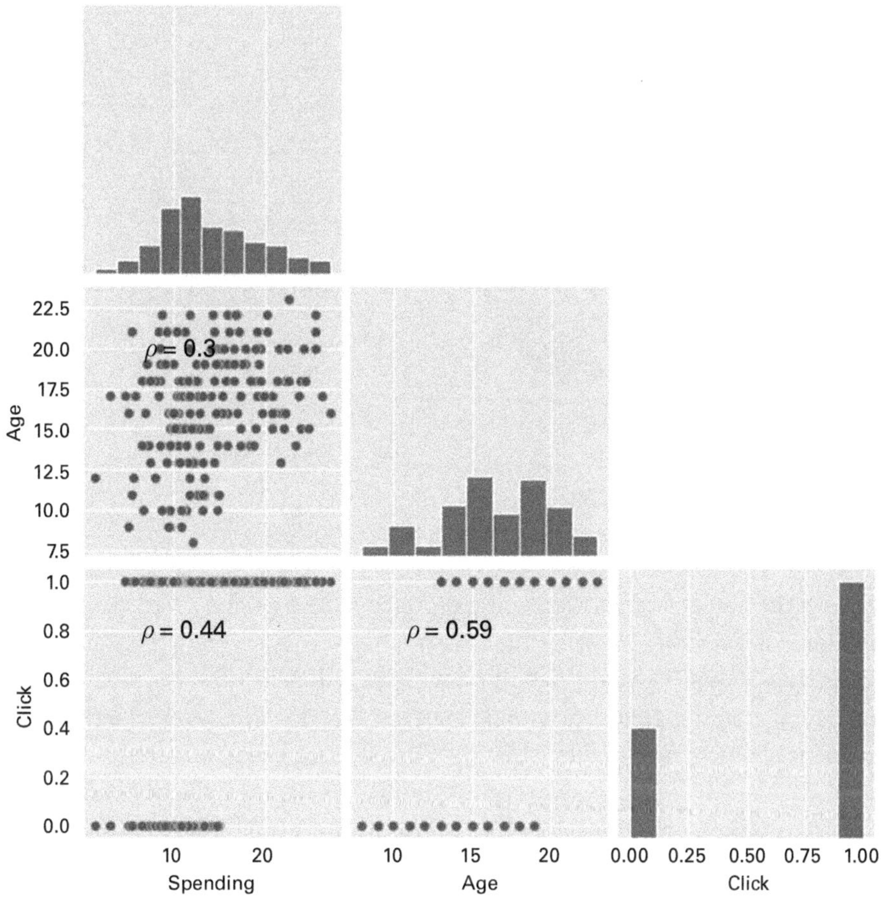

dataset. In machine learning, *class balance* refers to the distribution of classes within a dataset. A dataset is considered class balanced when each class is represented equally or nearly equally in the dataset. On the other hand, *class imbalance* occurs when one class is significantly more prevalent than the others. This can lead to biased models that perform poorly on minority classes because they have been exposed to fewer examples during training. Second, since the response variable is binary, from the scatter plots, it is not difficult to see that no regression line can fit the data well. Third, the two predictor variables Spending and Age are not significantly linear correlated.

7.3 What is Logistic Regression?

The fundamental concept behind logistic regression is to find a relationship between feature variables and the probability of a particular outcome of the target variable. In our motivating example, this outcome is modeled as a binary variable where 0

Figure 7.4 Logistic regression surface (i.e. logistic function)

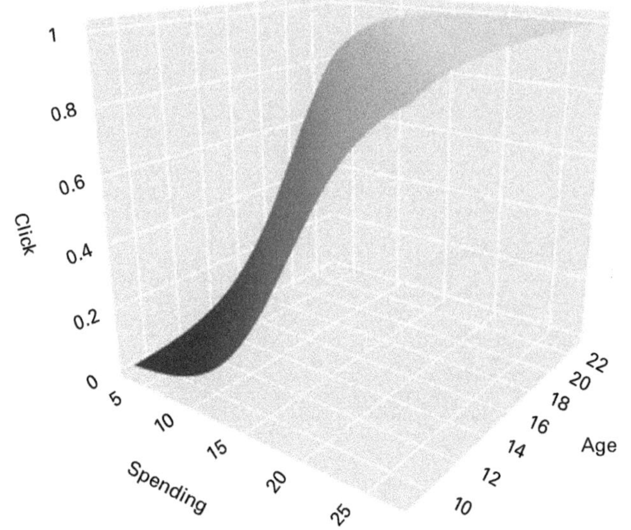

represents the absence of ad click and 1 represents the presence of ad click. Logistic regression achieves this by using the *logistic function* (also known as the *sigmoid function*). As shown in Figure 7.4, it is an S-shaped curve that can take any real-valued number and map it into a value between 0 and 1, but never exactly at those limits. This characteristic makes it suitable for estimating probabilities.

In mathematical terms, logistic regression models the *logit* (i.e. the logarithm of the odds) as a linear relationship with the feature variables, which means the logarithm of the odds ratio is modeled as a linear combination of the features. The *coefficients* (also known as *parameters* or *weights*) of the logistic regression algorithm must be estimated from the training data – this is typically done using a method called the *maximum likelihood estimation (MLE)*. Once the model is fitted, it can be used to predict the probabilities of the *positive* class, and by applying a threshold (like 0.5), we can decide the class assignment for each data point.

7.3.1 Odds and Logistic Function

Let the dataset be denoted by $\mathcal{D} = \{(\boldsymbol{x}_1, y_1), \cdots, (\boldsymbol{x}_N, y_N)\} = \{(\boldsymbol{x}_n, y_n)\}_{n=1}^{N}$, where $\boldsymbol{x}_n$ is a vector of feature values for the n th sample (also called the *feature vector* in machine learning), and y_n is the corresponding value of the target variable. In logistic regression, the total contribution of features for the n th sample is defined using the linear form as follows

$$z_n = \boldsymbol{w}^\top \boldsymbol{x}_n.$$

Let $p = \mathbb{P}(y_n = 1 \mid \boldsymbol{x}_n)$ be the probability of the sample to be clicked, then the odds that the click (event) occurs can be expressed as

$$\text{Odds of the Click} = \frac{p}{1-p}.$$

The aforementioned calculation aligns with the definition of *odds*, a concept in statistics and probability theory that quantifies the ratio of the likelihood of an event occurring to the likelihood of it not occurring. If we take the natural logarithm of the odds (then called the *logit*), the range of values lies in the real line, so we can use it to measure z_n, that is

$$\ln\left\{\frac{p_n}{1-p_n}\right\} = z_n.$$

If using z_n to represent the probability p, then it can be estimated by the following function, which is called the *logistic function*, so

$$p_n = \frac{e^{z_n}}{1+e^{z_n}}.$$

In other words, once the weight vector $\boldsymbol{w}$ is determined by the given data, we can obtain the logistic regression model to predict future advertisement clicks.

LOGISTIC FUNCTION

A logistic function (or sigmoid function) is a mathematical function having a characteristic S-shaped curve. For x on a real line, a logistic function $f(x)$ can be expressed as

$$f(x) = \frac{e^x}{1+e^x} = \frac{1}{1+e^{-x}}.$$

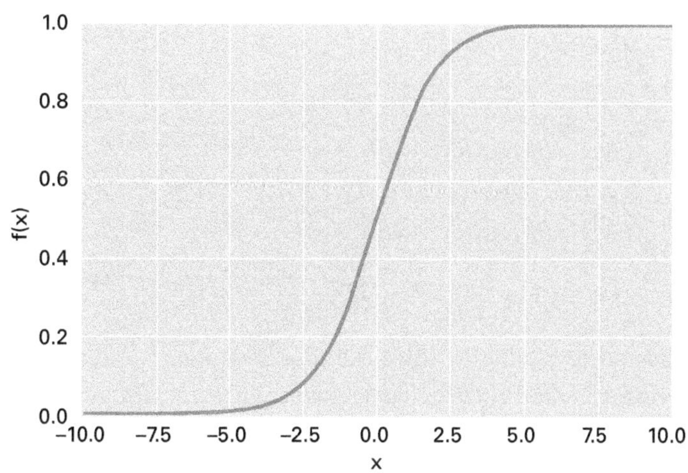

7.3.2 Estimating the Weights

The weights or coefficients in logistic regression are commonly estimated using the method of maximum likelihood estimation (MLE). This approach involves maximizing the likelihood function, which is a fundamental concept in statistical inference, particularly in the context of parameter estimation. Simply put, the likelihood function measures the probability of observing the given data under different parameter values of a statistical model. It is a function of the parameters of the model, given the observed data. In logistic regression, the MLE aims to find the weight values that make the observed data most probable.

For the n th sample, the probabilities of it being clicked and not clicked can be formulated as follows

$$p_n = \mathbb{P}(y_n = 1 \mid \boldsymbol{w}, \boldsymbol{x}_n) = \frac{e^{\boldsymbol{w}^\top \boldsymbol{x}_n}}{1 + e^{\boldsymbol{w}^\top \boldsymbol{x}_n}},$$

$$1 - p_n = \mathbb{P}(y_n = 0 \mid \boldsymbol{w}, \boldsymbol{x}_n) = \frac{1}{1 + e^{\boldsymbol{w}^\top \boldsymbol{x}_n}}.$$

As $y_n = 0$ or 1, it follows Bernoulli distribution, then the likelihood of $\boldsymbol{w}$ is given

$$\begin{aligned}
\mathcal{L}(\boldsymbol{w}) &= \mathbb{P}(y \mid \boldsymbol{w}, \boldsymbol{X}) \\
&= \prod_{n=1}^{N} \mathbb{P}(y_n \mid \boldsymbol{w}, \boldsymbol{x}_n) \\
&= \prod_{n=1}^{N} p_n^{y_n} (1 - p_n)^{1-y_n}.
\end{aligned}$$

The optimal $\boldsymbol{w}^*$ can be obtained by maximizing $l(\boldsymbol{w})$. However, directly calculating $l(\boldsymbol{w})$ is computationally difficult; instead, we can obtain $\boldsymbol{w}^*$ by maximizing the log-likelihood of $\boldsymbol{w}$, which can be given

$$\begin{aligned}
\mathrm{LL}(\boldsymbol{w}) &= \ln\{\mathcal{L}(\boldsymbol{w})\} \\
&= \ln\left\{\prod_{n=1}^{N} p_n^{y_n} (1 - p_n)^{1-y_n}\right\} \\
&= \sum_{n=1}^{N} [y_n \ln\{p_n\} + (1 - y_n) \ln\{1 - p_n\}].
\end{aligned}$$

Several methods are available to solve the aforementioned optimization problem, including Newton's method and stochastic gradient descent, among others. However, as these methods fall outside the primary scope of this discussion and are not the most critical aspects of logistic regression, they will not be explored in detail here.

7.4 Implementing Logistic Regression in Python

Estimating the weights or coefficients forms the basis of the logistic regression model. Let's now proceed to implement logistic regression in Python. In traditional statistical analysis, the entire dataset is typically used to develop a simple logistic regression model. However, in the realms of machine learning and data mining, this approach is frequently substituted with the division of observations into two distinct datasets: a training set and a test set.

The training set is employed to estimate the weights of the logistic regression model. This involves fitting the model to the training data, allowing it to learn the relationships between the features and the target variable. This process is also called model training. The test set serves as an independent evaluation mechanism. It is crucial for assessing the performance of the trained model on unseen data, ensuring it can generalize well beyond the training data and make accurate predictions for new instances.

In Python, the *scikit-learn* library can be used for training and evaluating logistic regression models. The first step in this process is to convert the loaded data into a NumPy ndarray, as this is the data format recognized and required by the *scikit-learn* library.

```
x = df.iloc[:, :-1].to_numpy()
y = df.iloc[:, -1].to_numpy()
```

Next, let's randomly divide the dataset into two parts: 70% for training and 30% for testing. The *train_test_split* function from the *model_selection* module in the *scikit-learn* library can be used. The argument *test_size* specifies the percentage of the original data that will be used for testing. The *random_state* argument is used to control the randomness in data split. By setting a specific value for the *random_state*, we can ensure that the code produces the same training and test sets every time it is run. This is crucial for reproducibility of results. Without a fixed *random_state*, each run of the code could lead to slightly different outcomes.

```
from sklearn.model_selection import train_test_split
x_train, x_test, y_train, y_test = train_test_split(x, y,
test_size=0.3, random_state=0)
```

The training and test sets of data after splitting can be visualized through the following codes, and the output is presented in Figure 7.5.

Figure 7.5 Visual summary of training and test sets

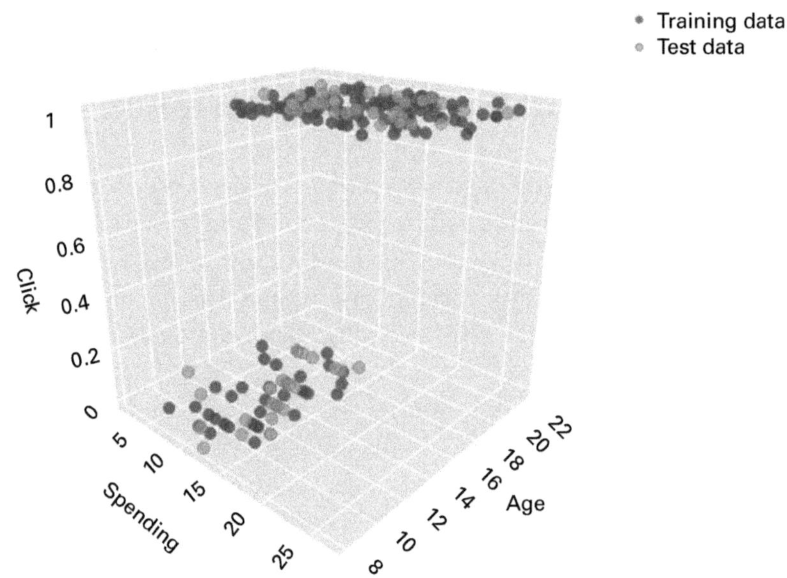


```
from plotly.offline import iplot, init_notebook_mode
init_notebook_mode(connected=True)
import plotly.graph_objs as go
import plotly.io as pio

fig_width = 800
fig_height = 600
pio.orca.config.default_width = fig_width
pio.orca.config.default_height = fig_height

plot_data_training = go.Scatter3d(
    x=x_train[:, 0],
    y=x_train[:, 1],
    z=y_train,
    opacity=0.75,
    mode="markers",
    marker=dict(color="#1f77b4", size=5,
    line=dict(color="#7f7f7f", width=1)),
    name="Training data",
)

```

```
plot_data_test = go.Scatter3d(
    x=x_test[:, 0],
    y=x_test[:, 1],
    z=y_test,
    opacity=0.75,
    mode="markers",
    marker=dict(color="#ff7f0e", size=5,
    line=dict(color="#7f7f7f", width=1)),
    name = "Test data",
)

data = [plot_data_training, plot_data_test]
layout = go.Layout(
    title="",
    autosize=True,
    width=fig_width,
    height=fig_height,
    margin=dict(l=65, r=50, b=65, t=90),
    scene ={
        "xaxis": {"title": "Spending"},
        "yaxis": {"title": "Age"},
        "zaxis": {"title": "Click"},
        "camera": {"eye": {"x": 1.5, "y":  1.65, "z": 0.9}},
        "aspectmode": "cube",
    },
    showlegend=True,
)
fig = go.Figure(data=data, layout=layout)
iplot(fig, image_width=fig_width, image_height=fig_height)
```

Now we could implement a logistic regression model using the *LogisticRegression* class from the *linear_model* module in the *scikit-learn* library. This class offers various solvers for addressing the optimization problem in estimating weights, including *lbfgs*, *newton-cg*, *liblinear*, *sag*, and *saga*. If no specific solver is designated, the default solver will be employed. Due to the random nature of the optimization (like random initialization of weights), the value of *random_state* needs to be specified.

```
from sklearn.linear_model import LogisticRegression
clf = LogisticRegression(random_state=0)
clf.fit(x_train, y_train)
```

After the logistic regression model is specified, the *fit* function can be used to train the model (i.e. estimating the weights using the training data). In this function, we need to specify the training feature data *x_train* and the training target variable data *y_train*.

Once the model is trained, we can use it for prediction. The *predict* method of the *LogisticRegression* class allows us to estimate the outcomes for new, unseen data. This predictive capability is fundamental to the utility of logistic regression in classification tasks. By inputting features of new samples (i.e. *x_test*) into the trained model, we can obtain predictions about the likelihood of each sample belonging to a particular class, thus enabling informed decision-making based on the model's learned patterns.

```
plot_data_training = go.Scatter3d(
    x=x_train[:, 0],
    y=x_train[:, 1],
    z=y_train,
    mode="markers",
    marker=dict(color="#1f77b4", size=5,
    line=dict(color="#7f7f7f", width=1)),
    name="Training data",
)

plot_data_test = go.Scatter3d(
    x=x_test[:, 0],
    y=x_test[:, 1],
    z=y_test,
    opacity=0.75,
    mode="markers",
    marker=dict(color="#ff7f0e", size=5,
    line=dict(color="#7f7f7f", width=1)),
    name="Test data",
)

xx = np.linspace(np.min(x_train[:, 0]), np.max(x_train
[:, 0]), 50)
yy = np.linspace(np.min(x_train[:, 1]), np.max(x_train
[:, 1]), 50)
xx_yy = np.array(np.meshgrid(xx, yy)).T.reshape(-1, 2)
X = pd.DataFrame(xx_yy, columns=["Spending", "Age"])

predictions_prob = clf. predict_proba(X.to_numpy())
```

```
predictions_prob = pd.DataFrame(predictions_prob).iloc[:, 1].values
predictions_prob = predictions_prob.reshape((50, -1))

plot_trace_prob = go.Surface(
    x=xx,
    y=yy,
    z=predictions_prob,
    name=“LR model”,
    showscale = False,
)

# plot predicted labels (training)
predictions_label_training = clf.predict(x_train)
plot_pred_label_training = go.Scatter3d(
    x=x_train[:, 0],
    y=x_train[:, 1],
    z=predictions_label_training,
    opacity=0.5,
    mode=“markers”,
    marker=dict(color=“#2ca02c”, size=5, line=dict(color=“#7f7f7f”, width=1)),
    name=“ Predicted label (training data)”,
)

# plot predicted labels (test)
predictions_label_test = clf.predict(x_test)
plot_pred_label_test = go.Scatter3d(
    x=x_test[:, 0],
    y=x_test[:, 1],
    z=predictions_label_test ,
    opacity=0.5,
    mode=“markers”,
    marker=dict(color=“#e377c2”, size=5, line=dict(color=“#7f7f7f”, width=1)),
    name=“Predicted label (test data)”,
)

data = [
    plot_data_training,
    plot_data_test,
    plot_trace_prob,
    plot_pred_label_training,
```

```
    plot_pred_label_test,
]

layout = go.Layout(
    title="",
    autosize=True,
    width=fig_width,
    height=fig_height,
    margin=dict(l=65, r=50, b=65, t=90),
    scene={
        "xaxis": {"title": "Spending"},
        "yaxis": {"title": "Age"},
        "zaxis": {"title": "Click"},
        "camera": {"eye": {"x": 1.5, "y": -1.65, "z": 0.9}},
        "aspectmode": "cube",
    },
    showlegend=True,
)

fig = go.Figure(data=data, layout=layout)
iplot(fig, image_width=fig_width, image_height=fig_height)
```

Figure 7.6 Training data, test data, logistic regression, and its predictions for the test data

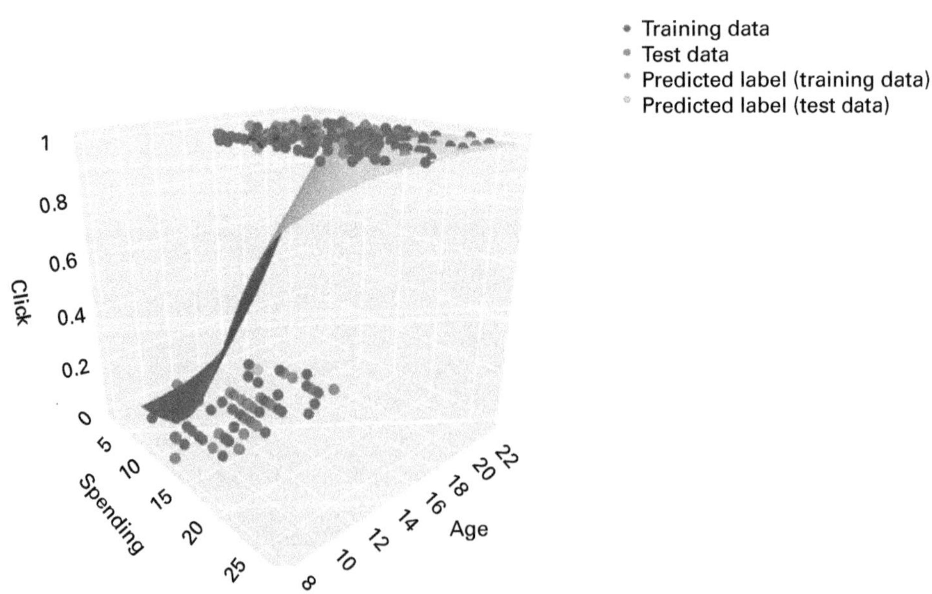

Figure 7.7 Output table that summarizes the ground truth, the predicted probabilities, and labels from the trained logistic regression model for the training data

	Label_GT	Label_Prob	Label_Pred
0	0.0	0.713198	1.0
1	1.0	0.954832	1.0
2	1.0	0.991380	1.0
3	0.0	0.064770	0.0
4	1.0	0.805269	1.0
5	1.0	0.999410	1.0
6	1.0	0.967737	1.0
7	1.0	0.870212	1.0
8	1.0	0.860574	1.0
9	1.0	0.980699	1.0

7.5 Model Evaluation

Model evaluation is a critical step in the machine learning workflow. It involves assessing the performance of a trained model to determine how well it has learned to make predictions on new data. There are numerous metrics available to evaluate the effectiveness of a trained machine learning model, and the choice of these metrics depends on the type of model and the specific problem it addresses. As our focus in this chapter is on developing logistic regression for a binary classification task (which involves distinguishing between two classes), we will explore the relevant evaluation metrics specifically suited for a two-class classification model in the following discussion.

First, let's examine the predictions made by the model on the training data. We will then compare these model predictions with the actual values, which, in machine learning terminology, is referred to as the *ground truth (GT)*.

```
y_prob_train = clf.predict_proba(x_train)[:, 1]
y_pred_train = clf.predict(x_train)
y_pred_test = clf.predict(x_test)

df_result_training = pd.DataFrame([y_train, y_prob_train,
y_pred_train])
df_result_training = df_result_training.T
df_result_training.columns = ["Label_GT", "Label_Prob",
"Label_Pred"]
df_result_training.head(10)
```

The data from the full table can be visualized using a histogram or a density plot.

```
prob_click = df_result_training.loc[df_result_training[“Label_GT”] == 1, “Label_Prob”]
prob_noclick = df_result_training.loc[df_result_training[“Label_GT”] == 0, “Label_Prob”]

fig, axes = plt.subplots(1, 2, figsize=(15, 5))

axes[0].hist(prob_click.values, bins=30, alpha=0.75, label=“Click”)
axes[0].hist(prob_noclick.values, bins=30, alpha=0.75, label=“No click”)
axes[0].legend(loc=“upper left”)
axes[0].set_xlabel(“$p$”)
axes[0].set_ylabel(“Frequency”)

sns.kdeplot(x=prob_click.values, ax=axes[1], label=“Click”)
sns.kdeplot(x=prob_noclick.values, ax=axes[1], label=“No click”)
axes[1].axvline(x=0.5, ymin=0, ymax=4, color=“g”, label=“Threshold”)
axes[1].legend(loc=“upper left”)
axes[1].set_xlabel(“$p$”)
axes[1].set_ylabel(“Density”)

plt.show()
```

Figure 7.8 Histogram and density which summarize the ground truth, the predicted probabilities, and labels from the trained logistic regression model for the training data

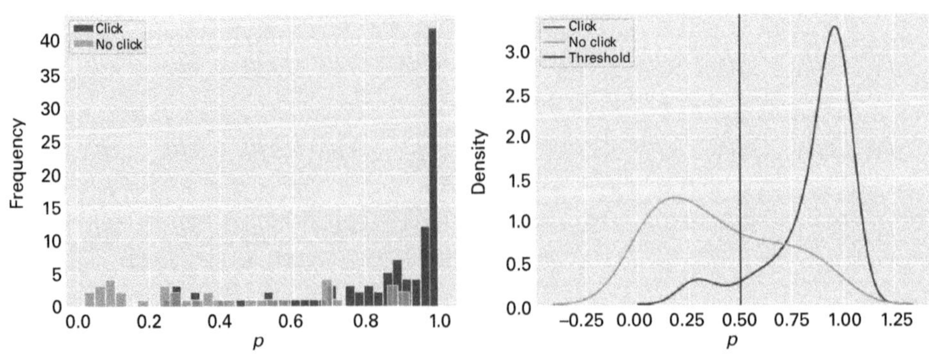

In the above density plot, we have assumed that the threshold for a random guess corresponds to a 50% probability of a click. This threshold can be modified based on domain-specific knowledge relevant to the application. Under this assumption, let's proceed to examine the model's predictions more closely. We will delve into analysing the data that the model has predicted correctly as well as the instances where its predictions were incorrect.

```
fig, axes = plt.subplots(2, 2, figsize=(15, 12))

sns.kdeplot(x=prob_click.values, ax=axes[0, 0], label="Click")
sns.kdeplot(x=prob_noclick.values, ax=axes[0, 0], label="No click")
axes[0, 0].axvline(x=0.5, ymin=0, ymax=4, color="g", label="Threshold")
xx = axes[0, 0].get_lines()[0].get_data()
shade = xx[0][xx[0] >= 0.5]
kde = xx[1][xx[0] >= 0.5]
axes[0, 0].fill_between(shade, kde, alpha=0.3, color="royalblue", label="TP")
axes[0, 0].legend(loc="upper left")
axes[0, 0].set_xlabel("$p$")
axes[0, 0].set_ylabel("Density")

sns.kdeplot(x=prob_click.values, ax=axes[0, 1], label="Click")
sns.kdeplot(x=prob_noclick.values, ax=axes[0, 1], label="No click")
axes[0, 1].axvline(x=0.5, ymin=0, ymax=4, color="g", label="Threshold")
xx = axes[0, 1].get_lines()[1].get_data()
shade = xx[0][xx[0] <= 0.5]
kde = xx[1][xx[0] <= 0.5]
axes[0, 1].fill_between(shade, kde, alpha=0.3, color="orange", label="TN")
axes[0, 1].legend(loc="upper left")
axes[0, 1].set_xlabel("$p$")
axes[0, 1].set_ylabel("Density")

sns.kdeplot(x=prob_click.values, ax=axes[1, 0], label="Click")
```

```
sns.kdeplot(x=prob_noclick.values, ax=axes[1, 0], label="No click")
axes[1, 0].axvline(x=0.5, ymin=0, ymax=4, color="g", label="Threshold")
xx = axes[1, 0].get_lines()[0].get_data()
shade = xx[0][xx[0] < 0.5]
kde = xx[1][xx[0] < 0.5]
axes[1, 0].fill_between(shade, kde, alpha=0.3, color="royalblue", label="FN")
axes[1, 0].legend(loc="upper left")
axes[1, 0].set_xlabel("$p$")
axes[1, 0].set_ylabel("Density")

sns.kdeplot(x= prob_click.values, ax=axes[1, 1], label="Click")
sns.kdeplot(x=prob_noclick.values, ax=axes[1, 1], label="No click")
axes[1, 1].axvline(x=0.5, ymin=0, ymax=4, color="g", label="Threshold")
xx = axes[1, 1].get_lines()[1].get_data()
shade = xx[0][xx[0] >= 0.5]
kde = xx[1][xx[0] >= 0.5]
axes[1, 1].fill_between(shade, kde, alpha=0.3, color="orange", label="FP")
axes[1, 1].legend(loc="upper left")
axes[1, 1].set_xlabel("$p$")
axes[1, 1].set_ylabel("Density")

plt.show()
```

The above plots show that, based on our threshold, we can evaluate how many positive and negative samples are correctly predicted by the trained logistic regression in the training data, where

- *True positive (TP)* represents, the model predicts positive, and its prediction is correct. Here in our project positive means click.
- *True negative (TN)* represents, the model predicts negative, and its prediction is correct. Here in our project negative means no click.
- *False positive (FP)* represents, the model predicts positive, but its prediction is incorrect.
- *False negative (FN)* represents, the model predicts negative, and its prediction is incorrect.

Figure 7.9 Density plots which compare the actual target values with those predicted by the logistic regression model for the training data

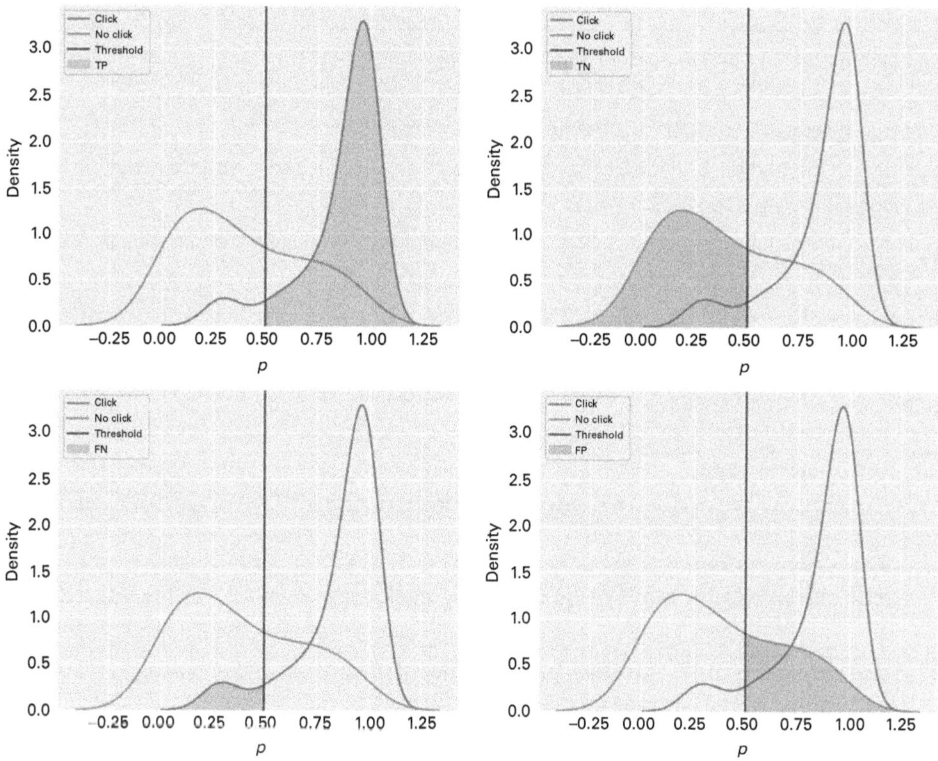

Figure 7.10 Visualized confusion matrix for the training data

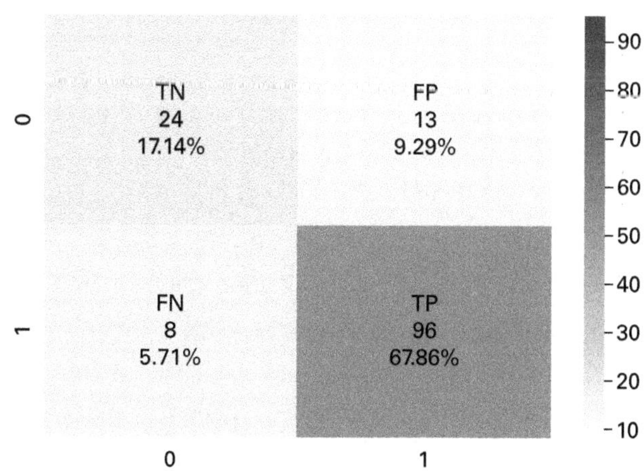

If we summarize these results into a tabular format, we can obtain the so-called *confusion matrix*, which compares the actual target values with those predicted by the model, providing insight into the types of errors being made.

```
from sklearn.metrics import confusion_matrix
cf_matrix = confusion_matrix(y_train, y_pred_train)
group_names = ["TN", "FP", "FN", "TP"]
group_counts = ["{0:0.0f}".format(value) for value in
cf_matrix.flatten()]
group_percentages = ["{0:.2%}".format(value) for value in
cf_matrix.flatten() / np.sum(cf_matrix)]
labels = [f"{v1}\n{v2}\n{v3}" for v1, v2, v3 in zip(group_
names, group_counts, group_percentages)]
labels = np.asarray(labels).reshape(2, 2)

fig = plt.figure()
sns.heatmap(cf_matrix, annot=labels, fmt="", cmap="Blues")
plt.show()
```

Based on the confusion matrix, the following evaluation metrics can be defined:

- *Accuracy* is the most intuitive performance measure and it is simply a ratio of correctly predicted observations to the total observations.

$$\text{Accuracy} = \frac{\text{TP} + \text{TN}}{\text{FP} + \text{FN} + \text{TP} + \text{TN}} = \frac{\text{TP} + \text{TN}}{\text{N}},$$

$$\text{Error Rate} = \frac{\text{FP} + \text{FN}}{\text{FP} + \text{FN} + \text{TP} + \text{TN}} = 1 - \text{Accuracy}.$$

- *Precision* is the ratio of correctly predicted positive observations to the total predicted positive observations. The question that this metric answers is, of all advertisements that are predicted to be clicked, how many actually are clicked?

$$\text{Precision} = \frac{\text{TP}}{\text{TP} + \text{FP}}.$$

- *Recall* or *true positive rate (TPR)* is the ratio of correctly predicted positive observations to the all observations in actual class. The question recall answers is that of all the advertisements that are truly clicked, how many did we predict?

$$\text{True Positive Rate (TPR)} = \text{Recall} = \frac{\text{TP}}{\text{TP} + \text{FN}},$$

$$\text{False Positive Rate (FPR)} = \frac{\text{FP}}{\text{FP} + \text{TN}}.$$

- *F1-score* is the harmonic mean of precision and recall. Unlike the arithmetic mean, the harmonic mean tends to be closer to the smaller of the two values of precision and recall, ensuring that a model must have a good balance of both to achieve a high F1 score. The F1 score ranges from 0 to 1, where a score of 1 indicates perfect precision and recall, and a score of 0 means that either the precision or the recall is zero. This score is particularly useful in scenarios where an equal balance between precision and recall is desired, or when dealing with datasets where one class is significantly underrepresented.

$$\text{F1-Score} = \frac{2 \times \text{Recall} \times \text{Precision}}{\text{Recall} + \text{Precision}}.$$

In Python, the *classification_report* function from the *metrics* module in the *scikit-learn* package is a convenient tool for computing the above evaluation metrics. Next, we will use this function to assess the performance of the trained logistic regression model on both the training and test sets.

```
from sklearn.metrics import classification_report

print("Training set")
print(classification_report (y_train, y_pred_train))

print("Test set")
print(classification_report (y_test, y_pred_test))
```

In the classification report output, the terms *macro avg* and *weighted avg* refer to two different methods of averaging the performance metrics (like precision, recall, and F1-score) across different classes. The macro average is calculated by first computing the metric independently for each class, and then taking the average of these metrics, treating all classes equally. On the other hand, the weighted average takes into account the imbalance in the dataset by weighting the metric score of each class by the number of true instances of that class.

For binary classification tasks, the *Area Under the Curve (AUC)* is another popular evaluation metric, which serves a different purpose compared to accuracy, precision, recall and F1-score. AUC provides an overall measure of a model's performance across all thresholds, whereas accuracy, precision, recall, and F1-score are typically calculated for a specific threshold. This makes AUC a useful metric when the optimal threshold is not known or when it's important to evaluate the model's performance across all thresholds. The Receiver Operating Characteristic (ROC) curve is created

Figure 7.11 Output of classification report for both training and test sets

```
Training set
              precision    recall  f1-score   support

           0       0.75      0.65      0.70        37
           1       0.88      0.92      0.90       103

    accuracy                           0.85       140
   macro avg       0.81      0.79      0.80       140
weighted avg       0.85      0.85      0.85       140

Test set
              precision    recall  f1-score   support

           0       0.93      0.61      0.74        23
           1       0.80      0.97      0.88        37

    accuracy                           0.83        60
   macro avg       0.87      0.79      0.81        60
weighted avg       0.85      0.83      0.82        60
```

by plotting the true positive rate (TPR) against the false positive rate (FPR) at various decision thresholds. As introduced earlier, the TPR is the proportion of actual positives correctly identified as such, while the FPR is the proportion of actual negatives incorrectly identified as positives. An ROC curve is a useful tool for comparing the performance of different binary classifiers. Since both TPR and FPR range from 0 to 1, the total area in the plot is then 1. The AUC of the model is the area beneath the ROC curve, and it also ranges from 0 to 1. A higher AUC indicates a better ability of the classifier to distinguish between positive and negative classes.

In the following toy example, when the trained model can perfectly predict positive and negative samples, the AUC is equal to 1. In Python, the functions *roc_curve* and *auc* are utilized to compute the FPR and TPR across various thresholds. Subsequently, these metrics are used to construct the ROC curve and calculate the AUC.

```
from sklearn.metrics import roc_curve, auc

# Generate perfect cases
y_worse = np.random.normal (0.7, 0.05, 1000)
y_train_new_01 = np.round (y_worse)

y_perfit = np.random.normal (0.3, 0.05, 1000)
y_train_new_02 = np.round(y_perfit)
```

```
y_perfit = np.concatenate((y_worse, y_perfit), axis=None)
y_train_new = np.concatenate((y_train_new_01, y_train_
new_02), axis=None)

fig, axes = plt.subplots(1, 2, figsize=[15, 5])

sns.kdeplot(y_perfit[y_train_new == 1], label="Click",
ax=axes[0])
sns.kdeplot(y_perfit[y_train_new == 0], label="No click",
ax=axes[0])
axes[0].axvline(x=0.5, ymin=0, ymax=4, color="g",
label="Threshold")
axes[0].set_xlabel("$p$")
axes[0].set_ylabel("Density")
axes[0].legend(loc="best")

fpr, tpr, thresholds = roc_curve(y_train_new, y_perfit)
roc_auc = auc(fpr, tpr)

axes[1].plot(fpr, tpr,
     label="Model (AUC={:0.2f})".format(roc_auc),
     linewidth=2)
axes[1].plot([0, 1], [0, 1],
     color="green",
     linestyle="--",
     label="Random (AUC=0.50)")
axes[1].set_xlabel("FPR", fontsize=13)
axes[1].set_ylabel("TPR", fontsize=13)
axes[1].legend (loc="best", fontsize=13)

plt.show()
```

The following toy example shows when the trained model's performance is poor, almost similar to a random guess like when we flip a fair coin, so its AUC is equal to 0.5.

```
# Generate worst cases
y_worse = np.random.normal(0.5, 0.2, 1000)
y_train_new_01 = 1 - np.round(y_worse)

y_perfit = np.random.normal(0.5, 0.2, 1000)
```

```
y_train_new_02 = np.round(y_perfit)

y_worse = np.concatenate((y_worse, y_perfit), axis=None)
y_train_new = np.concatenate((y_train_new_01, y_train_
new_02), axis=None)

fig, axes = plt.subplots(1, 2, figsize=[15, 5])

sns.kdeplot(y_worse[y_train_new == 1], label="Click",
ax=axes[0])
sns.kdeplot(y_worse[y_train_new == 0], label="No click",
ax=axes[0])
axes[0].axvline(x=0.5, ymin=0, ymax=4, color="g",
label="Threshold")
axes[0].set_xlabel("$p$")
axes[0].set_ylabel("Density")
axes[0].legend(loc="best")

fpr, tpr, thresholds = roc_curve(y_train_new, y_worse)
roc_auc = auc(fpr, tpr)

axes[1].plot(fpr, tpr,
      label="Model (AUC={:0.2f})".format(roc_auc),
      linewidth=2)
axes[1].plot([0, 1], [0, 1],
      color="green",
      linestyle="--",
      label="Random(AUC=0.50)")
axes[1].set_xlabel("FPR", fontsize=13)
axes[1].set_ylabel("TPR", fontsize=13)
axes[1].legend(loc="best", fontsize=13)

plt.show()
```

Now, returning to our advertisement click prediction project, the ROC curve and the AUC for the trained logistic regression model using the training data can be obtained as follows

```
fpr, tpr, thresholds = roc_curve(y_train, y_prob_train)
roc_auc = auc(fpr, tpr)

plt.figure(figsize=[7, 6])
plt.step(
```

```
    fpr, tpr,
    label="Logistic regression(AUC={:0.2f})".format(roc_auc),
    linewidth=2
)
plt.plot([0, 1], [0, 1],
    color="green",
    linestyle="--",
    label="Random (AUC=0.50)")
plt.xlabel("FPR", fontsize=13)
plt.ylabel("TPR", fontsize=13)
plt.legend(loc="lower right", fontsize=13)
plt.show()
```

It is worth noting that we employed the *step* function instead of the *plot* function in the above codes to illustrate the ROC curve in the above plot. Both functions serve their purpose, but using the *step* function offers the following advantages:

- Clarity in discrete changes: A continuous *plot* might imply a level of precision or smoothness in the model's performance that does not exist, while the *step* function makes it clear that the ROC curve is based on a finite set of threshold values. This can be particularly helpful when handling datasets or models that generate a limited number of distinct threshold levels (e.g. when predictions are not finely grained).
- Emphasis on decision thresholds: The *step* function can make it easier to see the exact point at which the TPR and FPR change, which is directly tied to the decision thresholds. This can be beneficial in applications where understanding the impact of changing these thresholds is crucial.

Figure 7.12 AUC of a perfect model

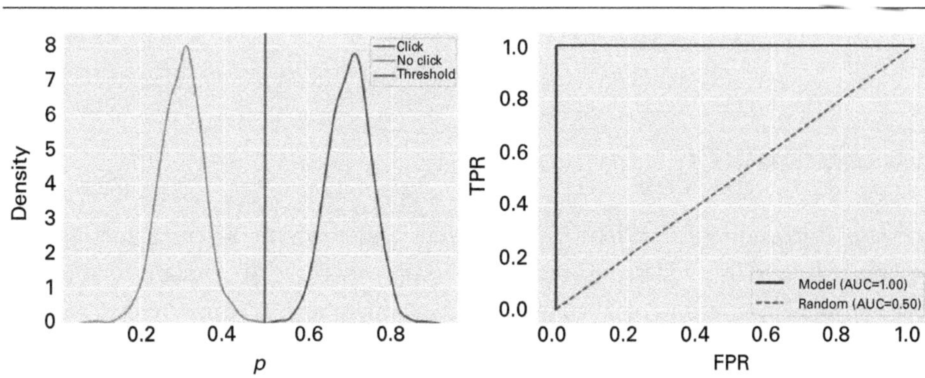

Figure 7.13 AUC of a poor model

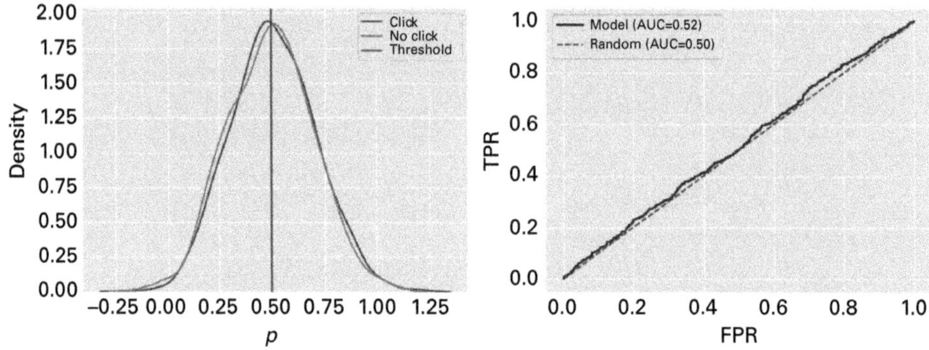

Figure 7.14 AUC of the trained logistic regression model on the training data

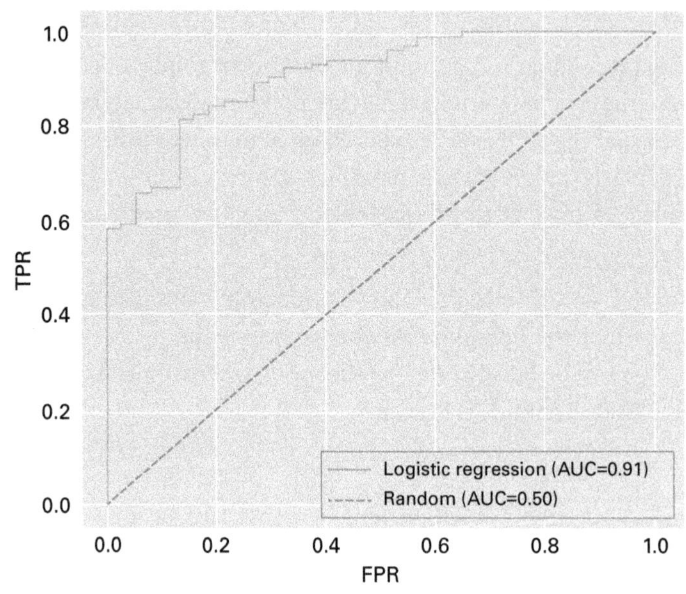

7.6 Summary

Logistic regression is a widely used statistics and machine learning method renowned for its effectiveness in predicting binary outcomes. Its versatility allows it to be applied to a range of business problems, including customer churn prediction, credit risk assessment, market segmentation, and forecasting the likelihood of a customer making a purchase. This chapter introduces binary logistic regression, highlighting its fundamental principles and applications. It is important to note that logistic regression is not limited to binary classification tasks. The model can be extended to handle multi-class classification problems, such as those encountered in multinomial logistic regression. In this extended form, the model is designed to estimate the probability of each class in the target variable based on a given set of features. The training or estimation of logistic regression involves maximizing the likelihood that the observed data is accurately represented by the model. This can be achieved in Python *scikit-learn* library and its *LogisticRegression* class from the *linear_model* module offers various solvers for addressing the optimization problem.

Logistic regression offers several advantages, including its ease of interpretation, interpretable decision boundaries, versatility for various classification tasks, computational efficiency with large datasets, a probabilistic approach that provides probabilities for outcomes, and lower susceptibility to overfitting when kept simple. However, it has limitations, as it struggles to capture complex data relationships as effectively as other algorithms like decision trees or neural networks, is sensitive to imbalanced data, and may exhibit reduced performance in high-dimensional feature spaces.

Several evaluation metrics for classification tasks have been introduced in this chapter. Metrics like confusion matrix, accuracy, precision, and recall can be applied not only in two-class classification tasks but also multi-class classifications. However, the metrics ROC and AUC are specifically for two-class classifications. These metrics can be easily calculated in Python using the *metrics* module from the *scikit-learn* library.

7.7 Exercise

In this exercise, you will implement logistic regression to determine whether a patient has heart disease and to speed up the diagnostic process based on the provided medical information about the patients. Use the *heart_disease.csv* dataset, which is created based on a publicly available heart disease dataset from the UCI Machine Learning Repository (https://archive.ics.uci.edu/dataset/45/heart+disease). This dataset contains medical information on patients and the diagnostic results indicating whether the patient has heart disease. Below is the description of the variables included in the dataset.

- **age:** age in years
- **sex:** sex
  - 1: male
  - 0: female
- **cp:** chest pain type
  - 0: typical angina
  - 1: atypical angina

    - 2: non-anginal pain
    - 3: asymptomatic
- **trestbps:** resting blood pressure (in mm Hg on admission to the hospital)
- **chol:** serum cholesterol in mg/dl
- **fbs:** (fasting blood sugar > 120 mg/dl)
    - 1: true
    - 0: false
- **restecg:** resting electrocardiographic results
    - 0: normal
    - 1: having ST-T wave abnormality (T wave inversions and/or ST elevation or depression of > 0.05 mV)
    - 2: showing probable or definite left ventricular hypertrophy by Estes' criteria
- **thalach:** maximum heart rate achieved
- **exang:** exercise induced angina
    - 1: yes
    - 0: no
- **oldpeak:** ST depression induced by exercise relative to rest
- **slope:** the slope of the peak exercise ST segment
    - 0: upsloping
    - 1: flat
    - 2: downsloping
- **ca:** number of major vessels (0-3) coloured by fluoroscopy
- **thal:**
    - 0: error (in the original dataset 0 maps to NaNs)
    - 1: fixed defect
    - 2: normal
    - 3: reversible defect
- **target (the label):**
    - 0: no disease
    - 1: disease

8 Neural Networks

Neural networks, also known as artificial neural networks (ANNs), the driving force behind modern AI and machine learning, have revolutionized fields like computer vision and natural language processing. Their potential to unlock actionable insights and optimize business practices is unquestionably valuable.

After studying this chapter, you should be able to:

- Understand the foundational concepts of neural networks, including artificial neurons, layers, and weights.
- Recognize the significance of neural networks in business analytics and their potential impact on decision-making.
- Gain insights into the popular types of neural networks, with a primary focus on Multi-Layer Perceptrons (MLPs).
- Comprehend the fundamental data preprocessing techniques essential for preparing data for neural networks, which include one-hot encoding, label encoding, and normalization.
- Acquire practical skills in implementing and using MLPs for solving real-world business problems.
- Learn how to evaluate and interpret the results generated by neural network models in a business context.
- Understand the strengths and weaknesses of neural networks in business settings.

8.1 What are Neural Networks?

Neural networks are computational models inspired by the human brain. They are designed to mimic the structure and functioning of the human brain in processing information, recognizing patterns, and making decisions. At the core of every neural network is the *(artificial) neuron*, the digital counterpart of biological neurons. These neurons act as information processors, taking in input data, applying mathematical operations, and generating output. Each neuron is associated with a *weight*, which determines the strength of its connection to other neurons. By adjusting these weights during training, neural networks can learn from data and adapt their behaviours.

Figure 8.1 Schematic view of a feedforward neural network and a recurrent neural network, where circles in blue represent input neurons, circles in grey represent hidden neurons, and circles in white represent output neurons

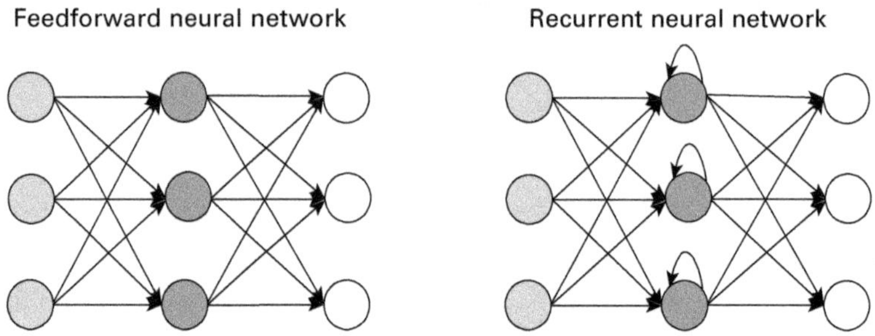

These artificial neurons are organized into layers: an input layer to receive data, one or more hidden layers for processing, and an output layer that produces the final result. It is this layered structure that gives neural networks their power, as they can capture intricate patterns and relationships within data that would be challenging for traditional algorithms to discern.

Neural networks come in various shapes and sizes, each tailored for specific tasks and challenges. Some of the most common types of neural networks include Feedforward Neural Networks (FNNs), Recurrent Neural Networks (RNNs), and Convolutional Neural Networks (CNNs). In Figure 8.1, we present a visual representation of an FNN and an RNN to emphasize their key differences. CNNs, with their unique representation, are not featured in this illustration. FNNs represent the simplest form of neural networks, characterized by a strictly feedforward architecture. They encompass an input layer, one or more hidden layers, and an output layer. Information flows unidirectionally, from the input layer to the output layer, devoid of any feedback loops. FNNs are typically employed in tasks where the sequential order of data is irrelevant, such as image classification or tabular data analysis. In contrast, RNNs embrace a recurrent architecture with feedback connections. They incorporate loops within their structure, allowing them to maintain a hidden state capable of capturing sequential dependencies in data. As a result, RNNs excel in tasks involving sequences, time series data, natural language processing, and speech recognition. CNNs, on the other hand, are meticulously crafted for the processing of grid-like data, such as images. Their architecture comprises convolutional layers that apply filters to localized portions of the input, followed by pooling layers to reduce dimensionality. CNNs shine when it comes to capturing spatial patterns in data, making them an indispensable choice for tasks like image recognition, object detection, and image generation. For a more comprehensive and detailed introduction to various advanced neural networks, please refer to Goodfellow et al. (2016) and Murphy (2022).

Figure 8.2 Summer events from a seaside resort company

8.2 Business Analytics Example: Consumer Segmentation

A seaside resort company specializes in providing budget-friendly, family-oriented holiday experiences and entertainment. As shown in Figure 8.2, their current objective is to establish a data-driven model for suggesting summer events, such as spa, shows, and outdoor activities, tailored to their existing customers who have already reserved accommodation. The primary aim is to harness valuable insights from past summer data to efficiently segment the customer base and utilize this knowledge to deliver personalized event recommendations to new bookings for the upcoming summer season. In the dataset provided, the target variable features three distinct categories representing summer events: spa, shows, and outdoor activities. This classification task falls under the category of multi-class classification. In the subsequent sections of this chapter, we are going to develop a simple neural network model to effectively categorize consumers.

8.3 Preliminary Analysis

Our first step involves importing the dataset. In this regard, we use the Pandas package to load the dataset into a Jupyter notebook, and then use the *head()* function to view the first five rows.

```
import pandas as pd

df = pd.read_csv("data/holiday_rental_consumer_segmentation.csv")
df.head()
```

Figure 8.3 Jupyter output of data header summary

◆	Price ◆	Size ◆	Bedroom ◆	Bathroom ◆	Floor ◆	Car_Parking ◆	Internet ◆	Location ◆	Pet ◆	Event ◆
0	420.0	292.5	3	1	2	Yes	No	Area_2	No	Spa
1	660.0	208.0	3	1	1	Yes	No	Area_1	No	Spa
2	660.0	194.0	3	2	2	Yes	No	Area_3	No	Spa
3	838.0	240.0	3	1	1	Yes	No	Area_1	No	Spa
4	900.0	360.0	3	2	1	Yes	No	Area_4	No	Spa

Figure 8.4 Jupyter output of *df.info()*

```
<class 'pandas.core.frame.DataFrame'>
RangeIndex: 191 entries, 0 to 190
Data columns (total 10 columns):
 #   Column       Non-Null Count  Dtype
---  ------       --------------  -----
 0   Price        191 non-null    float64
 1   Size         191 non-null    float64
 2   Bedroom      191 non-null    int64
 3   Bathroom     191 non-null    int64
 4   Floor        191 non-null    int64
 5   Car_Parking  191 non-null    object
 6   Internet     191 non-null    object
 7   Location     191 non-null    object
 8   Pet          191 non-null    object
 9   Event        191 non-null    object
dtypes: float64(2), int64(3), object(5)
memory usage: 15.0+ KB
```

The *info()* function can provide a summary of both the variables and observations contained within the loaded dataset.

```
df.info()
```

Referring to Figure 8.4, we observe the dataset consisting of 191 observations and 10 variables, comprising 9 features and the target variable *Event*. Notably, there are no instances of missing values across all features and observations. Hence, there is no requirement to handle missing data within this dataset. Also, in Figure 8.4, the variable types are visually represented. It is important to emphasize that these variable types are determined by the computer's interpretation and not by domain-specific knowledge. As a result, although a variable might be displayed as an integer under *Dtype*, it may actually represent a categorical variable. Therefore, it is advisable to conduct a thorough preliminary analysis to examine the unique values of each variable.

```
for col, col_dtype in zip(df.columns, df.dtypes):
    print(
      "====\n Variable: {0:} | Data type: {1:} | Unique values: {2:}\n".format(col, col_dtype, df[col].unique())
      )
```

In the above Python code, the *zip()* function is used to integrate two iterables (i.e. *df.columns* and *df.dtypes*) in an element-wise manner. This function yields an iterator of tuples where each tuple's *i*th element corresponds to the *i*th element from each of the input iterables. In our scenario, both *df.columns* and *df.dtypes* have equal lengths. However, if the lengths of the input iterables differ, the resulting iterator will align with the length of the shortest input iterable. The Jupyter output, as depicted in Figure 8.5, illustrates the examination of unique values for each variable within *df*, confirming the absence of missing or inconsistent values requiring attention. It is notable that numerical variables might be exempt from this assessment due to their large volume of unique values. Additionally, it is important to recognize that this type of visual inspection may not be practical for datasets with high dimensionality.

Various descriptive analytics can be conducted based on our analytical preferences and chosen methods. In the context of developing neural networks for this application, no specific assumptions are made regarding the features. However, other methods may impose certain assumptions about both the features and the target variable, such as linear regression and Naïve Bayes. In such cases, it is advisable to empirically validate these assumptions. For instance, we can check the distribution

Figure 8.5 Jupyter output of checking unique values of each variable in *df*

```
====
 Variable: Price | Data type: float64 | Unique values: [ 420.   660.   838.   900.   450.   485.   659.   440.   617.   545.
  665.   700.   570.   680.   950.   560.   600.   670.   510.   325.
  350.   470.   550.   639.   555.   780.   580.  1630.  1235.   599.
  790.  1250.   730.   635.   750.   945.  1065.  1160.  1170.   400.
  572.5  610.   800.   370.   620.  1300.   529.   480.   525.   500.
  699.   447.   575.   520.   539.   695.   720.   925.  1383.   785.
  708.   260.   645.   710.   462.   630.   649.   745.   650.   769.
  990.  1240.  1060.  1550.  1410.   595.   685.   860.  1750.  1200.
  820.   850.  1220.   840.   970.  1125.  1400.   747.   789.   869.
  770.   807.5  829.   760.   775.   870.   875.   890.  1000.   917.
 1745.   611.   585.5 1049.   749.   795.  1209.   476.   490.   605.
  930.   885.   880.   895.   955.   590.   715.   719.   589. ]

====
 Variable: Size | Data type: float64 | Unique values: [292.5  208.   194.   240.   360.   199.3  239.25 225.5  248.   175.
 201.6  157.5  187.25 226.   108.   205.   458.3  202.   363.   275.
 252.   300.   204.75  91.8  160.5   82.5  159.   318.   189.   154.5
 303.   295.   371.   402.5  412.5  225.   165.   216.   150.   187.5
 213.   200.   215.   342.   206.   298.   228.   132.5  108.75 180.
 147.65  95.25 156.   203.75 155.   181.5  151.8  171.   274.75 173.
 178.5  126.   217.5  177.   198.   140.85 140.   190.8  159.25 316.05
 235.   238.5  198.5  172.5  176.   220.5  182.   245.   127.5  483.35
 290.   249.75 322.5  444.   357.75 372.   375.   405.   202.3  350.
 340.   330.   498.   535.   660.   397.5  305.   321.   327.   358.
 327.5  354.25 345.   351.   400.   481.   525.   335.5  333.   361.55
 370.5  390.   341.25 450.   142.5  320.   558.75 337.5  256.8  170.
 143.5  266.   420.   202.5  572.   302.5  190.   270.   107.25 130.5
  97.5  100.75 139.35 249.5  333.5  312.7  272.5  285.   299.25 407.5
 232.3  250.5  384.3 ]

====
 Variable: Bedroom | Data type: int64 | Unique values: [3 2 4 5]

====
 Variable: Bathroom | Data type: int64 | Unique values: [1 2 3]

====
 Variable: Floor | Data type: int64 | Unique values: [2 1 3 4]

====
 Variable: Car_Parking | Data type: object | Unique values: ['Yes' 'No']

====
 Variable: Internet | Data type: object | Unique values: ['No' 'Yes']

====
 Variable: Location | Data type: object | Unique values: ['Area_2' 'Area_1' 'Area_3' 'Area_4']

====
 Variable: Pet | Data type: object | Unique values: ['No' 'Yes']

====
 Variable: Event | Data type: object | Unique values: ['Spa' 'Outdoor activities' 'Shows']
```

Figure 8.6 Jupyter output of *value_counts()* of the target variable *Event*

```
Event
Spa                   116
Shows                  55
Outdoor activities     20
Name: count, dtype: int64
```

of each numerical and categorical variable, encompassing both features and the target variable, and explore the correlation between numerical features, which can provide insights into potential relationships among them. These checks can be carried out using graphical representations or statistical measures, allowing for a comprehensive assessment of the data's characteristics.

As this project involves a classification task, it is imperative to check the distribution of classes within the target variable to ensure a certain level of balance. The *value_counts()* function can be useful in this regard, as demonstrated in Figure 8.6, where an imbalance in class distribution is evident; notably, *Outdoor activities* and *Shows* exhibit markedly fewer instances compared to *Spa*. Given the small dataset size of 191 observations, addressing imbalanced classification through upsampling is recommended. Further details on this technique will be elaborated upon in the subsequent data preprocessing section.

```
df["Event"].value_counts()
```

8.4 Data Preparation

Data preparation, also known as *data preprocessing*, aims to transform raw input data into an appropriate format for subsequent analysis. It typically involves merging data from multiple sources, dealing with missing values, correcting inconsistencies, removing noise and duplicates, selecting records and features that are relevant to the data mining task at hand, and encoding and scaling data for training and evaluating machine learning algorithms. In this section, we introduce a few important steps of data preparation using Python. More comprehensive details about data preparation are discussed by Han et al. (2011) and Tan et al. (2018).

8.4.1 Data Integration

Data integration, or sometimes *data fusion*, combines data from multiple sources to create a unified and consistent dataset for analysis. It can be a complex process depending on the volume, variety, and velocity of the available datasets. Understanding data formats and data types of each source is an important first step. Various tools and techniques can be used to facilitate this process, and here we simply discuss a few methods that are suitable for tabular data, which is the most popular data format in business analytics.

Tabular data is commonly represented in various formats such as comma-separated values (CSV), tab-separated values (TSV), Excel spreadsheet (XLS/XLSX), and database formats like SQL. Essentially, each column in these formats represents a variable, while each row represents an observation or sample. Therefore, three types of operations are commonly used for tabular data integration:

1 Merging tabular data by row (i.e. vertical concatenation)
2 Merging tabular data by column (i.e. horizontal concatenation)
3 Merging tabular data by key (i.e. integrating datasets based on the matched values of a specific variable shared by the merged datasets)

In Python, the *pd.concat()*, *append()*, and *pd.merge()* functions from the Pandas library are the methods for the above operations.

8.4.2 Data Cleaning

Data cleaning involves addressing missing values, correcting inconsistencies, removing noise and duplicates, and ensuring data integrity. In this section, we specifically focus on *missing values*, which refer to instances where data points are absent in a dataset. They may arise from various factors, including data entry errors, equipment malfunctions, non-responses in surveys, or intentional omission of information.

Detecting missing values is an integral part of data preparation. In Python, functions like *isnull()* or *isna()* can be used for this purpose. Alternatively, missing values can be visualized by examining the distribution of variables or inspecting unique values per variable (see Figure 8.5). It should be noted that missing values can be represented differently depending on the dataset and the data format. Common representations include empty cells in spreadsheets and placeholder values like *NA* or *NaN* (not a number) in programming languages such as Python and R.

There are several techniques to handle missing values:

- If only a few missing values are present, removing rows containing them can be an option using *df.dropna(axis=0)*.
- In cases where a variable contains a high percentage of missing values and is deemed unimportant in a business analytics scenario, removing the entire column can be a solution using *df.dropna(axis=1)*.
- Another approach is to replace the missing values with alternative values such as constants, means, medians, modes, or even predicted values using machine learning algorithms. *df.fillna()* function can facilitate this process.

8.4.3 Data Resampling

Data resampling is employed to mitigate class imbalance in a dataset. As mentioned in Chapter 7, *class imbalance* means that one class (referred to as the *minority class*) is notably underrepresented compared to another classes (the *majority class*). This class imbalance can result in biased models that exhibit poor performance in predicting the minority class.

There are two main approaches to data resampling for addressing class imbalance: over-sampling and under-sampling. *Over-sampling* involves augmenting the number of instances in the minority class, achieved through duplicating existing instances, generating synthetic instances, or a combination of both. Conversely, *Under-sampling* entails reducing the number of instances in the majority class to balance the class distribution. Within each approach, there are many methods, such as random sampling, Synthetic Minority Over-sampling Technique (SMOTE) (Chawla et al., 2002), Adaptive Synthetic Sampling (ADASYN) (He et al., 2008), and so on. While this section does not delve into the intricacies of each method, further details about resampling techniques can be found in the book by Good (2006). It is important to note that over-sampling may lead to overfitting while under-sampling may result in the loss of potentially useful information.

The following Python code shows that we perform a simple upsampling to minority classes in the data, and the upsampled data is verified by Figure 8.7.

```
from sklearn.utils import resample
my_random_seed = 100

# Separate majority and minority classes
df_majority = df.loc[df["Event"] == "Spa", :]
df_minority_1 = df.loc[df["Event"] == "Shows", :]
df_minority_2 = df.loc[df["Event"] == "Outdoor
activities", :]

# Upsample minority class
df_minority_upsampled_1 = resample(
     df_minority_1,
     replace=True, # sample with replacement
     n_samples=116, # to match majority class
     random_state=my_random_seed,
)

df_minority_upsampled_2 = resample(
    df_minority_2,
    replace=True, # sample with replacement
```

```
    n_samples=116, # to match majority class
    random_state=my_random_seed,
)

# Combine majority class with upsampled minority class
df = pd.concat([df_majority, df_minority_upsampled_1,
    df_minority_upsampled_2])

# Display new class counts
df["Event"].value_counts()
```

8.4.4 Data Encoding

Encoding means we convert the data values into a specified format or form. Decoding is the reverse process of encoding, which is to extract the information from the converted format. In the data preparation stage, data encoding is mainly for *feature encoding* and *label encoding*.

Figure 8.7 Jupyter output of *value_counts()* of the target variable *Event* after upsampling

```
Event
Spa                   116
Shows                 116
Outdoor activities    116
Name: count, dtype: int64
```

Figure 8.8 Illustration of one-hot encoding for categorical features of one feature vector, where the newly created binary features are highlighted in orange

Feature	1st record
Price	420
Size	292.5
Bedroom	3
Bathroom	1
Floor	2
Car_Parking	Yes
Internet	No
Location	Area_2
Pet	No

Feature	1st record
Price	420
Size	292.5
Bedroom	3
Bathroom	1
Floor	2
Car_Parking_Yes	1
Internet_Yes	0
Location_Area_2	1
Location_Area_3	0
Location_Area_4	0
Pet_Yes	0

One-hot encoding is a technique used in machine learning to represent categorical features as binary vectors. In one-hot encoding, each category or level of a categorical feature is converted into a binary feature with value 0 or 1. In other words, each newly created binary feature corresponds to one category of the original binary feature. Figure 8.8 provides an illustration of one-hot encoding for one feature vector, where the categorical features *Car_Parking*, *Internet*, *Location*, and *Pet* are converted into a set of binary features. For example, from Figure 8.5, we observe that feature *Location* has four unique values in the original data: *Area_1*, *Area_2*, *Area_3*, and *Area_4*. Then, four binary features are created to represent these four categories: *Location_Area_1*, *Location_Area_2*, *Location_Area_3*, and *Location_Area_4*. In the newly created binary features, if the value under *Location_Area_2* is 1, it means the category of *Location* in the original data is *Area_2*. In the meantime, the value of *Location_Area_1*, *Location_Area_3*, and *Location_Area_4* is 0. It should be noted that omitting the first or last binary feature in one-hot encoding is a common practice. This avoids redundancy and collinearity because the omitted binary feature does not provide any additional information that is not already captured in the remaining binary features. Therefore, the one-hot encoding results for feature *Location* are *Location_Area_2*, *Location_Area_3*, and *Location_Area_4*. As for *Car_Parking*, *Internet*, and *Pet*, each having two categories, their one-hot encoding results are *Car_Parking_Yes*, *Internet_Yes*, *Pet_Yes*, respectively.

In Python, we can use the *pandas.get_dummies()* function to perform one-hot encoding for categorical features. Apart from the input feature data, there are two important specifications of the function: *drop_first* is set to be *True* means dropping the first column, and *dtype* is set to *int64* means returns numerical values (i.e. 0 or 1) rather than Boolean values (*True* or *False*).

```
df_features = pd.get_dummies(df.iloc[:, :-1], drop_
  first=True, dtype="int64")
df_features.head ()
```

We can convert all the feature data frame *df_features* into a multidimensional array.

```
x = df_features.to_numpy()
```

As the target variable *Event* has more than two class labels (i.e. *Spa*, *Outdoor activities*, and *Shows*), we then perform *label encoding* to it to covert the class labels into numerical representations. In Python, we can use *LabelEncoder* from the scikit-learn package to encode the target variable.

Figure 8.9 Jupyter output of data header summary after performing one-hot encoding

◆	Price ◆	Size ◆	Bedroom ◆	Bathroom ◆	Floor ◆	Car_Parking_Yes ◆	Internet_Yes ◆	Location_Area_2 ◆	Location_Area_3 ◆	Location_Area_4 ◆	Pet_Yes ◆
0	420.0	292.5	3	1	2	1	0	1	0	0	0
1	660.0	208.0	3	1	1	1	0	0	0	0	0
2	660.0	194.0	3	2	2	1	0	0	1	0	0
3	838.0	240.0	3	1	1	1	0	0	0	0	0
4	900.0	360.0	3	2	1	1	0	0	0	1	0

Figure 8.10 Jupyter output of label encoding the target variable

```
['Outdoor activities' 'Shows' 'Spa']
[2 2 2 2 2 2 2 2 2 2 2 2 2 2 2 2 2 2 2 2 2 2 2 2 2 2 2 2 2 2 2 2 2 2 2 2 2
 2 2 2 2 2 2 2 2 2 2 2 2 2 2 2 2 2 2 2 2 2 2 2 2 2 2 2 2 2 2 2 2 2 2 2 2 2
 2 2 2 2 2 2 2 2 2 2 2 2 2 2 2 2 2 2 2 2 2 2 2 2 2 2 2 2 2 2 2 2 2 2 2 2 2
 2 2 2 2 2 1 1 1 1 1 1 1 1 1 1 1 1 1 1 1 1 1 1 1 1 1 1 1 1 1 1 1 1 1 1 1 1
 1 1 1 1 1 1 1 1 1 1 1 1 1 1 1 1 1 1 1 1 1 1 1 1 1 1 1 1 1 1 1 1 1 1 1 1 1
 1 1 1 1 1 1 1 1 1 1 1 1 1 1 1 1 1 1 1 1 1 1 1 1 1 1 1 1 1 1 1 1 1 1 1 1 1
 1 1 1 1 1 1 1 1 1 1 0 0 0 0 0 0 0 0 0 0 0 0 0 0 0 0 0 0 0 0 0 0 0 0 0 0 0
 0 0 0 0 0 0 0 0 0 0 0 0 0 0 0 0 0 0 0 0 0 0 0 0 0 0 0 0 0 0 0 0 0 0 0 0 0
 0 0 0 0 0 0 0 0 0 0 0 0 0 0 0 0 0 0 0 0 0 0 0 0 0 0 0 0 0 0 0 0 0 0 0 0 0
 0 0 0 0 0 0 0 0 0 0 0 0 0 0 0]
```

```
from sklearn.preprocessing import LabelEncoder
le = LabelEncoder()
le.fit(df["Event"])
print(le.classes_)
y = le.transform(df["Event"])
print(y)
```

8.4.5 Normalization

Normalization is a data preprocessing technique in machine learning. It refers to the process of rescaling the numerical features of a dataset to ensure that they all have similar scales or ranges. There are two main benefits to normalization. First, it helps prevent features with larger scales from dominating those with smaller scales during the training process. This is crucial for algorithms that rely on distances between data points, such as k-nearest neighbours (KNN) and support vector machines (SVM). Normalization ensures that features contribute equally to distance calculations, leading to more accurate results. Second, normalization can allow the model to explore the space more efficiently and converge to a better solution faster (Ioffe and Szegedy, 2015). This makes normalization a standard step for neural network algorithms because feature normalization may speed up the optimization process. However, it should be noted that normalization is not a necessary step for all machine learning algorithms and cannot guarantee a better model is obtained.

Two popular normalization techniques are worth introducing here: min-max scaling and z-score standardization. *Min-max scaling* (also known as *min-max normalization*) scales numerical features to a fixed range, typically between 0 and 1. Let x denote a numerical feature and its values over the dataset can be indexed by $n = 1, 2, \ldots, N$. Then the normalized feature $\tilde{x}_n$ can be obtained by

$$\tilde{x}_n = \frac{x_n - \min(x)}{\max(x) - \min(x)},$$

where min(x) and max(x) are the minimum value and the maximum value of x in the dataset. If scaling to a range between a and b, then the min-max can be calculated by

$$\tilde{x}_n = a + \frac{(x_n - \min(x))(b - a)}{\max(x) - \min(x)}.$$

The method *z-score standardization* transforms the features to have a mean of 0 and a standard deviation of 1. In other words, the output distribution is close to a standard normal distribution. It should be noted that it can behave badly if the original individual features do not more or less look like normally distributed data. The normalized feature $\tilde{x}_n$ using z-score standardization can be obtained by

$$\tilde{x}_n = \frac{x_n - \bar{x}}{\mathrm{std}(x)},$$

where $\bar{x}$ and std(x) is the mean and standard deviation of feature x in the dataset.

In Python, we can use the *MinMaxScaler* and *StandardScaler* functions from the *preprocessing* module from the scikit-learn package to perform min-max scaling and z-score standardization for numerical features. As demonstrated earlier, the first five columns in the variable x represent numerical features. In the following code, we apply z-score standardization to these numerical features.

```
from sklearn.preprocessing import StandardScaler
standard_scaler = StandardScaler()
standard_scaler.fit(x[:, :5])
x[:, :5] = standard_scaler.transform(x[:, :5])
```

Subsequently, we randomly split the pre-processed data into training and test sets using the *train_test_split* function from the *model_selection* module in scikit-learn. The argument *stratify=y* ensures that the training set maintains roughly the same class distribution as the entire dataset. This is achieved by strategically sampling data points from each class to preserve this proportional balance.

```
from sklearn.model_selection import train_test_split

x_train, x_test, y_train, y_test = train_test_split(
    x, y, test_size=0.4, random_state=my_random_seed,
stratify=y
)
```

It is worth emphasizing that data preparation in machine learning is a highly context-dependent process, with the specific steps varying significantly based on task requirements and dataset characteristics. Decisions such as data resampling, feature encoding, and normalization must be tailored to the problem at hand, as there is no one-size-fits-all approach. A critical consideration is whether to apply preprocessing to the training data exclusively or to the entire dataset. This consideration is crucial due to the risk of *data leakage*, where information from the testing data influences the model during training, leading to overly optimistic performance estimates. For example, normalizing the entire dataset is generally discouraged for this reason but may be justified in specific circumstances. The impact of preprocessing extends beyond immediate model performance, influencing the model's ability to generalize to the new data. Effective preprocessing enhances a model's capacity to perform well on both training and unseen data, while suboptimal choices can result in overfitting or underfitting. Ultimately, successful data preparation hinges on a deep understanding of the data and problem domain. By carefully evaluating preprocessing techniques, mitigating data leakage risks, and prioritizing generalization, practitioners can optimize model performance and reliability.

8.5 Multi-Layer Perceptrons

Several different neural network architectures can be explored for our project's specific task. In this context, we have opted for a straightforward model known as the *multi-layer perceptron (MLP)*. As illustrated in Figure 8.11, this model takes the form of a basic feedforward neural network comprising three distinctive layers: the input layer, the hidden layer, and the output layer. It is worth noting that in some references, this architecture is alternatively referred to as a *two-layer neural network* (with the input layer being excluded from the count).

Figure 8.11 Schematic view of a three-layer MLP for classification

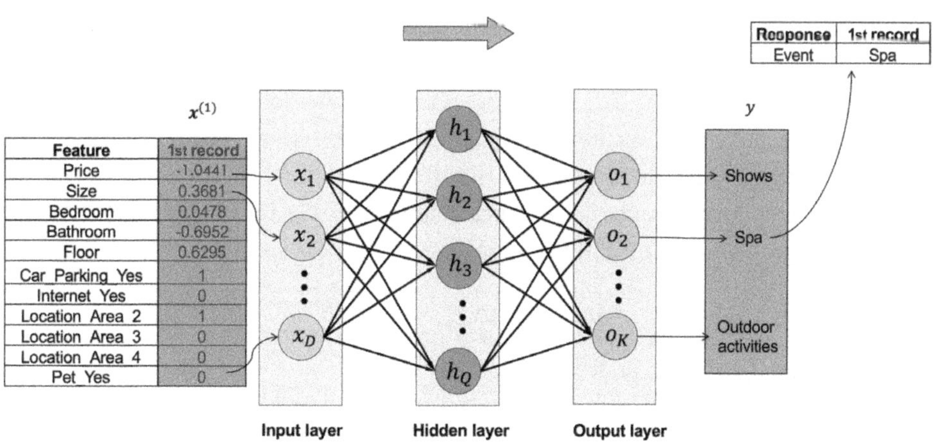

Each of these layers consists of a set number of nodes, with connections established sequentially from the input layer to the output layer. This arrangement defines the network as a feedforward type. Specifically, within this configuration, all nodes within a given layer are fully interconnected. This means that each node in the previous layer forms connections with every node in the subsequent layer, and conversely, each node in a later layer is linked to every node in the preceding layer. The encoded data serves as the input to our model, and as such, the number of nodes in the input layer aligns with the number of encoded features. Meanwhile, the nodes within the output layer are responsible for generating predictions for the various classes or values within the response variable. Consequently, the quantity of nodes in the output layer corresponds directly to the number of distinct classes or values within the response variable. In contrast, the number of nodes within the hidden layer is a flexible parameter that can be set according to our specific needs. It may be set to values such as 100 or 1,000, depending on the complexity of the task at hand. In the realm of machine learning, when human-defined parameters come into play, they are referred to as *hyperparameters*. The number of nodes within the hidden layer falls under this category, making it a crucial hyperparameter in the fine-tuning of our neural network model.

8.5.1 Mathematical Representation of MLP

Let's take a closer look at how the MLP processes input data, with a particular focus on an individual node within the hidden layer and then output layer. As shown in Figure 8.12, the output of a specific node in the hidden layer can be denoted as h_q. Here, the subscript q can take on any value from 1 to uppercase Q, where Q is the number of hidden nodes in the hidden layer. The value of h_q is determined by function γ, which operates on a linear combination of the input data, represented by x. There is a bias term in this equation. The function γ serves a critical role and is commonly referred to as the *activation function*. Its purpose is to perform intricate calculations that transform the signals at each node. A similar information processing pattern applies when we transition from the hidden layer to the output layer. For both the hidden and output layers, each node is associated with an activation function γ. In this context, the superscript '2' signifies that this particular γ function is tailored for the output layer, emphasizing its distinct role in shaping the model's predictions. Then the output of the MLP can be expressed as

$$o_k = \gamma^{(2)}\left(\sum_{q=1}^{Q} w_{kq}^{(2)} \gamma^{(1)}\left(\sum_{d=1}^{D} w_{qd}^{(1)} x_d + w_{q0}^{(1)}\right) + w_{k0}^{(2)}\right),$$

where w_{ij} is the weight that represents the connection between the neuron i and the neuron j of the previous layer.

Figure 8.12 Schematic view of MLP node computation by layer for classification

From the input layer to the hidden layer

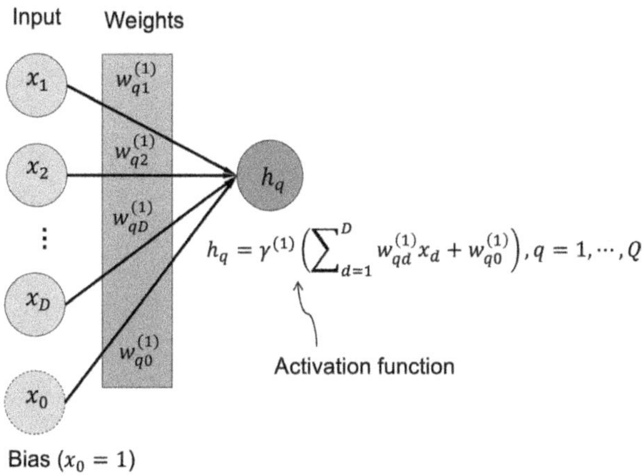

From the hidden layer to the output layer

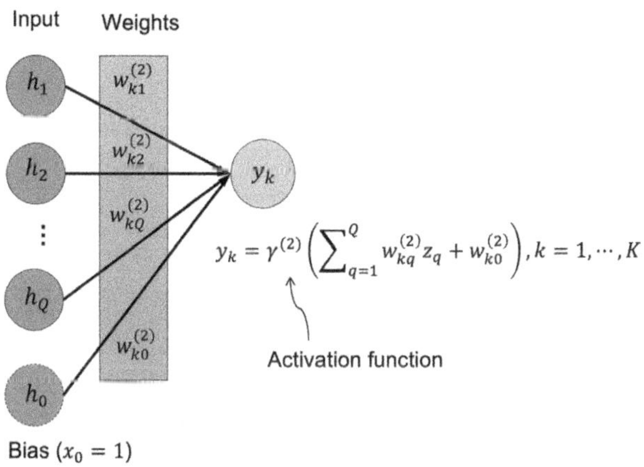

8.5.2 Activation Functions

Various activation functions are employed in different neural networks. The following list offers a brief summary of a few examples.

- Sigmoid (Logistic):

$$\gamma(u) = \frac{1}{1+e^{-u}}.$$

- Hyperbolic tangent (Tanh):

$$\gamma(u) = \frac{e^u - e^{-u}}{e^u + e^{-u}}.$$

- Rectified linear unit (ReLU):

$$\gamma(u) = \max\{0, u\}.$$

8.5.3 *Softmax for the Output Layer*

Thus far, a minor issue has been identified in the MLP setup. The model's objective is to determine whether a sample or consumer falls into one of the categories: *Spa*, *Shows*, or *Outdoor activities*, as represented by the target variable *Event*. However, based on our previous description of the model, it is not guaranteed that the output layer produces probability values. To rectify this, an additional step is necessary to enable predictions. As illustrated in Figure 8.13, this step involves applying the *softmax function* to generate probabilities for each class. Specifically, for observation $x^{(n)}$, the predicted probability for class k can be obtained by

$$p_k^{(n)} = \frac{e^{o_k^{(n)}}}{\sum_{k=1}^{K} e^{o_k^{(n)}}}.$$

Figure 8.13 Schematic view of a three-layer MLP for classification

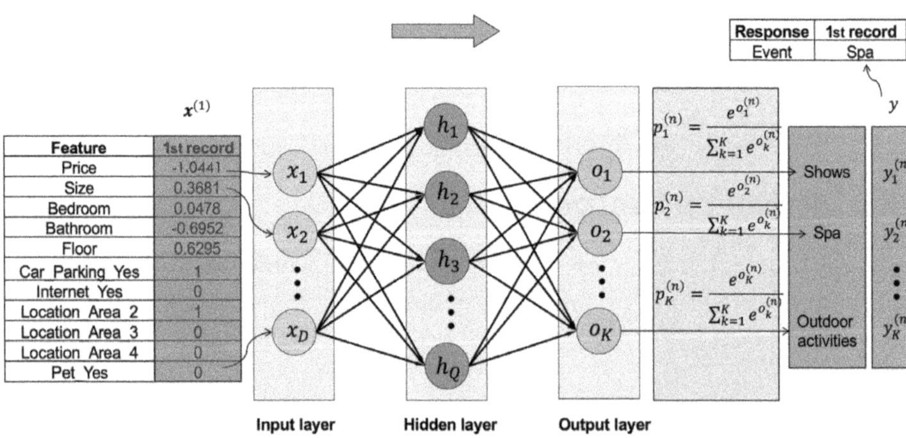

8.5.4 Loss Function

After mathematically representing the MLP, the next step is defining the appropriate loss function. This loss function serves as the objective used to train the model, which means fitting it to the training data. In our project, which involves multi-class classification, we employ the *cross-entropy* loss function. This function assesses the performance of a classification model producing output probabilities ranging between 0 and 1. For a single observation, it is defined as

$$-\sum_{k=1}^{K} y_k log\{p_k\},$$

where $y_k \in \{0,1\}$ and p_k shows the predicted probability of an observation is of class k, $k=1,\ldots,K$. For N observations, we have

$$L(\boldsymbol{W}^{(1)},\boldsymbol{W}^{(2)}) = -\sum_{n=1}^{N}\sum_{k=1}^{K} y_k^{(n)} \log\{p_k^{(n)}\}$$

$$= -\sum_{n=1}^{N}\sum_{k=1}^{K} y_k^{(n)} \log\left\{\frac{e^{o_k^{(n)}}}{\sum_{k=1}^{K} e^{o_k^{(n)}}}\right\}.$$

To address the optimization problem described above (i.e. minimizing the loss function), the gradient descent method can be employed. However, due to the substantial number of weights in the MLP, the direct computation of partial derivatives from the input layers to the output layers can be time-consuming. To tackle this challenge, the backpropagation (BP) is utilized in conjunction with gradient descent to estimate the weights. The discussion of BP involves a more in-depth mathematical derivation, which is beyond the scope of this book and, therefore, is not presented here. For a comprehensive discussion of the standard BP algorithm, you can refer to Chapter 5.3 in the book by Bishop (2006) or Chapter 13.3 of Murphy (2022).

8.6 Implementing MLP in Python

Now we can implement an MLP using the *MLPClassifier* class from the *neural_network* module in the scikit-learn library. It includes a few hyperparameters to specify: *hidden_layer_sizes* specifies the number of neurons in each hidden layer, controlling model complexity; *activation* specifies the activation function for neurons; *solver* specializes the optimization algorithm used for training (e.g. *adam*, *sgd*); *max_iter* sets the maximum number of iterations for training.

```
from sklearn.neural_network import MLPClassifier

mlp_clf = MLPClassifier(
    hidden_layer_sizes=(100, 100,),
    random_state=my_random_seed,
    max_iter=10000)
mlp_clf.fit(x_train, y_train)

y_predlabel_train = mlp_clf.predict(x_train)
y_predlabel_test = mlp_clf.predict(x_test)
```

To assess the performance of the MLP classifiers on both training and test sets, we employ the *classification_report* function from the *metrics* module. As illustrated in Figure 8.14, the classifiers exhibit excellent performance on both the training and test datasets, achieving 0.99 on the training data and 0.97 on the test data.

```
from sklearn.metrics import classification_report

print("Evaluation metrics in the train set:")
print(classification_report(y_train, y_predlabel_train))

print("Evaluation metrics in the test set:")
print(classification_report (y_test, y_predlabel_test))
```

It is important to recognize that neural networks are sensitive to their specifications such as architecture, activation functions, solver, and the number of iterations. Fine-tuning these hyperparameters can enhance the search for the optimal MLP model within the training set. In machine learning, *hyperparameter tuning* or *model tuning* is an important process for finding the optimal settings for a specific model's hyperparameters. These hyperparameters determine the model's learning process and overall performance, but unlike regular parameters learned from data, they must be set before training.

Several techniques are available for hyperparameter tuning, including grid search, random search, and Bayesian optimization. In grid search, all possible combinations of hyperparameter values are evaluated, although this approach can be slow and exhaustive. Random search, on the other hand, examines samples from random combinations, which is faster than grid search but may overlook optimal values. Bayesian optimization employs statistical techniques to efficiently explore the hyperparameter space based on past evaluations. There is no universally best hyperparameter tuning method as the choice of method depends on the specific model, data, and task at hand.

Figure 8.14 Classification report of the MLP for both training and test sets (without hyperparameter tuning)

```
Evaluation metrics in the train set:
              precision    recall  f1-score   support

           0       1.00      1.00      1.00        69
           1       0.97      1.00      0.99        70
           2       1.00      0.97      0.99        69

    accuracy                           0.99       208
   macro avg       0.99      0.99      0.99       208
weighted avg       0.99      0.99      0.99       208

Evaluation metrics in the test set:
              precision    recall  f1-score   support

           0       0.94      1.00      0.97        47
           1       0.98      1.00      0.99        46
           2       1.00      0.91      0.96        47

    accuracy                           0.97       140
   macro avg       0.97      0.97      0.97       140
weighted avg       0.97      0.97      0.97       140
```

Figure 8.15 Classification report of the MLP for the test set (with hyperparameter tuning)

```
Results on the test set:
              precision    recall  f1-score   support

           0       1.00      1.00      1.00        47
           1       1.00      1.00      1.00        46
           2       1.00      1.00      1.00        47

    accuracy                           1.00       140
   macro avg       1.00      1.00      1.00       140
weighted avg       1.00      1.00      1.00       140
```

The *model_selection* module from the scikit-learn library provides a few hyperparameter tuning options. The following code demonstrates how to utilize the *GridSearchCV* class to specify hyperparameter values and define the search space, encompassing all possible combinations of chosen hyperparameter values. For each combination, cross-validation is employed to assess the model's performance across different subsets of our data. Ultimately, the combination of hyperparameters yielding the highest overall performance, as per our chosen metric, is selected. By default, the evaluation metric used is accuracy. As illustrated in Figure 8.15, the model's generalization capability is enhanced following hyperparameter tuning.

```
from sklearn.model_selection import GridSearchCV

mlp_clf = MLPClassifier(max_iter=5000)

parameter_space = {
    "hidden_layer_sizes": [(50, 50, 50), (50, 100, 50), (100,)],
    "activation": ["tanh", "relu"],
    "solver": ["sgd", "adam"],
    "alpha": [0.0001, 0.05],
    "learning_rate": ["constant", "adaptive"],
}

clf = GridSearchCV(mlp_clf, parameter_space, cv=3, n_jobs=4)
clf.fit(x, y)

# Best parameters
print("Best parameters found:\n", clf.best_params_)

# All results
means = clf.cv_results_["mean_test_score"]
stds = clf.cv_results_["std_test_score"]
for mean, std, params in zip(means, stds, clf.cv_results_["params"]):
    print("%0.3f (+/-%0.03f) for %r" % (mean, std * 2, params))

y_pred_test = clf.predict(x_test)
print("Results on the test set:")
print(classification_report (y_test, y_pred_test))
```

8.7 Summary

Neural networks have revolutionized many fields. They exhibit remarkable flexibility, adapting to a diverse array of tasks, such as image recognition, natural language processing, and reinforcement learning. These networks excel in feature learning, being capable of automatically discerning relevant features from raw data, thereby reducing the need for manual feature engineering. Their ability to model complex, non-linear relationships in data is a significant advantage, making them apt for tasks involving intricate patterns. Furthermore, they can scale effectively, accommodating larger datasets to tackle big data challenges. They have frequently demonstrated state-of-the-art performance in various domains and facilitate transfer learning, where knowledge gained from one task can be leveraged for another, thus reducing the demand for extensive training data.

However, neural networks also present several limitations. Training neural networks, particularly deep neural networks, can be computationally demanding, necessitating access to high-performance GPUs or TPUs. Over-fitting is another concern, as neural networks can perform exceptionally well on training data but struggle with unseen data, requiring the use of regularization techniques and hyperparameter tuning. On the other hand, the process of hyperparameter tuning, including architecture selection and fine-tuning, can be time-consuming and require extensive experimentation. Furthermore, their complex nature often renders them as black boxes, making them less suitable for applications requiring transparency and interpretability.

In addition to classification tasks, neural networks can be utilized for regression tasks. In regression tasks, the typical loss function employed is Mean Squared Error (MSE), mirroring that of linear regression. The softmax function is dispensable in regression, as its role in converting outputs into a probability distribution across classes is irrelevant in this context. For implementation in Python, the scikit-learn package furnishes the *MLPRegressor* class tailored for constructing MLP models specifically for regression tasks. It bears resemblance to *MLPClassifier* but is customized for regression applications.

8.8 Exercise

In this exercise, you will implement the MLP to classify people's credit status (good or bad). Use the *german_credit.csv* file, which is created based on the original data provided by Prof. Hofmann from Universitat Hamburg on UCI Machine Learning Repository (https://archive.ics.uci.edu/dataset/144/statlog+german+credit+data). The data contains 20 variables for 1,000 past applicants for credit. These 20 variables represent the dataset's features, which provides identifying characteristics for each credit applicant. An additional column in each row represents the applicant's calculated credit risk, with 700 applicants identified as a low credit risk and 300 as a high risk.

The following is the description about the data.

- **Status of checking account: (qualitative)**
  - A11: ... < 0 DM
  - A12: 0 <= ... < 200 DM
  - A13: ... >= 200 DM / salary assignments for at least 1 year

- A14: no checking account

- **Duration in months:** (numerical)
  - Duration in months
- **Credit history:** (qualitative)
  - A30: no credits taken/all credits paid back duly
  - A31: all credits at this bank paid back duly
  - A32: existing credits paid back duly till now
  - A33: delay in paying off in the past
  - A34: critical account/other credits existing (not at this bank)
- **Purpose:** (qualitative)
  - A40: car (new)
  - A41: car (used)
  - A42: furniture/equipment
  - A43: radio/television
  - A44: domestic appliances
  - A45: repairs
  - A46: education
  - A47: (vacation does not exist?)
  - A48: retraining
  - A49: business
  - A410: others
- **Credit amount:** (numerical)
  - Credit amount
- **Savings account/bond:** (qualitative)
  - A61: ... < 100 DM
  - A62: 100 <= ... < 500 DM
  - A63: 500 <= ... < 1000 DM
  - A64: .. >= 1000 DM
  - A65: unknown/no savings account
- **Present employment since:** (qualitative)
  - A71: unemployed
  - A72: ... < 1 year
  - A73: 1 <= ... < 4 years

  - A74: 4 <= ... < 7 years
  - A75: .. >= 7 years
- **Installment rate in percentage of disposable income:** (numerical)
  - Installment rate in percentage of disposable income
- **Personal status and sex:** (qualitative)
  - A91: male : divorced/separated
  - A92: female : divorced/separated/married
  - A93: male : single
  - A94: male : married/widowed
  - A95: female : single
- **Other debtors:** (qualitative)
  - A101: none
  - A102: co-applicant
  - A103: guarantor
- **Present residence since:** (numerical)
  - Present residence since
- **Property:** (qualitative)
  - A121: real estate
  - A122: if not A121 : building society savings agreement/life insurance
  - A123: if not A121/A122 : car or other, not in attribute 6
  - A124: unknown/no property
- **Age in years:** (numerical)
  - Age in years
- **Other installment plans:** (qualitative)
  - A141: bank
  - A142: stores
  - A143: none
- **Housing:** (qualitative)
  - A151: rent
  - A152: own
  - A153: for free
- **Number of existing credits:** (numerical)
  - Number of existing credits at this bank

- **Job:** (qualitative)
  - o A171: unemployed/unskilled non-resident
  - o A172: unskilled resident
  - o A173: skilled employee/official
  - o A174: management/self-employed/highly qualified employee/officer
- **Number of people providing maintenance for:** (numerical)
  - o Number of people being liable to provide maintenance for
- **Telephone:** (qualitative)
  - o A191: none
  - o A192: yes, registered under the customer's name
- **Foreign worker:** (qualitative)
  - o A201: yes
  - o A202: no
- **Credit risk** (qualitative)
  - o 1: Good
  - o 2: Bad

Since the data contains both numerical and categorical features, you need to encode the categorical features into binary variables. You can use *pandas.get_dummies* to encode the categorical features and the target variable, or use the *OneHotEncoder* from scikit-learn for this purpose.

Also, encode the target variable as a dummy variable where 0 represents *Bad* and 1 represents *Good*. Next, split the data into training and test sets, with a test size of 0.4.

Train an MLP on the training data and make predictions on both the training and test sets. Create a confusion matrix to calculate the true positives, false positives, true negatives, and false negatives for predictions on both the training and test data.

Calculate the related evaluation metrics, such as accuracy, recall, and precision, for both the training and test data. Finally, calculate the AUC of your model's performance on the test data, and draw an ROC for your model.

9 K-Nearest Neighbours

This chapter introduces the k-nearest neighbours (or KNN for short) algorithm. It is a simple, yet effective machine learning algorithm that can be used for both classification and regression tasks, making it a versatile choice for various business analytics endeavours.

After studying this chapter, you should be able to:

- Learn what the KNN algorithm is and how it operates based on the principle of similarity or closeness to make predictions.
- Comprehend how the choice of K (i.e. the number of nearest neighbours considered) affects the performance of the algorithm.
- Gain knowledge of different distance metrics such as Euclidean distance and Manhattan distance and understand when to use them.
- Understand why feature scaling is important in KNN and how to apply it.
- Apply the KNN algorithm to solve real-world problems, interpret the results, and understand its limitations.
- Use Python to implement KNN for business analytics.

9.1 Main Idea of KNN

KNN falls in the supervised learning family of algorithms. It is a non-parametric and instance-based learning algorithm. Here *non-parametric* means it makes no explicit assumptions about the functional form of the model, avoiding the dangers of mismodelling the underlying distribution of the data. For example, suppose our data is highly non-Gaussian but the learning model we choose assumes a Gaussian form. In that case, our algorithm would make extremely poor predictions. On the other hand, *instance-based learning* (also called *memory-based learning*) means that the algorithm does not explicitly learn a model. Instead, it chooses to memorize the training instances which are subsequently used as 'knowledge' for the prediction phase. Concretely, this means that only when a query to our database is made will the algorithm use the training instances to spit out an answer.

As previously mentioned in this chapter, KNN is a versatile algorithm suitable for both classification and regression tasks. Simply put, KNN operates under the assumption that similar data points tend to share the same labels or values. When faced with a new data point, KNN identifies its k-nearest neighbours from the existing dataset. In classification tasks, the new data point is assigned the most frequently occurring class label among its neighbours. For regression tasks, the predicted value for the new point is determined as the average of the values held by its k-nearest neighbours. While KNN does necessitate the storage of the entire training dataset and requires careful selection of the optimal value for K, its merits lie in its ease of comprehension and its capability to handle intricate non-linear relationships. Consequently, KNN remains a popular choice for a wide range of machine learning applications.

9.2 Distance Metrics

Measuring similarity between data points in a multidimensional space is a critical aspect of various machine learning and data analysis methods, including KNN. The choice of distance metric for measuring similarity depends on the type of data you are working with and the characteristics of your problem. The following are some common distance metrics used to measure similarity.

Euclidean distance (or L_2 *norm*) is the most popular distance metric. It calculates the straight-line distance between two points in a Euclidean space, and it assumes that all features have equal importance. Let $\boldsymbol{x}$ denote the input feature vector for the new data, and let $\boldsymbol{x}_n$ denote the feature vector for the nth observation in the given data (i.e. the training data). These two feature vectors have the same size D. Then the Euclidean distance of these two data points can be calculated as below

$$\| \boldsymbol{x} - \boldsymbol{x}_n \|_2 = \sqrt{\sum_{d=1}^{D} (x^{(d)} - x_n^{(d)})^2}.$$

Manhattan distance (or L_1 *norm*) is another widely used metric. It measures the distance as the sum of absolute differences between the coordinates. It is often preferred when the data does not follow a Gaussian distribution and when outliers may be present. By following the same notations as those employed for feature vectors in the Euclidean distance, one can calculate the Manhattan distance as follows

$$\| \boldsymbol{x} - \boldsymbol{x}_n \|_1 = \sum_{d=1}^{D} | x^{(d)} - x_n^{(d)} |.$$

Minkowski distance (or L_p *norm*) is a generalization of both the Euclidean distance and the Manhattan distance. This metric provides a flexible approach to distance measurement, accommodating a wide range of scenarios. To compute the Minkowski distance, consider the following formula

$$\| \boldsymbol{x} - \boldsymbol{x}_n \|_p = \left[\sum_{d=1}^{D} | x^{(d)} - x_n^{(d)} |^p \right]^{1/p},$$

where p is a parameter that determines the order of the distance metric. It allows one to adjust the level of emphasis placed on different dimensions or features when measuring distance. For example, if $p = 1$, it considers each dimension independently like Manhattan distance; if $p = 2$, it gives equal importance to all dimensions, making it as the Euclidean distance.

9.3 Business Analytics Example: Fashion Item Recognition

There is an online retailer specializing in recycling donated fashion items, including clothing, footwear, and accessories. The company is highly motivated to enhance its inventory management processes and optimize its sales strategies. To support this endeavour, we have been provided with a comprehensive dataset containing 5,000 historical item images. Each image is a 28 × 28 greyscale representation, categorized into one of 10 distinct classes, as shown in Table 9.1.

Table 9.1 Classes in the donated fashion items dataset

Label (in the dataset)	Class
0	T-shirt/top
1	Trouser
2	Pullover
3	Dress
4	Coat
5	Sandal
6	Shirt
7	Sneaker
8	Bag
9	Ankle boot

This project aims to develop a machine learning model that automatically predicts the class type of a new fashion item donation, based solely on its image. This innovative solution will significantly improve the company's operational efficiency, particularly in inventory management. By automating the sorting process, we can optimize resource allocation, minimize manual sorting times, and ensure accurate categorization. Moreover, the model will empower data-driven decision-making, potentially boosting sales and driving sustainable growth for the company.

9.4 Preliminary Analysis

Similar to other projects, by using the Pandas package, we load the given dataset *fashion_mnist.csv* into a Jupyter notebook.

```
import pandas as pd

df = pd.read_csv("data/fashion_mnist.csv")
df.head()
```

As shown in Figure 9.1, the first column contains the image label, while the remaining 784 columns represent the pixel values of the image. In greyscale images, these pixel values are integers spanning from 0 (representing black) to 255 (representing white).

We can create a dictionary name it *label_map*, whose key is the label value and the key value is the corresponding fashion class show in data description.

```
label_map = {
    0: "T-shirt/top",
    1: "Trouser",
    2: "Pullover",
    3: "Dress",
    4: "Coat",
    5: "Sandal",
    6: "Shirt",
    7: "Sneaker",
    8: "Bag",
    9: "Ankle boot",
}
```

Furthermore, let's create a visual representation by randomly selecting 36 images from the dataset and presenting them in a 6 × 6 grid using subplots. Each subplot will include a title indicating the fashion class of the respective item. The following Python codes generate Figure 9.2.

Figure 9.1 Jupyter output of *fashion_mnist.csv* data loading and variable checking

	label	pixel1	pixel2	pixel3	pixel4	pixel5	pixel6	pixel7	pixel8	pixel9	...	pixel775	pixel776	pixel777	pixel778	pixel779
0	2	0	0	0	0	0	0	0	0	0	...	0	0	0	0	
1	9	0	0	0	0	0	0	0	0	0	...	0	0	0	0	
2	6	0	0	0	0	0	0	0	5	0	...	0	0	0	30	
3	0	0	0	0	1	2	0	0	0	0	...	3	0	0	0	
4	3	0	0	0	0	0	0	0	0	0	...	0	0	0	0	

5 rows × 785 columns

Figure 9.2 Image display of randomly sampled fashion items from the imported data

```
import numpy as np
import matplotlib.pyplot as plt

my_random_seed = 100
numbers_to_display = 36
num_cells = int(np.ceil(np.sqrt(numbers_to_display)))
np.random.seed(my_random_seed)
sample_index_list = np.random.choice(list(df.index),
numbers_to_display)

```

```
plt.figure(figsize=(10, 10))
for plot_index in range(numbers_to_display):
    sample_index = sample_index_list[plot_index]
    plt.subplot(num_cells, num_cells, plot_index + 1)
    frame = df.loc[sample_index, df.columns!="label"].
    to_numpy().reshape(28, 28)
    plt.imshow(frame, cmap="Greys")
    gt_label = label_map.get(df.iloc[sample_index,0])
    plt.title(gt_label)
    plt.tick_params(
        axis="both",
        which="both",
        bottom=False,
        left=False,
        labelbottom=False,
        labelleft=False,
    )

plt.subplots_adjust(hspace=0.5, wspace=0.5)
plt.show()
```

9.5 Implementing KNN in Python

Let's randomly divide the dataset into two parts: 60% for training and 40% for testing.

```
from sklearn.model_selection import train_test_split

x_train, x_test, y_train, y_test = train_test_split(
    df.iloc[:, 1:].to_numpy(),
    df.iloc[:, 0].to_numpy().flatten(),
    test_size=0.4,
    random_state=my_random_seed,
    stratify=df.iloc[: ,0].to_numpy(),
)
```

Next, we will create a KNN model using the *KNeighborsClassifier* class from the *neighbours* module in the scikit-learn library. In the parameter settings, *n_neighbours* sets the value of K, which determines the number of nearest neighbours used. By default, $K=5$. The *weights* parameter is set to *uniform*, meaning that all data points in a neighbourhood have equal weight. Furthermore, the *algorithm* parameter specifies the method used to find nearest neighbours, offering a faster alternative to linear search. The *metric* parameter defines the distance metric, with *minkowski* being the default, and *p* acts as the power parameter for the Minkowski metric. In our code example, we actually use the Euclidean distance as the value of *p* is 2.

```
from sklearn.neighbors import KNeighborsClassifier

knn = KNeighborsClassifier(
    n_neighbors=5,
    p=2,
    metric="minkowski",
    weights="uniform",
    algorithm="auto"
)
knn.fit(x_train, y_train)
y_pred_test_knn = knn.predict(x_test)
```

To assess the performance of the KNN predictions on the test set, we can make use of the *classification_report* function available within the *metrics* module. As illustrated in Figure 9.3, the model evaluation results reveal an accuracy of 0.81, which represents a noteworthy performance.

```
from sklearn.metrics import classification_report

print(classification_report(y_test, y_pred_test_knn))
```

Figure 9.3 Evaluation results of the KNN on the test set

```
              precision    recall  f1-score   support

           0       0.73      0.88      0.80       201
           1       0.98      0.94      0.96       200
           2       0.63      0.70      0.66       198
           3       0.91      0.81      0.86       205
           4       0.69      0.74      0.71       200
           5       0.95      0.73      0.83       196
           6       0.58      0.50      0.54       203
           7       0.81      0.95      0.88       207
           8       0.94      0.85      0.89       192
           9       0.91      0.94      0.93       198

    accuracy                           0.81      2000
   macro avg       0.81      0.80      0.81      2000
weighted avg       0.81      0.81      0.80      2000
```

KNN lacks a straightforward and easily interpretable explanation for its predictions. Unlike some other algorithms, it does not produce a model with coefficients or feature importances that facilitate interpretation. Consequently, comprehending the rationale behind assigning a specific class to a data point can be challenging. In scenarios with low-dimensional data, such as the well-known Iris Flower dataset (https://archive.ics.uci.edu/dataset/53/iris), it is common to visualize class decision boundaries over two feature dimensions, which aids in understanding the classifier's behaviours. However, this visualization technique becomes less practical for high-dimensional datasets, such as the one in our current project, due to visual complexity.

9.6 Summary

KNN is a simple and versatile machine learning algorithm. It is easy to understand and implement, making it an excellent choice for newcomers to machine learning. It does not require a training phase and can work with various types of data, making it suitable for classification and regression tasks. It can handle noisy data and outliers and does not make strong assumptions about data distribution, rendering it robust. However, KNN has some drawbacks. It can be computationally expensive, especially with large or high-dimensional datasets. The choice of the *K* value is critical, and it does not provide insights into feature importance. When it comes to implementing KNN in Python, the popular scikit-learn package offers a user-friendly solution. One important preprocessing step for KNN is standardizing numerical features to avoid bias within the feature space.

9.7 Exercise

In this exercise, you will implement the KNN to classify iris flowers and benchmark it with the MLP. Use the *iris.csv* dataset, which is based on a publicly available dataset from the UCI Machine Learning Repository (https://archive.ics.uci.edu/dataset/53/iris). This dataset is one of the earliest and most widely used in the literature on classification methods, playing a significant role in the fields of statistics and machine learning. The dataset comprises 50 samples from each of the three species of Iris: *Setosa*, *Virginica*, and *Versicolor*. Each sample includes measurements of four features: the length and width of the sepals and petals, all recorded in centimetres.

10 | Naïve Bayes

Naïve Bayes is one of the simplest yet surprisingly one of the most effective algorithms in machine learning. Named after the famous statistician, Thomas Bayes, this algorithm is rooted in probability theory and is found in many classification applications, from spam email filtering to sentiment analysis and even medical diagnosis. In this chapter, we will dive into the Naïve Bayes algorithm, explore its assumptions and limitations, and provide practical examples of how it can be implemented in real-world scenarios.

After studying this chapter, you should be able to:

- Explain how Bayes' theorem is applied in Naïve Bayes for classification tasks.
- Understand the key assumptions of Naïve Bayes and different Naïve Bayes classifiers.
- Implement a Naïve Bayes classifier in Python for a specific real-world scenario.
- Evaluate the strengths and limitations of Naïve Bayes in different practical applications.

10.1 Revisiting Bayes' Theorem

Let's begin by revisiting Bayes' theorem, a foundational concept in probability theory and statistics that enables us to refine our beliefs regarding the likelihood of an event occurring based on new evidence.

Consider two events or variables, denoted as A and B. Then the conditional probability of A given B can be computed by

$$\mathbb{P}(A \mid B) = \frac{\mathbb{P}(A, B)}{\mathbb{P}(B)} = \frac{\mathbb{P}(B \mid A) \times \mathbb{P}(A)}{\mathbb{P}(B)}.$$

In many statistics references, these probabilities are often interpreted as follows:

- $\mathbb{P}(A \mid B)$ referred to as the *posterior*, represents the probability of our hypothesis given the observed evidence. It is important to note that this is not directly computable but rather an updated probability based on new information.
- $\mathbb{P}(B \mid A)$ known as the *likelihood*, which quantifies the probability of the observed evidence occurring under the assumption that our hypothesis is true.

- $\mathbb{P}(A)$ termed the *prior*, indicates the initial probability of the hypothesis before taking into account any new evidence.
- $\mathbb{P}(B)$ referred to as the *marginal*, signifies the probability of the new evidence occurring under all possible hypotheses, regardless of whether they are true or not.

MONTY HALL PROBLEM

The Monty Hall problem is a renowned probability puzzle, named after Monty Hall, the host of the American television game show *Let's Make a Deal.* It is often used as an illustrative example when introducing the application of Bayes' theorem. Imagine yourself as a contestant on a game show, standing before three closed doors. Behind one of these doors hides an incredible prize, perhaps a brand new car. However, concealed behind the other two doors are decidedly less enticing offerings, often goats. You have no idea which door contains the coveted prize. You have the opportunity to select one of these three doors without any knowledge of what is hidden behind it. After making your choice, the game show host, Monty Hall, who happens to be privy to the contents behind all the doors, takes a pivotal step: he opens one of the other two doors, deliberately revealing a goat. It is crucial to note that Monty always selects a door with a goat behind it. Consequently, you are now left with only two doors: the one you initially chose and another unopened door. Now, here is the question: *Should you stick with your initial choice, or should you opt to switch to the other unopened door?* The answer to this problem is somewhat counterintuitive, leaving many people perplexed. The optimal strategy is to switch doors.

Let's first formulate the problem. We use D_1, D_2, D_3 to denote the event that the car is behind the first, second, and third door. As the car is randomly placed behind one of the doors, $\mathbb{P}(D_1) = \mathbb{P}(D_2) = \mathbb{P}(D_3) = \frac{1}{3}$. Then let H_1, H_2, H_3 denote the event that the host reveals a goat behind the first, second, and third door. Suppose if the host opened the third door and your initial choice was the first door, now we can calculate the conditional probability that the car is behind the first given the third door is opened by the host as follows

$$\begin{aligned}\mathbb{P}(D_1 \mid H_3) &= \frac{\mathbb{P}(H_3 \mid D_1)\mathbb{P}(D_1)}{\mathbb{P}(H_3)} \\ &= \frac{\mathbb{P}(H_3 \mid D_1)\mathbb{P}(D_1)}{\mathbb{P}(H_3 \mid D_1)\mathbb{P}(D_1) + \mathbb{P}(H_3 \mid D_2)\mathbb{P}(D_2) + \mathbb{P}(H_3 \mid D_3)\mathbb{P}(D_3)}\end{aligned}$$

$$= \frac{\frac{1}{2}\times\frac{1}{3}}{\frac{1}{2}\times\frac{1}{3}+1\times\frac{1}{3}+0\times\frac{1}{3}} = \frac{1}{3}.$$

Surprisingly, switching doors increases your probability of winning the prize to $\frac{2}{3}$, while sticking with your initial choice maintains a winning chance of only $\frac{1}{3}$.

10.2 Main Idea of Naïve Bayes

Naïve Bayes is a probabilistic machine learning algorithm that is particularly useful for classification tasks. Its basic idea is to classify data points into predefined classes based on the probability of a data point belonging to each class. Suppose there are total K classes in the target variable y and there are D features. The optimal decision of Naïve Bayes is made through the maximum a posterior (MAP), which can be simply expressed as follows

$$\mathbb{P}(y = c_k \mid \boldsymbol{x}_n) \geq \mathbb{P}(y = c_{-k} \mid \boldsymbol{x}_n),$$

where c_k represents class k, c_{-k} represents any class except class k, and x_n is the feature vector for observation n.

10.2.1 Assumption of Independence

The posterior probability can be decomposed by Bayes' theorem

$$\mathbb{P}(y = c_k \mid \boldsymbol{x}_n) = \frac{\mathbb{P}(\boldsymbol{x}_n \mid y = c_k)\mathbb{P}(y = c_k)}{\mathbb{P}(\boldsymbol{x}_n)}$$

$$\propto \mathbb{P}(\boldsymbol{x}_n \mid y = c_k)\mathbb{P}(y = c_k) \qquad \triangleright\ \boldsymbol{x}_n \text{ is given}$$

$$\propto \prod_{d=1}^{D}\mathbb{P}(x_n^{(d)} \mid y = c_k)\mathbb{P}(y = c_k). \quad \triangleright \text{ conditional independence.}$$

Naïve Bayes assumes that the features used to describe the data are conditionally independent, given the class label. In other words, it treats each feature as if it has no direct influence on any other feature when determining the class. Therefore, we just need to specify the prior and the likelihood probabilities.

10.2.2 Specification of the Prior

The prior $\mathbb{P}(y = c_k)$ can be specified directly from the target variable in the training set

$$\mathbb{P}(y = c_k) = \frac{\sum_{n=1}^{N} \mathbb{I}(y_n = c_k)}{N},$$

where $\mathbb{I}(\cdot)$ is the indicator function.

10.2.3 Specification of the Likelihood

The way we specify the likelihood $\mathbb{P}(x_d \mid y = c_k)$ differs between categorical and numerical features. For categorical features, suppose there are T distinct categories in feature $x^{(d)}$. The probability of category t in feature $x^{(d)}$ given class c_k in the target variable can be estimated as follows

$$\mathbb{P}(x^{(d)} = t \mid Y = c_k) = \frac{\sum_{n=1}^{N} \mathbb{I}(x_n^{(d)} = t, y_n = c_k) + \alpha}{\sum_{n=1}^{N} \mathbb{I}(y_n = c_k) + \alpha T},$$

where α is the called the *smoothing parameter*. If $\alpha = 1$, it is called the *Laplacian smoothing*.

For numerical features, the likelihood often takes the form of a probability density function. This function describes the probability of observing a specific value for $X^{(d)}$ given the class label. Different distributions can be used such as Gaussian, Laplace, log-normal, and so on.

For example, if feature $X^{(d)}$ is a numerical variable, the likelihood $\mathbb{P}(X^{(d)} = x \mid Y = c_k)$ is assumed to be Gaussian, then

$$\mathbb{P}(X^{(d)} = x \mid Y = c_k) = \frac{1}{\sqrt{2\pi\sigma_d^2}} \exp\left\{-\frac{(x - \mu_d)^2}{2\sigma_d^2}\right\},$$

where μ_d and σ_d^2 are the mean and variance of variable $X^{(d)}$, which can be obtained through maximum likelihood estimation.

We can write the likelihood function for variable $X^{(d)}$ as follows

$$L(\mu_d,\sigma_d^2;X_1^{(d)}=x_1^{(d)},\cdots,X_N^{(d)}=x_N^{(d)})=\prod_{n=1}^{N}\frac{1}{\sqrt{2\pi\sigma_d^2}}\exp\left\{-\frac{(x_n-\mu_d)^2}{2\sigma_d^2}\right\}$$

$$=(2\pi\sigma_d^2)^{-\frac{N}{2}}\prod_{n=1}^{N}\exp\left\{-\frac{(x_n-\mu_d)^2}{2\sigma_d^2}\right\}.$$

Therefore, the log-likelihood function is then

$$LL(\mu_d,\sigma_d^2;X_1^{(d)}=x_1^{(d)},\cdots,X_N^{(d)}=x_N^{(d)})=-\frac{N}{2}\ln\{2\pi\}-\frac{N}{2}\ln\{\sigma_d^2\}-\frac{1}{2\sigma_d^2}\sum_{n=1}^{N}(x_n-\mu_d)^2.$$

Thus, the maximum likelihood estimators of the mean and the variance are

$$\hat{\mu}_d=\frac{1}{N}\sum_{n=1}^{N}x_n,$$

$$\hat{\sigma}_d^2=\frac{1}{N}\sum_{n=1}^{N}(x_n-\hat{\mu}_d)^2.$$

There are different approaches to specify the likelihood of features, whether they are categorical or numerical. Selecting the appropriate method for specifying these likelihoods depends on the nature of the features. This choice is crucial to ensure the Naïve Bayes model effectively captures the data's characteristics and produces accurate classifications.

10.3 Business Analytics Example: Spam Email Detection

Spam email detection is a process involving the identification and filtering of unsolicited or unwanted emails, commonly referred to as 'spam' or 'junk' emails, effectively separating them from the legitimate messages residing in the inbox. Spam email detection safeguards a company's email ecosystem from the persistent menace of spam. This endeavour extends beyond mere inbox decluttering; it encompasses the broader objectives of enhancing productivity, fortifying security measures, and preserving valuable data assets.

Figure 10.1 Jupyter output of *email_spam.csv* data loading and variable checking

◆	the ◆	to ◆	ect ◆	and ◆	for ◆	of ◆	a ◆	you ◆	hou ◆	in ◆	... ◆	connevey ◆	jay ◆	valued ◆	lay ◆	infrastructure ◆	military ◆	allowing ◆	ff ◆	d
0	0	0	1	0	0	0	2	0	0	0	...	0	0	0	0	0	0	0	0	
1	8	13	24	6	6	2	102	1	27	18	...	0	0	0	0	0	0	0	1	
2	0	0	1	0	0	0	8	0	0	4	...	0	0	0	0	0	0	0	0	
3	0	5	22	0	5	1	51	2	10	1	...	0	0	0	0	0	0	0	0	
4	7	6	17	1	5	2	57	0	9	3	...	0	0	0	0	0	0	0	1	

5 rows × 3001 columns

To simplify the scenario, text mining techniques have been used to preprocess the email text and extract a few popular keywords. We are provided with a curated dataset consisting of 5,172 rows, with each row corresponding to an individual email. Our dataset in this example was created based on the open dataset from Kaggle: www.kaggle.com/datasets/balaka18/email-spam-classification-dataset-csv. Across these rows, there are 3,001 columns of data. The first 3,000 columns represent the frequency of popular keywords extracted from the email. The last column in this dataset is the target variable; it contains labels where '1' indicates spam, while those labelled '0' are classified as not spam. Next, we are going to implement a Naïve Bayes classifier in Python to deploy an effective spam email detection tool.

10.4 Preliminary Analysis

Using the Pandas package, we load the provided dataset *email_spam.csv* into a Jupyter notebook.

```
import pandas as pd
df = pd.read_csv("data/email_spam.csv")
df.head()
```

```
df.info()
```

```
df["target_spam"].value_counts()
```

As shown in Figure 10.3, the function *value_counts()* can further check the distributions of classes in the target variable. While spam emails have fewer occurrences, given the sufficient observations in the provided dataset, there is no need to perform resampling to balance the classes.

Figure 10.2 Jupyter output of data info summary

```
<class 'pandas.core.frame.DataFrame'>
RangeIndex: 5172 entries, 0 to 5171
Columns: 3001 entries, the to target_spam
dtypes: int64(3001)
memory usage: 118.4 MB
```

Figure 10.3 Jupyter output of the target variable checking

```
target_spam
0    3672
1    1500
Name: count, dtype: int64
```

10.5 Implementing Naïve Bayes in Python

We use stratified sampling to divide the dataset into two sets: 70% for training and 30% for testing.

```
from sklearn.model_selection import train_test_split
my_random_seed = 100
split_train_size = 0.7
x_train, x_test, y_train, y_test = train_test_split(
    df.iloc[:, :-1].to_numpy(),
    df.iloc[:, -1].to_numpy().flatten(),
    train_size=split_train_size,
    random_state=my_random_seed,
    stratify=df.iloc[:, -1].to_numpy().flatten(),
)
```

Next, the scikit-learn package can be used and its *naive_bayes* module offers a diverse collection of Naïve Bayes classifiers. Each of these tools is expertly tailored for distinct data types:

- *GaussianNB*: Ideal for numerical features, assuming Gaussian distributions.
- *CategoricalNB*: Specifically designed for categorical variables.
- *MultinomialNB*: Excels in text-based realms, particularly word counts.

As depicted in Figure 10.2, our data only contains numerical features and they are frequency of the popular keywords extracted by text mining techniques. This makes *GaussianNB* and *MultinomialNB* the ideal choices for our classification tasks. In the following, we implement both classifiers.

```
from sklearn.naive_bayes import GaussianNB

gnb = GaussianNB()
gnb.fit(x_train, y_train)
y_pred_test_gnb = gnb.predict(x_test)

from sklearn.naive_bayes import MultinomialNB

mnb = MultinomialNB()
mnb.fit(x_train, y_train)
y_pred_test_mnb = mnb.predict(x_test)
```

Figure 10.4 Evaluation results of the Gaussian Naïve Bayes and the Multinomial Naïve Bayes classifiers on the test set

```
=== GaussianNB ===
              precision    recall  f1-score   support

           0       0.98      0.94      0.96      1102
           1       0.87      0.96      0.91       450

    accuracy                           0.95      1552
   macro avg       0.93      0.95      0.94      1552
weighted avg       0.95      0.95      0.95      1552

=== MultinomialNB ===
              precision    recall  f1-score   support

           0       0.97      0.94      0.96      1102
           1       0.87      0.94      0.90       450

    accuracy                           0.94      1552
   macro avg       0.92      0.94      0.93      1552
weighted avg       0.94      0.94      0.94      1552
```

To evaluate the performance of both classifiers' predictions on the test set, we use the *classification_report* function within the *metrics* module.

```
from sklearn.metrics import classification_report

print("=== GaussianNB ===")
print(classification_report(y_test, y_pred_test_gnb,
zero_division=0))

print("=== MultinomialNB ===")
print(classification_report(y_test, y_pred_test_mnb,
zero_division=0))
```

Figure 10.4 displays the model evaluation results of the Gaussian Naïve Bayes and the Multinomial Naïve Bayes classifiers on the test set. The former demonstrates an accuracy of 0.95, while the latter achieves 0.94, both indicating a noteworthy level of performance.

The *naive_bayes* module of the scikit-learn package lacks an implementation of the Naïve Bayes classifier suitable for datasets with mixed data types, i.e. those containing both categorical and numerical features. To address this situation, we can use the MixedNB package (https://pypi.org/project/mixed-naive-bayes/), which provides an implementation of a mixed Naïve Bayes algorithm capable of handling both categorical and numerical data within a single classifier.

10.6 Summary

Naïve Bayes is a simple but effective probabilistic classifier. It leverages Bayes' theorem to make predictions based on the probability of data points belonging to different classes. Its strengths include ease of implementation, computational efficiency, and effectiveness in text classification, spam email detection, and sentiment analysis. However, Naïve Bayes relies on the naïve assumption of feature independence, which may not hold in real-world scenarios. This limitation can lead to suboptimal performance when complex relationships between features exist. It is also sensitive to irrelevant or noisy features, affecting its predictive accuracy. While it may not be suitable for every problem, it remains a popular choice in the machine learning toolbox. We can implement Naïve Bayes in Python using libraries like scikit-learn, which provides classes for different variants of Naïve Bayes such as Gaussian, Multinomial, and Bernoulli.

10.7 Exercise

Breast cancer is the most common cancer among women in the world. In this exercise, you will implement the Naïve Bayes algorithm to detect if tumours are malignant (cancerous) or benign (non-cancerous), and benchmark it against the KNN and MLP algorithms. Use the *breast_cancer.csv* dataset, which is created based on a publicly available dataset from Kaggle (www.kaggle.com/datasets/yasserh/breast-cancer-dataset).

11 Tree-Based Methods

Tree-based methods, encompassing decision trees, random forests, and gradient boosting decision trees, among others, are powerful techniques in machine learning for both classification and regression tasks. With their ability to handle complex relationships within data into interpretable tree structures, they have become useful tools across various domains. From predicting customer behaviour to optimizing supply chain operations, tree-based methods offer a versatile framework for tackling diverse business challenges.

After studying this chapter, you should be able to:

- Understand the foundational concepts of decision trees, such as nodes, splitting, pruning, and so on.
- Gain insights into popular tree-based ensemble methods like random forests and gradient boosting decision trees, understanding their strengths and weaknesses.
- Recognize the significance of tree-based methods in predictive modelling and their applicability in real-world scenarios.
- Comprehend the practical considerations involved in training and tuning tree-based models for optimal performance.
- Learn how to interpret predictions from tree-based methods and assess model performance metrics within a business context.

11.1 Decision Trees

Decision trees are the building blocks of tree-based methods. To demonstrate how a decision tree operates, we can use the scenario illustrated in Figure 11.1, which outlines the process of deciding on weekend activities. The construction of a basic decision tree involves posing a series of questions such as 'Is any homework left?', 'Any good movie?', 'Raining?', and so forth. The answers to these questions lead to different outcomes. Additionally, Figure 11.1 also highlights the critical components of a decision tree.

Figure 11.1 Example of decision tree for decision-making process

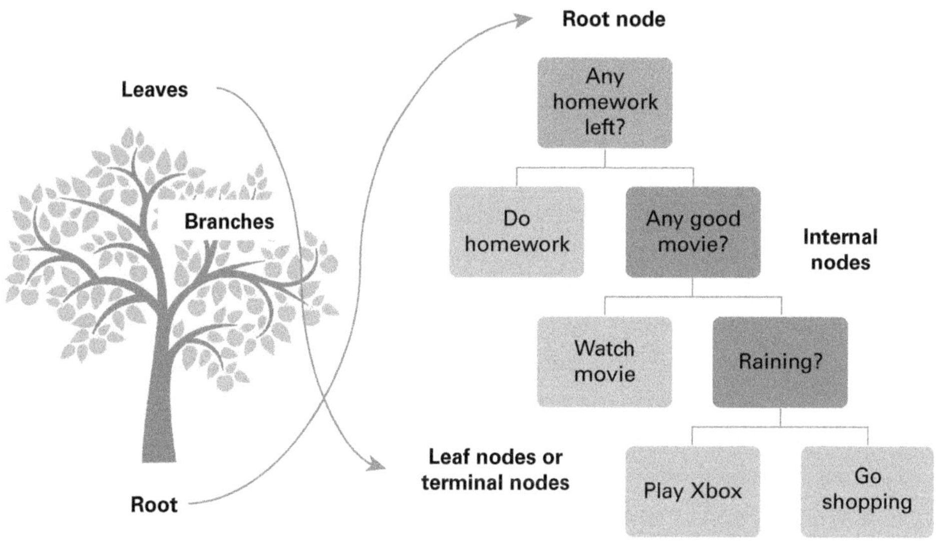

- *Root node*: The topmost node in the tree, represented by the question 'Any homework left?' This is the starting point for making decisions.
- *Leaf nodes* or *terminal nodes*: The nodes at the end of each path, such as 'Do homework', 'Watch movie', 'Play Xbox', 'Go shopping', etc. These represent the final decisions.
- *Internal nodes*: The nodes between the root and leaf nodes, such as 'Any good movie?' and 'Raining?' They represent features or attributes used for making decisions.

A *decision tree* is a directed, connected graph comprised of a single root node, internal nodes, and leaf nodes. The root node serves as the entry point, while each internal node, having exactly one predecessor (parent) and zero or more successors (children), represents a decision point based on a specific feature or attribute value. Leaf nodes, which have no successors, signify the final decisions or outcomes. Each node is connected via edges, with the *depth of a node* defined as the number of edges along the path from that node to the root. Conversely, the *height of the tree* is determined by the maximum number of edges found on any path from the root to a leaf. This structure facilitates hierarchical decision-making, enabling the breakdown of complex decisions into simpler, sequential steps represented by the nodes of the tree. Decision trees are usually visualized as tree-like diagrams that illustrate the decision-making process and its logic in a clear and intuitive manner. Alternatively, they can also be expressed through a sequence of if-else statements, offering a textual representation of the decision logic. This dual representation enhances the understanding and application of decision trees in various decision-making contexts.

Just as one might systematically ask a series of questions to determine weekend activities, the values of feature variables in a dataset can be used to construct a tree structure for classification purposes. Given a wide array of choices at each decision point, it becomes essential to employ a robust criterion to evaluate the efficacy of selecting a particular value of a given variable over the alternatives. This criterion is crucial for guiding the decision-making process within the tree structure. To facilitate this, methods such as Gini impurity and information entropy come into play. These measures allow us to quantify the level of uncertainty or disorder associated with a decision, thereby enabling the selection of the most informative features that lead to the highest degree of classification clarity.

Suppose there are K classes in the target variable y. In our example of car loan application, $K=2$ as the target variable *Class* has two classes: *Yes* and *No*. At a specific node, the frequency probability that the target variable can take class c_k can be denoted by $p_k \geq 0$, subject to $\sum_{k=1}^{K} p_k = 1$. Then

- *Gini impurity* is calculated by

$$\text{Gini}(p_1,\ldots,p_K) = \sum_{k=1}^{K} p_k(1-p_k) = 1 - \sum_{k=1}^{K} p_k^2.$$

- *Information entropy* (or shortly entropy) is calculated by

$$\text{Entropy}(p_1,\ldots,p_K) = -\sum_{k=1}^{K} p_k \log_2\{p_k\}.$$

These two measures have been used in the popular decision tree algorithms: *Classification and Regression Tree* (in short *CART*) (Breiman et al., 1984) uses Gini impurity; *ID3* (Quinlan, 1986) uses information gain based on information entropy; *C4.5* (Quinlan, 1993) uses the information gain ratio based on information entropy.

As mentioned earlier, decision trees can be used for addressing regression tasks, where the target variable is continuous. Unlike in classification, where the focus is on reducing impurity measures such as Gini impurity or information entropy, regression decision trees prioritize the minimization of error metrics. Specifically, these trees aim to minimize the sum of squared errors (SSE), the mean squared error (MSE), or the mean absolute error (MAE). This distinction is crucial, as it shifts the focus from sorting data into discrete categories to accurately predicting numerical values. The methodology for building the tree remains analogous to that of classification, with a significant difference: the criterion for splitting at each node is determined by the potential reduction in SSE or variance, ensuring that the branches resulting from each split are as homogeneous as possible with respect to the target variable.

The process of building a decision tree can be simply summarized by the following steps:

1. **Selecting the best feature to split on:** The first step involves identifying which feature within the dataset ought to be used to partition the data. This decision is made by using criteria such as Gini impurity, entropy (for classification tasks), and variance reduction (for regression tasks). The objective is to select the feature that most effectively segregates the dataset into distinct classes (for classification) or diminishes prediction error (for regression).
2. **Splitting the data:** Upon identifying the most suitable feature, the dataset is divided into subsets based on the values of that feature. For categorical features, these subsets may align with the feature's categories. For continuous features, a threshold value is generally employed to bifurcate the data into two segments.
3. **Creating decision nodes:** Each split creates a decision node in the tree, which corresponds to a question based on the feature split. These nodes act as the decision-making point and lead to further splits or to a leaf node.
4. **Repeating the process for subsets:** The division process is recursively executed on each subset, selecting the optimum feature for further segmentation and partitioning the dataset more finely. This procedure is reiterated for the ensuing subsets until a predefined stopping criterion is satisfied.
5. **Determining leaf nodes:** Eventually, the process reaches a point where further splitting is not beneficial or possible due to stopping criteria such as maximum tree depth, minimum samples per leaf, or minimal improvement in impurity or error. These stopping criteria are the hyperparameters of a decision tree. They allow early stopping of the tree growth earlier in the training process, which is also called *pre-pruning*. The idea behind pre-pruning is to prevent the tree from becoming overly complex and overfitting the training data by limiting how detailed the tree can get. It involves making decisions about when to stop the tree from growing before the tree fully develops. At this point, a leaf node is created. In classification, the leaf node represents the majority class among the samples in the leaf. In regression, it typically represents the mean or median target value of the samples in the leaf.
6. **Post-pruning the tree:** *Post-pruning* is an optional yet strategic step, which aims to identify and eliminate branches that minimally contribute to the model's predictive capacity, thus streamlining the model and potentially enhancing its generalization to new data. Techniques such as *cost-complexity pruning* are employed, in which a complexity parameter is adjusted to achieve an optimal balance between the tree's size and its accuracy on a validation set. Further details can be referred to in Hastie et al. (2009).

11.2 Implementing Decision Trees in Python

The implementation of decision trees in Python is straightforward. In the scikit-learn library, decision trees can be implemented through the *DecisionTreeClassifier* and *DecisionTreeRegressor* classes for classification and regression tasks, respectively.

In the following, we illustrate the application of decision trees for classification tasks using the dataset *car_loan_application.csv*. It contains car loan applications submitted to an automotive finance company. Each application includes feature variables such as *Age*, *Has_Job*, *Own_House*, *Credit_Rating*, and a *Class* label indicating approval or denial of the loan. To create a decision tree from this data, the algorithm would evaluate each attribute to determine how well it separates the loan applications into approved and denied categories.

```
import pandas as pd

df = pd.read_csv("data/car_loan_application.csv")
df
```

As shown in Figure 11.2, we are examining a particularly small dataset, consisting of merely 13 car loan applications. This dataset was deliberately constructed based

Figure 11.2 Car loan application dataset

	Age	Has_Job	Own_House	Credit_Rating	Class
0	young	False	False	fair	No
1	young	False	False	good	No
2	young	True	False	good	Yes
3	young	True	True	fair	Yes
4	young	False	False	fair	No
5	middle	False	False	fair	No
6	middle	False	False	good	No
7	middle	True	True	good	Yes
8	middle	False	True	excellent	Yes
9	middle	False	True	excellent	Yes
10	old	False	True	excellent	Yes
11	old	False	True	good	Yes
12	old	True	False	good	Yes
13	old	True	False	excellent	Yes
14	old	False	False	fair	No

on the illustrative example provided by Liu (2011) for educational purposes. In practice, many real-world business analytics datasets encompass a substantial number of feature variables and observations, which often result in 'bushy' trees. Such trees not only pose challenges for presentation in a book but also complicate the examination of intermediate results at each node, like impurity scores. However, it is important to acknowledge the adaptability of decision trees; they can be efficiently applied to datasets that are not only larger in scale but also more complex in dimensionality. This adaptability underscores their broad applicability across a variety of analytical scenarios.

Unlike many other machine learning algorithms, one-hot encoding is not strictly necessary for decision trees. This is because decision trees can inherently manage categorical data by splitting it based on the most effective feature value at each node. On the other hand, performing one-hot encoding can sometimes enhance the interpretability of decision trees, as it makes the splits based on specific categories more explicit. Alternatively, label encoding can be applied to categorical features when using decision trees. It assigns a unique integer to each category within a categorical feature, which may improve the model's performance, especially in cases where a categorical feature has an inherent ordinal relationship.

```
from sklearn.preprocessing import LabelEncoder

df_2 = df.copy()
col_select_category = df_2.select_dtypes(include=["bool",
"object"]).columns
label_encoder_tran = {}

for col in col_select_category:
    label_encoder_tran[col] = LabelEncoder()
    label_encoder_tran[col].fit(df_2[col].unique())
    df_2[col] = label_encoder_tran[col].transform
    (df_2[col].to_numpy())
    if col == "Class":
        label_names = label_encoder_tran[col].classes_
```

Figure 11.3 shows the pre-processed data after label encoding for both feature variables and the target variable. Given the exceptionally small size of the dataset, we will not be dividing the data into training and testing sets. Instead, we will construct a decision tree using the whole dataset. In the following codes, a CART tree is constructed using *DecisionTreeClassifier* class by specifying the argument *criterion* with *Gini*. The tree can be visualized with the aid of *export_graphviz* and *pydotplus*.

Figure 11.3 Car loan application data after label encoding

	Age	Has_Job	Own_House	Credit_Rating	Class
0	2	0	0	1	0
1	2	0	0	2	0
2	2	1	0	2	1
3	2	1	1	1	1
4	2	0	0	1	0
5	0	0	0	1	0
6	0	0	0	2	0
7	0	1	1	2	1
8	0	0	1	0	1
9	0	0	1	0	1
10	1	0	1	0	1
11	1	0	1	2	1
12	1	1	0	2	1
13	1	1	0	0	1
14	1	0	0	1	0

```
x = df_2.iloc[:, 0:4].to_numpy()
y = df_2.iloc[:, -1].to_numpy()

from sklearn.tree import DecisionTreeClassifier
from sklearn.tree import export_graphviz
import pydotplus
from IPython.display import Image

dtc = DecisionTreeClassifier(criterion="gini",
random_state=100)
dtc.fit(x, y)

dot_data = export_graphviz(
    dtc,
    out_file=None,
    feature_names=col_select_category[0:-1],
    class_names=label_names,
    filled=True,
```

```
        rounded=True,
        special_characters=True,
)

graph = pydotplus.graph_from_dot_data(dot_data)
Image(graph.create_png())
```

Figure 11.4 shows the visualized CART tree. It can predict a binary outcome based on two features: *Own_House* and *Has_Job*. The tree initially splits the data based on the *Own_House* feature. For instances where *Own_House* is less than or equal to 0.5 (i.e. *Own_House* is False), further differentiation is made based on the *Has_Job* feature. If *Has_Job* is also less than or equal to 0.5 (i.e. *Has_Job* is False), the tree predicts the class *No*, and the associated leaf node has an Gini impurity score of 0, indicating pure classification with all 6 samples belonging to the *No* class. Conversely, if *Has_Job* is large than 0.5 (i.e. *Has_Job* is True), the class is predicted as *Yes* with 3 samples, and again the Gini impurity is 0, showing that this node is also pure. On the other branch, where *Own_House* is larger than 0.5 (i.e. *Own_House* is True), the model directly predicts *Yes* without further splits, with an Gini impurity of 0 and 6 samples in this leaf node. The root node's Gini impurity of 0.48, which suggests some initial uncertainty, is reduced through subsequent splits. The 'value' arrays at each node show the distribution of samples across the two classes, providing a clear view of how the model arrives at its predictions.

The classifier also returns the impurity-based importance of a feature through its attribute *feature_importances_*. This importance is computed as the (normalized)

Figure 11.4 Visualized CART tree

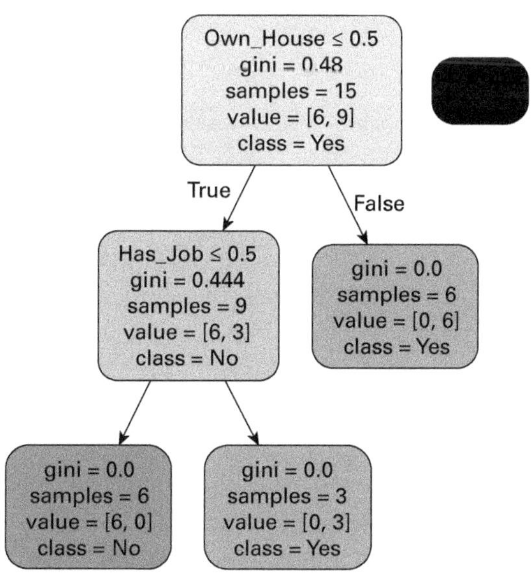

total reduction of the criterion brought by that feature. Impurity-based feature importance is a direct and interpretable method, facilitating feature selection. However, it has limitations, such as a bias toward features with many categories or high cardinality. Moreover, it can inaccurately represent the importance of correlated features or feature interactions and fails to provide the directionality of the feature's effects on the target variable. As such, while it can simplify models by identifying non-contributing features, its application requires careful interpretation to avoid misleading conclusions.

```
feature_importance = dtc.feature_importances_
print("feature_importance: {}".format(feature_importance))

feature_column = df_2.iloc[:, :-1].columns
print("feature_column: {}".format(feature_column))

x_features = pd.DataFrame(
    {
        "Feature": feature_column,
        "Importance": dtc.feature_importances_,
    }
)

x_features = x_features.sort_values("Importance", ascending=False)
x_features
```

Figure 11.5 Feature importance of the CART tree based on impurity reduction

```
feature_importance: [0.         0.56746193 0.43253807 0.        ]
feature_column: Index(['Age', 'Has_Job', 'Own_House', 'Credit_Rating'], dtype='object')
```

	Feature	Importance
1	Has_Job	0.567462
2	Own_House	0.432538
0	Age	0.000000
3	Credit_Rating	0.000000

Figure 11.5 shows that feature *Has_Job* has the highest importance score of approximately 0.567, suggesting that having a job is the most significant predictor among the features evaluated based on reduction of Gini impurity score. The next most important feature is *Own_House*, with a score of around 0.433, indicating that home ownership is also a strong predictor but less so than employment status. The features *Age* and *Credit_Rating*, on the other hand, have importance scores of 0, which implies that in the context of this particular model, they do not contribute to the predictive power regarding the target variable.

Alternatively, the use of the *permutation_importance* function, available through the *inspection* module of the scikit-learn library, presents a viable approach for computing importance scores via feature permutation. This technique, known as *permutation importance*, is notable for its ability to gauge the significance of input features in machine learning models, thus providing essential insights into which features most significantly impact the model's performance. The core concept of permutation importance lies in its strategy of randomly shuffling the values of a particular feature, thereby severing the direct link between the feature and the target outcome. This shuffle allows for an appraisal of the feature's standalone influence, highlighting its role in the model's predictive success. The primary benefit of this approach is its broad applicability, offering an isolated evaluation of each feature's significance. However, it is important to note a key limitation – permutation importance does not take into account the potential interactions or dependencies that may exist between features, which could lead to an incomplete understanding of feature dynamics within the model.

```
from sklearn.inspection import permutation_importance

result = permutation_importance(dtc, x, y,
scoring="accuracy", random_state=100)
print("feature_importance: {}".format(result.importances_
mean))
feature_column = df_2.iloc[:, :-1].columns
print("feature_column: {}".format(feature_column))

x_features = pd.DataFrame(
        {
          "Feature": feature_column,
          "Importance": result.importances_mean,
        }
)

x_features = x_features.sort_values("Importance",
ascending=False)
x_features
```

Figure 11.6 Feature importance of the CART tree based on permutation

```
feature_importance: [0.         0.24       0.30666667 0.        ]
feature_column: Index(['Age', 'Has_Job', 'Own_House', 'Credit_Rating'], dtype='object')
```

	Feature	Importance
2	Own_House	0.306667
1	Has_Job	0.240000
0	Age	0.000000
3	Credit_Rating	0.000000

In Figure 11.6, the feature importance values indicate the influence each feature has on the prediction of a model, assessed by feature permutation. The *Own_House* feature has the highest importance with a score of approximately 0.307, suggesting that whether a person owns a house or not is the most significant contributor to the model's predictions in the context of this dataset. Following this, the *Has_Job* feature holds an importance of about 0.240, indicating that employment status is also a critical factor but is less influential than home ownership in the model's decisions. On the other hand, *Age* and *Credit_Rating* show zero importance, implying that for the model in question, these features do not play a role in improving the predictive accuracy. This also means that changes to the *Age* and *Credit_Rating* data will have a trivial impact on the model's performance, perhaps because they do not carry information that differentiates the outcomes, or because their signal is captured by the other features which are more influential.

As mentioned earlier, due to the exceptionally small size of the dataset at hand, we will not be evaluating the performance of the developed decision tree. In subsequent sections of this chapter, we will explore a somewhat larger, real-world business analytics dataset to implement ensemble methods. Alongside this, as a benchmark, we will also implement and examine the performance of decision trees for comparative analysis.

11.3 Ensemble Methods

Ensemble methods are a special type of machine learning algorithms or techniques that leverage the strengths of multiple models to create a more robust and accurate final model like *crowd of wisdoms*. They achieve this by combining the predictions from multiple individual models, called *base learners*, into a single prediction.

Diversity among the base learners is very important as they should not all make the same mistakes on the same data points. By incorporating diverse perspectives, the ensemble can achieve better overall performance compared to any single model.

There are two main types of ensemble methods: bootstrap aggregation (in short bagging) and boosting. They differ in how they address the issues of bias and variance, which are two essential concepts in statistics and machine learning. *Bias* represents the model's tendency for systematic underperformance, failing to capture essential data patterns. It can be calculated as the difference between the expected prediction of the model and the true value. *Variance* refers to the model's prediction sensitivity to slight data shifts. It can be measured by checking how much the predictions for a given point vary between different versions of the model trained on different subsets of the dataset, then averaging these variations.

Bagging aims to decrease the model's variance through bootstrapping (sampling with replacement), creating several versions of the training dataset with some data points duplicated and others omitted. Each dataset variant trains a similar model, and the ensemble's final output is derived from averaging (for regression) or voting (for classification). It is analogous to students pooling diverse study insights for a more accurate collective answer. *Boosting*, on the other hand, focuses on reducing model bias by training models in sequence, with each new model focusing on previously mispredicted data points, effectively learning from prior errors. The ensemble's final decision comes from a weighted sum of individual model predictions, prioritizing models that correct the mistakes of their predecessors, similar to students sequentially addressing each other's study gaps for a unified comprehension. The choice between bagging and boosting hinges on the model's variance and bias. Bagging is preferable for high-variance models to bolster generalizability, whereas boosting is suited for high-bias models to improve accuracy. The book by Zhou (2012) on ensemble methods provides a comprehensive exploration of these techniques, detailing their theoretical underpinnings and practical applications to enhance prediction accuracy.

Table 11.1 Summary of popular tree-based ensemble methods

Ensemble method	Type	Reference
Random Forests	Bagging	Breiman (2001)
Adaptive Boosting (AdaBoost)	Boosting	Freund and Schapire (1995)
Gradient Boosting Decision Tree (GBDT)	Boosting	Friedman (2001)
eXtreme Gradient Boosting (XGBoost)	Boosting	Chen and Guestrin (2016)

Table 11.1 presents four popular tree-based ensemble methods. Random Forests uses bagging to reduce variance and improve model robustness. It creates a 'forest' of decision trees, each trained on random subsets of the data and features. By averaging their predictions, it mitigates overfitting commonly seen in single decision trees, ultimately enhancing overall prediction accuracy. AdaBoost employs boosting and sequentially trains a series of weak decision trees. Each subsequent model focuses more on instances that previous trees misclassified, while correctly classified instances receive less weight. This process iteratively improves prediction capabilities by building a strong model from a collection of weaker ones. Similar to AdaBoost, GBDT also uses boosting. It incrementally builds an ensemble of weak decision trees, where each tree corrects the errors made by the previous trees in the sequence, ultimately minimizing the loss function. XGBoost builds upon GBDT by incorporating advanced regularization techniques to prevent overfitting, along with efficient computation methods for improved scalability. Designed for enhanced performance and speed, XGBoost tackles large-scale data and complex modelling challenges effectively. These four methods encompass sophisticated techniques beyond this book's scope, aimed at demystifying mathematical concepts for wider accessibility. For detailed technical insights, please refer to the references in Table 11.1.

11.4 Implementing Tree-Based Ensemble Methods in Python

To implement tree-based ensemble methods in Python, we can use the scikit-learn library for Random Forests, AdaBoost, and GBDT, and the *xgboost* library for XGBoost. For the latter, it supports training models using both CPU and GPU. Further guidelines on installation can be found at the XGBoost website (https://xgboost.readthedocs.io/en/stable/).

Corporate credit rating prediction is a crucial task in finance, providing insights into the creditworthiness of companies. In the following, we use the *corporate_rating_moody.xlsx* dataset to implement a range of tree-based methods to predict corporate credit ratings as evaluated by Moody's Ratings. The dataset is derived from the Corporate Credit Rating Forecasting data available on Kaggle (www.kaggle.com/code/agewerc/corporate-credit-rating-forecasting).

```
import pandas as pd
df = pd.read_excel("data/corporate_rating_moody.xlsx")
df.info()
```

Figure 11.7 Summary of information of Moody's credit ratings data

```
<class 'pandas.core.frame.DataFrame'>
RangeIndex: 579 entries, 0 to 578
Data columns (total 29 columns):
 #   Column                                 Non-Null Count  Dtype
---  ------                                 --------------  -----
 0   Rating                                 579 non-null    object
 1   Rating agency name                     579 non-null    object
 2   Sector                                 579 non-null    object
 3   Current ratio                          579 non-null    float64
 4   Quick ratio                            579 non-null    float64
 5   Cash ratio                             579 non-null    float64
 6   Days of sales outstanding              579 non-null    float64
 7   Net profit margin                      579 non-null    float64
 8   Pre tax profit margin                  579 non-null    float64
 9   Gross profit margin                    579 non-null    float64
 10  Operating profit margin                579 non-null    float64
 11  Return on assets                       579 non-null    float64
 12  Return on capital employed             579 non-null    float64
 13  Return on equity                       579 non-null    float64
 14  Asset turn over                        579 non-null    float64
 15  Fixed asset turnover                   579 non-null    float64
 16  Debt equity ratio                      579 non-null    float64
 17  Debt ratio                             579 non-null    float64
 18  Effective tax rate                     579 non-null    float64
 19  Free cash flow operating cash flow ratio  579 non-null    float64
 20  Free cash flow per share               579 non-null    float64
 21  Cash per share                         579 non-null    float64
 22  Company equity multiplier              579 non-null    float64
 23  EBIT per revenue                       579 non-null    float64
 24  Enterprise value multiple              579 non-null    float64
 25  Operating cash flow per share          579 non-null    float64
 26  Operating cash flow sales ratio        579 non-null    float64
 27  Payables turnover                      579 non-null    float64
 28  Year                                   579 non-null    int64
dtypes: float64(25), int64(1), object(3)
memory usage: 131.3+ KB
```

Figure 11.8 Distribution of classes in the target variable

```
Rating
BBB    243
A      105
BB     102
B       87
CCC     34
AA       5
AAA      2
C        1
Name: count, dtype: int64

<IPython.core.display.Javascript object>
```

Figure 11.7 shows there are 28 features over 579 companies, including current ratio, quick ratio, cash ratio, days of sales outstanding, gross profit margin, among others. There are no missing values. The examination of the distribution of the target variable Rating reveals a notable class imbalance issue, as illustrated in Figure 11.8. Specifically, certain rating classes such as *C*, *CCC*, *AA*, and *AAA* are significantly under-represented in the dataset. Moreover, the distribution of observations across ratings somewhat resembles a bell-shaped curve, indicating that companies with the highest and lowest ratings are far fewer in number compared to those with medium grades. While upsampling can be a straightforward solution to address imbalance in some scenarios, it becomes challenging for classes like *C*, *AA*, and *AAA*, which have only a handful of observations each. Even with replacement, upsampling these classes would not yield a dataset with sufficiently diverse values. A potential solution involves aggregating the rating classes into broader categories, leveraging Moody's rating subcategory descriptions, to achieve a more balanced distribution.

```
df["Rating"].value_counts()
```

```
def categorize_rating(rating):
if rating in ["AAA", "AA"]:
    return "High quality (AAA/AA)"
elif rating == "A":
    return "Upper-medium (A)"
elif rating == "BBB":
    return "Medium (BBB)"
elif rating == "BB":
    return "Speculative (BB)"
elif rating == "B":
    return "Vulnerable (B)"
elif rating in ["C", "CC", "CCC"]:
    return "Poor standing (CCC/CC/C)"
df["Rating category"] = df["Rating"].apply(categorize_rating)
del df["Rating"]
del df["Rating agency name"]
df["Rating category"].value_counts()
```

Figure 11.9 Distribution of classes in the new target variable 'Rating category'

```
Rating
BBB    243
A      105
BB     102
B       87
CCC     34
AA       5
AAA      2
C        1
Name: count, dtype: int64

<IPython.core.display.Javascript object>
```

Figure 11.9 presents the distribution of the revised target variable 'Rating category'. While the issue of class imbalance persists, the redefined minority classes now encompass a significantly larger number of observations, making them more suitable for upsampling. This enhancement facilitates a more thorough exploration of patterns within the dataset, thereby increasing the likelihood of developing a more effective model. Subsequently, we proceed with upsampling to refine the dataset further.

```
from sklearn.utils import resample

most_frequent_category = df["Rating category"].value_counts().idxmax()
dfs = {
    category: df[df["Rating category"] == category]
    for category in df["Rating category"].unique()
}
random_seed_val = 100
upsampled_dfs = [
    resample(
        dfs[category],
        replace=True,
        n_samples=df["Rating category"].value_counts()[most_frequent_category],
        random_state=random_seed_val,
    )
    for category in dfs
    if category != most_frequent_category
]
upsampled_dfs.append(dfs[most_frequent_category])
balanced_df = pd.concat(upsampled_dfs)
```

Figure 11.10 showcases the summary of the upsampled dataset, which now consists of 1,458 observations. As a next step, akin to practices in other machine learning workflows, we plan to apply one-hot encoding to categorical features and normalization to numerical features. It is worth clarifying that these preprocessing steps are not strictly required for tree-based methods. Specifically, decision trees, as the base learners for tree-based ensemble methods, can intrinsically manage categorical features, and they do not rely on distance measures, making normalization less critical. However, we opt to proceed with one-hot encoding and normalization for two main reasons: (i) the dataset contains a nominal categorical feature with a wide range of categories, where one-hot encoding can enhance model interpretability; and (ii) GBDT and XGBoost, which employ numerical optimization techniques for model

Figure 11.10 Summary of information of upsampled credit ratings data

```
<class 'pandas.core.frame.DataFrame'>
Index: 1458 entries, 22 to 578
Data columns (total 28 columns):
 #   Column                                   Non-Null Count  Dtype
---  ------                                   --------------  -----
 0   Sector                                   1458 non-null   object
 1   Current ratio                            1458 non-null   float64
 2   Quick ratio                              1458 non-null   float64
 3   Cash ratio                               1458 non-null   float64
 4   Days of sales outstanding                1458 non-null   float64
 5   Net profit margin                        1458 non-null   float64
 6   Pre tax profit margin                    1458 non-null   float64
 7   Gross profit margin                      1458 non-null   float64
 8   Operating profit margin                  1458 non-null   float64
 9   Return on assets                         1458 non-null   float64
 10  Return on capital employed               1458 non-null   float64
 11  Return on equity                         1458 non-null   float64
 12  Asset turn over                          1458 non-null   float64
 13  Fixed asset turnover                     1458 non-null   float64
 14  Debt equity ratio                        1458 non-null   float64
 15  Debt ratio                               1458 non-null   float64
 16  Effective tax rate                       1458 non-null   float64
 17  Free cash flow operating cash flow ratio 1458 non-null   float64
 18  Free cash flow per share                 1458 non-null   float64
 19  Cash per share                           1458 non-null   float64
 20  Company equity multiplier                1458 non-null   float64
 21  EBIT per revenue                         1458 non-null   float64
 22  Enterprise value multiple                1458 non-null   float64
 23  Operating cash flow per share            1458 non-null   float64
 24  Operating cash flow sales ratio          1458 non-null   float64
 25  Payables turnover                        1458 non-null   float64
 26  Year                                     1458 non-null   int64
 27  Rating category                          1458 non-null   object
dtypes: float64(25), int64(1), object(2)
memory usage: 330.3+ KB
```

training, might benefit from normalized numerical features, as normalization can potentially accelerate the training process. This approach is supported by empirical evidence from the application of these preprocessing steps in other models.

```
balanced_df_features = pd.get_dummies(
    balanced_df.iloc[:, :-1], drop_first=True, dtype="int8"
)
balanced_df_features.head()

from sklearn.preprocessing import StandardScaler

x = balanced_df_features.to_numpy()
x[:, :26] = StandardScaler().fit_transform(x[:, :26])
print(x)
```

```
from sklearn.preprocessing import LabelEncoder

le = LabelEncoder()
le.fit(balanced_df["Rating category"])
print(le.classes_)
y = le.transform(balanced_df["Rating category"])
print(y)
```

In this project, we intend to implement all four of the discussed tree-based ensemble methods. Furthermore, as outlined in Section 11.2, our objective includes comparing the efficacy of tree-based ensemble methods against their fundamental components, decision trees, serving as a baseline for single-model performance. It's important to recognize that both decision trees and tree-based ensemble methods possess a number of hyperparameters, significantly influencing their performance. Consequently, fine-tuning these hyperparameters is imperative for a meaningful comparison. Accordingly, we plan to employ *GridSearchCV* for conducting cross-validation alongside hyperparameter tuning for these selected models. This strategy represents a more thorough and meticulous procedure, recommended when applying advanced methods to complex analytical tasks.

```
from sklearn.model_selection import GridSearchCV

model_cv_obj = {}
model_cv_results = {}
fold_cv = 10
no_jobs = -1

# Random forest
para_rf = {
    "max_depth": [10, 25, 50],
    "min_samples_leaf": [1, 5, 10],
    "min_samples_split": [2, 5, 10],
    "n_estimators": [100, 200, 500],
}
rf = RandomForestClassifier(random_state=random_seed_val)
model_cv_obj["RF"] = GridSearchCV(
    estimator=rf,
    param_grid=para_rf,
    n_jobs=no_jobs,
    cv=fold_cv,
```

```
    scoring="accuracy",
)

#AdaBoost
from sklearn.ensemble import AdaBoostClassifier

para_adaboost = {
    "learning_rate": [0.001, 0.01, 0.05, 0.1, 0.15],
    "n_estimators": [100, 200, 500],
}
adaboost = AdaBoostClassifier(random_state=random_seed_val)
model_cv_obj["AdaBoost"] = GridSearchCV(
    estimator=adaboost,
    param_grid=para_adaboost,
    n_jobs=no_jobs,
    cv= fold_cv,
    scoring="accuracy",
)

#GBDT
from sklearn.ensemble import GradientBoostingClassifier

para_gbdt = {
    "learning_rate": [0.001, 0.01, 0.05, 0.1, 0.15],
    "n_estimators": [100, 200, 500],
}
gbdt = GradientBoostingClassifier(random_state=random_seed_
val)
model_cv_obj["GBDT"] = GridSearchCV(
    estimator=gbdt,
    param_grid=para_gbdt,
    n_jobs=no_jobs,
    cv=fold_cv,
    scoring="accuracy",
)

# XGBoost
from xgboost import XGBClassifier

para_xgb = {
```

```
    “learning_rate”: [0.001, 0.01, 0.05, 0.1, 0.15],
    “max_depth”: [10, 25, 50],
    “min_child_weight”: [2, 3, 4],
    “gamma”: [0.0, 0.1, 0.2, 0.3, 0.4],
    “colsample_bytree”: [0.3, 0.4, 0.5, 0.7],
}
xgb = XGBClassifier(random_state=random_seed_val)
model_cv_obj[“XGBoost”] = GridSearchCV(
    estimator=xgb,
    param_grid=para_xgb,
    n_jobs=no_jobs,
    cv=fold_cv,
    scoring=“accuracy”,
)

#Decision tree
from sklearn.tree import DecisionTreeClassifier

para_dtc = {
    “criterion”: [“entropy”, “gini”],
    “max_depth”: np.arange(3, 10).tolist(),
    “min samples_leaf”: np.arange(3, 10).tolist(),
}
dtc = DecisionTreeClassifier(random_state=random_seed_val)
model_cv_obj[“DT”] = GridSearchCV(
    estimator=dtc,
    param_grid=para_dtc,
    n_jobs=no_jobs,
    cv=fold_cv,
    scoring=“accuracy”,
)

for algo in model_cv_obj.keys():
    print(algo)
    model_cv_obj[algo].fit(x_train, y_train)
    model_cv_results[algo] = model_cv_obj[algo].best_score_

model_cv_results
```

Figure 11.11 Comparison of tree-based methods

```
{'RF': 0.8435692541856925,
 'AdaBoost': 0.44438736681887364,
 'GBDT': 0.8394596651445967,
 'XGBoost': 0.8518645357686452,
 'DT': 0.727054794520548}
```

Figure 11.11 displays the results of the cross-validation for the fine-tuned models. While AdaBoost's underperformance merits additional analysis, the ensemble methods generally eclipse the solitary decision tree, with AdaBoost as the notable exception, confirming the value added by the ensemble strategy. The standout model is XGBoost, the most recent innovation among the evaluated models, delivering the best results. As a result, we have decided to proceed with XGBoost for making predictions on new datasets and for interpreting the importance of features. For the latter, we plan to employ feature permutation importance, a method analogous to that used in decision tree analysis, to assess the impact of individual features.

```
from sklearn.inspection import permutation_importance

fpi_dtc = permutation_importance(
    model_cv_obj[“XGBoost”], x, y, random_state=random_seed_val
)
df_fpi_dtc = pd.DataFrame(
{
    “Feature”: balanced_df_features.columns,
    “Importance Score”: fpi_dtc.importances_mean,
}
)
df_fpi_dtc.sort_values(“Importance Score”, ascending=False).head(15)
```

Figure 11.12 Top 15 important features of the XGBoost based on permutation

	Feature	Importance Score
2	Cash ratio	0.011934
15	Effective tax rate	0.009465
22	Operating cash flow per share	0.007545
3	Days of sales outstanding	0.007133
12	Fixed asset turnover	0.007133
23	Operating cast flow sales ratio	0.006036
13	Debt equity ratio	0.005624
17	Free cash flow per share	0.005487
21	Enterprise value multiple	0.004938
14	Debt ratio	0.004938
0	Current ratio	0.004938
1	Quick ratio	0.003841
9	Return on capital employed	0.003704
19	Company equity multiplier	0.003292
24	Payables turnover	0.002606

Figure 11.12 presents the top 15 important features from the XGBoost. The most influential feature, according to the importance score, is *Cash ratio*, with a score of 0.0119, suggesting that a company's liquidity plays a significant role in the model's predictions. Following this, *Effective tax rate* and *Operating cash flow per share* have importance scores of about 0.0095 and 0.0075, respectively, indicating their considerable, albeit lesser, influence compared to the cash ratio. *Days of sales outstanding* and *Fixed asset turnover* share an identical score of 0.0071, which points to the relevance of asset management and sales efficiency in the model's considerations. Further down the list, ratios such as *Debt equity*, *Free cash flow per share*, and *Enterprise value multiple* demonstrate moderate importance with scores around 0.0055 to 0.0049. Other features, including *Current ratio*, *Quick ratio*, and *Return on capital employed* have lower importance scores, suggesting they have a lesser but still non-negligible impact on the model's output. Due to the presentation space in the book, we only show top 15 features but one could check the importance scores for all the features.

11.5 Summary

This chapter delves into tree-based methods, illuminating both the fundamental decision trees and the more sophisticated ensemble techniques. We commenced with an exploration of decision trees – robust yet intuitively straightforward algorithms that delineate the predictor space into distinct, straightforward regions. In Python, the scikit-learn library's *DecisionTreeClassifier* and *DecisionTreeRegressor* stand out as the quintessential tools for crafting these models for classification and regression tasks, correspondingly.

A significant merit of decision trees lies in their exceptional interpretability. They reflect the nuances of human decision-making, rendering them transparent and straightforward to expound. As such, decision trees are emblematic of *white-box models*, characterized by their lucid and accessible logic. They competently contend with intricate, non-linear relationships amongst features, sans the necessity for data transformation, and they necessitate considerably less data preparation compared to alternative machine learning paradigms. However, absent meticulous tuning, decision trees are susceptible to overfitting, potentially crafting excessively intricate trees that struggle to generalize well. This is conventionally counteracted through the application of post-pruning.

Advancing in the chapter, we explored tree-based ensemble methods, which enhance decision tree efficacy by synthesizing multiple models, thus heightening both predictive acuity and robustness. Key ensemble methods, such as Random Forest, AdaBoost, GBDT, and XGBoost were discussed. In the Python ecosystem, the scikit-learn library provides for Random Forest, AdaBoost, and Gradient Boosting, whilst XGBoost is supported by its own specific library. These models are easily instantiated, trained, and employed to make predictions. Hyperparameter tuning, cross-validation, and feature importance evaluation are critical accompanying processes to optimize the model's performance. Although our illustrative examples have centred predominantly on classification tasks, their application to regression tasks is similarly approached.

11.6 Exercise

In this exercise, you will implement a decision tree and random forest to predict if a client would subscribe a term deposit in bank marketing. Use the *bank_marketing.csv* file, which is created based on a publicly available data on UCI Machine Learning Repository (https://archive.ics.uci.edu/dataset/222/bank+marketing).

The following are the description about the data:

- Input variables:
  - Bank client data:
    - **age** (numeric)
    - **job**: type of job (categorical: *admin.*, *blue-collar*, *entrepreneur*, *housemaid*, *management*, *retired*, *self-employed*, *services*, *student*, *technician*, *unemployed*, *unknown*)

  - **marital:** Marital status (categorical: *divorced*, *married*, *single*, *unknown*; note: *divorced* means divorced or widowed)
  - **education** (categorical: *basic.4y*, *basic.6y*, *basic.9y*, *high.school*, *illiterate*, *professional.course*, *university.degree*, *unknown*)
  - **default:** has credit in default? (categorical: *no*, *yes*, *unknown*)
  - **housing:** has housing loan? (categorical: *no*, *yes*, *unknown*)
  - **loan:** has personal loan? (categorical: *no*, *yes*, *unknown*)
- Related with the last contact of the current campaign:
  - **contact:** contact communication type (categorical: *cellular*, *telephone*)
  - **month:** last contact month of year (categorical: *jan*, *feb*, *mar*, ...)
  - **day_of_week:** last contact day of the week (categorical: *mon*, *tue*, *wed*, *thu*, *fri*)
  - **duration:** last contact duration, in seconds (numeric). Important note: this attribute highly affects the output target (e.g. if duration=0 then y=*no*). *Yet*, the duration is not known before a call is performed. Also, *after* the end of the call y is obviously *known*. Thus, this input should only be included for benchmark purposes and should be discarded if the intention is to have a realistic predictive model.
- Other attributes:
  - **campaign:** number of contacts performed during this campaign and for this client (numeric, includes last contact)
  - pdays: number of days that passed by after the client was last contacted from a previous campaign (numeric; 999 means client was not previously contacted)
  - **previous:** number of contacts performed before this campaign and for this client (numeric)
  - **poutcome:** outcome of the previous marketing campaign (categorical: *failure*, *nonexistent*, *success*)
- Social and economic context attributes:
  - **emp.var.rate:** employment variation rate - quarterly indicator (numeric)
  - **cons.price.idx:** consumer price index - monthly indicator (numeric)
  - **cons.conf.idx:** consumer confidence index - monthly indicator (numeric)
  - **euribor3m:** euribor 3 month rate - daily indicator (numeric)
  - **nr.employed:** number of employees - quarterly indicator (numeric)

- Target variable:
  - y: has the client subscribed a term deposit? (binary: *yes*, *no*)

12 Support Vector Machines

Support vector machines (SVMs) are a powerful and widely used machine learning algorithm suitable for both classification and regression tasks. They are particularly well-suited for high-dimensional data and can efficiently perform linear and non-linear classifications. In this chapter, we will explore the fundamental concepts and principles behind SVMs, and examine their applications for both classification and regression tasks within business analytics.

After completing this chapter, you should be able to:

- Explain the geometric interpretation of SVMs and the idea of finding the optimal hyperplane that maximizes the margin between classes for classification tasks.
- Describe the role of support vectors in defining the decision boundary and their significance in the SVM algorithm.
- Understand the kernel trick and how it allows SVMs to handle non-linear classification problems by implicitly mapping the data to higher-dimensional feature spaces.
- Comprehend the principles of the One-vs-Rest and One-vs-One approaches to transform a binary classifier into a multi-class classifier.
- Understand how the SVM can be extended for solving regression tasks.
- Apply SVMs to real-world business analytics problems, recognizing the scenarios where they are particularly effective.
- Implement SVMs using the machine learning libraries in Python.
- Critically assess the strengths and limitations of SVMs, compared to other machine learning algorithms.

12.1 What is a Hyperplane?

Grounded in theoretical advancements in statistical learning theory, SVMs have a rich history, with significant contributions from researchers such as Vladimir Vapnik and his collaborators. Primarily used for classification tasks, we will begin our discussion with binary classification, then extend it to multi-class classification, and finally generalize to regression.

SVMs rely on the hyperplane to effectively distinguish between data classes. In an SVM, a *hyperplane* is the decision boundary that divides the input data's feature space into two distinct regions, facilitating the binary classification of data points. Imagine we are going to sort a large pile of socks, which contains both green and blue socks. Each sock can be represented as a data point in a multidimensional feature space, where each dimension represents a characteristic or feature of the sock, such as brightness, texture, material, and so on. Let us adhere to the same notation convention as used previously and use D to represent the number of feature variables. We can visualize the data points as two separate groups, as shown in Figure 12.1, one for green socks and one for blue socks, along two-dimensional (left) or three-dimensional (right) plots, where x_1, x_2, x_3 are the corresponding features.

Here, the SVM functions as a sorter, which establishes the hyperplane that effectively segregates the majority of green socks on one side from blue socks on the other. In the two-dimensional plot, the hyperplane appears as a line (highlighted in orange); in the three-dimensional plot, it takes the form of a plane. Put simply, when handling linearly separable data, the hyperplane represents a flat space with one less dimension than the feature space: in two dimensions, a hyperplane is a flat one-dimensional space, basically a line; in three dimensions, a hyperplane is a flat two-dimensional space, which is a plane; in dimensions $D > 3$, visualizing a hyperplane becomes impossible, but the idea of a $(D-1)$ -dimensional flat space still holds.

Figure 12.1 The hyperplane for dividing green and blue socks: (left) two-dimensional scenario; (right) three-dimensional scenario

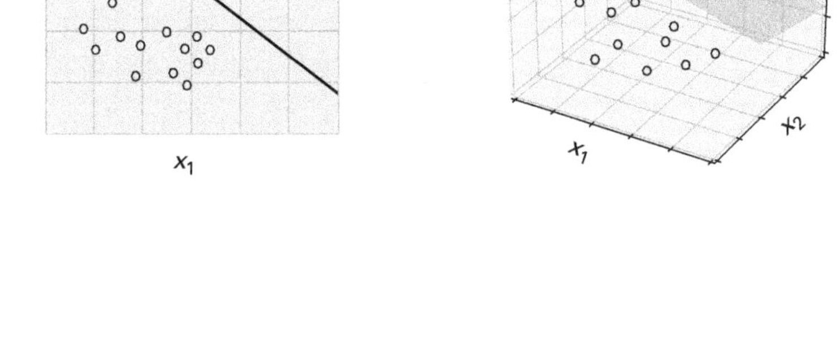

Figure 12.2 The hyperplane $2x_1 + 4x_2 + 1 = 0$ for dividing green and blue socks

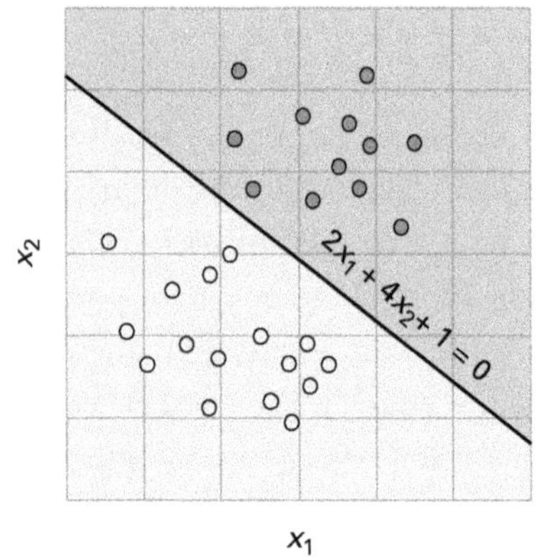

Mathematically, the *hyperplane function* $h(\cdot)$ can be defined as

$$h(\boldsymbol{x}) = \boldsymbol{w}^{\mathrm{T}}\boldsymbol{x} + b = w_1 x_1 + \cdots + w_D x_D + b,$$

where x is the D -dimensional feature vector, $\boldsymbol{w}$ is the weight vector and b is the bias term. The hyperplane satisfies the equation $h(\boldsymbol{x}) = 0$.

For instance, in two dimensions, a hyperplane is defined by the following equation

$$w_1 x_1 + w_2 x_2 + b = 0.$$

If $w_1 = 2$, $w_2 = 4$, and $b = 1$, as illustrated in Figure 12.2, the hyperplane becomes $2x_1 + 4x_2 + 1 = 0$. The blue region encompasses points where $2x_1 + 4x_2 + 1 > 0$ while the green region encompasses points where $2x_1 + 4x_2 + 1 < 0$. Suppose we have a new sock with a vibrant green hue and a rough texture, positioned below the hyperplane (i.e. on the negative side); in that case, we can classify it as a green sock.

12.2 Maximal Margin Classifier

If the given data can be effectively separated by a hyperplane, then there could be an infinite number of potential hyperplanes, as depicted in Figure 12.3. The crucial question to address is: which hyperplane is optimal? The selection of a specific hyperplane is strategic, aiming to create the widest possible 'buffer zone' between the two groups of socks. This 'buffer zone' is vital, particularly considering variations such as light green shades or colourful patterns in some socks. By intelligently positioning this hyperplane, the SVM ensures accurate allocation of the vast majority of socks to their respective groups, even amidst minor imperfections. Thus, it establishes itself as a remarkable sorting tool within the realm of laundry management.

Figure 12.3 Hyperplanes for dividing green and blue socks

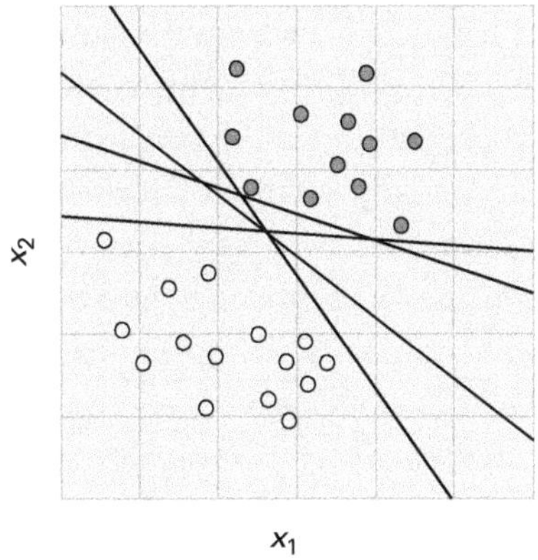

Figure 12.4 The maximal margin hyperplane

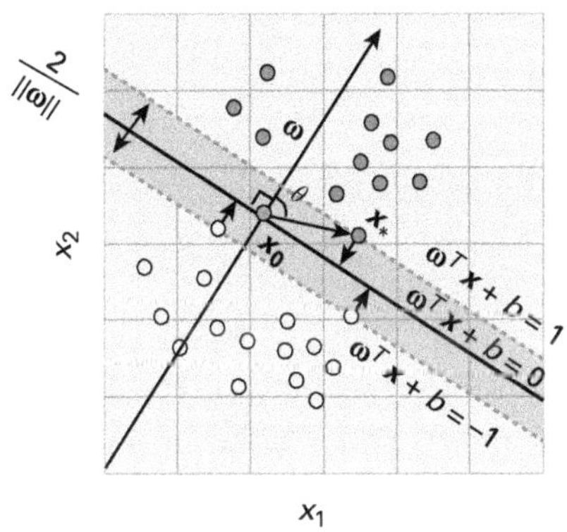

The strategy of establishing the widest possible 'buffer zone' for classification is known as the *maximal margin classifier*. The hyperplane that achieves this objective is referred to as the *maximal margin hyperplane*. Positioned farthest from the training data points, this hyperplane serves as the optimal decision boundary, effectively segregating instances belonging to different classes. The (perpendicular) distance from each training observation to a given separating hyperplane can be computed, with the smallest of these distances representing the minimal distance from the observations to the hyperplane, commonly referred to as the *margin*. As illustrated in Figure 12.4, the maximal margin hyperplane is shown as a solid line, and the margin is the distance from the solid line to either of the dashed lines. The blue point and two green points that lie on the dashed lines are called *support vectors*. These are the data points from the training data that lie closest to the hyperplane. Support vectors are named so because they 'support' the optimal hyperplane. If any of these points were moved or removed, the position of the hyperplane would also change. Support vectors play a significant role in SVMs because the classifier is trained based only on these points, rather than the entire dataset. This characteristic allows SVMs to be computationally efficient, especially in high-dimensional spaces where the number of support vectors can be substantially smaller than the total number of data points. Moreover, support vectors are informative for understanding the structure of the data and the performance of the SVM model. By analysing the support vectors, one can gain insights into which data points are most influential in determining the decision boundary and how well the model generalizes to unseen data.

For mathematical convenience, binary class labels in SVMs are typically denoted as $y_n \in \{-1, +1\}$, where $n = 1, \ldots, N$, $y_n = 1$ represents a blue point (i.e. a positive sample), while $y_n = -1$ represents a green point (i.e. a negative sample). Then a separating hyperplane has the property that

$$y = \begin{cases} +1, \text{ if } h(\boldsymbol{x}) > 0, \\ -1, \text{ if } h(\boldsymbol{x}) < 0. \end{cases}$$

Therefore, the classifier is

$$f(\boldsymbol{x}) = \text{sign}(h(\boldsymbol{x})) = \text{sign}(\boldsymbol{w}^\top \boldsymbol{x} + b),$$

where sign$(\cdot)$ represents the sign function.

From the definition of the hyperplane, we know that vector $\boldsymbol{w}$ is a *normal vector* because any vector that constitute two points on the hyperplane $(\boldsymbol{x} - \tilde{\boldsymbol{x}})$ is orthogonal with $\boldsymbol{w}$. That is $b + \boldsymbol{w}^\top \boldsymbol{x} = 0$, and $b + \boldsymbol{w}^\top \tilde{\boldsymbol{x}} = 0$, then $\boldsymbol{w}^\top(\boldsymbol{x} - \tilde{\boldsymbol{x}}) = 0$. If we denote the intersection of $\boldsymbol{w}$ with the hyperplane is $\boldsymbol{x}_0$, then the shortest distance from the point $\boldsymbol{x}_*$ to the hyperplane can be computed as below

$$\begin{aligned} d(\boldsymbol{x}_*, \text{hyperplane}) &= \| \boldsymbol{x}_* - \boldsymbol{x}_0 \| \cos(\theta) \\ &= \| \boldsymbol{x}_* - \boldsymbol{x}_0 \| \frac{\boldsymbol{w}^\top (\boldsymbol{x}_* - \boldsymbol{x}_0)}{\| \boldsymbol{w} \| \| \boldsymbol{x}_* - \boldsymbol{x}_0 \|} \\ &= \frac{\boldsymbol{w}^\top (\boldsymbol{x}_* - \boldsymbol{x}_0)}{\| \boldsymbol{w} \|} \\ &= \frac{\boldsymbol{w}^\top \boldsymbol{x}_* - \boldsymbol{w}^\top \boldsymbol{x}_0}{\| \boldsymbol{w} \|} \end{aligned}$$

$$= \frac{w^\top x_* + b}{\| w \|}$$

$$= \frac{h(x_*)}{\| w \|}.$$

Thus, for any point x lying on either the negative margin line ($w^\top x + b = -1$) or the positive margin line ($w^\top x + b = 1$), its distance to the hyperplane can be expressed as

$$\frac{| w^\top x + b |}{\| w \|}. \tag{12.1}$$

As shown in Figure 12.4, the distance between the negative margin line and the positive margin line is the maximal margin $\frac{2}{\| w \|}$, so we can formulate the maximal margin hyperplane as the solution to the following optimization problem

$$\max_{\mathrm{w},b} \frac{2}{\| w \|}, \tag{12.2}$$

$$\text{s.t. } y_n(w^\top x_n + b) \ge 1, \forall x_n \in \mathcal{D}. \tag{12.3}$$

The above optimization problem is equivalent to

$$\min_{\mathrm{w},b} \frac{1}{2} \| w \|^2, \tag{12.4}$$

$$\text{s.t. } y_n(w^\top x_n + b) \ge 1, \forall x_n \in \mathcal{D}. \tag{12.5}$$

Given that we have a quadratic objective function subject to linear constraints, this is a standard *quadratic optimization* problem. We can rewrite the optimization as an unconstrained problem using *Lagrange multipliers* as below

$$\begin{aligned}\min_{w,b,\alpha} \mathcal{L}(w,b,\alpha) &= \frac{1}{2} \| w \|^2 - \sum_{n=1}^{N} \alpha_n \left(y_n (w^\top x_n + b) - 1 \right) \\ &= \frac{1}{2} w^\top w - b \sum_{n=1}^{N} \alpha_n y_n - w^\top \sum_{n=1}^{N} \alpha_n y_n x_n + \sum_{n=1}^{N} \alpha_n,\end{aligned}$$

where $\alpha = [\alpha_1, \cdots, \alpha_N]^\top$ are Lagrange multipliers for the constraints $y_n(w^\top x_n + b) \ge 1$ and $\alpha_n \ge 0$ for $n = 1, \ldots, N$.

By taking the partial derivatives of $\mathcal{L}(w,b,\alpha)$ with respect to w and b, and setting to zero, we have

$$\frac{\partial}{\partial \boldsymbol{w}}\mathcal{L}(\boldsymbol{w},b,\boldsymbol{\alpha}) = \boldsymbol{w} - \sum_{n=1}^{N}\alpha_n y_n \boldsymbol{x}_n = 0,$$

$$\frac{\partial}{\partial b}\mathcal{L}(\boldsymbol{w},b,\boldsymbol{\alpha}) = -\sum_{n=1}^{N}\alpha_n y_n = 0. \tag{12.6}$$

Therefore, we have

$$\hat{\boldsymbol{w}} = \sum_{n=1}^{N}\alpha_n y_n \boldsymbol{x}_n,$$

$$0 = \sum_{n=1}^{N}\alpha_n y_n. \tag{12.7}$$

Substituting the above back to the Lagrangian yields the following

$$\max_{\alpha} \mathcal{L}(\hat{\boldsymbol{w}},\hat{b},\boldsymbol{\alpha}) = \frac{1}{2}\hat{\boldsymbol{w}}^\top\hat{\boldsymbol{w}} - b\sum_{n=1}^{N}\alpha_n y_n - \hat{\boldsymbol{w}}^\top\sum_{n=1}^{N}\alpha_n y_n \boldsymbol{x}_n + \sum_{n=1}^{N}\alpha_n,$$

$$= \frac{1}{2}\left(\sum_{n=1}^{N}\alpha_n y_n \boldsymbol{x}_n\right)^\top\left(\sum_{n=1}^{N}\alpha_n y_n \boldsymbol{x}_n\right) - b\underbrace{\sum_{n=1}^{N}\alpha_n y_n}_{=0}$$

$$-\left(\sum_{n=1}^{N}\alpha_n y_n \boldsymbol{x}_n\right)^\top\sum_{n=1}^{N}\alpha_n y_n \boldsymbol{x}_n + \sum_{n=1}^{N}\alpha_n,$$

$$= \sum_{n=1}^{N}\alpha_n - \frac{1}{2}\left(\sum_{n=1}^{N}\alpha_n y_n \boldsymbol{x}_n\right)^\top\left(\sum_{n=1}^{N}\alpha_n y_n \boldsymbol{x}_n\right)$$

$$= \sum_{n=1}^{N}\alpha_n - \frac{1}{2}\sum_{n=1}^{N}\sum_{m=1}^{N}\alpha_n\alpha_m y_n y_m \boldsymbol{x}_n^\top \boldsymbol{x}_m.$$

This is called the *dual form* of the objective. We want to maximize it with respect to α subject to the constraints $\sum_{n=1}^{N}\alpha_n y_n = 0$, and $\alpha_n \geq 0$ for $n = 1,\ldots,N$.

Since this is a convex objective, the solution must satisfy the *Karush-Kuhn-Tucker (KKT)* conditions, which tell us the following properties hold

$$\alpha_n \geq 0$$

$$y_n(\boldsymbol{w}^\top \boldsymbol{x}_n + b) \geq 1,$$

$$\alpha_n\left(y_n(\boldsymbol{w}^\top \boldsymbol{x}_n + b) - 1\right) = 0,$$

for $n = 1,\ldots,N$. The third KKT condition tells that either $\alpha_n = 0$ or $y_n(\boldsymbol{w}^\top \boldsymbol{x}_n + b) = 1$. If $\alpha_n = 0$, then $y_n(\boldsymbol{w}^\top \boldsymbol{x}_n + b) > 1$, indicating that the point $\boldsymbol{x}_n$ lies outside the margin and it does not affect the Lagrange function because $\alpha_n = 0$. Otherwise, if $\alpha_n > 0$, then

$y_n(\boldsymbol{w}^\top \boldsymbol{x}_n+b)=1$. This means the point $\boldsymbol{x}_n$ lies on the margin, it is the support vector and it will affect the Lagrange function because $\alpha_n>0$. Therefore, the final model is only affected the support vectors.

Also, when we obtain $\hat{\boldsymbol{w}} = \sum_{n=1}^{N} \alpha_n y_n \boldsymbol{x}_n$, the support vectors can be used to estimate $\hat{b}$

$$\hat{b} = \frac{1}{|\mathcal{S}|}\sum_{n\in\mathcal{S}}\left(\frac{1}{y_n} - \hat{\boldsymbol{w}}^\top \boldsymbol{x}_n\right),$$

where $\mathcal{S}$ represents the set of support vectors.

12.3 Soft Margin Classifier

Up to this point, we have assumed that our data is perfectly linearly separable. However, this scenario is highly idealistic. More often than not, classes overlap to some extent, making perfect separation unattainable. SVM can accommodate these non-separable instances by introducing what are known as *slack variables*. These variables allow for a certain flexibility in how strictly we adhere to the separation criteria, essentially showing how far a point can 'bend' the rules of separation. Mathematically, we have

$$y_n(\boldsymbol{w}^\top \boldsymbol{x}_n + b) \geq 1 - \xi_n,$$

Figure 12.5 The soft margin classifier

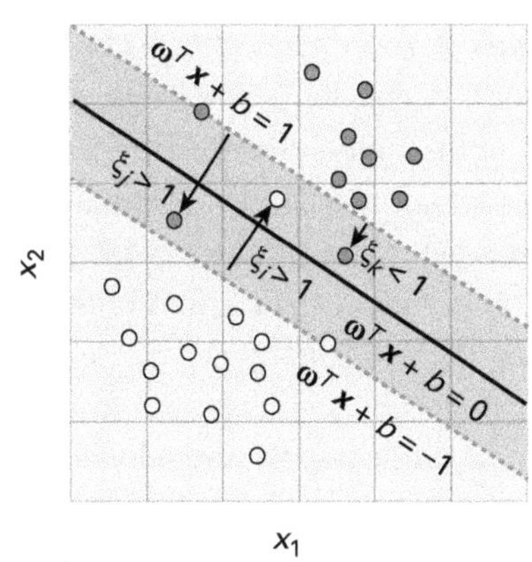

where $\xi_n \geq 0$ represents the slack variable for the point $\boldsymbol{x}_n$, which quantifies the extent to which the point may deviate from the separability condition, as depicted in Figure 12.5.

Then the SVM optimization problem becomes

$$\min_{\boldsymbol{w},b,\xi_n} \left\{ \frac{1}{2} \| \boldsymbol{w} \|^2 + C\sum_{n=1}^{N} \xi_n \right\}, \tag{12.8}$$

$$\text{s.t.} \quad y_n(\boldsymbol{w}^\top \boldsymbol{x}_n + b) \geq 1 - \xi_n, \forall \boldsymbol{x}_n \in \mathcal{D}, \tag{12.9}$$

$$\xi_n \geq 0, \forall \boldsymbol{x}_n \in \mathcal{D}, \tag{12.10}$$

where C is constant that balances the trade-off between maximizing the margin and minimizing the total loss from the slack variables $\sum_{n=1}^{N} \xi_n$.

The optimization problem above, incorporating slack variables, can be solved in a manner similar to that of the maximal margin classifier. This will entail additional Lagrange multipliers for the constraints involving slack variables. While the mathematical foundation underlying this optimization is noteworthy, it is not the primary focus of this chapter. Our aim is to simplify the mathematical aspects to make the discussion more accessible to a broader audience. For those interested in the detailed technical aspects, Bishop (2006), Deisenroth et al. (2020), and Murphy (2022) are comprehensive resources.

12.4 Kernel Tricks

Kernel tricks are a powerful tool in SVMs to handle data that is not linearly separable. This method works by projecting the original input data into a higher-dimensional feature space. In this transformed space, previously intertwined data points can be separated more easily. The idea behind this transformation involves mapping D-dimensional input vectors $\boldsymbol{x}_n$ to a higher-dimensional feature space using a nonlinear mapping function $\phi(\cdot)$. Consider a challenge scenario of dividing blue and green socks, as visualized in the right side of Figure 12.6. In their natural state, the socks are mixed together, making it difficult to separate them using a simple linear boundary. Employing the kernel trick is akin to wearing a pair of magical spectacles. Through these spectacles, blue socks emit a bright blue glow, and green socks emit a bright green glow, making them distinctly separable in this new, visually altered space. This transformed perspective, as illustrated in the right side of Figure 12.6, facilitates an easy division of the socks into two distinct categories, showcasing the power of the kernel trick to enhance the separability of data in a more complex feature space.

Figure 12.6 Non-linear transformation $\phi(\cdot)$ for the input data

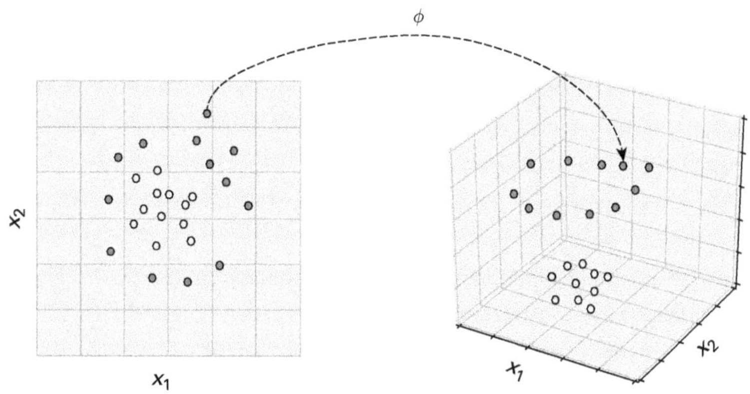

By incorporating the non-linear transformation $\phi(\cdot)$, the optimization problem becomes

$$\min_{w,b,\xi_n} \left\{ \frac{1}{2} \| w \|^2 + C\sum_{n=1}^{N} \xi_n^p \right\},$$

$$\text{s.t.} \quad y_n(w^\top \phi(x_n) + b) \geq 1 - \xi_n, \forall x_n \in \mathcal{D},$$

$$\xi_n \geq 0, \forall x_n \in \mathcal{D}.$$

In the context of maximal and soft margin classifiers, the optimization process enables the derivation of the weight vector $\hat{w}$ and bias $\hat{b}$. The key to the solution lies in the inner product of input feature vectors $x_n^\top x_m$ for $n,m = 1,\ldots,N$. By adding $\phi(\cdot)$, the solution of the above optimization is then based on $\phi(x_n)^\top \phi(x_m)$. This operation is effectively captured by the *kernel function*, denoted as $\kappa(\cdot,\cdot)$. The beauty of the kernel function lies in its ability to obviate the explicit representation of $\phi(\cdot)$. Thus, it facilitates operations in a transformed feature space, bypassing the direct computation of the transformation.

Some commonly used kernels include

- *Linear kernel*:

$$k(x_n, x_m) = x_n^\top x_m.$$

- *Sigmoid kernel*:

$$\tanh(\alpha x_n^\top x_m + r), \alpha > 0, r > 0.$$

- *Gaussian kernel*:

$$k(\boldsymbol{x}_n, \boldsymbol{x}_m) = \exp\left\{-\frac{\| \boldsymbol{x}_n - \boldsymbol{x}_m \|^2}{2\sigma^2}\right\}.$$

- *Radial kernel* or *radial basis function (RBF)*:

$$k(\boldsymbol{x}_n, \boldsymbol{x}_m) = \exp\left\{-\gamma \| \boldsymbol{x}_n - \boldsymbol{x}_m \|^2\right\}, \gamma > 0.$$

The selection of a kernel depends greatly on the specific problem and the characteristics of the data at hand. Different kernels excel at identifying distinct patterns and non-linear relationships within the dataset. A key benefit of using kernel functions lies in their ability to allow SVMs to handle non-linear data by implicitly mapping it to a higher-dimensional space. This is accomplished without the need for explicitly computing the mapping, which can be computationally demanding or unfeasible for data in very high dimensions.

12.5 One-vs-Rest and One-vs-One

Until now, our discussion on SVMs has focused on their application as binary classifiers. To adapt SVMs for multi-class classification tasks, two approaches are available: One-vs-Rest (OvR) and One-vs-One (OvO). It should be noted that these approaches are not exclusive to SVMs; they can be applied to convert any binary classification algorithm into a tool capable of addressing multi-class classification tasks.

The One-vs-Rest (OvR) is also referred to as One-vs-All (OvA). For each class k (where k ranges from 1 to K), the dataset is partitioned into two subsets: the positive examples consisting of instances belonging to class k, and the negative examples comprising instances from all the remaining classes. A binary classifier is then trained on this subset to discriminate between class k and the combined other classes. This process is repeated for all K classes, resulting in a total of K binary classifiers. When a new data point needs to be classified, it is passed through each of the K binary classifiers, and the decision scores or outputs from these classifiers are obtained. The data point is then assigned to the class whose corresponding binary classifier produces the highest decision score. This approach is computationally efficient, requiring only K binary classifiers to be trained, which is linear in the number of classes. However, it may face challenges with datasets having many classes or imbalanced class distributions, as it does not account for potential overlaps or similarities between the grouped other classes.

In the One-vs-One (OvO), $K(K-1)/2$ subsets of data are constructed, where each subset contains instances from only two of the K classes. For every such pair of classes, a binary classifier is trained on the corresponding subset to learn the decision boundary between those two classes. This process results in $K(K-1)/2$ binary classifiers being trained, with each classifier focusing on distinguishing between a unique pair of classes. When a new data point needs to be classified, predictions are obtained from all $K(K-1)/2$ binary classifiers. A voting strategy is then employed to determine the final class assignment. For each class, the number of binary classifiers that voted for that class is counted, and the data point is assigned to the class with the highest number of votes. The key advantage of the OvO method lies in its ability to potentially achieve better decision boundaries, especially for datasets with many classes or complex class distributions, by training classifiers specifically tailored to each pair of classes. However, this approach is computationally more expensive than the OvR method, as the number of binary classifiers grows quadratically with the number of classes. Consequently, the OvO method is generally preferred when dealing with datasets having a large number of classes, as the potential accuracy gains often outweigh the increased computational cost, while OvR may be more suitable for problems with fewer classes.

12.6 Implementing SVM Classifiers in Python

In this section, we use the Wine Quality dataset from the UCI Machine Learning Repository to illustrate the application of SVMs (https://archive.ics.uci.edu/dataset/186/wine+quality). This dataset contains physicochemical attributes of wine samples and a subjective quality rating assigned by experts. The goal is to develop a predictive model using this dataset to estimate the quality of a wine based on its chemical properties. This model can assist winemakers and retailers in making informed decisions about product development, inventory stocking, and marketing strategies. It can also enhance the customer's purchase experience by providing a scientifically estimated quality rating, helping to match consumer preferences with suitable wine products.

By using the Pandas package, we load the dataset *wine_quality.csv*, and we check the summary information of the data through the *info()* function.

```
import pandas as pd
df = pd.read_csv("data/wine_quality.csv")
df.info()
```

As shown in Figure 12.7, the data contains 6,497 observations over 13 variables. There are 12 features, most of which are numerical features, while variable *type* is a categorical variable. The target variable *quality* is by default recognized as the numerical variable. This suggests that it may be continuous or discrete with a number of categories. We will double check this further.

In addition, there are missing values in some variables: *fixed acidity*, *volatile acidity*, *citric acid*, *residual sugar*, *chlorides*, *pH*, *sulphates*. Here we could also use the

Figure 12.7 Summary information of *wine_quality.csv* by checking *df.info()*

```
<class 'pandas.core.frame.DataFrame'>
RangeIndex: 6497 entries, 0 to 6496
Data columns (total 13 columns):
 #   Column                Non-Null Count  Dtype
---  ------                --------------  -----
 0   type                  6497 non-null   object
 1   fixed acidity         6487 non-null   float64
 2   volatile acidity      6489 non-null   float64
 3   citric acid           6494 non-null   float64
 4   residual sugar        6495 non-null   float64
 5   chlorides             6495 non-null   float64
 6   free sulfur dioxide   6497 non-null   float64
 7   total sulfur dioxide  6497 non-null   float64
 8   density               6497 non-null   float64
 9   pH                    6488 non-null   float64
 10  sulphates             6493 non-null   float64
 11  alcohol               6497 non-null   float64
 12  quality               6497 non-null   int64
dtypes: float64(11), int64(1), object(1)
memory usage: 660.0+ KB
```

function *isna().sum()* to have a better view about the variables which have missing values. As the ratio of missing values for these variables are very small, we can simply remove those observations that contain any missing values using *dropna()*.

```
import pandas as pd
df = df.dropna()
```

Let's explore the distribution of the target variable *quality*. We have the option to use the *value_counts()* function for a direct summary, or, as an alternative, we can employ bar charts or histograms for a visual representation of the distribution.

```
import matplotlib.pyplot as plt
import seaborn as sns
%matplotlib inline
sns.set_style("whitegrid")

plt.figure(figsize=(8, 5))
sns.countplot(x=df["quality"])
plt.xlabel("Quality")
plt.ylabel("Frequency")
plt.show()
```

Figure 12.8 illustrates the distribution of wine quality ratings, which somewhat resembles a bell-shaped curve. This observation leads us to consider whether to approach the

Figure 12.8 Distribution of the target variable *quality*

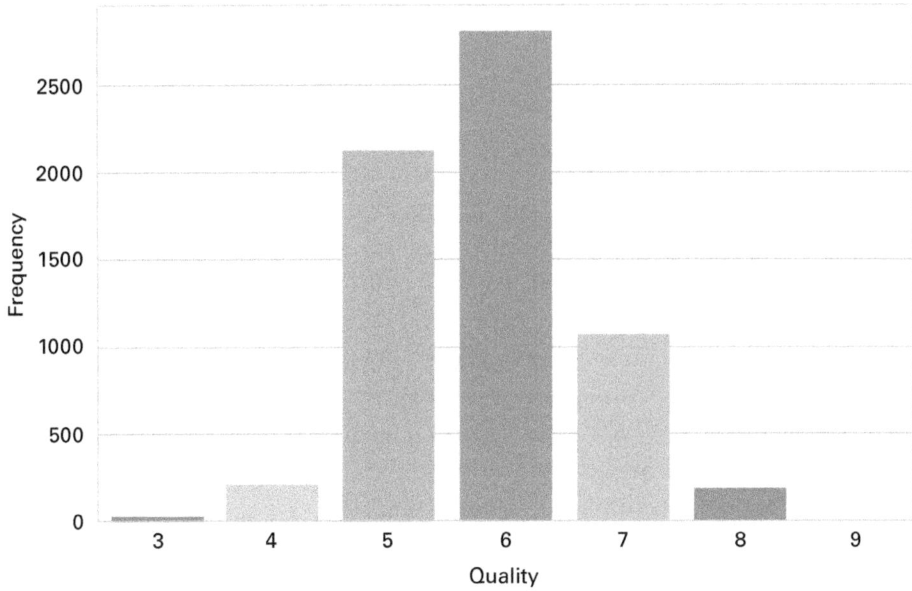

Figure 12.9 Distribution of the target variable *top quality*

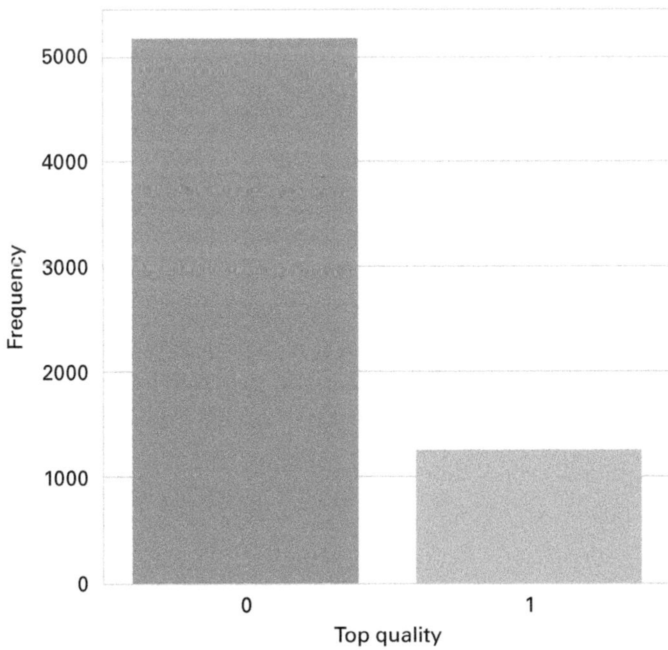

prediction of wine quality as a regression task, where the target variable quality is treated as continuous, or as a classification task, with quality considered as categorical. In the case of regression, the predicted quality ratings might be decimal values, necessitating rounding to the nearest integer. A challenge arises, however, with the potential for predictions to fall outside the expected range of 0 to 10 for wine quality ratings.

Alternatively, treating quality as a categorical variable frames our task as one of classification. We opt for this approach, wherein each quality rating corresponds to a distinct class. It is important to note the presence of class imbalance: certain ratings, such as 3, 4, 8, and 9, have significantly fewer observations compared to more common ratings like 5, 6, and 7. As explored in Chapter 8, class imbalance can be addressed through strategies like oversampling. For the sake of simplicity in this discussion, we could consider merging classes. For instance, rather than aiming to predict the precise quality rating, we could categorize wines as top quality based on whether their rating exceeds 6. This approach introduces a binary target variable, *top quality*. Figure 12.9 depicts the distribution of this binary classification, which, while not perfectly balanced, shows sufficient observations per class to proceed with the analysis.

```
df["top quality"] = [1 if x > 6 else 0 for x in
df["quality"]]
del df["quality"]
y = df["top quality"]

plt.figure(figsize=(5, 5))
sns.countplot(x=y)
plt.xlabel("top quality")
plt.ylabel("Frequency")
plt.show()
```

The correlation among numerical features can also be assessed. The heatmap in Figure 12.10 demonstrates that there is no strong linear correlation between the numerical features. Generally, when dealing with a large number of numerical features, a heatmap (as depicted in Figure 12.10) is preferred to a pairs plot (as seen in Figure 7.3), because it is more visually straightforward to pinpoint correlations.

```
plt.figure(figsize=(10, 10))
corr = df.iloc[:, 1:12].corr()
sns.heatmap(corr, annot=True, cmap="Blues")
plt.show()
```

Figure 12.10 Correlation of the numerical features

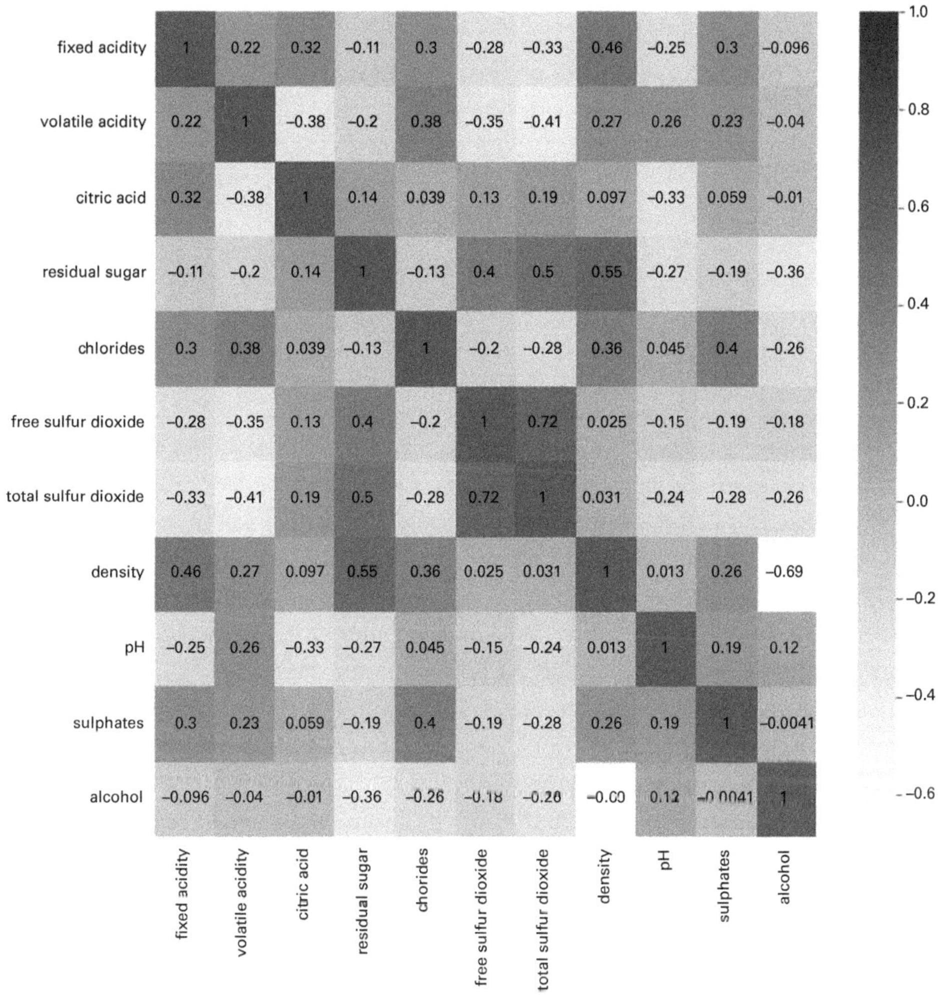

Next, we perform the one-hot encoding to the categorical feature *type* using *get_dummies()* and then perform the z-score normalization using *StandardScaler()* to the rest of numerical features.

```
#perform one - hot encoding to the categorical features
df_features = pd.get_dummies(df.iloc[:, :-1], drop_
first=True, dtype="int8")
df_features.head()

#perform z - score normalisation to the rest of numerical
features
```

```
from sklearn.preprocessing import StandardScaler
x = df_features.to_numpy()
x[:, :11] = StandardScaler().fit_transform(x[:, :11])
```

Then, similar to other models, we perform the stratified split of the pre-processed data to make them ready for model training and testing.

```
from sklearn.model_selection import train_test_split

random_seed_val = 100
x_train, x_test, y_train, y_test = train_test_split(
    x, y, test_size=0.4, stratify=y, random_state=random_
    seed_val
)
```

In terms of SVM classifiers, the scikit-learn library in Python offers several classes under its *svm* module, including *SVC*, *LinearSVC*, and *NuSVC*, Both *SVC* and *NuSVC* utilize the LIBSVM library (Chang and Lin, 2011) for their foundational computations, enabling the use of various kernel functions to create non-linear decision boundaries. This feature makes them well-suited to complex data patterns. Conversely, *LinearSVC* is a more rapid and memory-efficient choice, tailored specifically for linear kernels. Therefore, it is suitable for data where a linear decision boundary adequately ensures accurate classification. For the forthcoming SVM implementation, we will demonstrate using *SVC*, though the principles of using *LinearSVC* and *NuSVC* are similarly applicable.

To illustrate the kernel tricks, four different kernels are used. In other words, we have four different SVMs, which are specified through the argument *kernel* within *SVC*.

```
from sklearn.svm import SVC
from sklearn.metrics import accuracy_score

model_list = {}
model_list[“SVM (Linear)”] = SVC(gamma=“auto”,
kernel=“linear”)
model_list[“SVM (RBF)”] = SVC(gamma=“auto”, kernel=“rbf”)
model_list[“SVM (Poly)”] = SVC(gamma=“auto”, kernel=“poly”)
model_list[“SVM (Sigmoid)”] = SVC(gamma=“auto”,
kernel=“sigmoid”)
predictions_list = {}
results_list = {}
```

```
for algo in model_list.keys():
    print(algo)
    model_list[algo].fit(x_train, y_train)
    predictions_list[algo] = model_list[algo].predict(x_test)
    results_list[algo] = accuracy_score(y_test, predictions_
    list[algo])
```

The performance of SVMs can be compared. Figure 12.11 shows that the SVM with the RBF kernel achieves 83.60% accuracy, which outperforms other models.

```
plt.figure(figsize=(6, 4))
x_plot = [x for y, x in sorted(zip(results_list.values
(),results_list.keys()))]
y_plot = [y for y, x in sorted(zip(results_list.values(),
results_list.keys()))]
x_pos = [i for i, _ in enumerate(x_plot)]
plt.barh(x_pos, y_plot, color="royalblue")
plt.ylabel("Model")
plt.xlabel("Accuracy")
plt.yticks(x_pos, x_plot)
plt.show()
```

Figure 12.11 Performance comparison of SVMs with different kernels

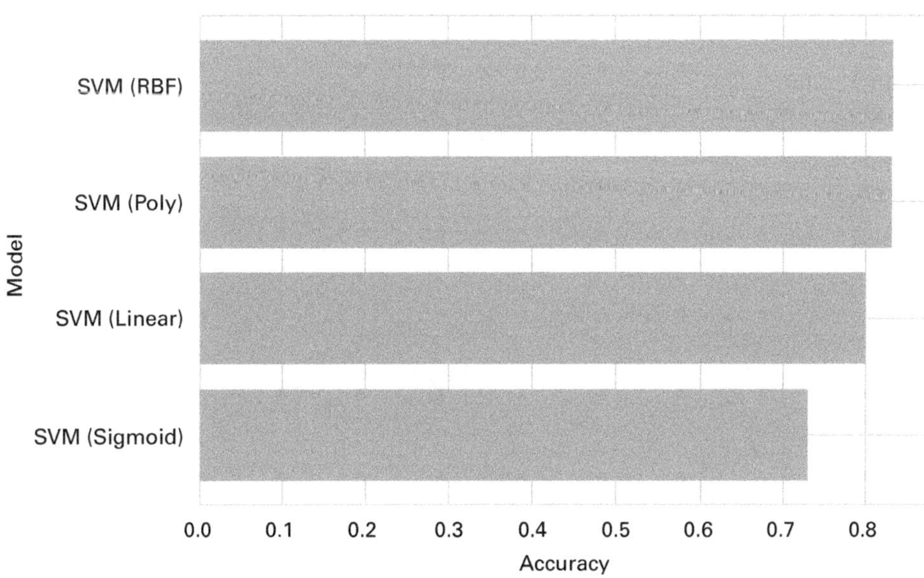

12.7 SVMs for Regression

As mentioned earlier, SVMs were initially developed for classification tasks but their concept was extended to deal with regression tasks. This extension then is called the *Support Vector Regression (SVR)*. Similar to other regression models, the SVR aims to fit a line (or hyperplane in higher dimensions) as close as possible to the data points, rather than separating them. Here the SVR focuses on finding a function that approximates the relationship between input variables and a continuous target variable while minimizing the prediction error within a specified tolerance. It introduces an ε *-tube* around the regression line, and data points within this tube are considered correct predictions and incur no penalty.

In Figure 12.12, the orange line represents the regression line, and the shaded grey area around the regression line represents the ε-tube, which defines a margin of tolerance within which deviations from the regression line are not penalized. In other words, errors within this margin are acceptable and do not contribute to the loss function.

$$\min_{w,b} \left\{ \frac{1}{2} \| \boldsymbol{w} \|^2 + C \sum_{n=1}^{N} l_\varepsilon (y_n - f(x_n)) \right\},$$

where $C > 0$ is a regularization constant, and $l_\varepsilon(\cdot)$ is the ε *-insensitive loss function*, given by

$$l_\varepsilon(y_n - f(x_n)) = \begin{cases} 0, & \text{if } | y_n - f(x_n) | \leq \varepsilon, \\ y_n - f(x_n) - \varepsilon, & \text{if } | y_n - f(x_n) | > \varepsilon, \end{cases}$$

where $\varepsilon > 0$ is an adjusting parameter.

Figure 12.12 SVM for regression

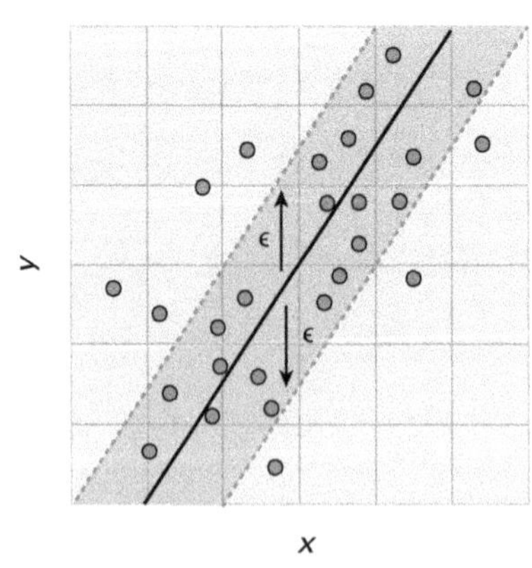

Figure 12.13 Comparison of the squared loss and ε-insensitive loss functions

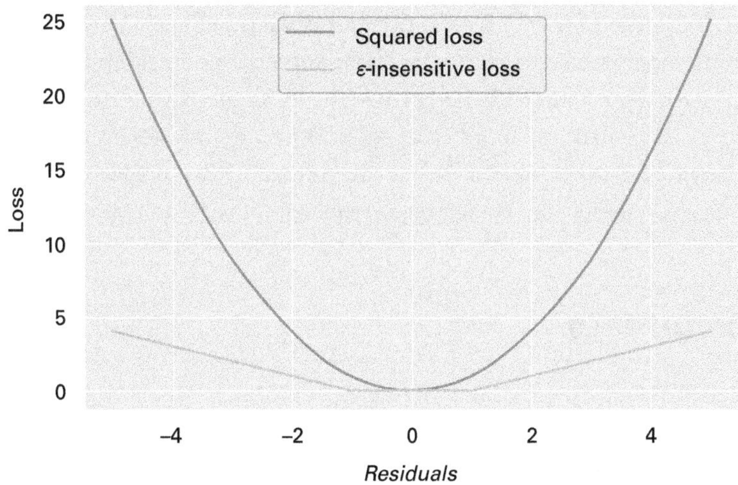

In the SVR, the choice of ε-insensitive loss function plays a crucial role in determining the model's behaviour and robustness as it introduces a margin of tolerance ε around the predicted value, within which no penalty is applied for errors. This allows the model to focus on significant deviations while ignoring minor discrepancies, making it more robust to noise and small fluctuations in the data. In contrast, as demonstrated in Figure 12.13, the squared loss function, which penalizes the square of the prediction error, is more sensitive to outliers and treats all errors proportionally to their magnitude. While squared loss emphasizes reducing large errors by penalizing them more heavily, ε-insensitive loss is better suited for applications where minor prediction errors can be tolerated, enabling a sparse and interpretable model in SVR.

Similar to SVM classification, slack variables can be added and SVR can also use kernel functions to handle non-linear relationships by mapping input features into higher-dimensional spaces where a linear regression function can be fit. Commonly used kernels include the linear, polynomial, and RBF. More in-depth discussions can be found in Bishop (2006), Deisenroth et al. (2020), and Murphy (2022).

12.8 Implementing SVR in Python

In terms of SVR implementation, the scikit-learn library provides three classes: *SVR*, *LinearSVR*, and *NuSVR*. The *SVR* class is the most widely used, supporting both linear and non-linear regression through kernel functions. Its versatility is enhanced by customizable parameters like the penalty term *C*, kernel type, and ε-insensitive loss margin, making it suitable for various regression tasks. For large datasets where linearity suffices, the *LinearSVR* class offers specialized efficiency by eschewing kernel functions. Compared to *SVR* with a linear kernel, it often exhibits faster training times. Alternatively, the *NuSVR* class provides a different parameterization using the *nu* parameter to control the number of support vectors and tolerance margin. This suite of classes empowers users to select the optimal SVR implementation based on factors such as computational efficiency, model complexity, and data characteristics.

12.9 Summary

SVMs are a popular type of supervised learning algorithms applicable to both regression and classification tasks. They excel in identifying the optimal hyperplane that segregates distinct classes within the input data, maximizing the margin between these classes and thereby establishing a clear decision boundary. This chapter has primarily concentrated on employing SVMs for classification purposes. The scikit-learn library in Python offers an extensive array of options for implementing SVM classifiers and regressors. Although the latter were not covered in this chapter, their application is quite similar to that of classifiers.

SVMs possess several advantages. They are well-suited to data in high-dimensional spaces and are memory-efficient during the prediction phase. Furthermore, they can manage non-linear data through the use of kernels. Nonetheless, selecting the appropriate kernel and interpreting the decisions made by SVMs can present challenges. Moreover, training SVMs can be computationally demanding for extensive datasets. Overall, SVMs are an excellent option for a variety of machine learning challenges, yet their limitations in terms of interpretability and training costs should be taken into account.

12.10 Exercise

This exercise revisits the consumer segmentation project in Chapter 8. You will develop an SVM to recommend summer events to the booked customers for a seaside resort company. Use the *holiday_rental_consumer_segmentation.csv* file, which contains 191 bookings with features such as price, size, bedrooms, bathrooms, floor, car parking, internet, location, pet, and the target variable is event. Since many classification models have been covered so far, it would be beneficial to compare the SVM against logistic regression, MLP, decision tree, random forest, AdaBoost, gradient boosting decision tree, Naïve Bayes, and KNN.

13 Principal Component Analysis

Principal component analysis (PCA) is a method to reduce data dimensions. As discussed in Chapter 4 on data wrangling, dimensions refer to the number of features or explanatory variables of our dataset. Why is reducing the number of explanatory variables useful? One could argue that having access to large datasets with many features (explanatory variables) in the age of big data should be beneficial. For instance, Tesco, the largest retailer in the UK, offers a Clubcard, which generates data based on customers' transactions. The Clubcard records more than 20 million daily transactions, which can be used to predict sales and optimize inventory management. Tesco stocks about 90,000 different products in its stores. Do we need sales data for all products to build forecasting models or is a subset sufficient?

LESS IS MORE

Principal component analysis is a powerful machine learning tool to reduce the number of variables needed to capture the information in a dataset.

More is not always better. First, explanatory variables might be highly correlated (e.g. substitutes or complements). Multicollinearity affects our ability to identify partial impacts of explanatory variables. This is not necessarily an issue if we aim to maximize model fit and predictability. However, including too many highly correlated explanatory variables is inefficient, as little information is added. The models might contain a considerable number of redundant variables. Second, model parameters are less stable if many explanatory variables enter the model. Simplifying models by reducing the number of parameters tends to be a good strategy. Third, speed and data storage might become an issue. These problems matter under certain conditions (e.g. trading algorithms, IT infrastructure).

An important application of dimensionality reduction refers to index construction. For instance, you could attempt to construct a 'healthy eating' index based on data on food consumption collected from surveys. Many indices – even widely applied measures – are poorly constructed. For instance, it is common to use equally weighted variables in index construction. A prominent example is the Human Development Index (HDI), which combines life expectancy, education, and gross domestic product (GDP) per capita into a single index value. Initially, an arithmetic mean was calculated, suggesting equal weighting of each dimension. Since 2010, a geometric mean has been used, and individual scores are derived differently. However, major issues remain, including how many dimensions are sufficient and which dimensions are more important.

PCA and related methods can address these limitations. In particular, we can derive weights (measures of importance) associated with each dimension. Moreover, the analysis provides tools that can be used to determine a sufficient number of so-called principal components. These principal components contain the key features of the data. How many dimensions are required to obtain a 'good understanding' of our dataset? Can we build a forecasting model using a much smaller number of principal components? Are these models more stable over time?

PCA tackles the problem that 'less is often more' in forecasting. Note that more dimensions mean that more parameters need to be estimated. Over time, these estimates tend to undergo fluctuations. Hence, parameter stability is an issue in many applications. It is common that models' predictability improves after applying PCA to reduce dimensions. PCA identifies (linear) patterns in data based on correlations between variables. It finds directions of maximum variance in high-dimensional data. Orthogonal axes (principal components) of a new subspace are directions of maximum variance. This chapter will explore these issues in detail. We will briefly explain the underlying theory and its implementation in Python and showcase the interpretation of results.

There are three commonly used methods to reduce dimensions. PCA only requires access to the data matrix $\mathbf{X}$. Hence, labels or a target variable $\mathbf{y}$ is unknown (and not needed). This approach refers to unsupervised learning, which differs from many machine learning tools covered thus far in the book. Basically, unknown features of the data are revealed through machine learning without our guidance. Other methods include linear discriminant analysis (LDA), which refers to supervised learning. LDA has many applications in financial services to assess default risk. Finally, the kernel principal component analysis (KPCA) is a non-linear method for more complicated problems. There are many closely related methods (e.g. Factor Analysis), but they do differ in subtle ways.

After a brief discussion of the theory and unsupervised learning, this chapter explores their applications in business analytics, such as index construction in the context of risk management. In summary, you will learn the following after completing this chapter:

- Knowing the main aspects of different types of learning.
- Understanding the underlying theory of PCA.
- Conducting a PCA analysis using NumPy.

- Using *scikit-learn* to derive principal components.
- Interpreting the outputs of PCA.
- Identifying the number of principal components required to capture the main features of data.

13.1 Unsupervised Learning

Thus far, the methods presented in this book required a target (dependent) variable y, which might be continuous, binary or categorical. For instance, the typical classification problem (e.g. whether a firm will default or survive) provides labels (e.g. binary outcomes). These labels constitute our dependent variable $\mathbf{y}$. To train our model, the dependent and a set of independent variables are required. For instance, a logistic regression takes a binary dependent variable and a data matrix $\mathbf{X}$ with k independent variables and a constant term. This setting is an example of supervised learning as the correct labels are provided. The model is trained and later used to classify test data. Hence, we know whether the model makes correct or incorrect predictions.

NO NEED TO TELL ME

Unsupervised learning means that we do not provide the true labels (dependent variable in a classification problem). The machine applies an algorithm to the data and identifies structures.

PCA does not require supervision, i.e. we do not have to present a dependent variable with classifications (labels). PCA can detect the 'main features' of the data based on correlations between all variables in the dataset. In this process, the problem is simplified as redundant information (i.e. correlated variables) is identified. The following section explains the underlying theory in more detail. Understanding the theory is useful but not essential. Hence, this section can be skipped at the first reading.

13.2 The Theory of PCA

The main idea is to reduce the number of dimensions (or features or explanatory variables) without losing essential information. Say we start with k dimensions in our original dataset. The idea is to transform our original dataset into a new feature subspace with dimension $l = k$. The transformation should preserve the main characteristics of the initial data. The transformed data can be used for further machine learning applications without the need to resort to the much larger original dataset. Hence, this process mitigates data storage requirements. Do we lose some information after transformation? Well, some information will be lost, but will it be essential? How can PCA 'learn' about the main features of a dataset?

Let's explore the steps moving from the original data to the principal components in more detail. The dataset has N observations labelled $i=1,\ldots,N$. Each observation has k features (explanatory variables or dimensions) written as a column vector $x_i = [x_{1i},\ldots,x_{1k}]^T$, where T refers to the transpose. The transpose of these N column vectors x_i could be regarded as rows in data matrix $\mathbf{X}$ with dimension $N \times k$. Note that PCA is sensitive to scaling; hence, the data matrix $\mathbf{X}$ needs to be standardized. You will see this step in the section on the implementation in Python.

The objective is to find a suitable transformation matrix $\mathbf{W}$ with dimension $k \times l$ with $l = k$ such that equation (13.1) holds.

$$z_i = \begin{bmatrix} z_{1i} \\ \vdots \\ z_{ki} \end{bmatrix} = x_i W \tag{13.1}$$

How do we find this transformation matrix $\mathbf{W}$? To proceed, we need to understand the eigendecomposition of a matrix. The following refers to the definition of eigenvectors and eigenvalues. The vector $\mathbf{v}$ is an eigenvector of a square $n \times n$ matrix $\mathbf{A}$ if it satisfies the linear equation (13.2), where λ is the associated eigenvalue of the eigenvector v.

$$Av = \lambda v \tag{13.2}$$

From linear algebra, we know that a real symmetric matrix, such as a covariance matrix, has real eigenvalues, and eigenvectors can be chosen such that they are orthogonal. Hence, these eigenvectors are uncorrelated by construction. Furthermore, a real symmetric matrix $\mathbf{A}$ can be decomposed as shown in equation (13.3).

$$A = Q \Lambda Q^T \tag{13.3}$$

In equation (13.3), Q refers to a matrix whose columns are orthogonal eigenvectors of $\mathbf{A}$, and Λ is a diagonal matrix whose entries are the eigenvalues of $\mathbf{A}$, illustrated in (13.4).

$$\Lambda = \begin{bmatrix} \lambda_1 & 0 & 0 & \ldots & 0 \\ 0 & \lambda_2 & 0 & \ldots & 0 \\ \vdots & \vdots & \vdots & \ldots & \vdots \\ 0 & 0 & 0 & \ldots & \lambda_n \end{bmatrix} \tag{13.4}$$

The PCA algorithm works as follows. First, we standardize the original dataset with k dimensions, i.e. we subtract the mean of variables and divide by their standard deviations. It should be noted that we need to be careful when working with time series data (e.g. non-stationary time series). Standardization is only meaningful when applied to stationary time series.

Second, we obtain the covariance matrix with dimension $k \times k$. By definition, the covariance matrix is real and symmetric. Third, we decompose the covariance matrix into its eigenvalues and eigenvectors in line with equation (13.3). Then, we sort the eigenvalues, starting with the largest. Finally, we derive the projection matrix $\mathbf{W}$ from the eigenvectors associated with the largest eigenvalues.

How are dimensions reduced in this process? Of course, we start with a covariance matrix of dimension $k \times k$. The eigendecomposition of the covariance matrix results in k eigenvalues, which we sort. The sorted eigenvalues provide a measure of their relative importance in terms of variance, which basically means information. Hence, we select a small number of important eigenvalues l, which reduces our dimension from k to l. Then, the data is transformed in line with equation (13.1), resulting in a subspace of dimension l. Now, let's see this method in action – back to Python.

PCA'S HISTORY

PCA predates the emergence of machine learning in the 1950s. Harold Hotelling developed PCA in 1933; however, earlier versions can be traced back to 1840 (Farebrother, 2022).

13.3 Implementation in Python

Many surveys contain a large number of variables. The Living Costs and Food Survey conducted in the UK is a good example, given its various applications in business, policy, and research. The full dataset can be obtained from the UK Data Service in various formats. A free registration is required via their website (https://ukdataservice.ac.uk/). The original dataset is downloaded in a data format, which can be opened in Stata, a commercial data analysis software. If you want to replicate this step, you can find a Stata do file to download from our website. We select a subset of the data, focusing on food purchases in large supermarkets. A data file containing 95 variables that capture the consumption of various food items is stored.

```
cd "C:\Users\..."
use "lcfs_2021_dvhh_ukanon.dta", clear
keep *L
save "data_import.dta", replace
```

We start with several import statements for Pandas, NumPy, and several additional objects from scikit-learn.

```
import pandas as pd
import numpy as np
from sklearn.model_selection import train_test_split
from sklearn.preprocessing import StandardScaler
```

Pandas can work with a wide range of data formats, including *dta* files. The following code imports Pandas and reads the *dta* dataset. The data is stored as a Pandas *DataFrame*. Inspecting the *DataFrame* shows 95 dimensions (variables on food consumption) based on 5,632 observations.

```
df = pd.read_stata('data_import.dta')
print(df.head())
```

Depending on your text editor or IDE, you might observe an error message stating that the data file was not found. This might occur even if the *dta* file is stored in the same folder as the Python script. To address this issue, we change the directory using the Python *os* library as follows.

```
import os
path = r'C:\Users\User\...'
os.chdir(path)
```

We define the data matrix **X**, which refers to the whole Pandas *DataFrame*. Note that we use the attribute *values* to convert the Pandas *DataFrame* into a *NumPy array*.

```
X = df.values
```

Next, we split the sample into 70% training and 30% test data using the *train_test_split()* function. Usually, we would use the function based on a predefined dependent variable y, which contains the classifications. In unsupervised learning, we do not have or need access to a dependent variable y. Moreover, the stratification of our random sample is not meaningful, as categories are not given.

```
X_train, X_test, y_train, y_test =
                train_test_split(X, y, test_size=0.3,
                stratify=y, random_state=0)
```

Instead, we only specify the data matrix, which provides the random sampling with the required split.

```
X_train, X_test =
    train_test_split(X, test_size=0.3, random_state=0)
```

Finally, we standardize the data using the *StandardScaler()* class.

```
sc = StandardScaler()
X_train_std = sc.fit_transform(X_train)
X_test_std = sc.transform(X_test)
```

To conduct the eigendecomposition of the covariance matrix, we first calculate the covariance matrix for the standardized variables in the data matrix **X**, which belongs to the training dataset. Note that the data matrix **X** has dimension $N \times k$. Hence, the transpose is needed to ensure that the covariance has the correct dimension $k \times k$. Using the linear algebra package, we derive the eigenvalues and their associated eigenvectors. A subsection of the eigenvectors defines our principal components. To determine the required number of principal components, we need a measure of importance, i.e. we determine the relative contribution of each component to the total variance.

```
cov_mat = np.cov(X_train_std.T)
eigen_vals, eigen_vecs = np.linalg.eigh(cov_mat)
print('\nEigenvalues \n%s' % eigen_vals)
```

The sum of all eigenvalues is equal to the total explained variance of the original data. Using the *sum()* function, we determine the total variance denoted *tot*. List comprehension offers an elegant way to provide a list of explained variances *i/tot* based on sorted eigenvalues. Note that each principal component's contribution to explaining the total variance refers to its eigenvalue relative to the total explained variance. The NumPy *np.cumsum()* function refers to a cumulative sum starting with one element and adding the next.

The first principal component explains 10.9% of the total variance, followed by the second, which accounts for 3.1%. Subsequent components drop in relevance to around 1%. Hence, combining two principal components captures 14.0% of the total variance. For many applications, this seems to be too low. Accordingly, a higher number of principal components might be required.

```
tot = sum(eigen_vals)
var_exp = [(i / tot) for i in sorted(eigen_vals,
reverse=True)]
cum_var_exp = np.cumsum(var_exp)
```

To illustrate the method, we select only the two most important principal components. The associated eigenvectors define the transformation matrix **W**. Again, using list comprehension, we organize eigenvalues and associated eigenvectors into tuples.

```
eigen_pairs = [(np.abs(eigen_vals[i]), eigen_vecs[:, i])
               for i in range(len(eigen_vals))]
```

Then, we sort the (eigenvalue, eigenvector) tuples from high to low and select the eigenvectors associated with the two largest eigenvalues. These define the transformation matrix **W**.

```
eigen_pairs.sort(key=lambda k: k[0], reverse=True)
w = np.hstack((eigen_pairs[0][1][:, np.newaxis],
               eigen_pairs[1][1][:, np.newaxis]))
print('Matrix W:\n', w)
```

Finally, we transform the data using a dot product and our transformation matrix **W**. Note that PCA was conducted based on the training data. We apply the same transformation matrix **W** to the test data.

```
X_train_pca = X_train_std.dot(w)
X_test_pca = X_test_std.dot(w)
```

PCA will perform well if the variables exhibit similar moments, which affects standardization and the covariance structure. This is not guaranteed and requires careful testing. In particular, when working with time series data, stochastic trends can lead to considerable changes in the covariance structure. This affects the reliability of PCA.

13.4 Alternative Implementation

Can we run PCA in *scikit-learn*? Yes, we can and hence reduce our work considerably. We use the *PCA* class based on our standardized training data *X_train_std*. The explained variance can be derived directly. Note that additional import statements are required for the alternative implementation.

```
from sklearn.decomposition import PCA
import matplotlib.pyplot as plt
```

The following code replicates our previous implementation.

```
pca = PCA()
X_train_pca = pca.fit_transform(X_train_std)
exp_var = pca.explained_variance_ratio_
```

Figure 13.1 Scatter plot of data after transformation

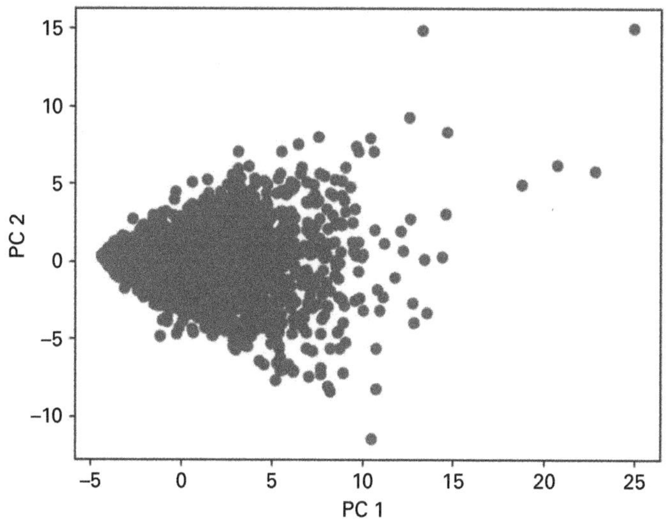

We can define the number of principal components needed and can change it easily. For instance, focusing on two principal components, the data is transformed. Finally, we can plot the data based on two principal components using a scatter plot.

```
pca = PCA(n_components=2)
X_train_pca = pca.fit_transform(X_train_std)
X_test_pca = pca.transform(X_test_std)
plt.scatter(X_train_pca[:, 0], X_train_pca[:, 1])
plt.xlabel('PC 1')
plt.ylabel('PC 2')
plt.savefig("PCA_transformed.png")
plt.show()
```

Figure 13.1 shows the scatter plot in the two-dimensional subspace. Sometimes, it is possible to identify clusters, but in this example, the explained variance remains at 14.0%, which is insufficient for most applications. Outliers should be considered, as discussed in Chapter 4. These might affect the reliability of PCA. Finally, Figure 13.1 indicates that *PCA 2* exhibits a higher variance with higher values of *PC 1*.

13.5 Visualization and Interpretation of PCA

PCA simplifies our higher-dimensional problem to a low-dimensional problem. It is often useful to plot the cumulative explained variance as a function of the number of principal components. We use the NumPy function *np.arange()* to construct the x-axis of the figure, i.e. counting the number of eigenvalues. The list of (eigenvalue, eigenvector) tuples is sorted by eigenvalues, and we focus on the largest 15 eigenvalues for the purpose of visualization. We plot the sorted eigenvalues and their explanatory power in terms of explained variance using a bar chart. The explained variance associated with the largest 15 eigenvalues is selected using slicing, *var_exp[:max_num]*. Note that *plt.step()* refers to a step function, which depicts the cumulative explained variance.

```
#Visualization and interpretation of PCA
#Max number of principal components
max_num = 15

#Construct x axis
x = np.arange(max_num)

plt.bar(x, var_exp[:max_num], alpha=0.5, align='center',
         label='Explained variance')
plt.step(x, cum_var_exp[:max_num], where='mid',
          label='Cumulative explained variance')
plt.ylabel('Explained variance')
plt.xlabel('Principal component')
plt.legend(loc='best')
plt.tight_layout()
plt.savefig('PCA_variance.png', dpi=300)
plt.show()
```

ALTERNATIVE IMPLEMENTATIONS

Given PCA's long history, there are many alternative implementations in other programming languages such as *Matlab* or *R* as well as statistical software packages, including *SPSS* and *Stata*.

Figure 13.2 Proportion of explained variance

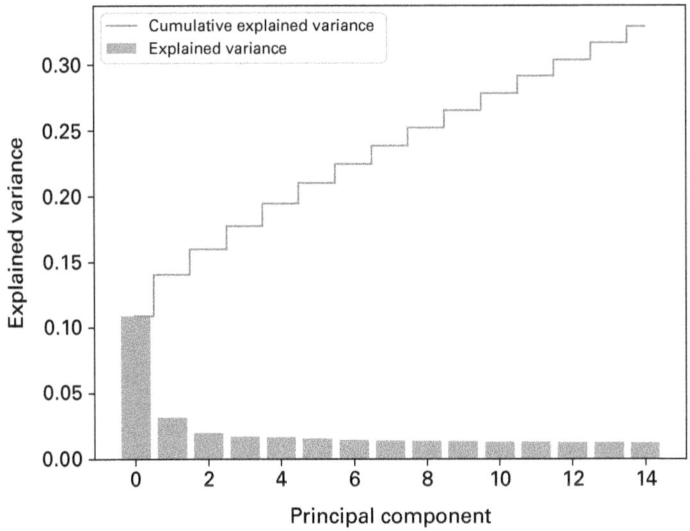

In many applications, restricting us to a few eigenvalues and their associated eigenvectors is sufficient to explain a large proportion of the total variance. However, as you can see from Figure 13.2, we need many principal components to capture the essential information contained in the original dataset. How many principal components are needed?

Answering this question will depend on the purpose of the model, which uses the principal components. For a classification problem (e.g. households in food poverty), a small number of principal components might be sufficient to separate the subgroups. In practice, there are many rules of thumb ranging from 85% to 95% of the explained variance.

An alternative visualization uses the sorted eigenvalues directly. This refers to a scree plot, which shows the eigenvalues on the vertical axis and the component number on the x-axis. Of course, the information provided is similar compared to plotting the explained variance. In our code, we use slicing with step –1 to reverse the order of the eigenvalues stored in the array *eigen_vals*.

```
plt.plot(eigen_vals[::-1])
plt.ylabel('Eigenvalue')
plt.xlabel('Component number')
plt.savefig('PCA_screeplot.png', dpi=300)
plt.show()
```

Figure 13.3 Scree plot

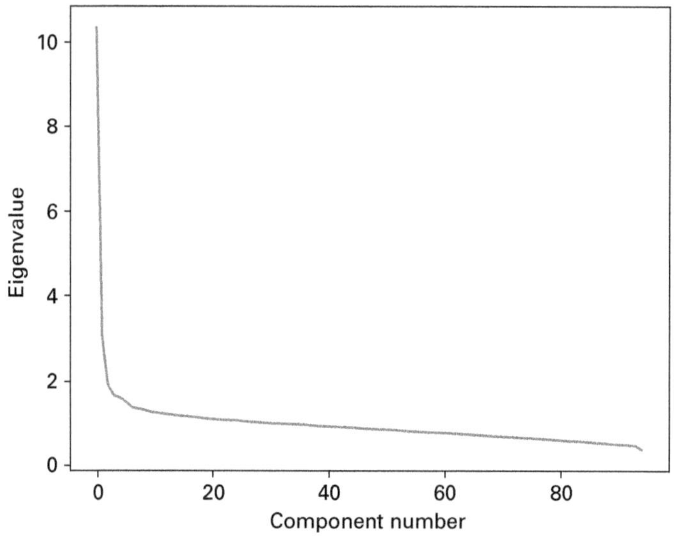

In most applications, eigenvalues drop very quickly to values below one. However, in our example, the decline is less pronounced, as shown in Figure 13.3.

13.6 Index Construction

In business applications, it is common to use indices to measure certain risks or other outcomes. Examples include ESG indices (environmental, social, and governance), the ease of doing business index, and climate risk indices, to name a few. One can regard an index as an extreme form of PCA, as all the information is contained in a single component.

Pesqué-Cela et al. (2021) discuss index construction in the context of measuring financial inclusion. They outline the main shortcomings of common indices. First, most indices seem to be constructed ad hoc without any data analysis. For instance, how many variables should be considered in an index? Second, the weights of each variable tend to be exogenous in the sense that weights are not based on the data.

Accordingly, one could use PCA to derive optimal weights, making the index endogenous and responsive to the data. Moreover, PCA could demonstrate the proportion of the explained variance captured by an index, i.e. a single principal component.

Finally, alternative methods related to Factor Analysis might be even better suited to address the construction of indices. As outlined by Pesqué-Cela et al. (2021), Confirmatory Factor Analysis, which is theory-driven, can be useful if the aim is to measure social constructs, i.e. latent (unobserved) variables. In this case, working with measurement models that permit error terms is the better approach compared to PCA.

The exercise highlights the use of PCA to construct indices that capture climate risk. PCA provides endogenous weights and indicates whether using a single index is adequate to capture climate-related risk factors.

13.7 Summary

This chapter introduced PCA and its applications in business analytics, including index construction and dimensionality reduction. PCA differs from other machine learning tools, which we have covered so far in the book, in that PCA does not require a dependent variable. PCA explores the data without further guidance, which refers to unsupervised learning.

PCA can be implemented in NumPy and *scikit-learn*. Before using these approaches, however, the data needs to be standardized. If variables are observed over time, standardization requires stationarity. This needs to be confirmed before PCA. In many applications, PCA is able to capture the information (i.e. the variance) of the data using a small subset of dimensions. Reducing dimensions tends to enhance parameter stability and, hence, the reliability of predictions.

TO REDUCE OR NOT TO REDUCE

Reducing dimensions can be useful in data visualization and model simplifications. The latter tends to lead to more reliable parameter estimates. However, principal components might be more difficult to interpret if the analysis aims to identify partial impacts of certain factors (e.g. price elasticity).

13.8 Exercise

This exercise applies PCA in the context of climate risk assessment. You will start with a large number of variables and use PCA to reduce dimensions. There are seven tasks as outlined below. The solutions provide codes and outputs, which are discussed in detail.

13.8.1 Data Import

Import the data from the CSV file *vul_data.csv* into Python. Using our new tools in the area of dimensionality reduction, we will attempt to construct an index that captures a country's exposure to climate risk. Please note that there are missing values (denoted nan). After importing the data, remove missing values from your Pandas *DataFrame*.

13.8.2 Define the Target Variable

The target variable is a dummy variable for countries at high risk, defined as being in the top 10% of all cases based on the variable VUL (ND-GAIN climate vulnerability index). HINT: define the top 10% quantile (name the variable high) and then define a -1/+1 dummy to flag high-risk countries. It is best practice to use y to denote the target variable.

13.8.3 Define a Set of Explanatory Variables

Now we define our data matrix X. We select all variables except VUL, N_VUL, and the identifiers for year and country.

13.8.4 Splitting the Sample

Now split the sample into 70% training and 30% test data. Finally, you need to standardize the data.

13.8.5 Calculate the Covariance Matrix and Eigenvalues

Next, calculate the covariance matrix and eigenvalues. How much of the observed variance is explained by the first principal component?

13.8.6 Plot Eigenvalues

Plot the eigenvalues and their explanatory power in terms of explained variance.

13.8.7 Transform the Data

Now, transform the data and plot the first two principal components. Can we separate the sub-groups with a straight line?

14 Cluster Analysis

Many methods covered in this book implicitly or explicitly assume that observations are independent of one another. For instance, regression analysis makes the assumption that residuals, i.e. the unexplained component, are random. All patterns contained in the data should be explained by the linear model. Crucially, observations should be identically and independently distributed (i.i.d. distributed). Frequently, this assumption is violated, affecting the reliability of ordinary least squares (OLS) estimates (e.g. significance tests).

Cluster analysis, in contrast, seeks patterns in a data set. Observations might be 'similar' and, hence, appear to be 'clustered'. There are many ways to define similarity or the lack of it, which we call distance. Cluster analysis does not require labelled data and can be considered unsupervised machine learning. At first glance, one might think that cluster analysis is similar to principal component analysis (PCA). Both methods do not rely on labelled data and try to detect patterns in a data set. However, the purpose differs. Principal component analysis attempts to reduce dimensions, capturing the essential features of a data set. Starting with a large set of explanatory variables (dimensions), PCA projects the data onto a much smaller number of principal components. In contrast, cluster analysis uses the current number of dimensions to determine the distance between observations. Observations that are close to each other form a cluster. In fact, cluster analysis often follows after a PCA reduces dimensions.

Cluster analysis has many applications in business analytics, including marketing (e.g. market segmentation), strategy (e.g. grand strategy clusters), and finance (e.g. forecasting and portfolio management). This chapter explores several applications for financial data to illustrate the use of cluster analysis following the research by Nanda et al. (2010), Aghabozorgi and Teh (2014), Babu et al. (2012), and Jaroonchokanan et al. (2022).

We start with the K-means algorithm, which we apply to cluster a data set of companies based on their financial or stock market performance. To obtain financial data, we use an API connected to Yahoo Finance. The Python package yfinance provides a convenient way to download financial data from Yahoo Finance using Python. APIs tend to undergo frequent changes which are not under our control. Hence, it is advisable to install the Python package yfinance in a virtual environment. This enables us to control the version and dependencies.

By default, clustering methods tend to be binary, i.e. an observation is either in a cluster or not. However, alternative methods based on fuzzy logic have emerged, such as Fuzzy C-means. We briefly outline this alternative approach. Finally, we present various methods to assess the validity of a cluster analysis. This is an essential step to ensure that your approach is reliable. In summary, you will learn the following after completing this chapter:

- Understanding the underlying theory of cluster analysis.
- The implementation of cluster analysis.
- Using scikit-learn to conduct cluster analysis.
- The validity of clusters using various indices to assess partitions.
- The application of cluster analysis to financial data.
- The limitations of cluster analysis in the context of portfolio management.

14.1 What is Cluster Analysis?

Let us assume that we have N observations and observe Q characteristics (e.g. income, credit card loans, home ownership, etc.). In general, the idea of clustering is as follows: observations within a cluster are similar, whereas observations that belong to different clusters are different. Algorithms differ in two main ways. First, how do we measure similarity or difference? Put differently, how do we define the distance between observations? Second, do we make a binary choice, i.e. is an observation either a member of the cluster or not a member, where membership is mutually exclusive? Alternatively, we can allow a fuzzy approach, i.e. observations can be in different clusters with varying degrees of belonging.

Next, we must decide or derive an 'optimal' number of clusters. Selecting too many clusters limits the usefulness of this approach, whereas selecting too few clusters might oversimplify the underlying patterns in our data. In many applications, theoretical considerations might justify clusters (e.g. cultural proximity in country-pair data for international trade flows).

Depending on the data structure (e.g. panel data), dynamics might need to be considered. Put differently, do observations move between clusters over time? How stable are clusters? These issues matter in the context of financial markets as most parameters exhibit time-varying behaviours (e.g. time-varying beta coefficients).

The next section provides a step-by-step guide for downloading data from companies' income statements and balance sheets before exploring different types of cluster analysis, starting with K-means. After considerable data wrangling in Pandas, we obtain a dataset covering the top 30 US-listed companies and their characteristics.

THE HISTORY OF CLUSTER ANALYSIS

The idea to identify observations that share similarities between them and group them into clusters originated in the 1930s. Early studies emerged in psychology and anthropology.

14.2 Data from Yahoo Finance

Chapter 4 on data wrangling introduced Yahoo Finance and the use of APIs. However, we focused only on share price data. The API has a lot more to offer, including data covering financials reported on companies' income statements and balance sheets. Before we proceed, it is a sensible idea to create and activate a new virtual environment, which we call Finance. Chapter 3, on Getting Started with Python, explains virtual environments and the use of the pip installer in more detail.

```
python -m venv Finance
Finance\Scripts\activate
pip install yfinance
```

We also install Pandas in our virtual environment. After the installations, we test our setup by requesting Microsoft's income statement.

```
import yfinance as yf
import pandas as pd
import numpy as np

#Test our installation
msft = yf.Ticker("MSFT")

#Income statement of Microsoft
df = msft.income_stmt
print(pdf.head())

print(type(df))
```

Our output confirms that the downloaded data refers to a Pandas *DataFrame*. Hence, our setup is completed successfully. Next, we need to define our sample. It is common to target a stock market index as a benchmark for portfolio analysis. We select the Dow Jones Industrial Average Stock Index with 30 constituents. Before we select variables (dimensions) for our cluster analysis, we need an overview of the available data. Hence, we download a sample dataset using the info attribute, which refers to a Python dictionary. Additional data, including historical data, is also available. However, the info attribute should be sufficient for our cluster analysis.

```
#All information on a ticker
print(msft.info)
```

We select a measure of size based on market capitalization (i.e. the number of shares outstanding times the current share price), marketCap (Mcap). We add profitability measures, including profit margins (profitMargins (Margin)), the return on assets (returnOnAssets (ROA)), and the return on equity (returnOnEquity (ROE)). To complement these accounting-based performance measures, we also obtain the market value of equity relative to the book value of equity (priceToBook (PTB)). This is a market-based multiple used in company valuation. Finally, we download beta coefficients (beta (Beta)), which capture the systematic risk of stocks based on the capital asset pricing model (CAPM).

The list *dj_list* contains the 30 constituents of the Dow Jones Industrial Average Stock Index. Starting with an empty Pandas *DataFrame*, the for loop runs through the list of 30 stocks. An instance of the class *Ticker()* is created, and the info attribute is applied, which provides all data in a dictionary. Next, we convert the dictionary into a Pandas *DataFrame* using the *pd.DataFrame.from_dict()* function. Note that the default setting is that the keys of the passed dictionary become the columns of the resulting *DataFrame*. The orientation of the data can be adjusted; however, the default setting is suitable for our data structure. Finally, each ticker's temporary *DataFrame* is appended to *dj_data*. The most recent data refers to the first row, which is selected using the *iloc[[0]]* method.

```
#Start with empty DataFrame
dj_data = pd.DataFrame()

for ticker in dj_list:
    #Create Ticker() instance
    ticker_inst = yf.Ticker(ticker)
    #Convert from dictionary to DataFrame
    temp = pd.DataFrame.from_dict(ticker_inst.info)
    #Take most recent data(first row)
    #Add and update main data
    dj_data = pd.concat([dj_data, temp.iloc[[0]]])
```

We select six variables and the ticker symbol. Market capitalization is expressed in USD billions and transformed using a natural logarithm. The latter is common in addressing outliers and the skewness of the size distribution. Finally, missing values are dropped, and the index is adjusted.

```
#List of variables
var_list = [
    'symbol',
    'marketCap',
    'profitMargins',
    'priceToBook',
    'returnOnAssets',
    'returnOnEquity',
    'beta'
    ]

#Replace marketCap in USD billions with log
dj_data['marketCap'] = np.log(dj_data['marketCap']/1000000000)

#Reassign DataFrame based on list of variables
dj_data = dj_data[var_list]

#Remove missing values
dj_data = dj_data.dropna()

#Remove index
dj_data.reset_index(drop = True, inplace = True)
```

This concludes our data download. If required, the *DataFrame* can be used in cluster analysis directly or converted into a NumPy array. The Python script data_download.py replicates these steps.

MORE DATA PLEASE

There are many free data sources available using APIs. Python tends to offer ready-made tools to access the data. Apart from Yahoo Finance, Financial Modeling Prep API offers a range of useful applications for financial data.

14.3 K-means: The Main Idea

K-means is one of the most common algorithms for deriving clusters. It has been applied in many areas, including marketing, finance, and operations research. This section illustrates the main idea of K-means before discussing its implementation in Python.

Say we have N observations labelled $i=1,2,\ldots,N$ and Q dimensions labelled $q=1,2,\ldots,Q$. Hence, observations refer to x_{iq}. Finally, we aim to identify $k=2^m$ clusters, where m is a positive integer. The algorithm starts with a single cluster that contains all observations. The mean vector determines the centre of this initial cluster.

Then, we split this initial cluster into two, and observations are allocated to the two clusters based on their distance from the two centres defined by the mean vectors. The process of splitting and allocating observations continues until $k=2^m$, i.e. our desired number of clusters is reached.

This algorithm is obviously sensitive to outliers as it relies on means. Hence, outlier detection before cluster analysis is an essential step, as outlined in Chapter 4. Moreover, missing values must be addressed using list-wise deletion (common in business applications) or imputation (standard in medical research due to small samples). Next, we explore the implementation in Python.

14.4 K-means: Implementation in Python

K-means can be implemented in Python directly following the description of the algorithm outlined in the previous section. However, scikit-learn offers ready-made classes and functions, which are sufficient for this type of cluster analysis. You might need to install scikit-learn depending on your virtual environment. In addition, we install Matplotlib for data visualization.

```
pip install scikit - learn
pip install matplotlib
```

It is useful to explore descriptive statistics for each variable in the data set prior to cluster analysis. As noted, K-means are sensitive to outliers; hence, inspecting the data is an essential step. If outliers are present (usually defined as values below or above the mean by more than three standard deviations), one might consider a winsorization to mitigate the impact of outliers.

The *describe()* method is applied to the *DataFrame* after removing the column with tickers. Descriptive statistics can be printed on the screen or exported as a LaTeX table. The latter requires the installation of Jinja2, which is a templating engine. Note that you do not need an import statement, but the *stats.to_latex()* function is dependent on Jinja2.

```
pip install Jinja2
```

Apart from printing the LaTeX table on the screen, we also export the output as a txt file, which is easier to import into LaTeX directly. Note that the booktabs package needs to be used in the LaTeX document.

```
#Descriptive statistics
print("\nDescriptive statistics:\n")

#Remove tickers
df = dj_data[var_list[1:]]
stats = df.describe()
print(stats)

#Export as LaTeX table
#This requires Jinja2
#Print to screen
output = stats.to_latex(
  formatters={"name": str.upper},
  float_format="{:.3f}".format,)

print(output)

des_table = open('des_table.txt', 'w')
print(output, file = des_table)
des_table.close()
```

Table 14.1 reports the descriptive statistics. Looking at the standard deviations, minimums, and maximums suggests that outliers should not be a major concern. Each variable exhibits considerable variability in the sample.

Table 14.1 Descriptive statistics

	Mcap	Margin	PTB	ROA	ROE	Beta
mean	5.600	0.149	20.688	0.073	0.686	0.913
std	1.029	0.148	67.313	0.053	2.181	0.329
min	3.724	-0.214	1.271	0.000	-0.711	0.384
25%	5.072	0.058	2.184	0.034	0.115	0.588
50%	5.453	0.120	6.928	0.067	0.218	0.993
75%	6.007	0.234	10.328	0.099	0.368	1.157
max	8.034	0.539	362.089	0.212	11.622	1.416

Finally, we save the *DataFrame* using the *to_pickle()* function as a pickle file for later use. This concludes our work in data_download.py.

```
#Save DataFrame
dj_data.to_pickle("data_cluster.pkl")
```

The Python script k_means.py provides the code for K-means cluster analysis using our data for the 30 constituents of the Dow Jones Industrial Average Stock Index. After list-wise deletion, the dataset contains six financial indicators, as shown in Table 14.1 for 28 stocks.

We start with several import statements, including Matplotlib for data visualization, NumPy, Pandas, and scikit-learn. If you use an older version of Matplotlib (older than version 3.2), an additional import statement is required for 3D figures, import mpl_toolkits.mplot3d.

```
import matplotlib.pyplot as plt
import numpy as np
import pandas as pd
from sklearn.cluster import KMeans
```

We start by loading the pickled data and checking the dataset. Tickers are used to label the data to identify the stocks. As tickers are just identifiers, they do not classify data. Hence, tickers do not contain any information, and we use the cluster analysis as an unsupervised machine learning tool.

```
#Load DataFrame
df = pd.read_pickle("data_cluster.pkl")
print(df)
```

For the purpose of data visualization, we select price-to-book ratios (PTB), beta coefficients (Beta), and return on assets (ROA) after analysing the correlation matrix. These three dimensions contain unique information, whereas other variables exhibit high correlation coefficients. The alternative approach would be to apply a principal component analysis using three principal components. However, the principal components are indices that are not easy to interpret.

```
#We use tickers as labels - no information
y = df['symbol']
X = df.iloc[:, 1:]

#Correlation matrix
print(X.corr())
```

Applying the attribute values to the *DataFrame* results in a NumPy array, which is assigned to **X**. To illustrate the impact of the number of clusters, we use two to five clusters for our data set. These are stored in the list estimators, which contains tuples of names and *KMeans()* instances.

```
#Select ROA, PTB, and Beta
#Convert to NumPy array
X = df[['priceToBook', 'returnOnAssets', 'beta']].values

#Select the number of clusters
estimators = [
    ("k_means_5", KMeans(n_clusters = 5)),
    ("k_means_4", KMeans(n_clusters = 4)),
    ("k_means_3", KMeans(n_clusters = 3)),
    ("k_means_2", KMeans(n_clusters = 2))
]
```

K-means are estimated and plotted in three dimensions. To compare different numbers of clusters, we use four subplots.

```
fig = plt.figure(figsize=(10, 8))
titles = [
    "Five clusters",
    "Four clusters",
    "Three clusters",
    "Two clusters"
    ]
for idx, ((name, est), title) in enumerate(zip(estimators, titles)):
    ax = fig.add_subplot(2, 2, idx + 1,
    projection="3d", elev = 45, azim = 50)
    est.fit(X)
    labels = est.labels_

    scatter = ax.scatter(X[:, 0], X[:, 1], X[:, 2],
    c=labels.astype(float), edgecolor = 'k')
    ax.xaxis.set_ticklabels([])
    ax.yaxis.set_ticklabels([])
    ax.zaxis.set_ticklabels([])
```

```
    ax.set_xlabel("PTB")
    ax.set_ylabel("ROA")
    ax.set_zlabel("Beta")
    ax.set_title(title)

plt.subplots_adjust(wspace = 0.05, hspace = 0.15)
plt.savefig("K_means.png")
plt.show()
```

Figure 14.1 shows our results. It is noted that the observation with the highest price-to-book ratio sits in its own cluster. Hence, even if they might not appear as outliers, extreme values have a pronounced effect on cluster analysis.

Figure 14.1 Different number of clusters using K-means

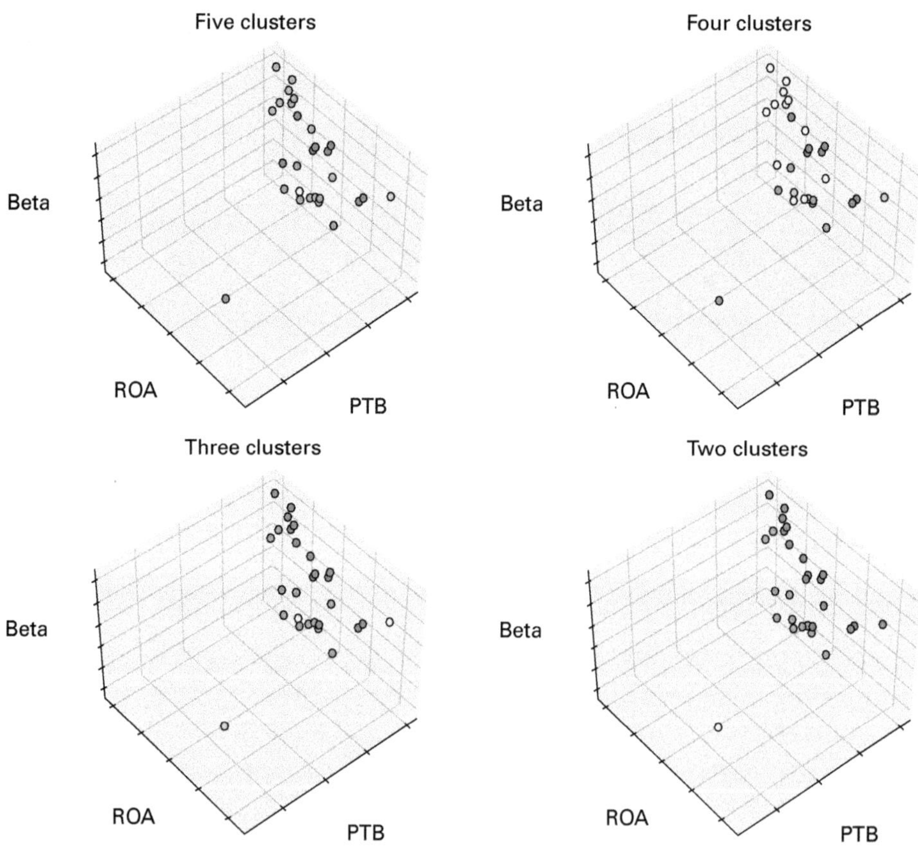

In many applications, K-means offers a useful starting point to explore clusters. However, its inherent limitations need to be considered. The following section provides an alternative approach, which is also applied to financial data based on fuzzy logic (Nanda et al., 2010).

14.5 Fuzzy C-means: The Main Idea

Most clustering methods, including K-means, determine cluster membership in a binary manner, i.e. observations are either in a particular cluster or not. There is no ambiguity. This approach is also called hard clustering.

Fuzzy logic offers an alternative perspective. Cluster membership is not binary but resembles a probability. This approach is called soft clustering. Accordingly, soft clustering algorithms assign a membership degree to each observation.

This section explores a simple algorithm, Fuzzy C-means (or FCM in short), which belongs to this strand of soft clustering methods. Dunn (1973) developed FCM, which was subsequently improved by Bezdek (2013).

FCM starts with an initial membership matrix denoted $U^{(0)}$, which assigns a random membership degree u_{ij} to each observation $j = 1,2,\ldots,N$. Note that $0 \le u_{ij} \le 1$, i.e. membership degrees resemble probabilities. Furthermore, $\sum_i^C u_{ij} = 1$, which states that for each observation j (row in the data matrix) membership degrees for each cluster $i = 1,2,\ldots,C$. The user selects the total number of clusters denoted C. Initially, i.e. at iteration $l = 0$, which is indicated in superscript (0), a random number is generated for each membership degree u_{ij}. To ensure that the condition $\sum_i^C u_{ij} = 1$ holds, we need to normalize the initial membership matrix $U^{(0)}$. We divide each membership degree u_{ij} with the respective row sum, normalizing the matrix as desired. Note that the membership matrix has dimension $N \times C$, where N refers to the number of observations.

We derive cluster centres denoted v_i with $i = 1,2,\ldots,C$ based on the initial membership matrix. It is common to combine the vectors v_i to form the cluster centre matrix V. Note that V has dimension $C \times q$, where q refers to the number of dimensions in the dataset (i.e. the number of variables). So, V captures the mean of each variable for each cluster. To derive cluster centres v_i, we apply the following equation (Zhou et al., 2014), where x_j refers to the j th row of the data matrix X with dimension $N \times q$. Hence, x_j are row vectors, i.e. $1 \times q$.

$$u_i = \frac{\sum_{j=1}^{N} u_{ij}^m x_j}{\sum_{j=1}^{N} u_{ij}^m} \tag{14.1}$$

Equation (14.1) uses the initial membership matrix $U^{(0)}$ to derive the cluster centres v_i, which are combined into the initial cluster centre matrix $V^{(0)}$. This equation refers to a weighted average, where the weights are the membership degrees to the power of m. The parameter $m>1$ refers to the fuzziness parameter. Most commonly, m is in the range $1.1 \leq m \leq 5$ (Zhou et al., 2014). A whole literature dedicated to setting the fuzziness parameter has emerged, and most studies seem to adopt a value of $m=2$, which we use as a default (Zhou et al., 2014).

Next, we determine each observation's Euclidean distance denoted d_{ij} from the cluster centres v_i. In theory, FCM can work with different distance measures as outlined by Eliyanto and Surono (2022). The Euclidean distance is by far the most common choice.

$$d_{ij} = \| x_j - v_i \| \qquad (14.2).$$

Finally, we move to the next iteration of the algorithm denoted $l=1,2,\ldots,L$ and update the membership matrix $U^{(1)}$ as follows.

$$u_{ij} = \frac{1}{\sum_{k=1}^{C} \left(d_{ij} / d_{kj}\right)^{\frac{2}{m-1}}} \qquad (14.3).$$

After updating the membership matrix $U^{(1)}$ based on equation (14.4), we derive the revised cluster centre matrix $V^{(1)}$ using equation (14.1). Distances are updated, followed by the membership matrix $U^{(2)}$. The algorithm continues until the maximum number of iterations L is reached or a stopping criterion is fulfilled.

A stopping criterion could be based on the objective (or loss) function $J(\mathrm{U}^{(l)}, \mathrm{V}^{(l)})$, which we try to minimize by selecting an optimal membership matrix.

$$J\left(\mathrm{U}^{(l)}, \mathrm{V}^{(l)}\right) = \sum_{i=1}^{C} \sum_{j=1}^{N} u_{ij}^{m} d_{ij}^{2}, \quad l = 1,2,\ldots,L \qquad (14.4).$$

It is common to base a stopping criterion on the extent of the adjustment to the membership matrix from iteration l to $l+1$ (Eliyanto and Surono, 2022). If the adjustments drop below a small value denoted ε the algorithm can be stopped.

$$\| u_{ij}^{(l+1)} - u_{ij}^{(l)} \|_{\infty} < \varepsilon \qquad (14.5).$$

Note that equation (14.5) refers to the infinity or maximum norm, i.e. the largest adjustment of the membership degree in absolute value over all observations and clusters triggers the stopping criterion. The following section demonstrates an implementation of FCM in Python without using any ready-made packages, such as fuzzy-c-means or FuzzyCMeans. The latter is an unstable development version at the time of writing.

14.6 Step-by-Step Implementation of Fuzzy C-means

It is useful to work through the FCM algorithm outlined in the previous section and implement it step-by-step. After importing standard libraries, we load our financial data from the pickle file. Ticker symbols are removed, and the Pandas *DataFrame* is converted into a NumPy array using the attribute values. We recommend using *print()* statements to check the structure of the data. These checks were commented out in the code.

```
import matplotlib.pyplot as plt
import numpy as np
import pandas as pd

#Load DataFrame
df = pd.read_pickle("data_cluster.pkl")
#print(df)

#Remove ticker symbols
df = df.iloc[:, 1:]

#Convert into NumPy array
data = df.values
#print(data)
```

Our data matrix (**data**) has dimension $N \times q$. Using the **shape** attribute, we obtain the dimension of the data matrix as a tuple. The first number is the number of rows, and the second entry refers to the number of columns. We can access the dimensions using **indexing**.

Next, we select the number of clusters and the fuzziness parameter m. Then, we start the algorithm using random numbers in the interval $[0,1]$ for each membership degree u_{ij}, which we collect in the membership matrix U. We derive the row sums and normalize the membership matrix U.

```
#print(data.shape)

#Number of clusters
clusters = 4

#Fuzziness parameter m
m = 2
```

```
#Initial cluster membership
#U refers to membership matrix
U = np.random.rand(data.shape[0], clusters)
#print(U)

#Probability that obs.is in one of the clusters
#Normalisation to ensure that row sum is one
row_sum = np.sum(U, axis=1)
#print(row_sum)

#Adds dimension as row_sum has shape(28,)
row_sum = row_sum[:, np.newaxis]

#Normalise U
U = np.divide(U, row_sum )
#print(U)
```

To replicate the algorithm, it is useful to test the equations and their implementation before deriving the metrics in loops or using vectorization. It is usually easier to spot mistakes working through a simple example. The following code replicates equation (14.1).

```
v1 = np.sum((U[:, 0]**m)[:, np.newaxis]*data, axis = 0)/
np.sum(U[:, 0]**m)
#print(v1)
```

After we are satisfied that the implementation works, we derive the cluster centre matrix V using a loop over all clusters. As we need this calculation several times, we define a function.

```
def cluster_centre(clusters, data, U):
    v = np.zeros((clusters, data.shape[1]))
    for i in range(clusters):
        v[i,:]=np.sum((U[:, i]**m)[:, np.newaxis]*data,
        axis = 0)
          /np.sum(U[:, i]**m)
    return v

#Call function
v = cluster_centre(clusters, data, U)
#print(v)
```

It is useful to define the structure of the cluster centre matrix V followed by replacing its entries in line with equation (14.1). Again, we test our code by calling the function and reviewing the output.

We define a function that updates the membership degrees in line with equation (14.4). Euclidean distances are derived inside the function's scope using NumPy's *linalg.norm()* function. Note that the default value for the order is two, which refers to the Euclidean distance. The dimension of the membership matrix U is defined, and entries are updated in line with equation (14.4).

Note that *np.newaxis* ensures that the resulting matrix has the correct dimension. The function returns the updated membership matrix U. Finally, we test our function by focusing on the first observation using indexing. Apart from the membership degree for all clusters, we also obtain the most likely cluster using the *np.argmax()* function.

```
def membership_degree(clusters, data, v, m):
  #Dimension of membership degree array
    U = np.zeros((data.shape[0], clusters))
    #Euclidean distance
    d = np.zeros((data.shape[0], clusters))
    for i in range(clusters):
        d[:, i] = np.linalg.norm(data - v[i,:], ord = 2,
        axis = 1)

    U = 1 / (d**(2/(m-1))*np.sum((1/d)**(2/(m-1)),
    axis = 1)[:, np.newaxis])
    return U

print(f"First observation is initially in cluster
{np.argmax(U, axis = 1)[0]}.")
print(f"It has membership degree of
{U[np.argmax(U, axis = 1)[0], 0]}.")

#Updated membership degree
U = membership_degree(clusters, data, v, m)
print(f"\nAfter updating, the first observation is
in cluster {np.argmax(U, axis = 1)[0]}.")
print(f"With membership degree of
{U[np.argmax(U, axis = 1)[0], 0]}.")
```

Without specifying a stopping criterion, we run the algorithm L=10 times using the following loop. The functions that update cluster centres and membership degrees are called at each iteration.

```
L = 10
for _ in range(L):
    v = cluster_centre(clusters, data, U)
    U_updated = membership_degree(clusters, data, v, m)
    print(U_updated[0, :])
    print(np.argmax(U_updated, axis = 1)[0])
    U = U_updated
```

This Python script implements the FCM step by step, and the file *fuzzy.py* contains the code developed in this section. It is a useful exercise to go through the equations without relying on ready-made solutions. Obviously, there are two major shortcomings. First, we do not implement a stopping criterion. Instead, the algorithm runs until the maximum number of iterations L is reached. Second, defining functions is certainly useful. However, we could refactor the code by defining our own class. The current functions become methods of the class. This improves the structure of the code, and it will be easier to apply our algorithm to a different dataset or problem.

14.7 The Fuzzy C-means Class

The keyword class starts our CMeans class. We store the number of clusters, the fuzziness parameter, iterations, the stopping criterion, the data, the cluster membership matrix, and the cluster centres matrix as attributes. Apart from the data, which needs to be a NumPy array, all other parameters are optional, and default or initial values are specified.

```
class CMeans():
    def __init__(self, data, clusters = 2, m = 2,
    L = 100, stop = 0.001):
        """
        clusters: Number of clusters
        m: Fuzziness parameter
        L: Iterations
        stop: Stopping criterion
        data: Data as a Numpy array
        U: Cluster membership matrix
        v: Cluster centres
        """
        self.data = data
        self.clusters = clusters
        self.m = m
```

```
        self.L = L
        self.stop = stop
        self.U = np.empty((self.data.shape[0],
        self.clusters))
        self.v = np.empty((self.clusters,
        self.data.shape[1]))
        self.reached = False
```

We suggest using docstrings to explain each method. The initial membership matrix refers to a normalized random matrix, which we derive in the initialization method. The attribute is updated; hence, there is no need for a return value.

```
    def initialisation(self):
        """
        Initial cluster membership matrix: random
        and normalised
        """
        U = np.random.rand(self.data.shape[0],
        self.clusters)
        row_sum = np.sum(U, axis=1)[:, np.newaxis]
        U = np.divide(U, row_sum )
        self.U = U
```

The method *cluster_centre()* determines the clusters' centres using class attributes. The updated cluster centre matrix V is stored on the attribute v.

```
    def cluster_centre(self):
        """
        Determines centres of clusters based on
        current cluster membership matrix
        """
        for i in range(self.clusters):
            self.v[i,:]=
            np.sum((self.U[:, i]**self.m)[:,np.newaxis]
            *self.data, axis = 0)/
            np.sum(self.U[:,i]**self.m)
```

The method *membership_degree()* updates the cluster membership matrix U. Using attributes removes the need for a return value.

```
    def membership_degree(self):
        """
        Updates cluster membership matrix
```

```
        """
        #Update cluster centres
        self.cluster_centre()
        #Euclidean distance
        d = np.zeros((self.data.shape[0],
        self.clusters))
        for i in range(self.clusters):
            d[:, i] = np.linalg.norm(self.data -
            self.v[i,:], ord = 2, axis = 1)

        self.U = 1 / (d**(2/(self.m-1))*
        np.sum((1/d)**(2/(self.m-1)),
        axis = 1)[:, np.newaxis])
```

The following method called *stopping_criterion()* extends our algorithm by implementing equation (14.5). The distance measure refers to the infinity norm. Each observation's distance to each centre of all clusters is assessed. If the infinity norm drops below the stopping criterion ε, the Boolean *self.reached* is triggered, and the string 'stop' is printed to the terminal. The latter is optional but helpful in testing the code. The Boolean *self.reached* is used in the iteration to ensure that the algorithm stops once the stopping criterion is fulfilled.

```
    def stopping_criterion(self):
        """
        Stopping criterion based on max adjustment
        """
        #Euclidean distance
        d = np.zeros(self.U.shape)
        #Update cluster membership matrix
        U_old = self.U[:]
        self.membership_degree()
        d = max(np.linalg.norm(self.U-U_old,
        ord = 2, axis = 1))
        if d <= self.stop:
            self.U = U_old
            self.reached = True
            print("stop")
```

The *fit()* method runs the iterations until the maximum number of iterations is reached or the stopping criterion is triggered. The latter is captured by the Boolean *self.reached* in the while loop.

```
    def fit(self):
        """
        Update until stopping criterion
        or max iteration reached
        """
        #Iteration left
        l = self.L

        while l and not self.reached:
            print(l)
            l -= 1
                self.stopping_criterion()
```

Finally, we test our FCM class extensively using several method calls and formatted strings. It is much easier to apply the FCM algorithm based on our class. The code has a clear structure and can be modified to address data-specific requirements (e.g. different distance measures or stopping criteria).

```
c_means = CMeans(clusters = 4, m = 2, data = data)

c_means.initialisation()
print(c_means.U)

c_means.cluster_centre()
print(c_means.V)

print(f"First observation is initially in cluster
{np.argmax(c_means.U, axis = 1)[0]}.")
print(f"It has membership degree of
{c_means.U[np.argmax(c_means.U, axis = 1)[0], 0]}.")

#Updated membership degree
c_means.membership_degree()
print(f"\nAfter updating, the first observation is
in cluster{np.argmax(c_means.U, axis = 1)[0]}.")
print(f"With membership degree of
{c_means.U[np.argmax(c_means.U, axis = 1)[0], 0]}.")

c_means.stopping_criterion()

c_means.fit()
```

The file fuzzy_2.py contains our FCM class. It would be useful to save the class in a separate script and import the class whenever the FCM algorithm is needed. The exercise at the end of this chapter will use and modify our FCM class. After conducting cluster analysis, it is good practice to check the validity of the derived clusters.

14.8 Assessing the Validity of Cluster Analysis

How good is our cluster analysis? This is actually not an easy question to answer as it depends on our knowledge of the true labels. Put differently, do we know the true membership of each observation, at least for a sub-sample (training data)?

In many applications, clustering is used without any knowledge of labels. Accordingly, the data is explored as an unsupervised machine learning exercise. In these cases, our assessment of the quality of clustering focuses on the main idea, i.e. observations within a cluster are more similar, whereas observations that belong to different clusters are more different.

This section explores two metrics commonly used if true labels are known or unknown. First, we introduce the Rand index with and without adjustments for random labelling (Rand, 1971). Second, we explain the Silhouette Coefficient, which is based on the ability of our analysis to identify clusters (Rousseeuw, 1987).

To illustrate the implementation, we load the Iris data, which contains the true labels stored in the array y. The data matrix has dimension $N \times q$, where the number of observations is $N = 150$ and four dimensions, i.e. $q = 4$ contain information.

```
import numpy as np
from sklearn import metrics
from sklearn.metrics import pairwise_distances
from sklearn import datasets
from sklearn.cluster import KMeans

#Load Iris dataset
X, y = datasets.load_iris(return_X_y = True)

#Three labels which are known
print(y)

#Data matrix with four dimensions
#150 observations
print(X.shape)
```

Based on the true labels, we know that three is the optimal number of clusters. Hence, we conduct a cluster analysis using the K-means method with three clusters. The labels derived from our analysis are stored in the variable *predict_y*. You notice that the numbering of the predicted clusters differs from the true labels. The actual number of a cluster is not meaningful (i.e. permutation is permitted). We need to compare how the classification differs.

Let's look at an example. Our dataset has $N=10$ observation. Thus, we can define the set $S=\{s_1,\ldots,s_N\}$. A clustering is a partition of this set S. For instance, the partition K might use $r=3$ clusters. For instance, $K=\{k_1,\ldots,k_r\}$ where $k_1=\{x_3, x_7, x_{10}\}$, $k_2=\{x_1, x_5, x_6, x_9\}$, and $k_3=\{x_2, x_4, x_8\}$. Finally, the true labels define the partition $Q=\{q_1,\ldots,q_l\}$ with $l=3$. For instance, the true labels could be $q_1=\{x_2, x_3, x_7, x_{10}\}$, $q_2=\{x_4, x_9\}$, and $q_3=\{x_1, x_5, x_6, x_8\}$. Obviously, our clustering is not perfect, which we can compare.

The Rand index assesses whether observations appear in the same or different clusters by comparing the true labels with predicted labels. It can be used unadjusted or adjusted, the latter accounting for the effect of partitions at random. The Rand index is in the range [0,1] and [−1,1] after adjustment. Low values indicate poor clustering, whereas high values suggest successful attempts. How do we score based on these metrics?

```
#Rand index
rand_index = metrics.rand_score(y, predict_y)
rand_index_adj = metrics.adjusted_rand_score(y, predict_y)
print(f"The Rand index is {rand_index}, and the
adjusted score is {rand_index_adj}.")

#K-means cluster analysis with 4 clusters
kmeans_model_4 = KMeans(n_clusters = 4).fit(X)
predict_4_y = kmeans_model_4.labels_
```

The Rand index is 0.880 and 0.730 after adjustment. These scores suggest that our K-means approach is rather effective in identifying the correct labels. If the true labels are unknown, we also do not know the correct number of clusters. This can be a considerable source of poor model performance. Fortunately, different predicted labels based on a range of parameters (e.g. the number of clusters or the fuzziness parameter) can be compared using the Silhouette Coefficient.

The Silhouette Coefficient takes values in the range [−1,1]. A high score suggests dense clusters with good separation. This metric compares the average distance between observations in nearby clusters and observations in the same cluster. This method is useful for comparing predictions based on different parameter values.

```
#The Silhouette Coefficient
silhouette_3 = metrics.silhouette_score (X, predict_y,
metric='euclidean')
```

```
silhouette_4 = metrics.silhouette_score (X, predict_4_y,
metric ='euclidean')
print(f"The Silhouette Coefficient is {round(silhouette_3, 3)}
with 3 clusters and {round(silhouette_4, 3)} with 4
clusters.")
```

The Silhouette Coefficient drops from 0.551 to 0.410 when we increase the number of clusters from three to four. Accordingly, comparing the Silhouette Coefficient for different numbers of clusters can identify an optimal number of clusters. Note that our calculation refers to the data matrix *X*; hence, true labels are not required.

The file validity.py provides the Python code for this section, which you might modify and use for this chapter's exercise. Whether the true labels are known or not, comparing validity measures can be useful in identifying better clustering. As discussed in this section, 'better' means that clusters are dense and observations are separated clearly.

14.9 Summary

This chapter briefly introduces cluster analysis without diving into a substantial body of literature on a vast number of methods. It is useful to understand hard and soft clustering as both approaches offer different logic for separating observations. Hard clustering is binary. Observations are either in a cluster or not. There is no ambiguity. In contrast, soft clustering regards cluster membership as a continuum.

This chapter covered the two most common methods, namely K-means and Fuzzy C-means, representing hard and soft clustering. It is essential to evaluate the performance of cluster analysis. Knowledge of the true labels is not a prerequisite for deriving useful performance metrics. The Silhouette Coefficient can be an effective tool in determining the optimal number of clusters by comparing various model specifications.

Finally, this chapter relied on ready-made and fully implemented tools as well as self-made Python classes that can handle fuzzy logic. This chapter's exercise explores the well-studied Iris dataset by applying our Fuzzy C-means approach.

14.10 Exercise

This exercise applies our Fuzzy C-means class, which you find in the Python file fuzzy_2.py. You can import the class into your own script or copy-paste the required code. Please try to answer the following questions.

The solution section offers a possible solution. Please note that solutions are not unique, as many alternative implementations exist. The solutions are available as a Python script named cluster_solution.py.

14.10.1 Load Data

Load the Iris data, which you find on scikit-learn. You will need the following import statement from scikit-learn import datasets. Define the data matrix denoted X and identify the true labels provided by the dataset.

14.10.2 Fuzzy C-means

Conduct a cluster analysis using Fuzzy C-means with four and five clusters. Save the predicted labels.

14.10.3 Optimal Number of Clusters

Compare the two models based on four and five clusters by calculating the Silhouette Coefficient.

PART THREE
Applications and Tools

15 Modelling Supply Chains: Use Cases

After learning about data management and covering many machine learning tools, it is time to walk through a few use cases step by step. The main challenge in practice is ensuring we deliver models and predictions in line with the client's requirements. Having conducted many projects, our main suggestion is to communicate clearly and discuss all requirements (data, privacy, measurement error, user interfaces, etc.) in advance. Many projects offer great technical solutions to problems nobody cares about or promise to deliver predictions that do not work in real life. Put differently, communication and planning are essential in designing and delivering models in business analytics.

COMMUNICATE PROJECT REQUIREMENTS

It is tempting to jump straight into fancy modelling, but ensure that you discuss the following issues with clients prior to investing time and money.

- What is the aim of the project (e.g. data visualization, predictions etc.)?
- What is the time frame and budget? Put differently, can you deliver the project and achieve the desired outcome?
- What data is needed (e.g. data input, formats, types)?
- How do end-users interact with the product (e.g. graphical user interfaces, web applications, integration)?
- What time horizon and accuracy are required for model predictions?

And most importantly, document everything in detail.

This chapter focuses on use cases in the context of supply chain management, which has become a major concern for companies and policymakers. Problems include finding optimal routes (e.g. minimizing transportation costs) and addressing risks due to political uncertainties such as blockades or climate change (e.g. extreme weather events). Moreover, data visualization of supply chains (e.g. the UK Maritime statistics) is another application. For instance, the UK's Department for Transport created a dashboard based on Microsoft Power BI that displays data from the Maritime Statistics.

Analysing supply chains can be challenging due to the data structure (e.g. multi-level, several actors) or the lack of data. Compared to other areas, such as financial data, data on the supply chain tends to be private or requires a subscription to data providers. Kaggle Data offers a free dataset, which illustrates a common data structure.

In many applications, data is observable, or we only have a statistical understanding of the problem (e.g. probability density function of prices, probability of conflicts, etc.). Hence, simulations play a major role in supply chain modelling.

Besides the lack of data, simulation can capture strategic interactions, which matter in supply chain modelling. Standard machine learning tools assume that actors cannot influence outcomes, i.e. nature is probabilistic. Statistical learning is based on this fundamental assumption. However, this assumption is no longer valid under certain conditions (e.g. limited number of actors, high market concentration). In such scenarios, nature is no longer probabilistic in the sense that states of the world have associated probabilities. In fact, such settings might become a 'game against the evil nature', i.e. an 'evil player' selects the worst possible action after you make your move. Simulations are an excellent tool for capturing strategic interaction.

Accordingly, subsequent sections introduce *SimPy*, a process-based discrete-event simulation framework. SimPy can be used to simulate supply chains and aid in decision-making. We will build a simple simulation of a supply chain and link it to strategic problems. Unfortunately, the Python library *Supplychainpy,* dedicated to supply chain analysis, modelling, and simulation, has not been updated since 2017. However, it still offers a good starting point for creating your own models.

This chapter starts with a brief discussion of common data structures in the context of supply chains. We will analyse the optimal routing problem. Next, SimPy is introduced, and we will build a supply chain simulation. Finally, this chapter's exercise explores an application in industrial economics through modelling a market and potential mergers. After completing this chapter, you will learn how to do the following:

- Analyse supply chain data.
- Model optimal routing problems.
- Use SimPy to simulate supply chains.
- Visualize supply chain data.
- Use models to support strategic decision-making.

15.1 Supply Chain Data Structure

Supply chains refer to distributing goods from one place to another. The purpose of this transport might be selling a finished product and delivering it to customers or moving inputs to the next step in the production process. Supply chains can operate inside an organization or between organizations (e.g. offshore outsourcing).

Regarding data structure, the origin and destination are discrete locations captured by a tuple, i.e. a pair indicating the start and end points. It is common to call these start and end points nodes. For instance, (A,B) captures the transport of a product from its origin A to its destination B. Commonly, costs are associated with moving products from A to B. In addition, constraints tend to apply (e.g. production capacities of plants, size of containers, etc.).

Accordingly, the resulting data structure might require multiple *DataFrames*, e.g. a matrix of origins and destinations capturing transportation costs between two nodes. Moreover, a second *DataFrame* stating capacity constraints, and so on. It is frequently helpful to illustrate a supply chain problem using graphs. Figure 15.1 shows two internal nodes (within a company) labelled B and C, where B is a production node and C might be a warehouse for distributing the final product. Customers are located at point D, and suppliers are at location A. Transportation costs γ apply to moving goods from B to C.

Supply chain management aims to minimize transportation costs or maximize profits. These optimization problems, together with a set of constraints, are usually linear problems. They can be solved using *linear programming*. However, more complex problems involving uncertainty (e.g. statistical knowledge of model parameters, risks of disruptions, etc.) benefit from simulating supply chains. The following section will introduce the Python package *pulp*, which offers tools for linear programming.

Figure 15.1 Illustration of a supply chain

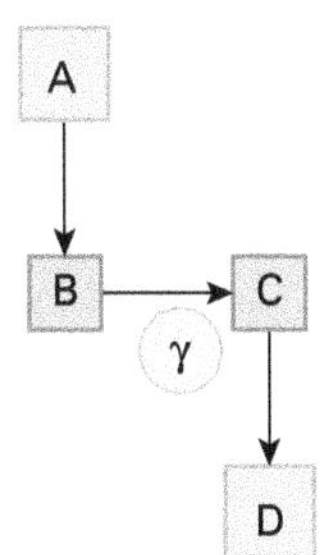

15.2 Production Planning

Supply chain optimization (e.g. finding optimal routes) is a common problem in business analytics. To get used to the Python package *pulp* and its syntax, we start this section with a trivial linear programming problem. The solution to this problem is obvious, but we learn from trying to implement the problem in Python about how *pulp* operates.

We create a virtual environment called *opt*, which we activate prior to installing the Python package *pulp*.

```
python -m venv opt
opt\Scripts\activate
pip install pulp
```

Let's start with a minimum working example to get used to *pulp*. After the import statement, we start a model, which is an instance of the *LpProblem()* class. The argument *sense* is set to –1, indicating a maximization problem. Note that the default setting is 1 for a minimization problem.

Outlining the deterministic model parameters (i.e. observed and known parameters) is good practice. Parameters include production capacities, variable costs, prices, and total demand.

```
import pulp as pp
#Default is a minimisation
#Set sense = -1 for maximising profit
model = pp.LpProblem("Optimal production", sense = -1)

#Model parameters
#Capacity constraints of factories
capacity = [
    1000,
    700
    ]

#Variable costs
var = [
    10,
    7]

#Price
price = 11

#Demand
demand = 1500
```

Next, we define two variables that capture the production in the two factories. These variables are continuous and have a lower bound of zero. Capacity constraints included in the list *capacity* above define the upper bounds.

```
#Define decision variables
#Lower and upper bounds
#Types
fac1 = pp.LpVariable('Factory 1', lowBound = 0,
upBound = capacity[0], cat = "Continuous")
fac2 = pp.LpVariable('Factory 2', lowBound = 0,
upBound = capacity[1], cat = "Continuous")
```

The objective function represents the company's profit calculated based on the total output times the price minus variable costs, which differ between the two factories. As stated in an inequality constraint, total production cannot exceed demand, which is added to the model using the += symbol.

The *solve()* method is applied to the model instance, and we print the results using the attribute *varValue*.

```
#Define objective function
model += price * (fac1 + fac2)
- var[0] * fac1 - var[1] * fac2

#Define constraint based on total demand
model += fac1 + fac2 <= demand

#Solve model
model.solve()
print(f"{fac1.varValue} in Factory 1 and
{fac2.varValue} in Factory 2.")
```

As expected, optimal production uses the factory with lower variable costs first until the production capacity is reached. This is followed by production in the more expensive facility until demand is met.

15.3 Finding an Optimal Route

Let's look at another problem. You run a company that has customers in five countries, say the UK ($j=1$), France ($j=2$), China ($j=3$), Japan ($j=4$), and India ($j=5$). Each market has a maximum level of demand denoted D_j, where $j=1,\ldots,5$ represents the five countries. The company owns a factory in the UK, which can produce all the output required for all markets. However, transportation costs and customs regulations

Table 15.1 Delivery costs: factory–market

Factory	UK	France	China	Japan	India
UK	1	2	5	4	3
India	3	3	2	2	1

make the delivery from the UK to all markets costly. The company can start another factory in India. Note that you can continue operations in the UK at no additional costs. Table 15.1 captures delivery costs from the UK and India to the five markets. How much are you willing to invest in India?

To answer this question, we need to compare two cases. First, the firm only produces in the UK and delivers to all five markets. Delivery costs per unit apply as described in Table 15.1. Demand in each country defines the minimum level that must be delivered. Without any optimization, we can calculate the total delivery costs in this case without outsourcing. Second, the firm outsources production to India and hence operates factories in the UK and India. In this case, we need to find optimal routes that minimize total delivery costs.

To formalize this problem, we start by importing *Pulp* and define two lists containing the locations of factories and markets. A dictionary defines the minimum deliveries in each market. The name of the market serves as a key. An array provides delivery costs between factories and markets in line with Table 15.1.

```
import pulp as pp

#Location of factories
factories = ["UK", "India"]

#Five markets
markets = ["UK", "France", "China", "Japan", "India"]

#Demand in each market
demand = {
    "UK": 100,
    "France": 150,
    "China": 200,
    "Japan": 90,
    "India": 80,
}

#Matrix (array) of delivery costs
```

```
delivery = [
        [1, 2, 5, 4, 3],
        [3, 3, 2, 2, 1],
]
```

Pulp offers the *makeDict()* function, which converts the array of delivery costs into a dictionary. The dictionary uses a list, i.e. a factory-market pair, as keys. A print statement checks the structure of the dictionary. Next, we create an instance called *model* of the *LpProblem()* class, which refers to a minimization problem by default.

Using list comprehension, we create a list of tuples for all factory-market pairs called *routes*. Finally, we define variables based on the routes using the *LpVariable.dicts()* function. We regard the demand as a minimum delivery requirement. Accordingly, we set zero as the lower bound and do not specify an upper bound. Furthermore, we assume that deliveries are in whole quantities (i.e. integers). Of course, these assumptions can be modified if required.

```
#Use keys in the new dictionary to capture delivery costs
#Rows refer to factories
#Columns refer to markets
costs = pp.makeDict([factories, markets], delivery, 0)

#Check the dictionary
print(costs)

#Create an instance of the cost minimisation problem
#Minimisation by default
model = pp.LpProblem("Outsourcing")

#List comprehension
#List of tuples for all factory-market pairs
routes = [(factory, market) for factory in factories
for market in markets]

#Check routes
print(routes)

#Dictionary containing routes
var_routes = pp.LpVariable.dicts('routes',
(factories, markets), lowBound = 0,
upBound = None, cat = "Integer")
print(var_routes)
```

Next, we add the objective function, which refers to the sum of delivery costs based on all possible routes. The *lpSum()* function is applied to a list. The list, in turn, is created from a list comprehension operation. Each quantity delivered from a factory to a market is multiplied by the associated cost using the factory-market key. We describe the objective function as the sum of delivery costs with outsourcing.

Next, we add constraints based on the minimum deliveries required for each market. Deliveries can be fulfilled from the UK or India; hence, we have to add both locations using list comprehension and the *lpSum()* function.

```
#Objective function added
model += (
    pp.lpSum([var_routes[factory][market]
    *costs[factory][market] for (factory, market)
    in routes]),
    "Sum of delivery costs with outsourcing",
)

#Minimum demand constraints
for market in markets:
    model += (
        pp.lpSum([var_routes[factory][market]
        for factory in factories]) >= demand[market],
        f"Total goods delivered to {market}",
    )
```

After specifying the outsourcing problem, we apply the *solve()* method to the model instance and print solutions. Using the *varValue* attribute, we access optimal values for each variable, which captures delivered quantities between each factory and market. Finally, the *value()* method is applied to the *objective* attribute to display the total delivery costs in the case of outsourcing. In summary, the model provides an optimal route selection, minimizing delivery costs when we operate factories in the UK and India.

```
#Solve model
model.solve()

print("Status:", pp.LpStatus[model.status])

#Show variables
for var in model.variables():
    print(var.name, "=", var.varValue)

#Optimised delivery costs with outsourcing
```

```
costs_out = model.objective.value()
print(f"Total costs using outsourcing = {costs_out}")
```

We derive delivery costs without outsourcing production to decide the maximum level we can invest in India. From the *costs* dictionary, we select all routes starting in the UK and add delivery costs for each market. Finally, the cost difference estimates the benefit of outsourcing, which is the upper bound we might be willing to invest in India.

```
#Comparison: UK production without outsourcing

costs_uk = 0

for market in markets:
   costs_uk += demand[market]*
          costs["UK"][market]

print(f"Total costs without outsourcing = {costs_uk}")
print(f"\nYou can invest up to
{round(costs_uk - costs_out, 0)}
in India to outsource production.")
```

This section demonstrated the use of *Pulp* to solve optimization problems in the context of managing production and deliveries. In many settings, however, we do not have all the information needed to formalize an optimization problem. In these cases, simulated data might be required to model different choices.

15.4 An Introduction to SimPy

SimPy provides a Python-based framework to create simulations in real-time. We use *process* functions or methods to structure our simulation. Processes *yield events*, which differs from a return value in 'normal' functions or methods. These processes exist in *environments*.

We recommend creating a virtual environment called *sim*. After activating the virtual environment, the *pip installer* ensures all the Python package SimPy's dependencies are taken care of. In addition, we also add NumPy and Matplotlib for data wrangling and visualization.

```
python -m venv sim
sim\Scripts\activate
pip install simpy
pip install numpy
pip install matplotlib
```

To get used to SimPy, our basic simulation focuses on creating customers randomly. Every minute, the probability that a customer enters the shop is denoted ARR, which is one of our model parameters. In total, we want to stop the simulation after 20 customers. We are interested in the time interval between customer arriving. Such so-called waiting time distributions matter in many applications (e.g. high-frequency trading patterns).

We start by importing SimPy, NumPy, and Matplotlib. Starting with model parameters, including the arrival probability and the total number of customers, is good practice. To collect the waiting times between customers, we create an array with all zeros and the dimensions required to capture information for all customers.

```
import simpy
import numpy as np
import matplotlib.pyplot as plt

#Model parameters
#Total number of customers
NUM = 20

#Probability of arrival
ARR = 0.05

#Collect data
interval = np.zeros(NUM)
```

In functions or methods, we are used to seeing the keyword *return*. However, SimPy uses processes, which are Python generators. The keyword refers to *yield*. Let's explore our *purchase* generator line by line.

We set our timer in minutes starting with zero followed by a *while* loop. This means the block inside the loop keeps running until an *event* occurs. While the process runs in discrete time, minutes are added, and a probability is calculated using a random number generator in NumPy. Then, we assess whether the probability is less than the arrival probability, which triggers an event, i.e. a customer enters the shop.

Two formatted strings follow, which display the customer's number referring to the environment instance *env* and its attribute *now*. The first customer gets the number 1. Hence, we need to refer to the index position 0 to update our data array by stating *env.now −1*. The timer is reset for the next customer, and the process yields *env.timeout(1)*. Basically, we refer to the environment instance created later in the script and apply the *timeout()* method, which pauses the process. Our counter for customers increases by one unit.

```
#Define process
def purchase(env, arrival = 0.1):
  #Start timer
  minutes = 0
  while True:
     #Generate a probability
     prob = np.random.rand()
     minutes += 1
     print(prob)
     if prob < arrival:
        print(f'Customer number
              {env.now} arrived.')
        print(f'It took {minutes}
              minutes.')
        #Add data
        interval[env.now-1] = minutes
        #Reset timer
        minutes = 0
        yield env.timeout(1)
```

Figure 15.2 Simulated time between customers

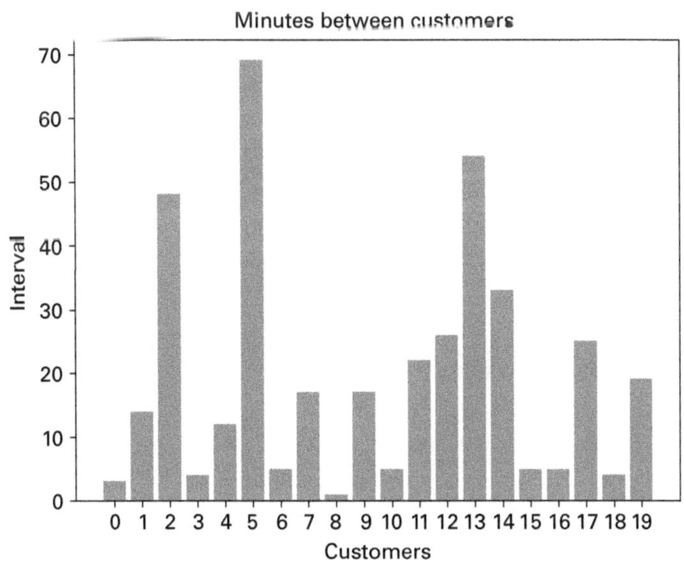

Next, we create the environment instance and specify our process using the *process()* method. Finally, the *run()* method is called, and we specify that we stop after observing 20 customers.

```
#Create an Environment() instance
env = simpy.Environment()

#Run the process until reaching 20 customers
env.process(purchase(env, arrival = ARR))
env.run(until = NUM + 1)
```

Finally, we analyse our simulated dataset stored in the array of waiting times between customers. It might be useful to calculate the cumulative waiting time. A bar chart visualizes the waiting time between customers in minutes. This concludes our first simulation in SimPy, which you find in the Python script *basic.py*. Figure 15.2 plots an example of waiting times between customers.

```
#Explore data
x = np.arange(NUM)

#Cumulative time
cumulative_time = np.cumsum(interval)

#Bar chart of waiting times
plt.title(“Minutes between customers”)
plt.xlabel(“Customers”)
plt.ylabel(“Interval”)
plt.xticks(range(NUM))
plt.bar(x, interval, color = ‘red’)
plt.savefig(‘CS_arrival.png’)
plt.show()
```

15.5 Building a Supply Chain Model

After covering the basics, we attempt to model a more complex problem in SimPy using several classes and process methods, which interact (e.g. waiting for a process to complete before restarting a process).

Let’s assume that we run a store that sells rice. Customers arrive randomly and buy between one and three units of rice. The initial stock is 100. We receive shipments to replenish our stock. A container ship with a capacity of 15 units starts from our port. However, the length of the sea journey varies, disrupting our supply chain.

This model's objective is to predict the rice stock. Simulated stock levels are collected for data visualization or further statistical analysis. In practice, such simulations are run many times to derive simulated probability density functions. These can be used to calculate percentiles (e.g. value at risk) or define cutoff points (e.g. stop loss criteria in trading algorithms).

The script *supply.py* starts with our usual import statements followed by the model parameters defining the total number of purchase events (i.e. customers arrive and buy quantities of rice) and the initial stock. The list *stock* is appended with simulated levels of stock.

```
import simpy
import numpy as np
import matplotlib.pyplot as plt

#Parameters
NUM = 1000

#Collect data
stock = [100]
```

In contrast to our first example, which used process functions, we recommend object-oriented programming by defining several classes for more advanced simulation. Process methods apply to instances of classes. In most cases, it is useful to commence a process when initializing an instance of the class. We accomplish this task in the *dunder init* method. The *Store()* class captures our rice inventory. The attribute *stock* provides access to current levels of stock, starting with the initial level of 100. To work with processes, we need to refer to the environment instance called *env*, which we pass as an argument. Finally, we start the process method called *run()* by applying the *process()* method to the environment instance. Accordingly, when we initialize an instance of the *Store()* class, we also trigger the process method *run()*.

The *run()* process method rolls a dice (i.e. generates a probability) and adjusts the stock if a customer arrives. The quantity purchased can be in the interval from one to three units. A uniform distribution applies. If a customer arrives, the process is paused for one period, and then the dice roll restarts. The reduced stock level is added to our list for further data analysis.

```
class Store():
  """
  Store models stock of rice
  Customers arrive randomly
  """
  def __init__(self, env):
```

```
    """
    Stock of rice in store and
        start process
    """
    self.env = env
    self.stock = 100
    self.start = env.process(self.run())

  def run(self):
    while True:
      #Generate a probability
      prob = np.random.rand()
      if prob < 0.1:
        print(f'Customer number {env.now}
                 arrived.')
        self.stock -= np.random.randint(1, 3)
        print(f'Current stock {self.stock}.')
        stock.append(self.stock)
        yield env.timeout(1)
```

To restock our store, we need to send container ships. The *Ship()* class refers to the environment instance and starts a process method. The ship has a capacity of 15 units as requested. The process method *run()* starts the ship at time zero and triggers the process method *on_sea()*. The sea journey varies from a lower bound of 7 to an upper bound of 13. During this time, the process is paused. The *run()* process method restarts after the wait, the ship is unloaded, and the stock levels are adjusted by the ship's storage capacity. Note that we include the instance *store* as an argument of the *run()* process method. The *Ship()* class implicitly assumes that the *stock* attribute exists, i.e. *store* is an instance of the *Store()* class. This is a common approach in programming. Of course, in more advanced projects, one needs to write tests that ensure that the alleged attributes actually exist. Frequently, one changes the name of an attribute in the original class without realizing that this attribute was used in a different class. Tests will highlight the issue swiftly.

```
class Ship():
  def __init__(self, env, store):
    """
    Refer to the environment and
    start the process
    """
    self.env = env
    self.capacity = 15
```

```
    self.start = env.process(self.run(store))

  def run(self, store):
    while True:
      print(f"Ship starts at {env.now}")
      #Waiting until the journey is completed
      yield env.process(self.on_sea())

      #Ship reached and unloaded rice
      store.stock += self.capacity
      print(f"Ship reaches at {env.now}")
      print(f"Store has {store.stock}
                 units of rice.")
      yield env.timeout(1)

  def on_sea(self):
    """
    Travel time
    """
    time = np.random.randint(7, 13)
    yield self.env.timeout(time)
```

Finally, we create the *Sim()* class, which initializes our simulation. It is very convenient to do this in a separate class. Again, we refer to the environment instance. The store instance is saved as an attribute as well as a ship instance. Once we initialize an instance of the *Sim()*, a store and ship emerge and their processes commence.

```
class Sim():
  """
  Sim class initialises the store and ship
  """
  def __init__(self, env):
    self.env = env
    self.store = Store(self.env)
    self.ship = Ship(env = self.env,
        store = self.store)
```

The final step consists of the creation of an environment and simulation instance. The *run()* process method applied to the environment instance commences the simulation and stops until the required number of events.

```
#Create an environment and simulation
env = simpy.Environment()
```

```
sim = Sim(env)
env.run(until = NUM)
```

The *np.array()* function converts our list with stock levels into a NumPy array, which we plot as a line chart.

```
#Line chart of stock
plt.title("Stock of rice in store")
plt.xlabel("Purchase events")
plt.ylabel("Stock")
plt.plot(np.array(stock), color = 'blue')
plt.savefig('CS_stock.png')
plt.show()
```

Figure 15.3 demonstrates that our current restocking approach is unsustainable in the long term. After adjusting model parameters (e.g. adding an additional ship or increasing the initial stock level), simulations can test whether our decisions will sustain adequate stock levels.

15.6 Facilitating Decision-Making

The methods covered in this book can enhance your ability to forecast a target variable or uncover relationships between variables. However, you need to provide sufficient data to train your machine learning algorithms. As discussed in Chapter 4,

Figure 15.3 Stock of rice in store

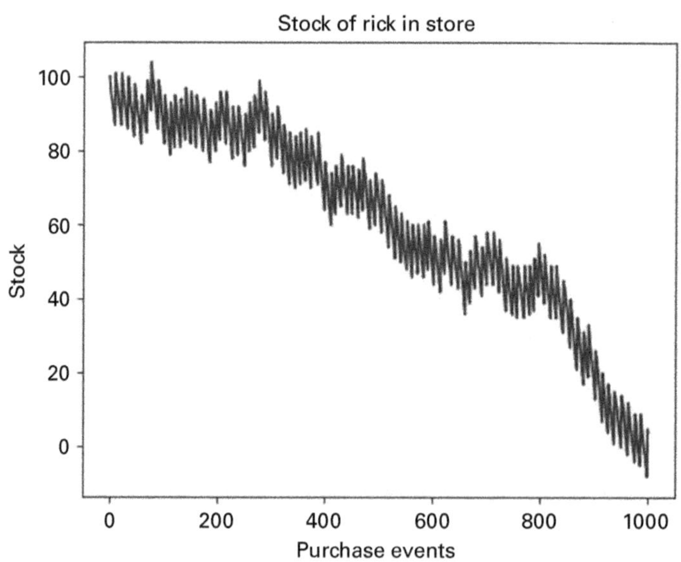

many issues, including outliers and measurement problems, need to be addressed before more advanced data analysis can commence.

In many applications, access to data might be limited, or we might only have a probabilistic understanding of data. In supply chain management, some data is public, such as commodity prices, outputs, and stock of raw materials, but most data is commercially sensitive and hence not in the public domain. So, we need to combine our knowledge of data with simulation techniques to capture the essence of our problem. Accordingly, before building a model, you should ask yourself the following questions.

WHAT DO WE KNOW ABOUT THE PROBLEM?

It is good practice to start asking yourself a few fundamental questions.

- What is the target (dependent) variable (e.g. transportation costs)?
- What is the objective (e.g. cost minimization)?
- What are the variables (e.g. choice of routes)?
- What other parameters do we need to consider (e.g. quotas, tariffs)?
- Which variables can be observed (e.g. quotas, tariffs, possible routes)?
- Should we treat some variables as random (e.g. transportation costs might vary captured by a probabilistic model)?
- What is the scope of the model?

The last question is essential as we must define your model's limitations. Many factors might matter but are outside the scope and hence assumed to be exogenous (e.g. model parameters).

Developing a model that captures the essence of your problem requires a lot of practice. Due to their limited scope and knowledge, models need to simplify reality. However, there is a risk of oversimplification. The 'holy grail' of modelling is finding the right balance of a tractable model without omitting important features and unnecessary complexity.

Let's walk through another example by trying to answer the questions outlined above. We developed a simulation that captures the shipments of rice. Due to the random voyage time, shipments might take between seven and thirteen units of time (say weeks). The company buys the rice at the current market price, which is loaded onto the ship and then stays on board for several weeks. During this period, the company is exposed to changes in rice prices (long position in rice). Let's assume that the company can charge a premium of 10% on top of the wholesale price. How much money might the company lose in the worst case, defined as the 5th percentile?

Our target variable is a value-at-risk measure, assuming that rice prices drop to their 5th percentile during the voyage. Our objective is to derive a risk measure. We do not intend to model countermeasures (e.g. hedging instruments) now. Moreover, we do not make any additional choices, i.e. no additional variables are added at this stage (e.g. increasing the number of ships). Model parameters include the markup of 10%, creating a buffer if prices drop. We could use additional data, including commodity price data provided by the UK National Statistics and the FAO (Food and Agriculture Organization of the United Nations). You can also find Cargo Calculators if you want to explore actual distances and routes.

The csv file *rice_data.csv* contains data on prices and stock relative to annual consumption. The *read_csv()* function imports the data as a *DataFrame*. After removing redundant columns, Figure 15.4 visualizes the dataset with a subplot of the two time series. Commodity prices tend to exhibit spikes, i.e. sharp price jumps as supply tends to be more difficult to adjust. Hence, demand shocks have a pronounced impact on prices. The increase in stock relative to annual consumption has diminished the likelihood of spikes over time.

```
import pandas as pd
import matplotlib.pyplot as plt

#Import csv files as DataFrame
file = "rice_data.csv"
df = pd.read_csv(file)
print(df.head())

#Remove redundant columns
df = df[['Time', 'price', 'stock']]
print(df.head())

#Plot time series
#Set index
df = df.set_index('Time')
fig1, axes = plt.subplots(nrows=2, ncols=1)
axes[0].set_title('Price of rice')
axes[1].set_title('Stock of rice')
df.price.plot(ax = axes[0], color = 'blue')
df.stock.plot(ax = axes[1], color = 'red')
plt.tight_layout()
fig1.savefig("CS_price.png")
plt.show()
```

Figure 15.4 Prices and stock of rice

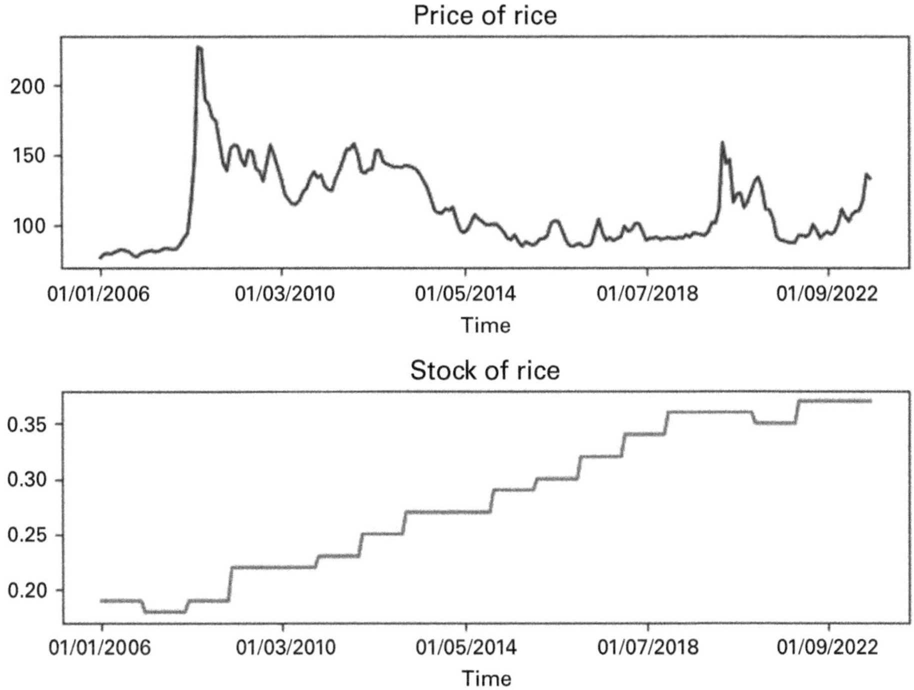

Analysing the time series data can reveal parameters (e.g. drift component, predicted volatility), which can be used for model calibration. Simplifying assumptions could include the type of diffusion equation (e.g. rice prices follow a random walk) employed. In practice, we combine observed and simulated data to enhance our understanding of a problem and capture possible strategic decisions.

15.7 Summary

This chapter explored several use cases in the context of supply chain management. If data can be observed, the Python package *Pulp* offers useful tools to model optimization problems with constraints. Linear programming and route optimization are classic areas in business analytics and supply chain modelling.

However, data is frequently private, i.e. unobserved, or we need to capture a degree of randomness in our models (e.g. disruptions in supply chains). The Python package SimPy provides a toolbox for modelling processes in environments. Accordingly, we explored process functions and methods, which are based on Python *generators*. Processes can interact by disrupting other processes. These interactions can mimic waiting times in real-life settings. Model calibration relies on observed data to enrich simulated data by providing more relevant parameter values or assumptions of stochastic behaviour.

Finally, we need to remind ourselves that our statistical models assume a probabilistic nature. Put differently, we exclude the possibility that our actions can alter the fabric of our probabilistic world (e.g. modifying outcomes of events or their probabilities). This is a realistic assumption in many settings (e.g. we are small actors with limited impact on our environment). However, if the number of actors is small (e.g. a limited number of companies in an industry), strategic interactions will alter outcomes. Consequently, we do not play a game of dice; we play against the 'evil nature' that might wish to harm our prospects. So be careful and understand the game you are playing.

After more than 20 years of consulting experience, the following advice is crucial. Many clients tend to push business analysts to confirm their perspective. Try to push back. Models need to be allowed to contradict your initial perceptions.

DO NOT USE A MODEL TO JUSTIFY A DECISION YOU ALREADY MADE

You can force any model based on observed data, simulated data, or a combination of the two to reaffirm your beliefs. The desired outcome of a model can be imposed by the modeller, e.g. changing parameters or assumptions. A model can only provide insights if you stay objective.

This chapter's exercise explores strategic interactions in more detail. You will attempt to model a market, including prices and quantities sold. Companies are allowed to merge and form larger entities. Will mergers occur under certain conditions? Will you spark a merger wave? Let's find out.

15.8 Exercise

15.8.1 Modelling Mergers

Your task is to develop a model that predicts mergers between companies in an industry. If you are familiar with game theory, we are playing a Cournot game with heterogeneous firms. Our objective is to answer the question of whether the highest-valued firm will acquire the cheapest firm in the industry. Let's start with the basic model setup.

Your model should have the following variables:

- Firms select quantities x_i where i refers to firms (Cournot game).
- They can make a cash bid b_k where k refers to transactions.

The model has the following parameters:

- $\alpha > 0$ and $\beta > 0$ are demand parameters as outlined in equation (15.1).
- $\rho > 0$ is a discount rate (cost of capital).
- The market starts with N firms.
- Each firm has marginal costs: c_i with $i=1, 2,\ldots, N$. Marginal costs differ between firms (heterogeneous firms).

To simplify our model, we make a few additional assumptions:

- (A1) We assume an infinite time horizon; $t = 1, 2, \ldots$.
- (A2) Discounting with $\rho > 0$ applies.
- (A3) We only permit cash mergers, i.e. the bidder offers cash to acquire a target firm.

As this is a Cournot game, the market price P is determined by the sum of quantities sold by the N firms operating in the market.

$$P = \alpha - \beta \sum_{i=1}^{N} x_i \quad \text{with} \quad \alpha > 0, \beta > 0 \tag{15.1}$$

Then, we derive the profit of each firm denoted r_i.

$$\begin{aligned} r_i = (P - c_i)x_i &= \alpha x_i - \beta \sum_{j=1}^{N} x_j \cdot x_i - c_i x_i \\ &= \alpha x_i - \beta \sum_{j=1, i \neq j}^{N} x_j \cdot x_i - \beta x_i^2 - c_i x_i \end{aligned} \tag{15.2}$$

We derive the first-order conditions, which is a system of N equations with the following structure.

$$\frac{dr_i}{dx_i} = \alpha - \beta \sum_{j=1, i \neq j}^{N} x_j - 2\beta x_i - c_i = 0, \quad i = 1, 2, \ldots, N \tag{15.3}$$

Or written differently.

$$\frac{dr_i}{dx_i} = \alpha - \beta \sum_{j=1}^{N} x_j - \beta x_i - c_i = 0, \quad i = 1,2,\ldots,N \tag{15.4}$$

Let $N\bar{x} = \sum_{j=1}^{N} x_j$ and $\bar{c}$ refers to average marginal costs. Summing the N equations yields the following.

$$N\alpha - N\beta\sum_{j=1}^{N}x_j - \beta\sum_{i=1}^{N}x_i - \sum_{i=1}^{N}c_i = 0$$

$$\alpha - \beta N\overline{x} - \beta\frac{1}{N}\sum_{i=1}^{N}x_i - \frac{1}{N}\sum_{i=1}^{N}c_i = 0$$

$$\alpha - \beta N\overline{x} - \beta\overline{x} - \overline{c} = 0 \quad (15.5)$$

Hence, we obtain the average quantity x^{-}.

$$\beta\overline{x}(N+1) = \alpha - \overline{c}$$

$$\overline{x} = \frac{\alpha - \overline{c}}{\beta(N+1)} \quad (15.6)$$

The market price then follows.

$$p = \alpha - \beta N\overline{x} = \alpha - \beta N\frac{\alpha - \overline{c}}{\beta(N+1)}$$

$$= \alpha - \frac{N}{N+1}(\alpha - \overline{c}) \quad (15.7)$$

For $N \to \infty$ it follows that $p \to \overline{c}$ as expected. Then, we can obtain the individual first-order condition for each firm.

$$\frac{dr_i}{dx_i} = \alpha - \beta N\overline{x} - \beta x_i - c_i = 0$$

$$x_i^* = \frac{\alpha - c_i}{\beta} - N\overline{x} \quad (15.8)$$

Based on assumptions A1 and A2, we can derive the firm value v_i, which refers to a perpetuity (i.e. steady-state profit without future growth).

$$v_i = \frac{r_i}{\rho} \quad (15.9)$$

A merger happens if the bid exceeds the standalone value $b_k > v_i$. Finally, we need to accumulate cash in each firm. In each round, the firm's profit is added to cash (retained earnings).

$$cash_{it} = r_i \cdot t \quad (15.10)$$

The condition for a cash merger with bidder i and target k suggests that the bid exceeds the target firm's standalone value.

$$r_i \cdot t = b_k > \frac{r_k}{\rho} \quad (15.11)$$

You will try to implement this model step-by-step, working through the following tasks. Possible solutions are provided (see the Python script *merger.py*) and discussed.

15.8.2 Start the Simulation

You can work with any Python package you prefer. Start with setting up the simulation. The number of firms should be $N = 100$. Parameters can be set at $\alpha = 20$, $\beta = 0.1$, and the discount rate should be $\rho = 0.1$. Create a distribution of marginal costs c_i for the $N = 100$ firms. We suggest using a normal distribution with a mean of one and a standard deviation of one.

15.8.3 Average Quantity and Market Price

Write two functions to calculate the average quantity $\bar{x}$ based on equation (15.6) and the market price p as described in equation (15.7).

15.8.4 Optimal Outputs, Adjust the Size of the Market, and Derive the Price

Next, we use equation (15.8) to determine the optimal output of each firm given their marginal costs. Call this function and remove the firm with the most negative output recursively. Basically, for the firm with the highest marginal costs, optimal output will be negative. This firm leaves the market. This affects the average quantity produced. Hence, optimal quantities need to be recalculated. You continue this process until all firms exhibit a positive optimal output. Finally, you can calculate the resulting market price using equation (15.7).

15.8.5 Distribution of Firm Values

To obtain firms' values, we derive the profit in a period and apply the discount rate in line with (15.9). The resulting array of firm values can be visualized using a histogram.

15.8.6 Will the Highest-Valued Firm Acquire the Cheapest Firm in the Industry?

To answer this question, you will need to derive the cash positions of companies based on their period profits, assuming that all profits are retained. If a firm acquires another firm, the companies not involved in the merger also benefit as the price increases for all. These positive externalities tend to make mergers unprofitable. What is your answer in this case?

16 User Interfaces and Web Applications

How do people interact with your code? Can you repackage your Python script and embed it in easy-to-use applications? This chapter briefly introduces graphical user interfaces (GUIs) and web applications. Natural or graphical interfaces (NUIs or GUIs) offer intuitive controls to users so they can work with software without needing to understand the code's inner workings. User interfaces are the main entry point and can be provided by mobile, desktop, and web-based applications. As this is a substantial area with a vast literature, this chapter restricts itself to Python-based user interfaces.

Python is not the best choice for cross-platform applications (i.e. running the same code without modifications on mobile apps, desktops, and websites). The combination of C# and .NET dominates the user interface market, and Python applications tend to be fed into other systems using application programming interfaces (APIs). Many models developed in Business Analytics need to be accessible throughout an organization. Not every user must understand the underlying Python script or machine learning tools. User interfaces enable a user-friendly environment to provide input (e.g. personal data) and receive outputs (e.g. predictions).

Most models developed in Business Analytics are not designed with the end-user in mind. The focus tends to be on predictability or model fit without much concern for user interaction. However, the 'packaging' or front end needs to be considered to create successful products. Moreover, a good front-end development (i.e. a user interface) can simplify our back-end application. For instance, a well-designed GUI guides users to provide the desired input (e.g. a horizontal slider only permits integers), making checking input less onerous in the application's back-end.

Python offers many packages dedicated to creating user interfaces. Tkinter is an easy tool to create GUIs, whereas more advanced designs might benefit from PyQt5. GUIs developed with Tkinter run on Windows and Mac OS. This chapter introduces the main features offered by Tkinter. We demonstrate the relationship between GUIs and the back-end application. Thinking about this interaction is essential in the process of product development.

Python has been used in web development in many large-scale projects, including Netflix and Airbnb. There are two prominent Python-based frameworks, Flask and Django. The latter is a full-stack framework ideal for large projects, whereas Flask is a useful choice for smaller projects. If you are new to web development, Flask is the easier framework for creating your first web application. Accordingly, this chapter focuses on Flask and also covers a very brief introduction to HTML (HyperText Markup Language). We aim to expose you to the primary process of creating user interfaces for desktop or web applications. This matters in the process of product development. Understanding the basics is helpful in avoiding costly design mistakes, as back-end development needs to consider end-users' inputs and requirements.

In summary, you will learn how to do the following after completing this chapter:

- Understand the basics of user interfaces.
- Build GUIs in Tkinter.
- Create buttons, frames, and entry widgets.
- Link buttons to Python functions.
- Design menu bars.
- Work with popup menus and windows.
- Create a static website using Flask.

16.1 An Introduction to Tkinter

Tkinter offers a wide range of tools to create graphical user interfaces (GUIs) in Python. These GUIs can execute a Python-based back-end application such as a machine learning tool. In addition, end-users can interact with the GUI, input data, or visualize model outputs. GUIs run as desktop applications on Windows and macOS; however, Tkinter is not compatible with mobile applications.

Applying the following command, you can use the pip installer to download the Tkinter package and its dependencies. Alternatively, if you use Anaconda, open the Anaconda Power Shell and type in the second line of code.

```
pip install tk
conda install -c anaconda tk
```

We only need the following import statement to use Tkinter.

```
import tkinter as tk
```

The installation succeeds if the import statement does not cause an error message. In addition, you can run the following test, which creates a basic GUI.

```
tk._test()
```

Note that the GUIs created might look very small. Make sure that you do not overlook your creations. The following section explores the basic features of Tkinter.

16.2 Building Your First GUI

In this section, you will create your first GUI. Arguably, the first attempt is very basic, but it contains the key ingredients of any GUI in Tkinter. We import Tkinter and initialize an instance of the *Tk()* class. This creates the root, our main canvas. Using the *title()* method on our root instance enables a title which we can modify. Finally, we adjust the size of our canvas using the *geometry()* method.

```
import tkinter as tk

#Starts root
root = tk.Tk()
root.title('My first GUI')

#Size
root.geometry("500x600")
```

If you try to execute the code until now, you will not see any GUI emerging. Why is that? The problem is that Python runs the script, which does not trigger any error messages. However, the end is reached after running the script, and Python exits. To keep our application open, we need to continue running our script. We achieve this by applying the *mainloop()* method to root, which you find at the end of this section.

To create a structure for our GUI, it is useful to define frames. Frames can hold other objects, such as buttons or labels. Hence, we initialize an instance of the *Frame()* class. The argument refers to our canvas called root. There are two methods to place objects on your canvas: the *grid()* and the *pack()* method.

The *pack()* method lets Python decide where to put your object. This is an acceptable approach for simple GUIs. However, if you deal with a large number of objects, more control over placing items is required. The *grid()* refers to a matrix starting in the top left corner of your canvas. By referring to row and column numbers, objects can be placed in relation to each other. Note that the numbers represent orders, i.e.

row 7 is on the right of row 4. It is about the order, not the absolute reference to a grid position. So, the objects placed at (0,0) and (3,4) have the same relative position as the two objects at (2,2) and (6,9).

```
#Frames
frm = tk.Frame(root)
frm.grid(column = 0, row = 0)
```

You can create and place an item in one line of code. However, separating the initialization and positioning is a useful approach. It makes it easier to spot positions if you have to deal with many items.

To add text, we can use labels. An instance of the *Label()* class is created and placed using the *grid()* method.

```
#Labels
label_frm = tk.Label(frm, text = "Hello World!")
label_frm.grid(column = 0, row = 0)
```

To add functionality to our GUI, we initialize a button instance and place it next to the label. Buttons require a command, which refers to a function or method. This command is executed if the user clicks on the button. In contrast to calling a function or method, you notice that open and closed brackets are not added. Hence, we state *root.destroy* instead of *root.destroy()*. You can add brackets and observe what happens. The GUI does not seem to be displayed. However, this is not quite what happens. The GUI is created and displayed, but immediately, the method *root.destroy()* is called. The *destroy()* deletes the root instance instantaneously. By removing brackets, Python waits until the user clicks on the button to call the function or method.

```
#Buttons
button_frm = tk.Button(frm, text = "Exit",
command = root.destroy)
button_frm.grid(column = 1, row = 0)
```

Finally, the following code, which defines the GUI, must be placed at the end of the script. This ensures the GUI exists until the user wants to end the application.

```
#Mainloop at the end
root.mainloop()
```

Figure 16.1 shows our first GUI attempt. The following section explores more advanced features, including menu bars, standard in most desktop applications.

Figure 16.1 Our first GUI

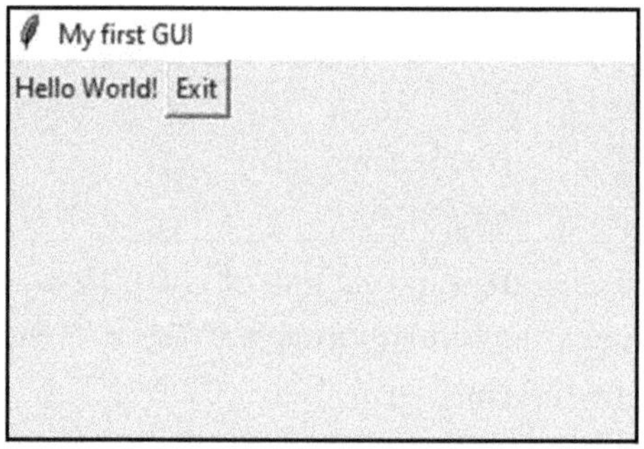

16.3 Designing Menu Bars

Menu bars offer an easy way to add many functions to a GUI. Virtually all commercial software applications use menu bars, as it is easy to structure different functions. In this example, we start with a simple menu bar, which has a File menu that handles creating a new stock portfolio, saving current data and loading portfolios. The second menu refers to investing (Invest), which splits into a buy and sell sub-menu structure. Finally, users have a choice to buy or sell stocks or bonds.

In accordance with the previous section, we create a basic GUI, modify its title, and add a frame. The frame is not required but can be used to add additional features later.

```
import tkinter as tk

#Starts root
root = tk.Tk()
root.title(‘Menu bars’)

#Size
root.geometry(“500x600”)

#Frames
frm = tk.Frame(root)
frm.grid(column = 0, row = 0)
```

Buttons require a command. It is common to create a GUI while the back-end application is still unfinished. Hence, creating a *do_nothing()* function is helpful, which prints a string to the terminal to test whether the button works as expected.

```
def do_nothing():
   print(“Do nothing!”)
```

Next, we initialize an instance of the *Menu()* class, which is placed on root. Then, we create the *file_menu*, which refers to the menu bar. The *tearoff* option can be enabled. It permits the user to move the menu. We add three commands to the file menu using the *add_command()* method. The exit command refers to the destroy method, which exits the application. However, the new, save, and load commands connect to our test function. The chapter's exercise demonstrates linking a back-end application to these menu items.

The *add_separator()* method provides a nice feature to highlight the exit option on the menu bar. The *add_cascade()* method completes the construction of the file menu.

```
menubar = tk.Menu(root)

#File menu
file_menu = tk.Menu(menubar, tearoff = 0)
file_menu.add_command(label = "New",
command = do_nothing)
file_menu.add_command(label = "Save",
command = do_nothing)
file_menu.add_command(label = "Load",
command = do_nothing)
file_menu.add_separator()
file_menu.add_command(label = "Exit",
command = root.destroy)
menubar.add_cascade(label = "File",
menu = file_menu)
```

The invest menu offers two sub-menus for buying and selling. The approach is similar except that we place menu bars on different levels.

```
#Invest menu
invest_menu = tk.Menu(menubar, tearoff = 0)
menubar.add_cascade(label = "Invest",
menu = invest_menu)
```

The buying options include investing in stocks and bonds. All options refer to our placeholder function for initial testing.

```
#Adds submenu to Buying
buy_sub_menu = tk.Menu(menubar, tearoff = 0)
buy_sub_menu.add_command(label = "Stocks",
command = do_nothing)
buy_sub_menu.add_command(label = "Bonds",
command = do_nothing)
invest_menu.add_cascade(label = "Buy",
menu = buy_sub_menu)
```

The sell sub-menu has a similar structure. This approach allows for the design of more complex menu bars. It is common to start with a GUI that contains the application's main features prior to completing the back end.

```
#Adds submenu to Selling:
sell_sub_menu = tk.Menu(menubar, tearoff = 0)
sell_sub_menu.add_command(label = "Stocks",
command = do_nothing)
sell_sub_menu.add_command(label = "Bonds",
command = do_nothing)
invest_menu.add_cascade(label = "Sell",
menu = sell_sub_menu)
```

The following code adjusts the configuration using the *config()* method. This step is essential to ensure that the menu bar is correctly displayed.

```
#Root configuration for menu bar
root.config(menu = menubar)
```

The script ends with the *mainloop()* method.

```
#Mainloop at the end
root.mainloop()
```

Figure 16.2 illustrates the menu bar, which is a lot more sophisticated. There are many ways to modify this GUI based on end-users' requirements. The Python script *menu_bar.py* provides the code for this section.

Figure 16.2 Menu bars

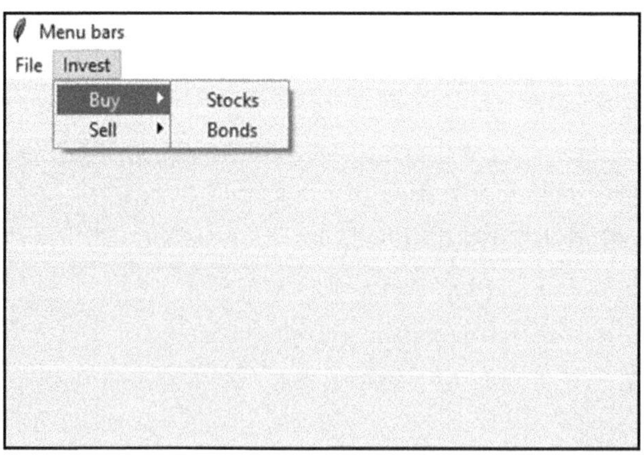

Figure 16.3 New window to handle user input

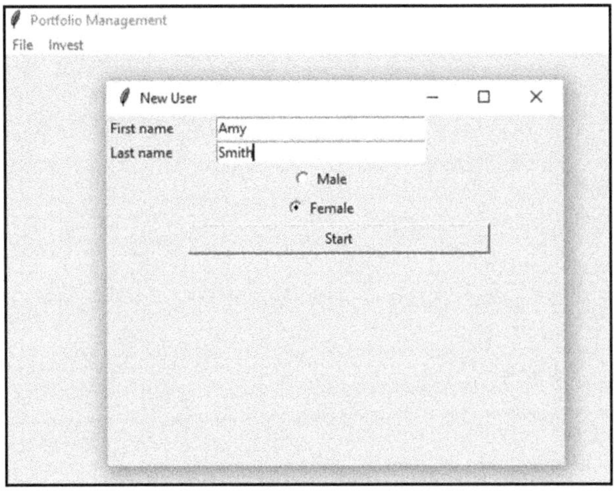

16.4 User Inputs

This section deals with user input. In this example, we add functionality to our menu bar. In particular, once a user clicks on the file menu and selects the New command, a popup window emerges. The user can add first and last names. A radio button selects the gender. The input is submitted by pressing the start button, which closes the popup window. Figure 16.3 demonstrates the popup window that permits user input.

How do we build this application? Starting with the Python script *menu_bar.py*, we need to add additional functions for the New command and the Start button. These new functions replace our placeholder function.

Starting with the *new_user()* function, we create a popup window which enables users to input their data. The *new_user_window* is an instance of the *Toplevel()* class. Note that the keyword global declares that *new_user_window* is a global variable. This means we can use the object *new_user_window* outside its scope (i.e. the current function). This is important as we need to close the window once the user presses the start button, which will be handled in a separate function.

The new window gets a separate title, and we adjust the size. To manage users' input, three global variables are created. In Tkinter, we need to declare that the first and last name are string variables, which is not very Pythonian as Python is dynamically typed. Next, we create and place an entry widget, i.e. an instance of the *Entry()* class. To the left of the entry widgets, labels display their meaning.

Gender refers to an integer *IntVar()* selected using a radio button. We can set a default position that will be displayed when the popup window emerges. A list of tuples captures the options for the radio button, placed using the *grid()* method. Note the use of the information about the position (int(option[1])) contained in the tuples when allocating the options.

```
def new_user():
    #New window
    global new_user_window
    new_user_window = tk.Toplevel()
    new_user_window.title('New User')

    #Size of widget
    new_user_window.geometry("400x300")

    #Create global variables
    global f_name
    global l_name
    global gender

    f_name = tk.StringVar()
    l_name = tk.StringVar()

    #Entry: first and last name
    f_name_entry = tk.Entry(new_user_window,
    width = 30,textvariable = f_name)
    f_name_entry.grid(row = 0, column = 1, padx = 20)

    l_name_entry = tk.Entry(new_user_window,
    width = 30, textvariable = l_name)
    l_name_entry.grid(row = 1, column = 1, padx = 20)

    #Labels for entry
    f_name_label = tk.Label(new_user_window,
    text = "First name")
    f_name_label.grid(row = 0, column = 0)

    l_name_label = tk.Label(new_user_window,
    text = "Last name")
    l_name_label.grid(row = 1, column = 0)

```

```
    #Radio button
    gender = tk.IntVar()
    gender.set('1')

    #Options for radio button as list of tuples
    OPTIONS = [('Male', '0'), ('Female', '1')]

    for option in OPTIONS:
          radio_button = tk.Radiobutton(new_user_window,
                text = option[0], variable = gender, \
          value = option[1])
          radio_button.grid(row = int(option[1]) + 2,
                column = 1)

    #Create start button
    start_button = tk.Button(new_user_window,
    text = "Start", command = start_button_function)
    start_button.grid(row = 4, column = 1,
    columnspan = 2, ipadx = 115, padx = 10, pady = 1)
```

Finally, the new window gets a Start button that saves users' inputs and closes the entry window. Note that the *start_button_function()* is used inside the *new_user()* function. Hence, it must be placed first in our script. When clicking the start button, user input is obtained using the *get()* method. Note that the variables *f_name_get*, *l_name_get*, and *gender_get* are local, i.e. they have scope inside the function. Hence, we need to consider adding user input to global variables.

After user input is stored in local variables, the window is closed. We added a print statement to test our code by displaying users' data on the terminal. These print statements are useful tests in the development phase of the project. Removing these statements and adding proper tests in more advanced applications is common.

```
def start_button_function():
   """Function for start button"""
   #Get first and last name from entry widget
   f_name_get = f_name.get()
   l_name_get = l_name.get()

   #Get gender
   gender_get = gender.get()

   #Close new_game_window
   new_user_window.destroy()
```

```
    #CHECK
    print(f"{f_name_get} {l_name_get} is
      a {gender_get}.")
```

It is easy to forget to link the *new_user* function to our New command on the file menu.

```
file_menu.add_command(label = "New",
command = new_user)
```

The Python script *user_input.py* provides the code for this part of our GUI development. Please feel free to modify the code and experiment with various options. That is the best way to learn more about GUI development.

16.5 Loading and Saving Data

Our GUI captures functionality using a well-structured menu bar. The file menu contains the New command that opens an entry window. Users provide their personal data and start the application. At the moment, local variables store users' data, requiring further development. Accordingly, we need to refactor our *start_button_function()* to find a better way to save users' input in a Python object. This is an essential step as our local variables, due to the way Tkinter works, cannot be saved and loaded directly.

A key feature of applications is the ability to save and load data. This section adds this functionality to our GUI, starting with the Python script *user_input.py*. The chapter on clustering introduced the Python pickle package, which we used to save and load a Pandas *DataFrame*. This section revisits the pickle package, which offers a convenient way to handle our data requirements without needing more advanced database management (e.g. SQL).

First, we create a basic User class. The attributes store users' inputs once the start button is pressed. This action creates an instance (i.e. a new user). Second, we modify our *start_button_function()*. Third, we add a *save()* and *load()* function, which we connect to the respective commands on the menu bar.

Starting with import statements, you notice that our User class is imported from the *user.py* script, which is located in the same folder (otherwise, the import statement needs modification). We prefer separating classes and functions. Separation and testing procedures will become much more important in complex applications.

```
import tkinter as tk
import pickle

from user import User
```

We create a basic *User()* class and define three attributes that store users' inputs. The import statement allows us to use the *User()* class in our main script.

```
class User():
  def __init__(self, f_name, l_name, gender):
     self.f_name = f_name
     self.l_name = l_name
     self.gender = gender
```

In the *start_button_function()*, we declare the global variable user, which refers to an instance of the *User()* class. The instance is initialized, and all attributes are assigned based on the user's input. Finally, we modify our print statement to check whether the attributes work as intended.

```
def start_button_function():
     """Function for start button"""
     #Get first and last name from entry widget
     f_name_get = f_name.get()
     l_name_get = l_name.get()

     #Get gender
     gender_get = gender.get()

     #Close new_game_window
     new_user_window.destroy()

     #Create global variables
     global user

     #Initialise user
     user = User(f_name = f_name_get,
     l_name = l_name_get, gender = gender_get)

     #CHECK
     print(f"{user.f_name} {user.l_name} entered {user.gender}.")
```

Next, the *save()* function defines a list of objects that should be stored. At the moment, we only have the user instance, which contains our data. It is easy to modify the code by adding new objects for storage. We use the *dump()* method to output our object to a pickle file. Finally, we display a test statement on the terminal to check our function.

```
def save():
    """Saves objects; overwrites any existing file;
    default file 'portfolio.pkl'"""
    obj = [user]
    with open('portfolio.pkl','wb') as output:
        pickle.dump(obj, output, pickle.HIGHEST_PROTOCOL)

    #CHECK
    print(f"{user.f_name} SAVED.")
```

The *load()* function opens the pickle file and unpacks its content using the *load()* method from the pickle package. We declare that user is a global variable and assign this variable to the stored object in our list. A test statement concludes this function.

```
def load():
    """Loads objects"""
    with open ('portfolio.pkl', 'rb') as input:
    obj = pickle.load(input)
    global user
    user = obj[0]

    #CHECK
    print(f"{user.f_name} LOADED.")
```

The last step is to link our new functions to the Save and Load commands in the file menu of our menu bar. The Python script *load_save.py* provides the code for this section. Ensure you run the modified application a few times and start playing with it.

```
file_menu.add_command(label = "Save", command = save)
file_menu.add_command(label = "Load", command = load)
```

Now we have developed a basic GUI that runs on desktops with Windows or macOS. This basic GUI can be linked to our machine learning tools to enable end-users to change model parameters, underlying data, and export model outputs. This chapter's exercise will explore these extensions further.

16.6 An Introduction to Flask

After more than 20 years of coding and data analytics, it is hard to deny that clients have moved more and more to web-based applications. The main reasons include the rise of cloud computing, software as a service (SaaS), and outsourcing of IT departments. Web-based applications are easier to run and integrate into existing infrastructure. Of course, many issues exist, such as privacy and security concerns. Web development is a vast and rapidly expanding area requiring familiarity with various programming languages, such as JavaScript and SQL. At least a basic understanding of HTML and CSS is essential in most projects.

For business analytics, the focus tends to be on back-end development (e.g. a machine learning model to enhance the predictability of inventories). However, product development requires a basic understanding of how models can be made more accessible.

This section offers a brief introduction to Flask. Hence, we can stick to Python to develop a lightweight web application. However, learning a bit about databases is essential for data-heavy applications.

Having worked on many web-based machine learning applications, we strongly recommend setting up a virtual environment. Too many things out of our control can affect the functionality of our web applications, including changes to package versions, dependencies, or APIs for data feeds. A virtual environment offers some protection and control. Hence, in our target folder, we open the command line. Then, we create and activate the virtual environment called web as follows.

```
python -m venv web
web\Scripts\Activate
```

We use the pip installer to install the latest version of Flask.

```
pip install flask
```

Finally, we open the Python shell by typing python on the command line and try importing flask (import flask). If we do not trigger an error message, the installation is successful. Note that the virtual environment needs to be active for this to work. Hence, check whether the name of the virtual environment is displayed in brackets in front of the command line. Now, we are ready to start our first web application.

16.7 Developing Your First Web Application

To get used to flask, a minimum working example is a good start. The Python script *basic_web.py* contains the following code.

```
from flask import Flask

app = Flask(__name__)

@app.route("/")
```

```
def hello_world():
    return "<p>Hello, World!</p>"
```

After importing the *Flask()* class from the Python package flask, we create an instance, which refers to our application (app). The *argument __name__* with double underscores specifies the module name. At the moment, we only have one Python script.

The route determines the navigation on the website. Note the use of the decorators indicated by @. The argument ("/") refers to the root page of the website. We display the famous 'Hello World!' string using HTML.

To run the application, we have to modify the settings using the following two lines of code in the command line. Please ensure that your virtual environment is active while performing this process step. The lines of code need to be executed separately. Basically, we tell Python where to find our application in the first line, and the second line sets the debug mode. The latter is useful when developing the web application as changes to our code are displayed instantaneously without the need to restart the server.

```
set FLASK_APP = basic_web.py
set FLASK_DEBUG = 1
```

After changing the settings, we can run our server using the following command in the command line.

```
flask run
```

Where can we find our website? Your terminal displays the following: 'Running on http://127.0.0.1:5000', i.e. the location of your website is the so-called localhost. You can open any web browser and type the address shown in the terminal. Alternatively, you can go to 'localhost:5000'. Note that the number after the colon refers to the port number. This should display our test string on the website.

You can modify the test string in your code and save the Python script. When you refresh your browser, the updated content should be displayed on localhost. This works without restarting our server because we are in debug mode.

There is a more convenient way to run our application. We add the following code to our Python script, which checks whether we run the script directly, i.e. it becomes the 'main' script. If the statement is true, we apply the *run()* method to our application and set the debug mode to true.

```
if __name__=='__main__':
    app.run(debug = True)
```

We stop our server using CTRL+C to test this simplified approach. Using python *basic_web.py* starts our server directly. In line with our desktop application, we need to handle user input. For instance, a user could provide a ticker symbol to receive the current share price. Restricting ourselves to HTML and Python, we can use forms to permit user input. First, we need to modify our import statement. Starting with the Python script *basic_web.py*, we modify the import statement. The revised code is saved under the name *stock_web.py*.

```
from flask import Flask, render_template
```

In the folder where you keep the Python script *stock_web.py*, create a new folder called templates. You must store your templates, i.e. HTML files, in the templates folder. Otherwise, Python would not be able to find your HTML files. We create a basic HTML file in the templates folder, which we might call home.html.

```
<!DOCTYPE html>
<html>
<body>

<h1>Portfolio Management</h1>
<p>Enter ticker symbol</p>

</body>
</html>
```

Instead of returning a string that uses HTML, we use the *render_template()* function. The argument refers to the name of our template. The template's name is a string, requiring double or single quotation marks.

```
@app.route ("/")
def home():
    return render_template('home.html')
```

This code should create a website like Figure 16.4.

Figure 16.4 Using HTML templates in flask

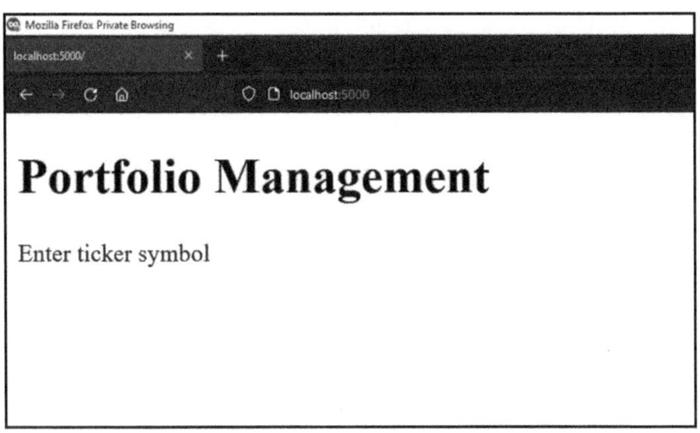

To permit user input, we add a form to our HTML template home.html. The POST method sends data from the user to our server. The attribute action refers to a new route, which we need to define later. After providing data, the user moves to http://localhost:5000/lookup.

A label is added to ensure that the user knows what is requested. Finally, the input is defined as a text. If we wish, a submit button can be displayed. Otherwise, user input is sent to the server after pressing the return key.

```
<!DOCTYPE html>
<html>
<body>

<h1>Portfolio Management</h1>
<p>Enter ticker symbol</p>

   <form action = "/lookup" method = "POST">
   <center>
     <label for = "Ticker"> Add ticker here :</label>
     <input type = "text" name = "Ticker">
     <!--Adding a submit button-->
     <input type = "submit">
   </center>
   </form>

</body>
</html>
```

Let's go back to our Python script. We have to add the new route to avoid an error message. Basically, we require the endpoint for the data request. To add the route, we use the decorator and also specify the attribute methods, providing a list for the POST and GET methods. These methods handle user inputs and data requests.

The *lockup()* function requests the data from our form, which is converted into a Python dictionary applying the *to_dict()* method. So we can operate with the key-value pairs of the dictionary. We obtain the ticker symbol provided by the user and assign it to the variable stock. The return value renders a new HTML template, which we must create in the following step. Finally, we ensure we can use the variable stock by passing it into the template.

```
@app.route("/lookup", methods = ['GET', 'POST'])
def lookup():
   #Dictionary
   output = request.form.to_dict()
   #Use keys
```

```
    stock = output["Ticker"]
    #stock = stock ensures it can be used in the template
    return render_template('output.html', stock = stock)
```

Flask uses Jinja2 as its web template engine, enabling loops, if-else statements, and a lot more in HTML templates. For instance, our HTML template can respond to conditions. If users submit a ticker symbol as requested, a message that retrieves the data submitted using placeholders can be displayed. The syntax resembles Python (e.g. formatted strings use a similar placeholder using {}). Note that structures such as loops or if statements need to be closed (e.g. {%*endfor*%}).

The if statement checks whether the variable stock contains a string. The first message is displayed in this case, asking the user to verify the input. The else statement requests that a ticker symbol needs to be submitted.

```
<!DOCTYPE html>
<html>
<body>

<h1>Portfolio Management</h1>
<p>Check your ticker</p>
  <center>
  {% if stock %}
     <h2>Is {{stock}} the correct ticker?</h2>
  {% else %}
     <h2>No ticker submitted</h2>
  {% endif %}
  </center>
</body>
</html>
```

Figure 16.5 shows the input form located on the website's root. Users can add a ticker symbol and submit their request.

Figure 16.5 Forms for user input

Figure 16.6 Response to user input

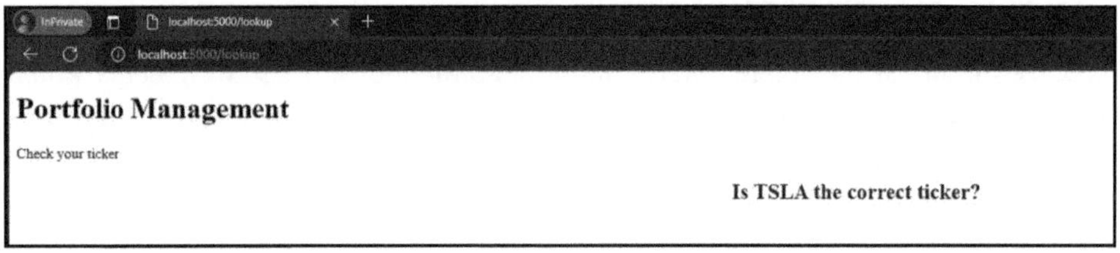

After clicking the submit button, users are relocated to receive a response. The template displays the correct message as the user provides an input (i.e. the string is not empty). Figure 16.6 displays the http://localhost:5000/lookup.

This concludes our brief introduction to web applications. Our website can handle user input and display a response based on the data provided. These principles can be easily extended to integrate our machine learning tools. For instance, we could verify whether the ticker symbol exists in Yahoo Finance. If the ticker matches an existing stock, share prices or other financial data can be requested through the yfinance API.

16.8 Summary

This chapter introduces Tkinter and Flask. After completing this chapter, you will not become an expert in GUIs or web development, as there is much more to learn, which goes beyond the scope of a book on business analytics. However, based on our experience working on various projects, a basic understanding of front-end development is helpful.

You need to know enough about the main features of GUIs or templates to understand clients' requirements. With the widespread use of tablets and mobile apps, most users will struggle to run your code in Python directly. Offering products that provide sophisticated solutions in Business Analytics but, at the same time, are easy to operate and integrate into existing frameworks is a strong value proposition.

If you got excited about web development, we suggest exploring freeCodeCamp, which covers HTML, CSS, JavaScript, and Python for web applications.

PRODUCT DEVELOPMENT

Selling a business analytics tool often requires developing a graphical user interface (GUI), which could be web-based or an application for devices such as laptops or mobiles. Developing a user-friendly GUI can simplify your Python code by guiding user input and limiting mistakes. For instance, model parameters can be restricted to ensure convergence of your algorithm.

16.9 Exercise

This exercise focuses on making our Roulette and gambler's ruin simulation, which we developed in the chapter on data wrangling, more user-friendly. We suggest starting with the GUI created by the Python script *load_save.py* to reduce duplication. Moreover, you can re-use the game simulation captured in *gambler.py*. The script *gambler_gui.py* demonstrates a possible solution.

16.9.1 Modify the Menu Bar

Your task is to change the title to 'Betting Simulation' to capture the GUI's purpose. Next, rename the invest menu to 'simulation' (or similar) and remove the sub-menus for buying and selling. Finally, add a command to start the simulation, which points to the placeholder function (*do_nothing()*). This new command should be part of the simulation menu.

16.9.2 Modify the User() Class

The simulation uses the following parameters and default settings:

- games = 100
- money = 100
- initial_bet = 1

Your task is to change the attributes of the *User()* class to capture the parameters for the simulation.

16.9.3 Adjust Functions

As we changed attributes of the *User()* class, our functions need to be updated. First, adjust the *new_user()* function to ensure it works with the new attributes. The radio button might not be the best choice for the *initial_bet* attribute. Second, the *start_button_function()* requires modifications in line with the revised attributes. Test your revised code.

16.9.4 Display Results

Finally, display the wealth (i.e. the money attribute of the user) of the gambler after all games are played based on your simulation. We suggest that the start command in the simulation menu initializes the simulation based on the parameters provided by the user. You can reuse the Python script *gambler.py* after revising the *betting()* function. You have to obtain the simulated position, which is an array, and refer to the last entry using indexing. Finally, you can use an entry widget to display the gambler's wealth at the end of the simulation.

ANSWERS TO EXERCISES

This section provides answers to exercises in Chapters 1–16. As some exercises may have multiple viable answers, readers' responses may differ from those presented here. Such variations are perfectly acceptable.

Chapter 1

1. There are four types of analytics: descriptive, diagnostic, predictive, and prescriptive. Descriptive analytics summarizes what happened in the past; diagnostic analytics explores their causes; predictive analytics forecasts future scenarios; and prescriptive analytics provides recommendations for action based on these insights. Together, they enable businesses to understand historical patterns, diagnose issues, predict future trends, and make informed decisions. For further details, please refer to section 1.2 in Chapter 1.
2. Machine learning is a branch of artificial intelligence that focuses on enabling computers to learn from and make decisions based on data. Broadly speaking, there are three types of machine learning: supervised learning, unsupervised learning, and reinforcement learning. In supervised learning, algorithms are trained using labelled data to make predictions. In unsupervised learning, algorithms mainly discover hidden patterns or structures in unlabelled data. In reinforcement learning, algorithms learn to make a sequence of decisions by receiving feedback in the form of rewards or penalties. For further details about these three types and their representative applications, please refer to section 1.4.
3. There are six key stages involved in the CRISP-DM, including business understanding, data understanding, data preparation, modelling, evaluation, and deployment. Details about each stage can be found in section 1.6.
4. An IDE is a software application that provides comprehensive facilities to computer programmers for software development. It typically integrates a variety of tools into one cohesive package, facilitating an integrated experience for development.

Chapter 2

1

(a) $\lim_{x\to-\infty}\dfrac{4}{x^2}=0$.

(b) $\lim_{x\to c}(x^2+10)=c^2+10$.

(c) $\lim_{x\to c}\dfrac{x^3+4x^2-3}{x^2+5}=\dfrac{\lim_{x\to c}(x^3+4x^2-3)}{\lim_{x\to c}(x^2+5)}=\dfrac{c^3+4c^2-3}{c^2+5}$.

(d) $\lim_{x\to2}\dfrac{x^3-8}{x^2-4}=\lim_{x\to2}\dfrac{(x-2)(x^2+2x+4)}{(x-2)(x+2)}=\lim_{x\to2}\dfrac{x^2+2x+4}{x+2}=3$.

2 The cost of producing one more bike a week when 10 are produced is about $c'(10)$. Since $c'(x) = 3x^2 - 12x + 10$, then $c'(10) = 3 \times 100 - 12 \times 10 + 10 = 190$. The additional cost will be about £190.

3

(a) $y' = 4x^3 + 12$.

(b) $y' = 3x^2 + 6x - 5$.

(c) $y' = \dfrac{4x}{(x^2+1)^2}$.

(d) $y' = x^3 + x^2 + x + 1$.

(e) $y' = -\left(1-\dfrac{x}{7}\right)^6$.

(f) $y' = 8(2x - 5)^3(x + 1)^7(3x - 4)$.

4

(a) $UV = \begin{bmatrix} 20 & 18 \\ 29 & 14 \\ 27 & 14 \end{bmatrix}$.

(b) $UV = \begin{bmatrix} 35 \\ 6 \\ 49 \end{bmatrix}$.

(c) $U^{\mathrm{T}}V = \begin{bmatrix} 0 & 5 & 8 \\ 0 & -5 & 6 \\ 2 & 9 & 0 \end{bmatrix}$.

5

(a) $UV = \begin{bmatrix} 3 & 4 \\ 4 & 6 \end{bmatrix}$, and $VU = \begin{bmatrix} 1 & 2 \\ 3 & 8 \end{bmatrix}$, so $UV \neq VU$.

(b) $(U + V)^2 = U^2 + UV + VU + V^2$. Since $UV \neq VU$, $(U + V)^2 \neq U^2 + 2UV + V^2$.

(c) $(U + V)(U - V) = U^2 + VU - UV - V^2$. Since $UV \neq VU$, $(U + V)(U - V) \neq U^2 - V^2$.

6 As $U^2 = \begin{bmatrix} 1 & 0 \\ c & 1 \end{bmatrix}\begin{bmatrix} 1 & 0 \\ c & 1 \end{bmatrix} = \begin{bmatrix} 1 & 0 \\ 2c & 1 \end{bmatrix}, U^3 = \begin{bmatrix} 1 & 0 \\ c & 1 \end{bmatrix}\begin{bmatrix} 1 & 0 \\ c & 1 \end{bmatrix}\begin{bmatrix} 1 & 0 \\ c & 1 \end{bmatrix} = \begin{bmatrix} 1 & 0 \\ 3c & 1 \end{bmatrix}$,

then $U^k = \begin{bmatrix} 1 & 0 \\ kc & 1 \end{bmatrix}$. This result can be easily proved using mathematical induction.

7 Let B_i denote the die shows i, $\mathbb{P}(B_i) = 1/6$ for $i = 1, 2, \ldots, 6$ and

$$\mathbb{P}(A \mid B_1) = 0, \quad \mathbb{P}(A \mid B_2) = 0, \quad \mathbb{P}(A \mid B_3) = 2^{-3},$$

$$\mathbb{P}(A \mid B_4) = \binom{4}{3} 2^{-4}, \quad \mathbb{P}(A \mid B_5) = \binom{5}{3} 2^{-5}, \quad \mathbb{P}(A \mid B_6) = \binom{6}{3} 2^{-6}.$$

Then we have

$$\mathbb{P}(A) = \sum_{i=1}^{6} \mathbb{P}(A \mid B_i)\mathbb{P}(B_i) = \frac{1}{6}\left(\frac{1}{8} + \frac{4}{16} + \frac{10}{32} + \frac{20}{64}\right) = \frac{1}{6}.$$

8

(a) The sample space is $\{BBB, BBG, BGB, BGG, GBB, GBG, GGB, GGG\}$, then we have $\mathbb{P}(A \cap B) = 1/8 = \mathbb{P}(A)\mathbb{P}(B)$, and $\mathbb{P}(B \cap C) = 3/8 = \mathbb{P}(B)\mathbb{P}(C)$.

(b) No, because $\mathbb{P}(A \cap C) \neq \mathbb{P}(A)\mathbb{P}(C)$.

(c) No.

9 Let $Y = X^2$. Then, the probability mass function of Y is given by

$$\mathbb{P}(Y = 1) = \mathbb{P}(X = -1) + \mathbb{P}(X = 1) = 0.5; \quad \mathbb{P}(Y = 0) = \mathbb{P}(X = 0) = 0.5.$$

Hence, $\mathbb{E}[X^2] = \mathbb{E}[Y] = 1 \times 0.5 + 0 \times 0.5 = 0.5$.

10

(a) Since the PDF must integrate to 1, so $\int_0^1 f(x)dx = 1$. This implies

$$\int_0^1 (ax + bx^2)dx = \frac{a}{2} + \frac{b}{3} = 1.$$

On the other hand, we have

$$\mathbb{E}[X] = \int_0^1 xf(x)dx = \int_0^1 (ax^2 + bx^3)dx = \frac{a}{3} + \frac{b}{4} = 0.6.$$

Solving the system of the above equations, we obtain $a = 3.6$ and $b = -2.4$.

(b) Using the results from (a), we obtain

$$f(x) = \begin{cases} 3.6x - 2.4x^2, & 0 < x < 1, \\ 0, & \text{otherwise.} \end{cases}$$

Thus,

$$\mathbb{P}(X < 1/2) = \int_0^{1/2} f(x)dx = \int_0^{1/2} (3.6x - 2.4x^2)dx = 0.35.$$

(c) As $\text{Var}[X] = \mathbb{E}[X^2] - \mathbb{E}[X]^2$, here we know

$$\mathbb{E}[X^2] = \int_0^1 x^2 f(x)dx = \int_0^1 (3.6x^3 - 2.4x^4)dx = 0.42,$$

and $\mathbb{E}[X] = 0.6$.

Thus,

Var[X] = 0.42 – 0.62 = 0.06.

Chapter 3

We import the *random* Python package and create a random number resembling a probability. This concludes task 3.16.1.

```
import random

#Generate a random number from 0 to 1
num = random.random()
print(num)
```

Next, we create the player class. Note that we can indicate the expected data type when we specify the attributes. However, this does not enforce the data type, as Python remains dynamically typed.

```
class Player():
    def __init__(self, name, army: int):
        self.name = name
        self.army = army
```

This completes our task 3.16.2. Next, we initialize two players, which addresses task 3.16.3.

```
amy = Player(name = "Amy", army = 5)
tom = Player(name = "Tom", army = 4)
```

'Amy' can roll the dice five times. So, we need to create random numbers five times and derive a score by adding them up. A loop with the *range()* function might be a good start. We can use the *army* attribute to reveal the number of armies of each player. As discussed, the *range()* function is exclusive, starting at 0. The index in the loop can have any name, for instance, *i*. We start with a score for 'Amy' at zero and add random numbers one by one inside the loop. Note that $a+ = 1$ is the same as $a = a + 1$.

```
amy_score = 0
for i in range(amy.army):
    amy_score += random.random()
```

We repeat the same for 'Tom' and print a statement to the terminal.

```
tom_score = 0
for i in range(tom.army):
    tom_score += random.random()

print(f"Amy has a score of {amy_score} and
Tom scores {tom_score}.")
```

As we reuse the same code, defining a *score* function might be better. This is more elegant and concise. We use *player* as the argument. The function assumes that *player* refers to an instance of the *Player()* class because the function relies on the attribute *army*.

```
def score(player):
    player_score = 0
    for i in range(player.army):
        player_score += random.random()
    return player_score
```

Finally, we announce the winner by applying the score function and with the help of branching. This concludes task 3.16.4.

```
amy_score = score(amy)
tom_score = score(tom)

if amy_score == tom_score:
  print(“Nobody wins.”)
elif amy_score > tom_score:
  print(“Amy wins.”)
else:
  print(“Tom wins.”)
```

Chapter 4

The following code demonstrates a possible solution using a function that does the betting. You could achieve similar outcomes using your own class or other approaches. We use the random number generator in NumPy to mimic the spin (0 to 36).

Branching is used to determine whether the gambler wins or loses. This triggers an adjustment of the bet. The while loop keeps the game running as long as the gambler has sufficient cash or the maximum number of games is reached.

```
import numpy as np
import matplotlib.pyplot as plt

#Random integers
#Note 0 is inclusive to 37 is exclusive
spin = np.random.randint(0, 37)

#Parameters
games = 100
money = 100
initial_bet = 1

def betting(money, games = 100, initial_bet = 1):
    #Player’s position
    position = np.zeros(games + 1)
    position[0] = money
    #Initial bet
    bet = initial_bet
    idx = 0
    while money > bet and idx < games:
```

```
        #Spin the wheel
        spin = np.random.randint(0, 37)
        #Update index
        idx += 1
        if spin % 2 == 0 and spin !=0:
            money += bet
            bet = initial_bet
        else:
            money -= bet
            bet *= 2
        #Update position
        position[idx] = money
    return position

#Play game
position = betting(money = 1000, games = 5000)

plt.plot(position)
plt.savefig('DW_position.png')
plt.show()
```

Figure A.1 plots the realization of a gambler's position. In this example, the strategy did not end well. Survival chances depend on the initial cash position and the initial bet.

Figure A.1 Simulated position of gambler

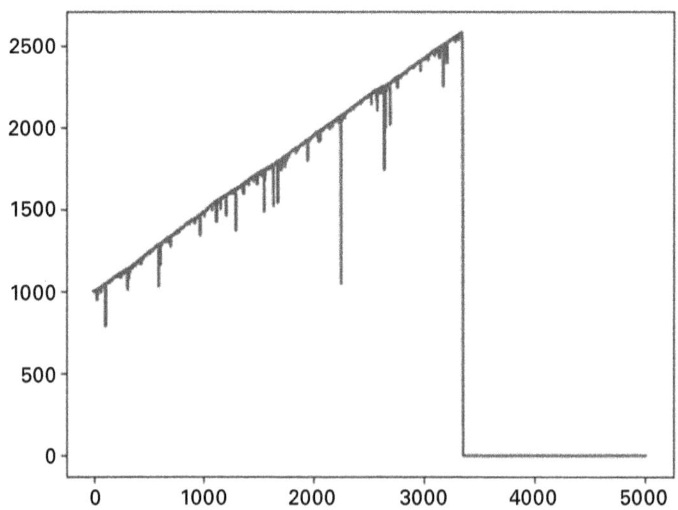

Chapter 5

We import Python packages, including Pandas, Matplotlib, and Seaborn and read the CSV file. As we have time series data, we use *Year* as an index. The *astype()* method with the argument *int* converts floats to integers. Finally, we inspect the dataset, which concludes task 5.6.1.

```
import pandas as pd
import seaborn as sns
import matplotlib.pyplot as plt

#Import data as DataFrame
df = pd.read_csv("gdp.csv")

#Set index
df = df.set_index(df['Year'])

#Change float to integer for Year
df = df.astype(int)

#Inspect the data
print(df.head())
print(df.tail())
```

Next, we plot the GDP per capita of each country using a line chart, which addresses task 5.6.2.

```
#Multiple lines
sns.lineplot(data = df[['ARG', 'AUS', 'AUT', 'BRA', 'GBR']])

plt.savefig('DV_gdp.png')
plt.show()
```

Figure A.2 demonstrates long-term growth in all countries; however, Latin American countries in this sample have performed worse.

Figure A.2 Long-term trends in GDP per capita

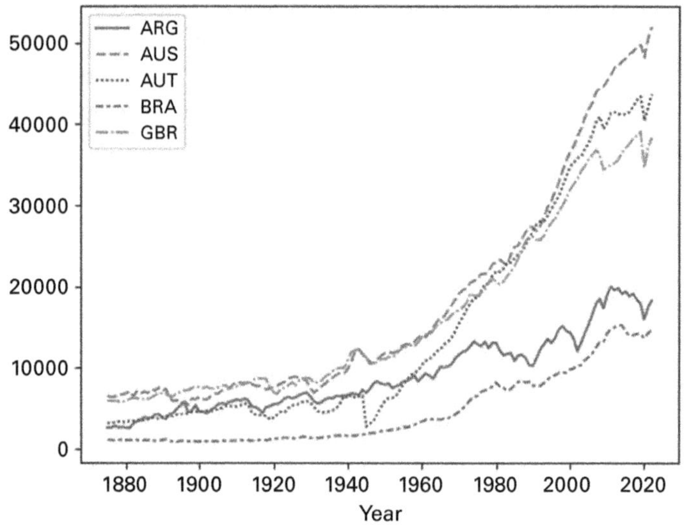

Next, we import NumPy and apply a log transformation to all columns containing GDP per capita data. We add the column *DVI*, which refers to the sigma convergence measure. This measure takes the standard deviation of countries' GDP per capita in each year. The *std()* method with the option *axis = 1* generates the desired convergence measure. Finally, a line chart depicts sigma convergence over time.

```
import numpy as np
#Log transformation
df[[‘ARG’, ‘AUS’, ‘AUT’, ‘BRA’, ‘GBR’]] =
np.log(df[[‘ARG’, ‘AUS’, ‘AUT’, ‘BRA’, ‘GBR’]])

#Standard deviation of log GDP per capita in each year
df[‘DIV’] = df[[‘ARG’, ‘AUS’, ‘AUT’, ‘BRA’, ‘GBR’]].std(axis = 1)

#Plot measure of convergence
sns.lineplot(data = df[‘DIV’])
plt.savefig(‘DV_convergence.png’)
plt.show()
```

Figure A.3 Long-term trends in GDP per capita

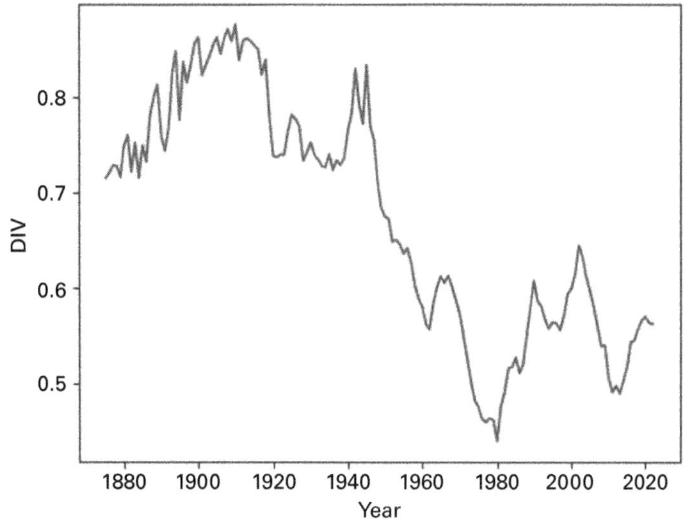

Figure A.3 demonstrates strong convergence from WWII until the 1980s, followed by more divergence. These periods coincide with the so-called second phase of globalization after WWII and a more recent shift due to higher trade barriers and less overseas investment. Our task 5.6.3 is completed, but questions remain. Are we heading into another phase of deglobalization?

Chapter 6

We create and activate a virtual environment, which we call *stats*, and install *Statsmodels*.

```
python -m venv stats
stats\Scripts\activate
pip install statsmodels
```

Pandas and NumPy should be included as dependencies when you install Statsmodels; hence, you do not need separate commands for installation. This completes task 6.7.1.

Next, we import a few packages – not all might be needed for the tasks. Using the *read_csv()* function, we import and check the data as a *DataFrame*. We notice a large number of missing values. These steps address task 6.7.2.

```
import pandas as pd
import numpy as np
import statsmodels.formula.api as smf
from statsmodels.iolib.summary2 import summary_col

#Import csv files as DataFrame
file = "health.csv"
df = pd.read_csv(file)
print(df.head())
```

Applying the method *dropna()* removes missing values from the dataset. The adjusted *DataFrame* is reassigned to the variable *df*, which concludes task 6.7.3.

```
#Remove missing values
df = df.dropna()
print(df.head())
```

We run several linear regressions to explain the dependent variable, health expenditure denoted *h_exp*, applying the *ols()* method from the Python package *Statsmodels*.

```
#Regression model
model = smf.ols('h_exp ~ DHI + pop + r_gdp', data = df)
res = model.fit()
print(res.summary())
```

In this example, we include the digital healthcare index (*DHI*), population (*pop*), and real GDP per capita (*r_gdp*). Richer countries, measured by real GDP per capita, spend more on health, whereas countries with a large population tend to spend less. Finally, the digital provision of health care seems to reduce health expenditure.

All coefficients significantly differ from zero, indicated by p-values of 0.000. The model explains 45.2% (adjusted R-squared) of the observed variability in health expenditures. Given the small number of variables, the explained proportion is quite considerable.

Chapter 7

Let's first load the dataset and perform the initial check of the data.

```
import pandas as pd
df = pd.read_csv("data/heart_disease.csv")
df.shape
df.dtypes
```

In the above codes, *df.shape* shows this is a small dataset only containing 303 observations and 14 variables, and *df.dtypes* shows that all the variables are numerical variables.

We can then split the data into training and test sets, where test size is 0.4.

```
my_random_seed_number = 10

x = df.iloc[:, :-1].to_numpy()
y = df.iloc[:, -1].to_numpy()

from sklearn.model_selection import train_test_split

x_train, x_test, y_train, y_test = train_test_split(
    x, y, test_size=0.4, random_state = my_random_seed_
    number, stratify=y
)
```

Next, use *LogisticRegression* from the scikit-learn library to train a logistic regression model.

```
from sklearn.linear_model import LogisticRegression

clf = LogisticRegression(random_state = my_random_seed_
number, max_iter=5000)
clf.fit(x_train, y_train)
```

The trained model can then make predictions with both the training data and the test data.

```
y_pred_label_train = clf.predict(x_train)
y_pred_label_prob_train = clf.predict_proba(x_train)[:, 1]
y_pred_label_test = clf.predict(x_test)
y_pred_label_prob_test = clf.predict_proba(x_test)[:, 1]
```

Then, calculate the related evaluation metrics (accuracy, recall, precision) for both the training and the test data.

```
from sklearn.metrics import recall_score
from sklearn.metrics import precision_score

print("Compute evaluation metrics(training)")
print("Average accuracy : %0.4f" % clf.score(x_train,
y_train))
print(
```

```
    "Average recall: %0.4f" % recall_score(y_train, y_pred_label_train, average="macro")
)
print(
     "Average precision: %0.4f"
     % precision_score(y_train, y_pred_label_train, average="macro")
)

print("Compute evaluation metrics(test)")
print("Average accuracy: %0.4f" % clf.score(x_test, y_test))
print(
    "Average recall: %0.4f" % recall_score(y_test, y_pred_label_test, average="macro")
)
print(
    "Average precision: %0.4f"
    % precision_score(y_test, y_pred_label_test, average="macro")
)
```

Alternatively, we can use *classification_report* to obtain a summarized result.

```
from sklearn.metrics import classification_report

print(classification_report(y_train, y_pred_label_train))
print(classification_report(y_test, y_pred_label_test))
```

Finally, we can use *roc_curve* and *auc* from *sklearn.metrics* to calculate the AUC of the model performance in the test data, and define a function to draw an ROC graph of the model.

```
from sklearn.metrics import roc_curve, auc

fpr, tpr, thresholds = roc_curve(y_test, y_pred_label_prob_test)
roc_auc = auc(fpr, tpr)

def plot_roc_curve(fpr, tpr):
    fig, ax = plt.subplots(figsize=(5, 5))
```

```
        ax.step(fpr, tpr, color="Orange", label="ROC curve(area = %0.4f)" % roc_auc)
        ax.plot([0, 1], [0, 1], color="RoyalBlue", linestyle="--")
        ax.set_xlim([0.0, 1.0])
        ax.set_ylim([0.0, 1.0])
        ax.set_xlabel("False Positive Rate")
        ax.set_ylabel("True Positive Rate")
        ax.set_title("Receiver Operating Characteristic (ROC) Curve")
        ax.legend(loc="lower right")
        plt.show()
        fig.savefig("ml_logistic_regression_exercise_plot_roc.pdf")

plot_roc_curve(fpr, tpr)
```

Chapter 8

Let's first load the dataset and perform the initial check of the data. Please note that the original dataset does not contain a header; therefore the *header* specification is set to be *None* in the *pd.read_csv()* function.

```
import pandas as pd

df = pd.read_csv("data/german_credit.csv", header=None)
df.info()
```

In the data description, we know the following variables represent the columns (same sequence) in the dataset so we can assign these variable names to the columns in the imported dataset: Status of checking account, Duration in months, Credit history, Purpose, Credit amount, Savings account/bond, Present employment since, Installment rate in percentage of disposable income, Personal status and sex, Other debtors, Present residence since, Property, Age in years, Other installment plans, Housing, Number of existing credits, Job, Number of people providing maintenance for, Telephone, Foreign worker, Credit risk.

```
df.columns = [
    "Status of checking account",
    "Duration in months",
```

```
    "Credit history",
    "Purpose",
    "Credit amount",
    "Savings account/bond",
    "Present employment since",
    "Installment rate in percentage of disposable income",
    "Personal status and sex",
    "Other debtors",
    "Present residence since",
    "Property",
    "Age in years",
    "Other installment plans",
    "Housing",
    "Number of existing credits",
    "Job",
    "Number of people providing maintenance for",
    "Telephone",
    "Foreign worker",
    "Credit risk",
]
df.head(5)
```

The distribution of the classes in the target variable is then checked to ensure they are balanced. As shown in Figure A.4, although not perfectly balanced, they are acceptable.

```
import matplotlib.pyplot as plt

%matplotlib inline

plt.hist(df["Credit risk"])
plt.xlabel("Credit risk")
plt.ylabel("Frequency")
plt.show()
```

Using the following codes, we can check the unique values of the numerical variables.

```
for col in df.select_dtypes(include=["int64"]):
    print("{}: {}".format(col, df[col].unique()))
```

Figure A.4 Distribution of classes in the target variable *Credit risk*

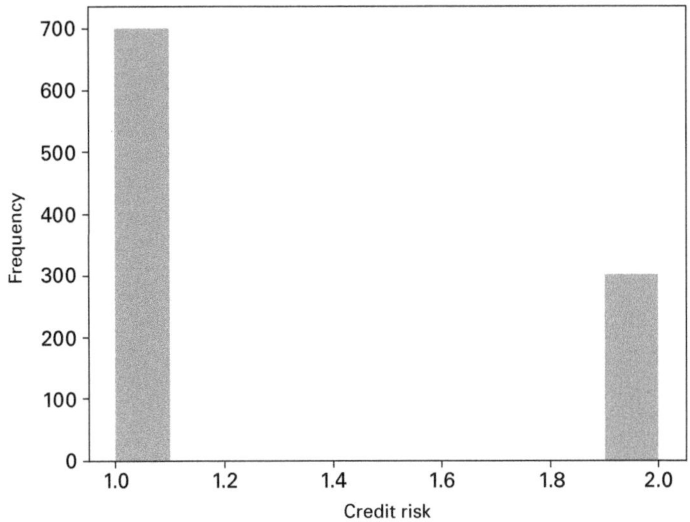

We can then convert numerical features to categorical type if they contain only a limited number of unique values. In this example, we set the threshold to 5, but this number can be adjusted as needed.

```
for col in df.select_dtypes(include="int64"):
    if len(df[col].unique()) <= 5:
        df[col] = df[col].astype("category")

for col in df.select_dtypes(include="object"):
    df[col] = df[col].astype("category")
```

Next, we perform one-hot encoding. Figure A.5 shows that the numerical features have been moved to the first two columns. Additionally, after performing one-hot encoding on the entire dataset df, the target variable has also been encoded, with 0 representing *Bad* and 1 representing *Good*.

```
df2 = pd.get_dummies(df, drop_first=True)
df2.head(5)
```

We can convert the dataset into NumPy array and then perform standardization for the numerical variables.

Figure A.5 Dataset after performing one-hot encoding

	Duration in months	Credit amount	Age in years	Status of checking account_A12	Status of checking account_A13	Status of checking account_A14	Credit history_A31	Credit history_A32	Credit history_A33	Credit history_A34	...	Number of existing credits_2	Number of existing credits_3	Number of existing credits_4
0	6	1169	97	False	False	False	False	False	False	True	...	True	False	False
1	48	5951	22	True	False	False	False	True	False	False	...	False	False	False
2	12	2096	49	False	False	True	False	False	False	True	...	False	False	False
3	42	7882	45	False	False	False	False	True	False	False	...	False	False	False
4	24	4870	53	False	False	False	False	False	True	False	...	True	False	False

5 rows × 55 columns

```
x = df2.iloc[:, :-1].to_numpy()
y = df2.iloc[:, -1].to_numpy()

from sklearn.preprocessing import StandardScaler

ss = StandardScaler().fit(x[:, :2])
x[:, :2] = ss.transform(x[:, :2])
```

Then, the data is split through stratified sampling into a training set and a test set, where the test size is 0.4.

```
from sklearn.model_selection import train_test_split

my_random_seed_number = 100

x_train, x_test, y_train, y_test = train_test_split(
    x, y, test_size =0.4, random_state=my_random_seed_
    number, stratify=y
)
```

To simplify the discussion, we just implement an MLP using the default hyperparameter setting in scikit-learn without further fine-tuning the model.

```
from sklearn.neural_network import MLPClassifier

clf = MLPClassifier(random_state=my_random_seed_number,
max_iter=5000)
clf.fit(x_train, y_train)

y_pred_label_train = clf.predict(x_train)
y_pred_label_prob_train = clf.predict_proba(x_train)[:, 1]

y_pred_label_test = clf.predict(x_test)
y_pred_label_prob_test = clf.predict_proba(x_test)[:, 1]
```

Create two data frames, each containing three columns: *Label_GT* (ground truth from the dataset), *Label_Pred_Prob* (probability of your model's prediction), and *Label_Pred* (your model's predicted label).

```
df_result_train = pd.DataFrame([y_train, y_pred_label_prob_
train, y_pred_label_train])
df_result_train = df_result_train.T
df_result_train.columns = ["Label_GT", "Label_Pred_Prob",
"Label_Pred"]
```

```
df_result_train.head()

df_result_test = pd.DataFrame([y_test, y_pred_label_prob_test, y_pred_label_test])
df_result_test = df_result_test.T
df_result_test.columns = ["Label_GT", "Label_Pred_Prob", "Label_Pred"]
df_result_test.head()
```

Use *confusion_matrix* to calculate the TP, FP, TN, FN of both the training data and the test data.

```
from sklearn.metrics import confusion_matrix

print("Training")
print(confusion_matrix(y_train, y_pred_label_train))
print("--\n")

print("Test")
print(confusion_matrix(y_test, y_pred_label_test))
```

Calculate the related evaluation metrics (accuracy, recall, precision) for both the training and the test data.

```
from sklearn.metrics import recall_score
from sklearn.metrics import precision_score

print("Compute evaluation metrics (training)")
print("Average accuracy: %0.4f" % clf.score(x_train, y_train))
print(
    "Average recall: %0.4f" % recall_score(y_train, y_pred_label_train, average="macro")
)
print(
    "Average precision: %0.4f"
    % precision_score(y_train, y_pred_label_train, average="macro")
)

print("Compute evaluation metrics(test)")
print("Average accuracy: %0.4f" % clf.score(x_test, y_test))
```

```
print(
    "Average recall: %0.4f" % recall_score(y_test, y_pred_label_test, average="macro")
)
print(
    "Average precision: %0.4f"
    % precision_score(y_test, y_pred_label_test, average="macro")
)
```

Alternatively, we can use the *classification_report* function.

```
from sklearn.metrics import classification_report

print(classification_report(y_train, y_pred_label_train))
print(classification_report(y_test, y_pred_label_test))
```

Finally, we use *roc_curve* and *auc* from *sklearn.metrics* to calculate the AUC of the model performance in the test data, and draw a ROC graph of the model, as shown in Figure A.6.

```
from sklearn.metrics import roc_curve, auc

fpr, tpr, thresholds = roc_curve(y_test, y_pred_label_prob_test)
roc_auc = auc(fpr, tpr)

def plot_roc_curve(fpr, tpr):
    fig, ax = plt.subplots(figsize=(5, 5))
    ax.step(fpr, tpr, color="Orange", label="ROC curve (area = %0.4f)" % roc_auc)
    ax.plot([0, 1], [0, 1], color="RoyalBlue", linestyle="--")
    ax.set_xlim([0.0, 1.0])
    ax.set_ylim([0.0, 1.0])
    ax.set_xlabel("False Positive Rate")
    ax.set_ylabel("True Positive Rate")
    ax.set_title("Receiver Operating Characteristic (ROC) Curve")
    ax.legend(loc="lower right")
    plt.show()
    fig.savefig("ml_logistic_regression_exercise_plot_roc.pdf")

plot_roc_curve(fpr, tpr)
```

Figure A.6 Plot of ROC for the MLP on the test data

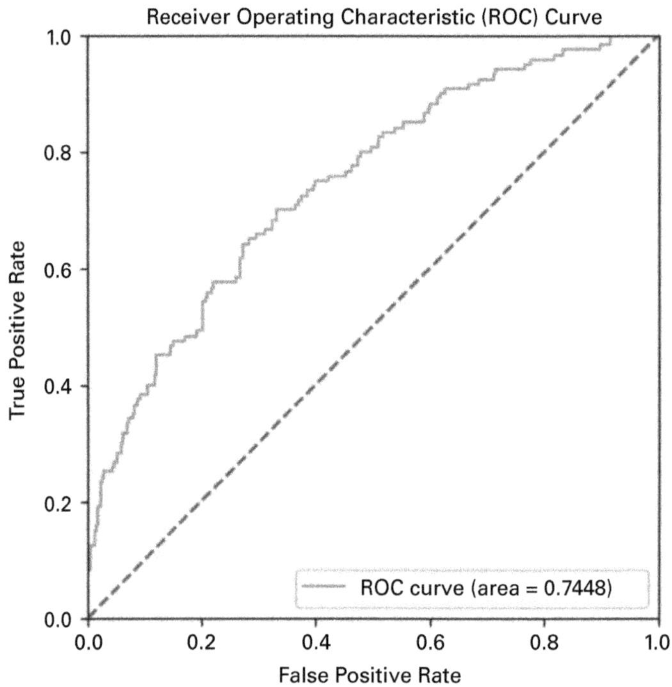

Chapter 9

Let's first load the dataset, and check data dimension and variable types.

```
import pandas as pd

df = pd.read_csv("data/iris.csv")
df.info()
```

Then split the data with the stratified sampling into a training set and a test set, with test size 40%.

```
from sklearn.model_selection import train_test_split

my_random_seed = 100

x = df.iloc[:, 0:-1].to_numpy()
y = df.iloc[:, -1].to_numpy().flatten()

```

```
x_train, x_test, y_train, y_test = train_test_split(
    x,
    y,
    test_size =0.4,
    random_state=my_random_seed,
    stratify=y,
)
```

Develop KNN and MLP, and compare their performance on the test data. As illustrated in Figure A.7, KNN demonstrates performance comparable to that of MLP.

```
from sklearn.neighbors import KNeighborsClassifier

knn = KNeighborsClassifier(
    n_neighbors=5, p=2, metric="minkowski",
    weights="uniform", algorithm="auto"
)
knn.fit(x_train, y_train)
y_pred_test_knn = knn.predict(x_test)

from sklearn.neural_network import MLPClassifier

mlp_clf = MLPClassifier(random_state=my_random_seed,
max_iter=2000)
mlp_clf.fit(x_train, y_train)
y_pred_test_mlp_clf = mlp_clf.predict(x_test)
```

```
from sklearn.metrics import classification_report

print("KNN ----------------\n")
print(classification_report(y_test, y_pred_test_knn))

print("MLP ----------------\n")
print(classification_report(y_test, y_pred_test_mlp_clf))
```

Figure A.7 Evaluation results of the KNN and MLP on the test set

```
KNN ----------------
                  precision    recall  f1-score   support

    Iris-setosa        1.00      1.00      1.00        20
Iris-versicolor        0.95      0.95      0.95        20
 Iris-virginica        0.95      0.95      0.95        20

       accuracy                            0.97        60
      macro avg        0.97      0.97      0.97        60
   weighted avg        0.97      0.97      0.97        60

MLP ----------------
                  precision    recall  f1-score   support

    Iris-setosa        1.00      1.00      1.00        20
Iris-versicolor        1.00      0.95      0.97        20
 Iris-virginica        0.95      1.00      0.98        20

       accuracy                            0.98        60
      macro avg        0.98      0.98      0.98        60
   weighted avg        0.98      0.98      0.98        60
```

Chapter 10

Let's first load the dataset, and check data dimension and variable types.

```
import pandas as pd

df = pd.read_csv("data/breast_cancer.csv")
df.info()
```

We then split the data with the stratified sampling into a training set and a test set, with test size 30%.

```
from sklearn.model_selection import train_test_split

my_random_seed = 100

x = df.iloc[:, 1:].to_numpy()
y = df.iloc[:, 0].to_numpy().flatten()

x_train, x_test, y_train, y_test = train_test_split(
    x,
    y,
    test_size=0.3,
    random_state=my_random_seed,
    stratify=y,
)
```

Develop Gaussian, Naïve Bayes (GNB), KNN, and MLP, and compare their performance on the test data. As illustrated in Figure A.8, GNB outperforms the other two algorithms.

```
from sklearn.naive_bayes import GaussianNB

gnb = GaussianNB()
gnb.fit(x_train, y_train)
y_pred_test_gnb = gnb.predict(x_test)

from sklearn.neighbors import KNeighborsClassifier

knn = KNeighborsClassifier(
    n_neighbors=5, p=2, metric="minkowski",
    weights="uniform", algorithm="auto"
)
knn.fit(x_train, y_train)
y_pred_test_knn = knn.predict(x_test)

from sklearn.neural_network import MLPClassifier

mlp_clf = MLPClassifier(random_state=my_random_seed, max_iter=2000)
mlp_clf.fit(x_train, y_train)
y_pred_test_mlp_clf = mlp_clf.predict(x_test)
```

```
from sklearn.metrics import classification_report

print("GNB ------------------\n")
print(classification_report(y_test, y_pred_test_gnb))

print("KNN ------------------\n")
print(classification_report(y_test, y_pred_test_knn))

print("MLP ------------------\n")
print(classification_report(y_test, y_pred_test_mlp_clf))
```

Figure A.8 Evaluation results of the GNB, KNN and MLP on the test set

```
GNB ----------------
              precision    recall  f1-score   support

           B       0.96      1.00      0.98       107
           M       1.00      0.92      0.96        64

    accuracy                           0.97       171
   macro avg       0.98      0.96      0.97       171
weighted avg       0.97      0.97      0.97       171

KNN ----------------
              precision    recall  f1-score   support

           B       0.92      0.95      0.94       107
           M       0.92      0.86      0.89        64

    accuracy                           0.92       171
   macro avg       0.92      0.91      0.91       171
weighted avg       0.92      0.92      0.92       171

MLP ----------------
              precision    recall  f1-score   support

           B       0.90      0.96      0.93       107
           M       0.93      0.83      0.88        64

    accuracy                           0.91       171
   macro avg       0.92      0.90      0.90       171
weighted avg       0.91      0.91      0.91       171
```

Chapter 11

Let's first load the dataset and perform the initial check of the data.

```
import pandas as pd
df = pd.read_csv(“data/bank_marketing.csv”, sep=“;”)
df.info()
```

We then check the distribution of classes in the target variable, and find the classes are not balanced. Therefore, resampling can be performed.

```
df[“y”].value_counts()
```

As there are 41,188 observations in the dataset and the minority class contains 4,640 entries, we can consider either upsampling or downsampling. Let's proceed with downsampling as follows.

```
from sklearn.utils import resample
my_random_seed = 100

#Separate majority and minority classes
```

```
df_majority = df.loc[df[“y”] == “no”, :]
df_minority = df.loc[df[“y”] == “yes”, :]

#Downsampling
df_majority_downsampled = resample(
    df_majority,
    replace=False, # sample with replacement
    n_samples=df_minority.shape[0], # to match majority class
    random_state=my_random_seed,
)
df_majority_downsampled

df_downsampled = pd.concat([df_majority_downsampled,
df_minority])
df_downsampled.reset_index(drop=True, inplace=True)
df = df_downsampled.copy()
```

Next, we perform the one-hot encoding, convert the data into NumPy array format, and split the data into a training set and a test set.

```
df = pd.get_dummies(data=df, drop_first=True, dtype=“int8”)
feature_name = df.columns.tolist()

feature_name.remove(“y_yes”)
x = df[feature_name].to_numpy()
y = df[“y_yes”]

from sklearn.model_selection import train_test_split

split_train_size = 0.7
x_train, x_test, y_train, y_test = train_test_split(
    x, y, train_size=split_train_size, random_state=
    my_random_seed, stratify=y
)
```

First, we will develop a decision tree. Since decision trees have several hyperparameters that can significantly impact their performance, we will use *GridSearchCV* to fine-tune the model based on the training data.

Figure A.9 Visualization of the fine-tuned decision tree

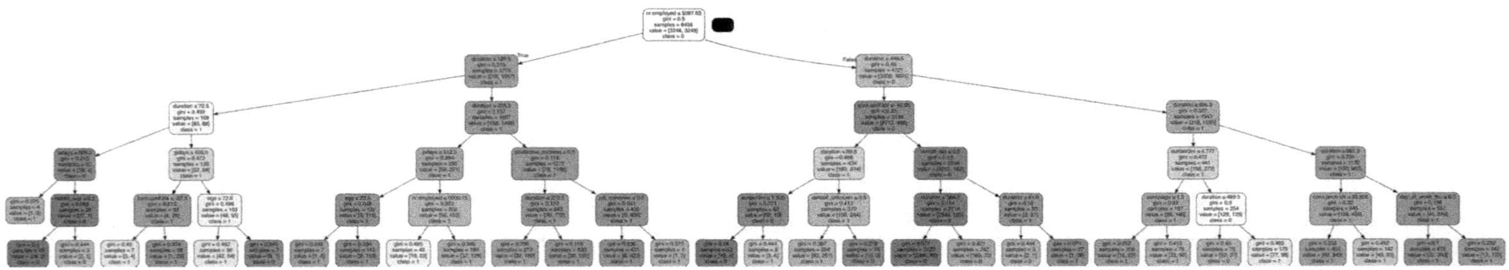

```
from sklearn.model_selection import GridSearchCV
from sklearn.tree import DecisionTreeClassifier
import numpy as np

dtc_param = {
    "criterion": ["entropy", "gini"],
    "max_depth": np. arange(3, 10).tolist(),
    "min_samples_leaf": np.arange(3, 10).tolist(),
}

n_folds = 5

dtc = DecisionTreeClassifier(random_state=my_random_seed)

dtc_cv = GridSearchCV (
    estimator=dtc, param_grid=dtc_param, cv=n_folds,
    scoring="accuracy"
)

dtc_cv.fit(x_train, y_train)

dtc = DecisionTree Classifier(random_state = my_random_seed,
**dtc_cv.best_params_)
dtc.fit(x_train, y_train)
```

We can also visualize the fine-tuned decision tree, as shown in Figure A.9.

```
label_names = df["y_yes"].value_counts().index.tolist()
label_names = [str(x) for x in label_names]
label_names

from sklearn.tree import export_graphviz
import pydotplus
from IPython.display import Image

dot_data = export_graphviz(
    dtc,
    out_file=None,
    feature_names = feature_name,
    class_names = label_names,
    filled=True,
```

```
    rounded=True,
    special_characters=True,
)

graph = pydotplus.graph_from_dot_data(dot_data)
Image(graph.create_png())
```

Then, we evaluate the model's performance based on its predictions for the test data, with the accuracy 0.88, indicating a good model obtained.

```
y_test_pred = dtc.predict(x_test)

from sklearn.metrics import classification_report

print(classification_report(y_test, y_test_pred))
```

We can also use the *eli5* package to explain the predictions made by the fine-tuned decision tree. As Figure A.10 shows, duration, nr.employed, and cons.conf.idx are the most important features.

```
import eli5

eli5.show_weights(dtc, feature_names=feature_name)
```

Figure A.10 Feature importance of the fine-tuned decision tree

Weight	Feature
0.5014	duration
0.3317	nr.employed
0.1130	cons.conf.idx
0.0199	month_oct
0.0117	euribor3m
0.0089	pdays
0.0053	default_unknown
0.0038	cons.price.idx
0.0012	age
0.0011	poutcome_success
0.0009	campaign
0.0007	day_of_week_thu
0.0003	month_sep
0.0002	job_unknown
0	job_self-employed
0	job_housemaid
0	job_student
0	job_technician
0	job_retired
0	job_management
	... 32 more ...

Following similar steps, we then develop a random forest model. The fine-tuned random forest achieves an accuracy of 0.89, which is slightly better than the decision tree.

```
from sklearn.ensemble import RandomForestClassifier

rf_param = {
    “criterion”: [“entropy”, “gini”],
    “max_depth”: np.arange(3, 10).tolist(),
    “min_samples_leaf”: np.arange(3, 10).tolist(),
}

rf = RandomForestClassifier(random_state=my_random_seed)

rf_cv = GridSearchCV(estimator=rf, param_grid=rf_param,
cv= n_folds, scoring=“accuracy”)
rf_cv.fit(x_train, y_train)

rf = RandomForestClassifier(random_state=my_random_seed,
**rf_cv.best_params_)
rf.fit(x_train, y_train)

y_test_pred_rf = rf.predict(x_test)
print(classification_report(y_test, y_test_pred_rf))
```

Also, the *eli5* package can be used for random forest to show the important features in the fine-tuned model, though they may different to the decision tree.

```
eli5.show_weights(rf, feature_names=feature_name)
```

Chapter 12

Let’s first load the dataset and perform the initial check of the data.

```
import pandas as pd

df = pd.read_csv(“data/holiday_rental_consumer_segmentation.
csv”)
df.info()
```

As the classes in the target variable are not balanced, we will perform upsampling. Next, we will apply one-hot encoding to the categorical features, standardization to the numerical features, and label encoding to the target variable.

```
from sklearn.utils import resample

df_label = df["Event"].value_counts()

df_spa = df.loc[df["Event"] == "Spa",]
df_shows = df.loc[df["Event"] == "Shows",]
df_outdoor = df.loc[df["Event"] == "Outdoor activities",]

df_shows_upsampled = resample(df_shows, replace=True, n_samples=df_label["Spa"])
df_outdoor_upsampled = resample(df_outdoor, replace=True, n_samples=df_label["Spa"])

df2 = pd.concat([df_spa, df_shows_upsampled], ignore_index=True)
df2 = pd.concat([df2, df_outdoor_upsampled], ignore_index=True)

df2["Event"].value_counts()

from sklearn.preprocessing import StandardScaler
from sklearn.preprocessing import LabelEncoder

x = pd.get_dummies(df2.iloc[:, :-1], drop_first=True, dtype="int8").to_numpy()
x[:, :5] = StandardScaler().fit_transform(x[:, :5])
y = LabelEncoder().fit_transform(df2["Event"])
```

Next, develop models using logistic regression, neural networks, decision tree, random forest, AdaBoost, gradient boosting, mixed Naïve Bayes, KNN, and SVM to segment consumers. Compare their performance using five-fold cross-validation. Additionally, you can further fine-tune these models through cross-validation.

```
random_seed_val = 100
model_list = {}

from sklearn.linear_model import LogisticRegression
```

```
model_list["LR"] = LogisticRegression(random_state=random_seed_val)

from sklearn.neural_network import MLPClassifier
model_list["MLP"] = MLPClassifier(
    random_state=random_seed_val, activation="logistic", max_iter=10000
)

from sklearn.tree import DecisionTreeClassifier
model_list["DT (CART)"] = DecisionTreeClassifier(
    criterion="gini", random_state=random_seed_val
)

from sklearn.ensemble import RandomForestClassifier
model_list["RF"] = RandomForestClassifier (
    criterion="entropy", random_state=random_seed_val
)

from sklearn.ensemble import AdaBoostClassifier
model_list["AB"] = AdaBoostClassifier(random_state=random_seed_val)

from sklearn.svm import SVC
model_list["SVM (Linear)"] = SVC(gamma="auto", kernel="linear")
model_list["SVM (RBF)"] = SVC(gamma="auto", kernel="rbf")
model_list["SVM (Poly)"] = SVC(gamma="auto", kernel="poly")

from mixed_naive_bayes import MixedNB
model_list["MNB"] = MixedNB(categorical_features=list(range(5, 11)))

from sklearn import neighbors
model_list["KNN"] = neighbors.KNeighborsClassifier(
    n_neighbors=5, p=2, metric="minkowski", weights="uniform", algorithm="auto"
)

```

```
from sklearn.model_selection import cross_val_score
import numpy as np

k_fold = 5
results_cv = {}
for algo in model_list.keys():
    print(algo)
    results_cv[algo] = np.mean(cross_val_score(model_list[algo], x, y, cv=k_fold))

results_cv
```

We can visualize the model performance comparison, as shown in Figure A.11.

```
import matplotlib.pyplot as plt

%matplotlib inline
import seaborn as sns

sns.set_style(“whitegrid”)

x_plot = [x for y, x in sorted(zip(results_cv.values(), results_cv.keys()))]
y_plot = [y for y, x in sorted(zip(results_cv.values(), results_cv.keys()))]
x_pos = [i for i, _ in enumerate(x_plot)]

plt.barh(x_pos, y_plot, color=“royalblue”)
plt.ylabel(“Model”)
plt.xlabel(“Accuracy”)
plt.title(“Model performance(CV=5)”)

plt.yticks(x_pos, x_plot)
plt.show()
```

Figure A.11 Performance comparison of SVMs with different kernels against other classification models

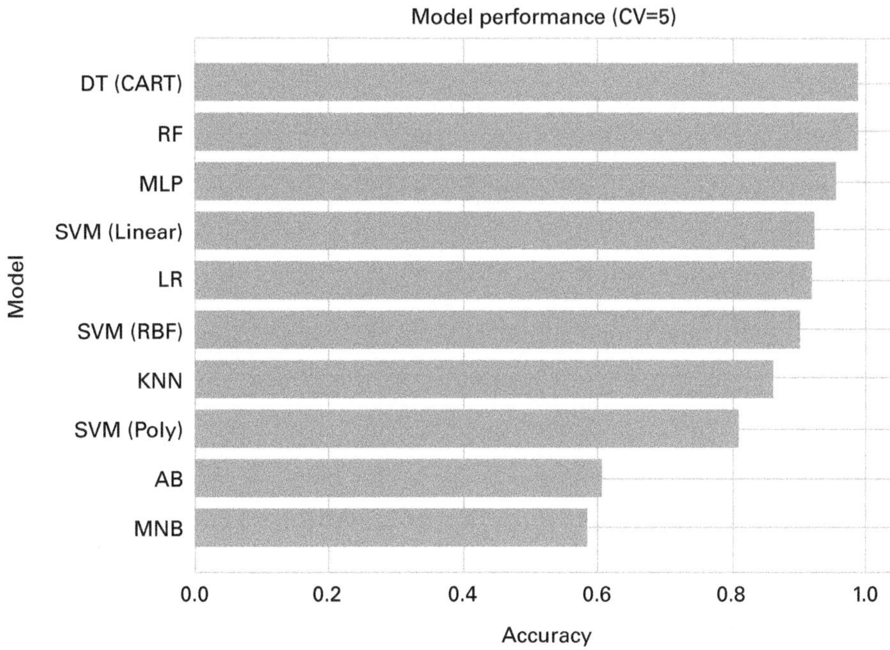

Chapter 13

We start with the usual import statements, including Pandas, NumPy, scikit-learn, and Matplotlib.

```
import pandas as pd
import numpy as np
import matplotlib.pyplot as plt
from sklearn.model_selection import train_test_split
from sklearn.preprocessing import StandardScaler
```

Then, we import the data and drop missing values, as requested in the task 13.8.1.

```
#Import data
df = pd.read_csv("vul_data.csv")

#Drop missing values
df = df.dropna(how='any')
```

To complete task 13.8.2, we define the variable high, which measures the 90th percentile of the variable VUL. The ND-GAIN index refers to the variable VUL. Hence, countries in the top 10% of cases exhibit high climate risk according to this index. Using indexing and the *iloc[]* method on the Pandas Series, we obtain a NumPy array called vul that contains the values of the ND-GAIN index. Finally, using the NumPy function np.where(), the dummy is created.

```
#Countries in top 10% based on VUL measure
high = df.VUL.quantile(.9)

#Take values for index
vul = df.iloc[:, 2].values

#Dummy for high - risk country
y = np.where(vul >= high, 1, -1)
```

Task 13.8.3 is easy to accomplish.

```
#Define data matrix
X = df.iloc[:, 4:].values
```

Next, we split the sample and standardize our data in line with task 13.8.4.

```
#We split the sample into 70% training and 30% test data
X_train, X_test, y_train, y_test =
    train_test_split(X, y, test_size=0.3,
    stratify=y,
    random_state=0)

#Standardisation
sc = StandardScaler()
X_train_std = sc.fit_transform(X_train)
X_test_std = sc.transform(X_test)
```

Task 13.8.5 requires the calculation of the covariance matrix. Eigenvalues and associated eigenvectors are obtained. Eigenvalues are sorted, and the explained variance is derived. The first principal component explains 22.4% of the variance, which is considerable. However, this level is still far below the standard threshold, around 85% to 95%. Hence, one needs to question whether a single index adequately measures climate risk.

```
#Covariance matrix
cov_mat = np.cov(X_train_std.T)
eigen_vals, eigen_vecs = np.linalg.eigh(cov_mat)
```

```
print('\nEigenvalues \n%s' % eigen_vals)

#Sort eigenvalues
tot = sum(eigen_vals)
var_exp = [(i / tot) for i in sorted(eigen_vals,
reverse=True)]
cum_var_exp = np.cumsum(var_exp)
```

Next, we plot the eigenvalues and the explained variance to complete task 13.8.6.

```
#Plot eigenvalues
plt.bar(range(1, 27), var_exp, alpha=0.5, align='center',
        label='individual explained variance')
plt.step(range(1, 27), cum_var_exp, where='mid',
         label='cumulative explained variance')
plt.ylabel('Explained variance ratio')
plt.xlabel('Principal component index')
plt.legend(loc='best')
plt.tight_layout()
plt.savefig('PCA_Task_Fig1.png', dpi=300)
plt.show()
```

Figure A.12 shows that combining two or three principal components would be required to explain at least 40% of the total variance.

Figure A.12 Explained variance to capture climate risk

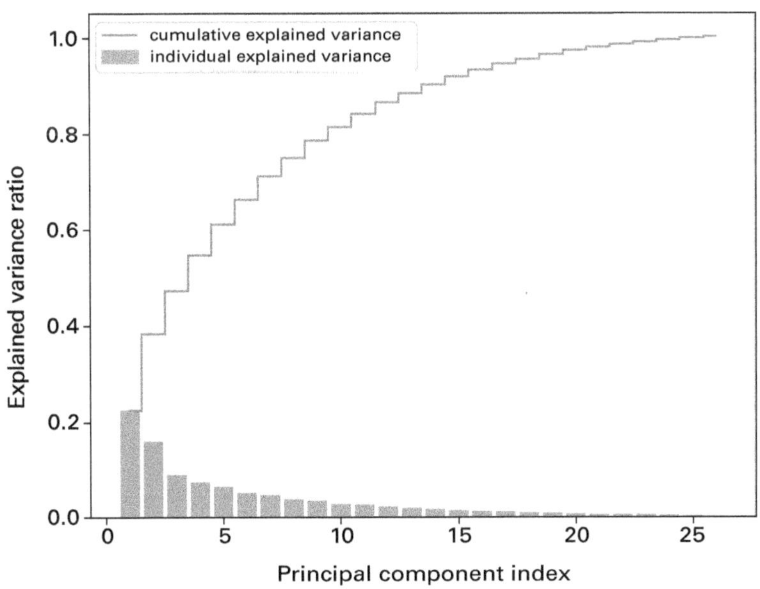

Finally, we transform the data and plot the transformed data using two principal components, which addresses task 13.8.7.

```
#List of (eigenvalue, eigenvector) tuples
eigen_pairs = [(np.abs(eigen_vals[i]), eigen_vecs[:, i])
               for i in range(len(eigen_vals))]

#Sort the (eigenvalue, eigenvector) tuples from high to low
eigen_pairs.sort(key = lambda k: k[0], reverse=True)
w = np.hstack((eigen_pairs[0][1][:, np.newaxis],
                  eigen_pairs[1][1][:, np.newaxis]))
print('Matrix W:\n', w)

X_train_std[0].dot(w)
```

Figure A.13 illustrates that we cannot separate the high- and low-risk countries using only two principal components. However, accepting some errors, a 'rough' identification might be achievable.

In summary, our PCA shows that using a single index to capture climate risk is insufficient. We can use these initial findings to construct our own measures, which might be superior in identifying countries at risk.

Figure A.13 Transformed data using two principal components

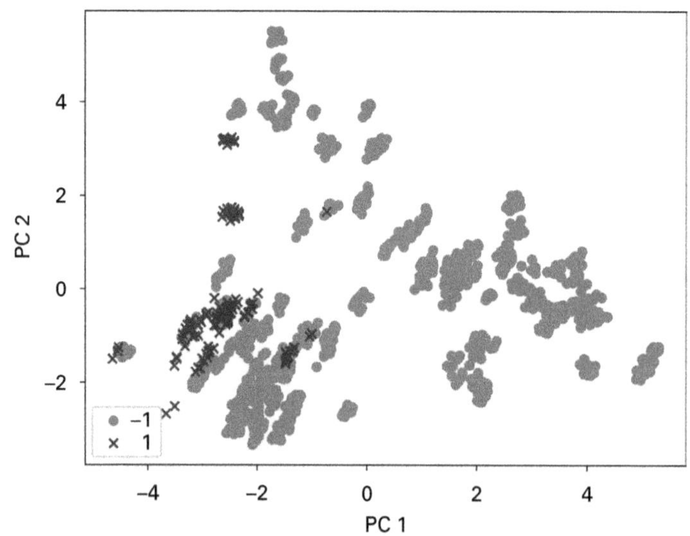

Chapter 14

We start with the usual import statements. It is convenient to load the data into the data matrix and the array containing the true labels. Using print statements, we check the structure of the data, which completes task 14.10.1.

```
import numpy as np
from sklearn import metrics
from sklearn.metrics import pairwise_distances
from sklearn import datasets
from sklearn.cluster import KMeans

#Load Iris dataset
X, y = datasets.load_iris(return_X_y=True)

#Check the data structure
print(X)
print(f"\nThese are the true labels {y}.")
```

Next, we copy-paste our FCM class or use an import statement. Then, we define an instance of the class with four and five clusters. Note that we need to run the *initialize()* method before the *fit() method*.

```
#Fuzzy c_means with four or five clusters
c_means = CMeans(clusters = 4, m = 2, data = X)

c_means.initialisation()
print(c_means.U)

c_means.cluster_centre()
print(c_means.v)

c_means.membership_degree()
print(c_means.U)

c_means.fit()

#Labels
labels_4 = np.argmax(c_means.U, axis = 1)
print(labels_4)

#Increase to 5 clusters
```

```
c_means_5 = CMeans(clusters = 5, m = 2, data = X)
c_means_5.initialisation()
c_means_5.fit()

#Labels
labels_5 = np.argmax(c_means_5.U, axis = 1)
print(labels_5)
```

Note that we need to obtain the labels from the cluster membership matrix. We select the cluster with the highest membership degree using the *np.argmax()* function. This concludes task 14.10.2.

Finally, we calculate the Silhouette Coefficient for both model specifications.

```
silhouette_4 = metrics.silhouette_score(X, labels_4,
metric=‘euclidean’)
silhouette_5 = metrics.silhouette_score(X, labels_5,
metric=‘euclidean’)
print(f"The Silhouette Coefficient is
{round(silhouette_4, 3)} with 4 clusters
and {round(silhouette_5, 3)} with 5 clusters.")
```

As expected, the Silhouette Coefficient drops when we move from four to five clusters. This concludes task 14.10.3.

Chapter 15

We start with the usual import statements. This simulation can be constructed in NumPy as processes are not required. We define the parameter values as suggested and create the distribution of marginal costs. Each firm's marginal costs are drawn from a normal distribution and stored in the array *costs*. This concludes task 15.8.2.

```
"""
Cournot game with heterogeneous agents
"""
import numpy as np
import matplotlib.pyplot as plt

"""Setup"""
N = 100 #Number of firms
costs = [] #Array of marginal costs; empty list

"""Random seed"""
```

```
np.random.seed(7) #Initialize random number generator

"""Set default parameters"""
alpha = 20
beta = 0.1
rho = 0.1 #Discount rate

"""Distribution of marginal costs"""
mu_c = 1
sigma_c = 1

for _ in range(N):
    costs.append(abs(np.random.normal(mu_c, sigma_c)))
```

[numbers=left,language=Python]

Next, we implement equations (15.6) and (15.7), completing task 15.8.3.

```
""""Average quantity"""
def average_quantity(costs: list, alpha: int, beta: int,
N: int):
    return (alpha - np.mean(costs))/(beta * (N + 1))

"""Market price"""
def market_price(costs: list, alpha: int, N: int):
    return alpha - N/(N + 1) * (alpha - np.mean(costs))
```

[numbers=left,language=Python]

Task 15.8.4 derives the optimal output for each firm. Using a while loop, firms with negative outputs are dropped individually. The loop stops if the firm with the lowest output exhibits a positive output. Finally, we recalculate the market price.

```
"""Optimal output"""
"""
Returns the outputs, which can be
negative in the case of high-cost firms
"""
def optimal_output(costs: list, alpha: int, beta: int,
N: int):
    output = []
    av_quant = average_quantity(costs, alpha, beta, N)
    for cost in costs:
        output.append((alpha - cost)/beta - N * av_quant)
```

```
    return output

"""Call function"""
out = optimal_output(costs, alpha, beta, N)

"""Remove firm with most negative output recursively"""
while min(out) < 0:
    #Remove costs that belong to the firm
    with the smallest output
    del costs[out.index(min(out))]
    N -= 1 #Reduce the number of firms by one
    out = optimal_output(costs, alpha, beta, N)

"""Market price"""
price = market_price(costs, alpha, N)
```

Task 15.8.5 determines firm value based on revenues and applying the discount rate. We use a histogram to illustrate the distribution in the sample.

```
"""Period revenue"""
def firm_revenue(price: int, costs: list, out: list):
    rev = []
    for idx in range(len(out)):
        rev.append((price - costs[idx]) * out[idx])
    return rev

revenue = firm_revenue(price, costs, out)

"""Firm value"""
def firm_value(revenue: list, rho: int):
    return[rev/rho for rev in revenue if rev > 0]

value = firm_value(revenue, rho)

"""Distribution of firm value"""
data = value
#fixed bin size
bins = np.arange(0, max(data), 1.5)

plt.xlim([min(data), max(data)])

plt.hist(data, bins=bins, alpha=0.5)
```

```
plt.title('Distribution of firm value')
plt.xlabel('Firm value')
plt.ylabel('Count')
plt.show()
```

To address task 15.8.5, we start with the accumulation of cash based on firms' profits. Cash positions increase over time. We develop a function called *best_target*. This function identifies the best target for the bidder. The best target maximizes the bidder's increase in firm value. The function returns the index position of the best target. Finally, our simulation will answer the question.

```
"""Accumulation of cash"""
def cash(revenue: list, time: int = 1):
    return[rev * time for rev in revenue]

time = 1
cash_stock = cash(revenue, time)

"""Cash mergers"""
"""
The best_target function identifies the best target for bidder.
This target maximises the bidder's increase in value.
It returns the index position of the best target
"""

def best_target(costs: list, revenue: list, value: list,
    cash_stock: list, N: int, alpha: int, beta: int):
    benefit_for_bidder = []
    for __ in range(N):
        #Copies of lists
        N_copy = N
        costs_copy = costs[:]
        revenue_copy = revenue[:]
        value_copy = value[:]
        cash_copy = cash_stock[:]

        #Checks conditions for any firm in the list
        cash_merger = max (cash_copy) > value_copy[__]
        #Boolean whether cash merger is possible
```

```
        pre_merger_value = value[revenue_copy.index(max(cash_copy))]
        #Bidder
        target_value = value_copy[_ _] #Values of i's firm

        if cash_merger:
            del costs_copy[value_copy.index(value_copy[__])]
            #Remove costs that belong to target firm i
            N_copy -= 1 #Reduce the number of firms by one

            #Outputs, price, and value after merger
            out_new = optimal_output(costs_copy, alpha, beta, N_copy)
            price_new = market_price(costs_copy, alpha, N_copy)
            revenue_new = firm_revenue(price_new, costs_copy, out_new)
            value_new = firm_value(revenue_new, rho)

            post_merger_value = max(value_new)
            benefit_for_bidder.append(post_merger_value
            - pre_merger_value - target_value)
        else:
            benefit_for_bidder.append (0)
    return benefit_for_bidder.index(max(benefit_for_bidder))

index_bidder = cash_stock.index(max(cash_stock))
index_target = best_target(costs, revenue, value,
cash_stock, N, alpha, beta)
index_cheapest = value.index (min(value))

"""FIRST INSIGHT: The cheapest target is not the best target"""
print(f"Is the statement that the highest valued firm will\n \
      acquire the lowest valued firm correct ?\n
      Answer: {index_target == index_cheapest}")
```

Chapter 16

We start with the usual import statements. At the moment, we still rely on the *User()* class imported from *user.txt*. The title of the GUI reflects its new purpose.

```
import tkinter as tk
import pickle

from user import User

# Starts root
root = tk.Tk()
root.title('Betting Simulation')
```

The menu bar provides a simulation menu with a new command that starts the simulation. This new command refers to the placeholder function as the back-end needs adjustment prior to linking any function.

```
# Simulation menu
sim_menu = tk.Menu(menubar, tearoff = 0)
sim_menu.add_command(label = "Start",
command = do_nothing)
menubar.add_cascade(label = "Simulation",
menu = sim_menu)
```

This concludes task 16.9.1. Next, we modify the *User()* class to permit users to modify parameters for the simulation.

```
class User():
  def __init__(self, games, money, bet):
    self.games = games
    self.money = money
    self.bet = bet
```

This concludes task 16.9.2. Next, we revise the *new_user()* function by updating the attributes (e.g. revised entry widgets and labels) and changing the radio button to a standard entry widget, as there are many options for the value of the bet.

```
def new_user():
    #New window
    global new_user_window
    new_user_window = tk.Toplevel()
    new_user_window.title('New Simulation')

    #Size of widget
```

```
    new_user_window.geometry("400x300")

    #Create global variables
    global games
    global money
    global bet

    games = tk.StringVar()
    money = tk.StringVar()
    bet = tk.StringVar()

    #Entry: number of games, money, and value of bet
    games_entry = tk.Entry(new_user_window, width = 30,
    textvariable = games)
    games_entry.grid(row = 0, column = 1, padx = 20)

    money_entry = tk.Entry(new_user_window, width = 30,
    textvariable = money)
    money_entry.grid(row = 1, column = 1, padx = 20)

    bet_entry = tk.Entry(new_user_window, width = 30,
    textvariable = bet)
    bet_entry.grid( row = 2, column = 1, padx = 20)

    #Labels for entries
    games_label = tk.Label(new_user_window,
    text = "Number of games")
    games_label.grid(row = 0, column = 0)

    money_label = tk.Label(new_user_window,
    text = "Initial wealth")
    money_label.grid(row = 1, column = 0)

    bet_label = tk.Label(new_user_window,
    text = "Value of each bet")
    bet_label.grid(row = 2, column = 0)

    #Create start button
    start_button = tk.Button (new_user_window,
    text = "Start", command = start_button_function)
    start_button.grid(row = 4, column = 1,
    columnspan = 2, ipadx = 115, padx = 10, pady = 1)
```

There are a few things to consider further. First, we assume that all inputs are string variables (*tk.StringVar()*). We could consider changing the data type. Your back-end will need to convert the strings to integers. This is quickly done; however, users might input invalid strings that cannot be converted to integers. Second, instead of using entry widgets, you could restrict user input to integers by offering horizontal sliders that capture users' choices.

The next step is to revise the *start_button_function*. This is easier to complete as we only need to modify the attributes and our checking message.

```
def start_button_function ():
    """Function for start button"""
    #Get first and last name from entry widget
    games_get = games.get()
    money_get = money.get()
    bet_get = bet.get()

    #Close new_game_window
    new_user_window.destroy()

    #Create global variables
    global user

    #Initialize user
    user = User(games = games_get, money = money_get,
    bet = bet_get)

    #CHECK
    print(f"You want to play {user.games} games.")
    print(f"\nYou have initial wealth {user.money}
    and bet {user.bet}.")
```

Are we done with task 16.9.3? Not quite, as testing the code triggers error messages. Our print statements in our functions that handle saving and loading data still refer to the old attributes of the user instance, which need to be revised as follows.

```
def save():
    """Saves objects; overwrites any existing file;
    default file 'portfolio.pkl'"""
    obj = [user]
    with open('portfolio.pkl', 'wb')as output:
        pickle.dump(obj, output,
        pickle.HIGHEST_PROTOCOL)

```

```
    #CHECK
    print(f"{user.games}SAVED.")


def load():
    """Loads objects"""
    with open('portfolio.pkl', 'rb') as input:
        obj = pickle.load(input)
    global user
    user = obj[0]

    #CHECK
    print(f"{user.games} LOADED.")
```

Task 16.9.4 illustrates the complexity of working with front- and back-end at the same time. First, we modify the *betting()* function and remove all unnecessary code from *gambler.py*.

```
import numpy as np
import matplotlib.pyplot as plt

def betting(money, games = 100, initial_bet = 1):
    #Player's position
    position = np.zeros(games + 1)
    position[0] = money
    #Initial bet
    bet = initial_bet
    idx = 0
    while money > bet and idx < games:
        #Spin the wheel
        spin = np.random.randint(0, 37)
        #Update index
        idx += 1
        if spin % 2 == 0 and spin != 0:
            money += bet
            bet = initial_bet
        else:
            money -= bet
            bet *= 2
        #Update position
        position[idx] = money
    return position
```

Now, we can import the function.

```
from gambler import betting
```

We add a display, which sits in its own frame. The entry widget will report the user's wealth after running the simulation.

```
current_frame = tk.LabelFrame(root, text = ‘Simulation result’)
current_frame.grid( row = 1, column = 1, \
sticky=‘W’, padx = 5, pady = 10, ipadx = 100, ipady = 30)

fin_position_label = tk.Label(current_frame,
text = “Financial Position”).grid(row = 0, column = 0)
cash_display = tk.Entry(current_frame, width = 10,
borderwidth = 5)
cash_display.grid(row = 1, column = 1)
cash_label = tk.Label(current_frame,
text = “Wealth”).grid(row = 1, column = 0)
```

Finally, we define our *start_simulation()* function, which runs the simulation based on the parameter values provided by the user. Note that this is not a perfect implementation as we must assume that the user instance exists, i.e. the new command is used prior to running the simulation. Furthermore, we assume that users' inputs can be converted to integers.

In practice, we must ensure that our code addresses these potential cases by modifying how data is entered and adding checks (e.g. warning messages).

```
def start_simulation():
    position = betting(money = int(user.money),
    games = int(user.games), initial_bet = int(user.bet))
    cash_display.delete(0, “end”)
    cash_display.insert(0, position[-1])
```

Finally, we link the function to our start command in the simulation menu.

```
sim_menu.add_command(label = “Start”, command = start_simulation)
```

Figure A.14 Displaying the result of simulations

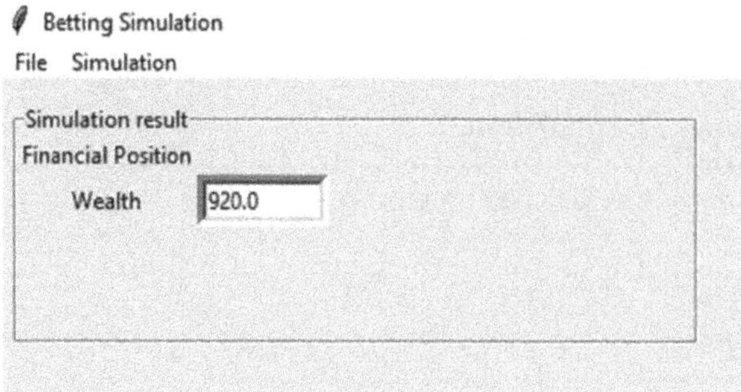

Figure A.14 demonstrates how the GUI displays the result of simulations. Of course, many additional features (e.g. charts) can be added.

BIBLIOGRAPHY

Aghabozorgi, S and Y W Teh. Stock market co-movement assessment using a three-phase clustering method, *Expert Systems with Applications*, 2014, 41 (4), 1301–14

Babu, M S, N Geethanjali, and B Satyanarayana. Clustering approach to stock market prediction, *International Journal of Advanced Networking and Applications*, 2012, 3 (4), 1281

Bezdek, J C (2013) *Pattern Recognition with Fuzzy Objective Function Algorithms*, Springer Science & Business Media

Bishop, C M (2006) *Pattern Recognition and Machine Learning*, Springer-Verlag, Berlin/Heidelberg

Boyd, S and L Vandenberghe (2018) *Introduction to Applied Linear Algebra: Vectors, matrices, and least squares*, Cambridge University Press

Breiman, L. Random forests, *Machine Learning*, 2001, 45 (1), 5–32

Breiman, L, J Friedman, C Stone, and R Olshen (1984) *Classification and Regression Trees*, CRC

Casella, G and R Berger (2002) *Statistical Inference*, Thomson Learning, 2nd edn

Chawla, N V, K W Bowyer, L O Hall, and W P Kegelmeyer. SMOTE: Synthetic minority over-sampling technique, *Journal of Artificial Intelligence Research*, 2002, 16 (1), 321–57

Chang, C-C and C-J Lin. LIBSVM: A library for support vector machines, *ACM Transactions on Intelligent Systems and Technology*, 2011, 2, 1–27

Chen, T and C Guestrin. Xgboost: A scalable machine learning system for both regression and classification problems, *Proceedings of the 22nd ACM SIGKDD International Conference on Knowledge Discovery and Data Mining*, 2016, 785–94

Deisenroth, M P, A A Faisal, and C S Ong (2020) *Mathematics for Machine Learning*, Cambridge University Press

Domingos, P (2015) *The Master Algorithm: How the quest for the ultimate learning machine will remake our world*, Basic Books, New York, 1st edn

Dunn, J. A fuzzy relative of the isodata process and its use in detecting compact well-separated clusters, *Journal of Cybernetics*, 1973

Eliyanto, J and S Surono. The suitable distance function for fuzzy c-means clustering, *AIP Conference Proceedings*, 2022, 2578 (1)

Farebrother, R W. Notes on the prehistory of principal components analysis, *Journal of Multivariate Analysis*, 2022, 188, 104814

Freund, Y and R Schapire. A decision-theoretic framework for boosting and aggregating, *Machine Learning*, 1995, 38 (2), 237–70

Friedman, J H. Greedy function approximation: A gradient boosting machine, *Annals of Statistics*, 2001, 1189–232

Good, P I (2006) *Resampling Methods: A practical guide to data analysis*, Birkhäuser, 3rd edn

Goodfellow, I, Y Bengio, and A Courville (2016) *Deep Learning*, MIT Press

Han, J, M Kamber, and J Pei (2011) *Data Mining: Concepts and techniques*, Morgan Kaufmann, 3rd edn

Hass, J, C Heil, M Weir, and P Bogacki (2022) *Thomas' Calculus*, Pearson, 15th edn

Hastie, T, R Tibshirani, and J Friedman (2009) *The Elements of Statistical Learning: Data mining, inference and prediction*, Springer, 2nd edn

Hayashi, F (2011) *Econometrics*, Princeton University Press

He, H, Y Bai, E A Garcia, and S Li. ADASYN: Adaptive synthetic sampling approach for imbalanced learning, *Proceedings of International Joint Conference on Neural Networks*, Hong Kong, June 1–8, 2008, 1322–28

Ioffe, S and C Szegedy. Batch normalization: Accelerating deep network training by reducing internal covariate shift, *ICML'15: Proceedings of the 32nd International Conference on Machine Learning*, 2015, 37, 448–56

Jaroonchokanan, N, T Termsaithong, and S Suwanna. Dynamics of hierarchical clustering in stocks market during financial crises, *Physica A: Statistical Mechanics and its Applications*, 2022, 607, 128183

Kling, G, U Volz, V Murinde, and S Ayas. The impact of climate vulnerability on firms' cost of capital and access to finance, *World Development*, 2021, 137, 105131

Liu, B (2011) *Web Data Mining*, Springer, 2nd edn

McKinney, W (2012) *Python for Data Analysis: Data wrangling with Pandas, NumPy, and IPython*, O'Reilly Media

Molin, S (2019) *Hands-On Data Analysis with Pandas: Effciently perform data collection, wrangling, analysis, and visualization using Python*, Packt Publishing Ltd

Murphy, K P (2022) *Probabilistic Machine Learning: An introduction*, MIT Press

Nanda, S R, B Mahanty, and M K Tiwari. Clustering Indian stock market data for portfolio management, *Expert Systems with Applications*, 2010, 37 (12), 8793–98

Pesqué-Cela, V, L T, D Luo, D Tobin, and G Kling. Defining and measuring financial inclusion: A systematic review and confirmatory factor analysis, *Journal of International Development*, 2021, 33 (2), 316–41

Quinlan, J R. Induction of decision trees, *Machine Learning*, 1986, 1, 81–106

Quinlan, J R (1993) *C4.5: Programs for Machine Learning*, Morgan Kaufmann

Rand, W M. Objective criteria for the evaluation of clustering methods, *Journal of the American Statistical Association*, 1971, 66 (336), 846–50

Ross, S (2009) *Introduction to Probability Models*, Academic Press, 10th edn

Rousseeuw, P J. Silhouettes: A graphical aid to the interpretation and validation of cluster analysis, *Journal of Computational and Applied Mathematics*, 1987, 20, 53–65

Rudin, W (1976) *Principles of Mathematical Analysis*, McGraw-Hill, 3rd edn

Silver, D, A Huang, C J Maddison, A Guez, L Sifre, G van den Driessche, J Schrittwieser, I Antonoglou, V Panneershelvam, M Lanctot, S Dieleman, D Grewe, J Nham, N Kalchbrenner, I Sutskever, T Lillicrap, M Leach, K Kavukcuoglu, T Graepel, and D Hassabis. Mastering the game of Go with deep neural networks and tree search, *Nature*, 2016, 529 (7587), 484–89

Stigler, S M. Gauss and the invention of least squares, *Annals of Statistics*, 1981, 465–74

Strang, G (2023) *Introduction to Linear Algebra*, Cambridge University Press, 6th edn

Tan, P-N, M Steinbach, A Karpatne, and V Kumar (2018) *Introduction to Data Mining*, Pearson, 2nd edn

Thomas, G and R Finney (1992) *Calculus and Analytic Geometry*, Addison-Wesley, 8th edn

Vasicek, O. An equilibrium characterization of the term structure, *Journal of Financial Economics*, 1977, 5 (2), 177–88

Zhou, K, C Fu, and S Yang. Fuzziness parameter selection in fuzzy c-means: The perspective of cluster validation, *Science China Information Sciences*, 2014, 57, 1–8

Zhou, Z-H (2012) *Ensemble Methods: Foundations and algorithms*, CRC Press

INDEX

Page numbers in *italic* indicate figures or tables